MW00624178

THE BOOK OF

REVELATION

Understanding the Future

David Hocking

THE BOOK OF REVELATION
Understanding the Future
© 2014 HFT Publications

Revision and updating of THE COMING WORLD LEADER that was published in 2000 AD

Copyright 2014 by HFT Publications
PO Box 3927 Tustin, CA 92781
1-800-75-BIBLE

Printed in the United States of America

ISBN   9780988243163

2

CONTENTS

PRELUDE

Students of world history are keenly aware that the nations of the world are facing enormous challenges and difficulties that were simply unknown in the past. The age of nuclear power has brought with it some frightening possibilities and realities.

Some sociologists and scientists are now speaking of the terrifying prospect of nuclear war and the end of human civilization as we know it. Movies, magazines, television, and Internet communications have pictured and described a holocaust of destruction and devastation previously thought impossible. Today it is a reality facing us all. The cries for world peace have become stronger with each passing decade.

In the midst of all these terrifying realities stands a problem for which there does not seem to be an answer. It is the problem of leadership – some would call it a crisis. Leaders have failed us. Politicians have lied to us. No matter who is elected or comes to power by force, the world situation rarely changes for the better. It seems that human history is out of control. The question is often asked, "Who can bring world peace?"

Various religious groups, past and present, have challenged us with the need for a world leader, someone who can bring peace to planet earth. There have been many suggestions and attempts to bring such a leader to the world's attention and support. The cry for leadership continues, and the world seems ready, if not desperate, for it.

One of the most remarkable books in all of literature is found in the Bible. The Old Testament (often called the Tanakh or Jewish Bible) contains 39 books that are filled with predictions and prophecies about the future of humanity. The New Testament with its 27 books introduces us to the Messiah (meaning *"anointed One"*) and teaches us that He is the One Who will one day bring peace to this troubled world.

The last book of the New Testament is the most fascinating and amazing of all – THE BOOK OF REVELATION. It contains 22 chapters that were written by the Apostle John, a dedicated and devoted follower of the Messiah. He was a prisoner on the Island of Patmos, exiled by Roman authorities for his outspoken teachings concerning the coming of the Messiah, and the impact of His life, death, and resurrection. It was John the Apostle to whom Jesus committed the care of His mother, Miriam (Mary), at the time of His death (He was crucified by the Romans).

The correct and complete title of this amazing book is THE REVELATION OF JESUS CHRIST! The word *"revelation"* is a translation of the Greek word *apocalypse*, a word meaning "unveiling" or "to take the cover off." While there are many fascinating events in the book, its primary purpose is to reveal the glory and majesty of the Messiah!

INTRODUCTION

The Book of Revelation is prophecy; the majority of its teachings remain unfulfilled. It has a long history of different interpretations and while somewhat interesting to read and understand, the Book remains a mystery to the average person.

CAN WE REALLY UNDERSTAND THIS BOOK?

Many people believe that a normal person without scholastic credentials or knowledge of Hebrew and Greek may find it almost impossible to understand.

The major viewpoints of church history fall into the following categories:

> **HISTORICAL** – this view sees the Book of Revelation as a series of events that have already taken place, but serve as an example to future believers, especially those who find themselves alive at the time of the Second Coming of Messiah.

> **SYMBOLICAL** – this view is often referred to as the "allegorical" view. It sees the book as an expression of spiritual truth in symbolical language. The events are not to be taken as literal history but simply as illustrations of spiritual principles and insights.

> **SPIRITUAL** – this view (closely related to the "symbolical" view) sees the events in the Book as descriptive of the continual conflict between Christianity and paganism. It is sometimes called the "preterist (Latin word meaning "past")" view.

LITERAL – this view sees the Book of Revelation as describing both past and future events. It understands the use of symbolic language, but unless the context emphasizes that its words are "only" symbolical, it is to be taken literally, describing both fulfilled and unfulfilled prophecy. (It is sometimes called the "futuristic" view, as it believes that from Revelation 4:1 until the end of the Book is all future.)

The Bible has a great deal of teaching that can be most difficult for modern man to understand. For one thing, it quotes voluminously from the Jewish Bible. Unless a person studies the context of those quotations, he or she will find it most confusing and difficult.

Some of the best kept secrets about understanding the Bible are found within the pages of the Bible itself. There are four "secrets" that a person needs to know in order to have a greater understanding of Biblical teachings.

1. <u>FAITH</u> - If we approach the Bible with preconceived ideas about its accuracy or reliability, doubting that it is the Word of God, our chances of understanding its message will be extremely limited.

Hebrews 11:3 – *"Through <u>faith</u> we understand that the worlds were framed by the word of God, so that things which are seen were not made of things which do appear."*

Hebrews 11:6 says: *"But without <u>faith</u> it is impossible to please Him; for he that cometh to God must believe that He is, and that He is a rewarder of them that diligently seek Him."*

It is faith that causes a person to pray to God and ask for His help in understanding the Bible. God wants us to know the message of Revelation more than we personally want to understand it.

Psalm 119:18 says *"Open Thou mine eyes, that I may behold wondrous things out of Thy law."*

The Hebrew word translated *"wondrous"* refers to that which is too difficult for normal human brains to comprehend.

Psalm 119:169 adds: *"Let my cry come near before Thee, O LORD; give me understanding, according to Thy word."*

A CLEAN LIFE – It appears from many verses in the Bible that the ability to understand the Bible comes **from moral purity**.

Psalm 66:18 says: *"If I regard iniquity in my heart, the Lord will not hear me."*

I Peter 2:1-3 adds: *"Wherefore laying aside all malice, and all guile, and hypocrisies, and envies, and all evil speakings, As newborn babes, desire the sincere milk of the word, that ye may grow thereby: If so be ye have tasted that the Lord is gracious."*

James 3:17 states: *"But the wisdom that is from above is first pure, then peaceable, gentle, and easy to be entreated, full of mercy and good fruits, without partiality, and without hypocrisy."*

When there is sin in our hearts that remains unconfessed and unforsaken, it is a barrier to our ability to interpret the Bible.

10

OBEDIENCE – Those who obey the teachings of the Bible have a better understanding of the Bible than those who do not. Jesus said (John 7:17): *"If any man will do His will, he shall know of the doctrine, whether it be of God, or whether I speak of Myself."*

Psalm 119:100 – *"I understand more than the ancients, because I keep Thy precepts."*

STUDY - It takes time, patience, and effort, but there is no substitute for it. In Acts 17:11, the Apostle Paul commended the believers at Berea with these words: *"These were more noble than those in Thessalonica, in that they received the word with all readiness of mind, and searched the scriptures daily, whether those things were so."*

A classic passage on the importance of study is found in II Timothy 2:15: *"Study to shew thyself approved unto God, a workman that needeth not to be ashamed, righty dividing the word of truth."*

The Greek word that is translated *"study"* is the word for "diligence." Those who study carefully the Scriptures have no reason to be embarrassed in that they engage in such study with an intensity and effort that is rewarded by God Himself. Correct interpretation is based on careful study, being diligent, and working at it.

WHAT ABOUT ALL THE DIFFERENT INTERPRETATIONS OF THE BOOK OF REVELATION?

Naturally, the one you listen to and believe – you believe has the correct interpretation! Sometimes you will hear people say that there are "many different interpretations" of the Bible itself. Well, there may be different applications that people make, but there is only one correct interpretation, and that is the one God originally made when it was written. When we speak of the "inspiration" of the Bible, we are not talking about the infallibility of the writers. The Bible does not teach that. It is not the writers that are inspired, but rather the writings themselves. II Timothy 3:16-17 says: *"All scripture is given by inspiration of God, and is profitable for doctrine, for reproof, for correction, for instruction in righteousness: That the man of God may be perfect, throughly furnished unto all good works."*

The writers of the Bible are not considered to be the real "Author" of the words of the Bible. The true Author is the Holy Spirit of God Who, according to the Bible itself, controlled the writers so that what was written was exactly what God wanted. Consider the teaching of II Peter 1:20-21:

"Knowing this first, that no prophecy of the scripture is of any private interpretation. For the prophecy came not in old time by the will of man: but holy men of God spake as they were moved by the Holy Ghost."

In Hebrews 1:1-3 we read these remarkable words: *"God, Who at sundry times and in divers manners spake in time past unto the fathers by the prophets, Hath in these last days spoken unto us by His Son, Whom He hath appointed Heir of all things, by Whom also He made the worlds; Who being the brightness of His glory, and the express image of His Person, and upholding all things by the word of His power, when He had by Himself purged our sins, sat down on the right hand of the Majesty on high."*

The above passage teaches that God spoke directly and audibly to the *"fathers"* (like Abraham, Isaac, and Jacob) through the words of the prophets to whom God spoke directly.

In verse 2, it begins *"hath in these last days"* – but the Greek grammar says something very different – it says *"hath in the last of these days."* The *"days"* are referring to the times of God speaking audibly and directly. There is coming a time according to these verses when *"these days"* will be brought to an end. When that day comes, it will be a message from God about the Messiah, His Son, and our Savior. Apparently, His Son will be known for His true identity as *"God manifest in the flesh"* (I Timothy 3:16). It is very important that we understand that this last book of the Bible - THE REVELATION OF JESUS CHRIST – is God's final revelation to us! That's why we read in Revelation 22:18-19 these serious words:

"For I testify unto every man that heareth the words of the prophecy of this book, If any man shall add unto these things, God shall add unto him the plagues that are written in this book: And if any man shall take away from the words of the book of this prophecy, God shall take away his part out of the book of life, and out of the holy city, and from the things which are written in this book."

PROPHECY EVENTS

There are four major events of Bible prophecy about which we gain information by the study of the Book of Revelation.

1. The Rapture of the Church

2. The Great Tribulation

3. The Second Coming of the Messiah

4. The Millennial Kingdom

Many will say that the subject of the Rapture of the Church is not found in the Book of Revelation. A few even argue that the Rapture is not mentioned in the entire Bible!

WHAT DO PEOPLE BELIEVE ABOUT THE RAPTURE?

1. <u>The No Future Rapture View</u>

2. <u>Mid-Tribulation View</u> – the two witnesses of Revelation 11 are symbolic of the church being raptured at the middle of the tribulation.

3. <u>The Pre-Wrath Rapture View</u> - It will happen just before the seven last plagues that are listed in Revelation 16. Revelation 16:1 speaks of 7 bowls of wrath that summarize the final plagues that are coming on the planet.

4. <u>The Partial Rapture View</u> - Only Spirit-filled believers will be raptured; carnal believers will go through the tribulation.

5. <u>Post Tribulation Rapture View</u> – proponents see the Rapture as the same event as the Second Coming of Messiah at end of the tribulation.

6. <u>Pre-Tribulation View</u> – The Rapture will come before the Tribulation begins!

It is the position of this book that the Rapture of the Church will occur BEFORE the tribulation begins! Many object to this belief and offer their objections to it.

SIX MAJOR OBJECTIONS TO THE PRE-TRIBULATION RAPTURE

1. The word "Rapture" does not appear in the Bible!

However, it does appear in the Latin Bible. The Latin verb (*rapturo*) translates the Greek word *harpazo* that appears in I Thessalonians 4:17 and is translated with the English words *"caught up."*

I Thessalonians 4:16-17 – *"For the Lord Himself shall descend from heaven with a shout, with the voice of the archangel, and with the trump of God: and the dead in Christ shall rise first: Then we which are alive and remain shall be <u>caught up</u> to meet the Lord in the air: and so shall we ever be with the Lord."*

2. Believers will be protected but not removed!

In Revelation 3:10 we read: *"Because thou hast kept the word of My patience, I also will keep thee from the hour of temptation, which shall come*

15

upon all the world, to try them that dwell upon the earth."

Consider the following facts about this verse in the Book of Revelation

(1)   The term *"them that dwell upon the earth"* is always used of unbelievers in the Book of Revelation.

(2)   The term *"the hour of temptation"* is worldwide. Also, the Greek language has the definite article in front of the word *"hour"* and the word *"temptation"* – it is referring to a specific time in God's prophetic program.

(3)   The word *"from"* is not the Greek word *"apo"*, but is the Greek word *"ek"* which means "out of". It teaches "removal" not simply protection!

(4)   If believers were being protected then we have a huge problem in Revelation, because most believers are killed during the tribulation. Conclusion: Church Age Believers will be removed from the coming tribulation.

3. The Wrath of 1 Thessalonians 5:9 refers to hell, not the Tribulation!

Consider carefully the following issues:

(1)   The Pre-Trib view is that the coming wrath IS the day of the Lord, not hell at all.

(2)   Even if wrath does refer to hell, it doesn't change the Pre-Trib view for Jesus will deliver us from the wrath of hell as well.

(3)   Revelation 6:17 announces the opening of the sixth seal as the great day of His wrath, and confirms that the Day of the Lord is the great day of His wrath.

(4)   Revelation 16:1 describes the wrath of God in the pouring out of the seven bowls on earth. All of these are the wrath of God, and believers are NOT appointed to this wrath.

(5)   I Thessalonians 5:1-9 is quite clear. It follows the teaching on the Rapture in I Thessalonians 4:16-17. The opening verses of chapter 5 speaks of the coming *"day of the LORD"* – NOT hell! And, in verse 9 we read: *"For God hath not appointed us to wrath, but to obtain salvation by our Lord Jesus Christ."*

4. The words of I Thessalonians 4:17 *"to meet the Lord in the air"* connect with the end of the tribulation, NOT before the tribulation! The Rapture is the same event as the Second Coming!

This major objection focuses on the words of Matthew 25:1-13 and believes that it requires the Second Coming of the Messiah to occur at the end of the tribulation. We believe that this is correct in its understanding. However, it does not mean that it is the same event as taught in I Thessalonians 4:16-17.

Consider the following facts:

(1)   Matthew 25 is speaking of a "marriage" on the earth, the bride's future home. The meeting in the air speaks of going to the Bridegroom's home when we are raptured.

(2)   Matthew 8:11 says we are going to sit down with Abraham, Isaac and Jacob, but they are not resurrected until the end of the tribulation period (according to Daniel 12).

(3)   At the Rapture we meet the Lord in the air, but at the Second Coming we are with the Lord on the earth.

(4)   At the Rapture the Bible says the Lord comes FOR His saints, but at the Second Coming He comes WITH His saints.

5. In 1 Thessalonians 4:16 the Lord will descend with a trumpet at the Rapture. I Corinthians 15:51-52 speaks of the "Last Trumpet". The 7th trumpet begins to blow at the middle of the tribulation and blows until the end. So, if the Lord doesn't come until the last trumpet is blown, He would have to come after the tribulation.

However, we have the following facts:

(1) Our Lord is contrasted as the "last Adam" (I Corinthians 15), but Jesus was not the last man to exist on the earth. He was last in some sense as it deals with theology here.

(2) The seventh trumpet of the book of Revelation is not the last trumpet to be blown. Psalm 98:6 says the rejoicing of God's people will be with trumpets (Psalm 81:3-4). (The words that speak of blowing trumpet on a feast day – is to be a statue for Israel forever).

(3) Zechariah 9:14 speaks of coming victory of our Lord, and says He will blow the trumpets. But in Revelation the seven trumpets are blown by seven angels. The LAST trumpet is not referring to the

last one ever to be blown. They will be blown during the millennial reign.

6. The first resurrection is for believers only, and does not happen until after the tribulation!

Consider the following facts:

The resurrection of Old Testament believers is after the tribulation (Daniel 12), and has no reference to the resurrection of the Church.

The resurrection of tribulation believers (Revelation 20) who will be martyred comes after the tribulation but it is also called the first resurrection. But there is no mention of Church age believers. Applying English to Greek grammatical statements is a problem. We think "first" means first and never second, but it could be first in some sense. Believers will be with the lord forever. The "first" resurrection will include Old Testament believers who are resurrected at the end of the Tribulation, and the Tribulation Martyrs; The "first" resurrection also includes the Church Age believers who are resurrected at the Rapture when the dead in Christ will rise first.

The Rapture passages reveal the dead will be raised and some will be alive and remain, and they shall be changed. Who are those Gentile believers who are alive and remain, if Revelation says all the Gentile believers are martyred during the tribulation? Even

Paul thought he would be among those who are *"alive and remain."*

WHY BELIEVE IN THE RAPTURE?

1. Because the Bible teaches it. God said it, that settles it whether you believe it or not!

2. Because it is the hope of resurrection. Problems showing up in old age – we want to be like Him, and we shall be like Him, for we shall see Him as He is!

3. Because it guarantees a future reunion of believers – family and friends!

4. Because it promises that we will be with the Lord forever!

5. Because according to the Bible it brings great comfort to all believers – comfort one another with the hope of the Rapture! I don't know when He is coming, but I know <u>Who</u> is coming. Watch and be ready!

A BOOK ABOUT JESUS CHRIST
Revelation 1:1-3

"The Revelation of <u>Jesus Christ</u>, which God gave unto Him, to shew unto His servants things which must shortly come to pass; and He sent and signified it by His angel unto His servant John: who bare record of the word of God, and of the testimony of Jesus Christ, and of all things that he saw. Blessed is he that <u>readeth</u>, and they that <u>hear</u> the words of this prophecy, and <u>keep</u> those things which are written therein; <u>for the time is at hand</u>."

THE TITLE OF THE BOOK
The Revelation of Jesus Christ

There are several things we learn from the Book of Revelation. One concerns the glorious event in the future that we call "<u>The Second Coming of the Messiah</u>." There is also a good deal of information given to the Apostle John and to future readers of the Book about what is going to take place in the future when these events will occur on planet earth.

However, the primary thing we should learn from the study of this amazing Book is <u>the glory and majesty of our coming Messiah</u>, <u>our blessed Lord YESHUA</u> (abbreviated Jewish name of "Jesus" which translates His Greek name – *Yesous*).

THE <u>USAGE</u> OF DESCRIPTIONS OF THE MESSIAH IN THE BOOK OF REVELATION

The faithful witness (1:5)
The firstborn from the dead (1:5)
The ruler over the kings of the earth (1:5)
The Alpha and Omega (1:8)
The Beginning and the End (1:8)
The One Who i<u>s</u>, Who w<u>as</u>, and Who i<u>s t</u>o come (1:8)
The Almighty (1:8)
The First and the Last (1:11, 17)
The Son of Man (1:13)
<u>He Who lives</u> (1:18)
He Who holds the seven stars in His right hand, and
      Who walks in the midst of the seven golden
      lampstands (2:1)
He Who has the sharp two-edged sword (2:12)
Son of God (2:18)
He Who has eyes like a fame of fire (2:18)
He Who has His feet like fine brass (2:18)
He Who has the seven spirits of God (3:1)
He Who is h<u>oly</u> (3:7)
He Who is <u>true</u> (3:7)
He Who has the key of David (3:7)
The Amen (3:14)
The <u>Faithful</u> and <u>true Witness</u> (3:14)
The Beginning of the creation of God (3:14)
The Lion of the tribe of Judah (5:5)
The root of David (5:5; 22:16)
The Lamb (5:6, 8, 12, 13; 6:1, <u>16 – 28 times!</u>)
<u>Lord, holy and true</u> (6:10)
<u>Lord God Almighty</u> (15:3)
King of the saints (15:3)

23

The Word of God (19:13)
KING of kings and LORD of lords (19:16)
Bright and Morning Star (22:16)
Lord Jesus (22:20)
Lord Jesus Christ (22:21)

Yes, we have 33 descriptions of our Lord Jesus Christ – the Messiah of Israel! He is the centerpiece of the Book, the focus of all things, past, present, and future!

THE UNIQUENESS OF THIS BOOK (1:1-3)

"The Revelation of Jesus Christ, which God gave unto Him, to shew unto His servants things which must shortly come to pass; and He sent and signified it by His angel unto his servant John: Who bare record of the word of God, and of the testimony of Jesus Christ, and of all things that he saw. Blessed is he that readeth, and they that hear the words of this prophecy, and keep those things which are written therein: for the time is at hand."

This Book of Revelation is unique in the WAY it was given (1:1-2). The opening verse tells us immediately that God the Father gave this message to His Son, Jesus Christ, Who, in turn, sent it to John by means of an angel. According to Revelation 22:16, Jesus claims to have sent His angel to give this message to John for the churches.

John is the one *"Who bare record to the word of God, and of the testimony of Jesus Christ, and of all things that he saw."* The words *"I saw"* and/or *"I heard"* appear over <u>sixty times in the book, some 44</u> of those times referring to separate and distinct visions that were given to him.

<u>Verse 1</u> tells us that one of the key ways by which this message was communicated to John was <u>by</u> "<u>signs</u>" – for we read *"He sent and <u>signified</u> it by His angel unto His servant John."* That statement alone declares that there is a great deal of <u>symbolic language in the book</u>.

This Book of Revelation is also unique in the <u>WORTH</u> of this message to our hearts by simply reading its contents. <u>Revelation 1:3 says</u>:

"Blessed is he that <u>readeth</u>, and they that <u>hear</u> the words of this prophecy, and <u>keep</u> those things which are written therein; for the time is at hand."

The promised blessing emphasizes the importance of the message of this Book <u>as it mentions three groups of people</u>:

1. The one who <u>reads</u> it

Before the Bible was printed so that we could each have our own copy, an important function of a church leader (or pastor) was to read its message. The apostle Paul told Timothy (I Timothy 4:13): *"Till*

I come, give attendance to reading." It is important for all of us today to understand the critical nature of someone "reading" the Bible!

2. Those who <u>hear</u> it

The change from "he" to "those" indicates that one person was to read the book in the hearing of others. Those who would listen to the public reading of this book would also receive a blessing from its message.

3. Those who <u>keep</u> the things written in it

, obey
, guard

This does not refer to keeping the book in a safe place. It refers to <u>obedience</u> – <u>responding</u> to the message in our hearts and <u>applying the challenges</u> in this book t<u>o the way we live our lives</u> in this world.

HOW CLOSE ARE WE TO THE EVENTS OF THIS BOOK?

The Book is also unique in the <u>WORDS</u> that emphasize the urgency of its message – *"<u>the time is at hand</u>."* Verse one speaks of the *"<u>things which must shortly come to pass</u>"* and verse three says *"<u>for the time is at hand</u>."*

The word *"shortly"* or *"quickly"* appears several times in the Book.

• 1:1 – *"must shortly come to pass"*
  2:5 – *"or else I will come unto thee quickly"*
  2:16 – *"I will come unto thee quickly"*
  3:11 – *"Behold, I come quickly"*
  11:14 – *"the third woe cometh quickly"*
  22:7 - *"Behold, I come quickly"*
  22:12 – *"And, behold, I come quickly"*
  22:20 – *"Surely I come quickly"*

The words *"I come quickly"* are found in Revelation 2:5, 16; 3:11; 22:7, 12, 20. We also have the words *"I will come on thee as a thief"* in Revelation 3:3 and *"Behold, I come as a thief"* in Revelation 16:16. II Peter 3:10 also says: *"But the day of the Lord will come as a thief in the night."* The Apostle Paul added in I Thessalonians 5:2: *"the day of the Lord so cometh as a thief in the night."* The idea of coming *"quickly"* is that which is sudden, soon, and surprising! No time for additional preparation!

There are eight grammatical forms of the word translated *"quickly."* The Greek noun *tachos* refers to speed or quickness and is only used with the preposition *en* – and speaks of that which is of short duration, or soon, or suddenly – used in Revelation 1:1 and 22:6 – translated often in the King James Bible with the word *"shortly."* This noun form is found 7 times in the New Testament.

Two forms of the word are used as adjectives: the word *tachos* found once in James 1:19 – *"let every man be swift to hear"* and the word *tachinos* which is used twice in II Peter 1:14 and 2:1.

27

Five forms of the word are used as adverbs. The word *tachu* is used 11 times and in Revelation 2:5, 16; 3:11; 11:14; 22:7, 12, 20. The word *tacha* is found twice in Romans 5:7 and Philemon 1:15.

The word *tacheos* is found 10 times in the New Testament; the word *tachion* is used 5 times and is a comparative form of the words meaning *"more quickly"* as in Hebrews 13:19, 23. The final form of the word is *tachista* and is a superlative of the other words meaning the *"quickest"* or the *"soonest possible"* and is found once in Acts 17:15 and translated in English as *"with all speed."*

These eight forms of a Greek word are used 39 times in the New Testament and refer to speed, suddenness, and surprise.

The phrase *"the time is at hand"* refers to the season or opportunity for these events to unfold. The specific *"time"* involved is the time for God's judgment and wrath to be poured out upon the earth. If there has been a delay (and there certainly has been – for almost 2000 years!), it is for the salvation of people.

In II Peter 3:8-10a we read the following:

"But, beloved, be not ignorant of this one thing, that one day is with the Lord as a thousand years, and a thousand years as one day. The Lord is not slack concerning His promise, as some men count slackness; but is longsuffering to us-ward, not

willing that any should perish, but that all should come to repentance. But the day of the Lord will come as a thief in the night..." 6/9/15

We also learn in <u>Acts 1:6-8</u> about the concern of the disciples concerning future events and promises:

"*When they therefore were come together, they asked of Him, saying, Lord, wilt Thou at this time restore again the kingdom to Israel? And He said unto them, It is not for you to know the times or the seasons, which the Father hath put in His own power. But ye shall receive power after that the Holy Ghost is come upon you: and ye shall be witnesses unto Me both in Jerusalem, and in all Judea, and in Samaria, and unto the uttermost part of the earth.*"

In <u>Matthew 24:32-36</u> we read: "*Now learn a parable of the fig tree; when his branch is yet tender, and putteth forth leaves, ye know that summer is near: So likewise ye, when ye shall see all these things, know that it is near, even at the doors. Verily I say unto you, This generation shall not pass, till all these things be fulfilled. Heaven and earth shall pass away, but My words shall not pass away. But of that day and hour knoweth no man, no, not the angels of heaven, but My father only.*"

In <u>Matthew 25:13</u> it says: "*Watch therefore, for ye know neither the day nor the hour wherein the Son of man cometh.*"

29

In the prophecy of Luke 21:20-24 we read:

"And when ye shall see Jerusalem compassed with armies, then know that the desolation is nigh. Then let them which are in Judea flee to the mountains; and let them which are in the midst of it depart out; and let not them that are in the countries enter thereinto. For these be the days of vengeance, that all things which are written may be fulfilled. But woe unto them that are with child, and to them that give suck, in these days! For there shall be great distress in the land, and wrath upon this people. And they shall fall by the edge of the sword, and shall be led away captive into all nations: and Jerusalem shall be trodden down of the Gentiles, until the times of the Gentiles be fulfilled."

Another closely related prophecy speaks in Romans 11:25 of the following:

"For I would not, brethren, that ye should be ignorant of this mystery, lest ye should be wise in your own conceits; that blindness in part is happened to Israel, until the fullness of the Gentiles be come in."

Notice carefully these two passages relating to Biblical prophecy:

Luke 21:24 – *"the times of the Gentiles"*

Romans 11:25 – *"the fullness of the Gentiles"*

Are these two phrases speaking of the same thing or event? Probably not. In Romans 11:11-12 we learn the meaning of the *"fullness of the Gentiles"*:

"I say then, Have they stumbled that they should fall? God forbid: but rather through their fall salvation is come unto the Gentiles, for to provoke them to jealousy. Now if the fall of them be the riches of the world, and the diminishing of them the riches of the Gentiles; how much more their fullness?"

The *"fullness of the Gentiles"* is referring to the salvation of the Gentiles which will continue until the end of the tribulation period, for there will be a multitude of Gentiles who will come to faith in the Messiah during the tribulation (according to Revelation 7).

The phrase *"times of the Gentiles"* is referring to Gentile domination of the city of Jerusalem. When does that take place? Many Bible teachers teach that it takes place at the Roman destruction of Jerusalem in 70 AD, and has continued until 1967 when the army of Israel took possession of the Temple Mount.

The Jewish people are no longer *"captive in all nations"* but as of 1948 are back in possession of the land. However, in the conquest of the Temple Mount in 1967, General Moshe Dayan was worried that the entire Muslim world would revolt and attack Israel if the Temple Mount did not stay in

Muslim hands. On that Mount we find the Mosque called "The Dome of the Rock" and the structure known as "The Al Aqsa Mosque." Even though Israel conquered it in 1967, the decision was made to give the control of the Temple Mount into the hands of the Great Muslim Council. That decision has been a constant pain to the Jewish people.

SO, IS THIS THE TIME ABOUT WHICH THE BOOK OF REVELATION SPEAKS IN REVELATION 1:3?

Jesus told us to *"watch and be ready."* That should be enough. Too much speculation keeps us from doing what He said to do while we wait. Guessing is a waste of time. We are obviously closer today than we were yesterday.

As we study the Book of Revelation we must always remember that it is not primarily a book telling us how to set dates or develop a chronological table of events, but rather an unveiling of the Person, work, and majesty of the Messiah, our blessed Lord Yeshua! It is a book that gives us hope and joy. It draws us closer to our Savior, inspiring us to love Him more and to anticipate that glorious day when He shall return in power and great glory!

GOD'S FINAL MESSAGE TO THE CHURCHES
Revelation 1:4-11

The specific churches to which this message was sent by the Apostle John are located in western Turkey today, and they include:

EPHESUS (2:1-7)
SMYRNA (2:8-11)
PERGAMOS (2:12-17)
THYATIRA (2:18-29)
SARDIS (3:1-6
PHILADELPHIA (3:7-12)
LAODICEA (3:13-22)

THE <u>SOURCE</u> OF THIS MESSAGE
Revelation 1:4-6

"John to the seven churches which are in Asia: Grace be unto you, and peace, from Him which is, and which was, and which is to come; and from the seven spirits which are before His throne; And from Jesus Christ, Who is the faithful witness, and the first begotten of the dead, and the prince of the kings of the earth. Unto Him that loved us, and washed us from our sins in His own blood, and hath made us kings and priests unto God and His Father; to Him be glory and dominion forever and ever. Amen."

It is from GOD the FATHER!

He is the One which is and which was and which is to come. Past, present, and future – He is the only and eternal God, no beginning or end – He has always existed. The Bible's opening statement in Genesis 1:1 says *"In the beginning God created the heaven and the earth."* No more needs to be said. The Bible does not set out to prove His existence, but rather assumes it. Nothing has meaning or purpose without it.

It is from the seven spirits!

There are two major views regarding this fact:

1. It refers to the SEVEN ANGELS that are mentioned throughout the Book of Revelation!

2. It refers to the HOLY SPIRIT OF GOD!

Those who believe that the word *"seven"* is referring to the sevenfold characteristics of the Holy Spirit seem most comfortable with their interpretation. They usually quote from the passage in Isaiah 11:1-2:

"And there shall come forth a rod out of the stem of Jesse (father of King David), *and a Branch shall grow out of his roots: And the spirit of the LORD shall rest upon Him, the spirit of wisdom and understanding, the spirit of counsel and might, the spirit of knowledge and of the fear of the LORD."*

Some scholars and teachers believe sincerely that this passage speaks of seven characteristics of the Holy Spirit. However, the Hebrew text of these verses does not speak of "seven" characteristics, but rather speaks of "six" and they are organized into three couplets:

The spirit of wisdom and understanding
The spirit of counsel and might
The spirit of knowledge and of the fear of the LORD

These angels are called *"ministering spirits, sent forth to minister for them who shall be heirs of salvation"* (Hebrews 1:14). Notice that the Book of Revelation pictures them *"before the throne"* of God – ready to do whatever the LORD GOD asks them to do.

It is from Jesus Christ!

The Book of Revelation unveils before our eyes the glory and majesty of our coming Messiah, the blessed Lord Yeshua, Son of the living God! But, the book also speaks of our Messiah as the One Who gives the final instructions to the churches.

1. His <u>PLACE</u> of authority

Three titles are given to Him to emphasize His authority that is behind these final words to the churches:

HIS <u>STABILITY</u> – *"the faithful witness"*

We can rely upon His credibility. To Pilate in John 18:37 He said: *"Thou sayest that I am a king. To this end was I born, and for this cause came I into the world, that I should bear witness unto the truth. Every one that is of the truth heareth My voice."*

In Revelation 3:14 He is called *"the faithful and true witness."*

HIS <u>SUPERIORITY</u> – *"the first begotten of the dead"*

In Colossians 1:18 we read: *"And He is the Head of the body, the church: Who is the beginning, the firstborn from the dead; that in all things He might have the preeminence."*

The Greek word is *prototokos* and is a word of rank or position. It is found five times in reference to the glory and majesty of Jesus Christ:

> **Romans 8:29** – *"that he might be the firstborn among many brethren"*
>
> **Colossians 1:15** – *"the firstborn of every creature"*
>
> **Colossians 1:18** – *"the firstborn from the dead; that in all things He might have the preeminence."*

Hebrews 1:6 – *"And again, when He bringeth in the first begotten into the world, He saith, And let all the angels of God worship Him."*

Revelation 1:5 – *"the first begotten of the dead"*

HIS <u>SOVEREIGNTY</u> – *"the Prince of the kings of the earth"*

In Revelation 11:15 we read: *"And the seventh angel sounded; and there were great voices in heaven, saying, The kingdoms of this world are become the kingdoms of our Lord, and of His Christ; and He shall reign forever and ever."*

Revelation 19;16 proclaims: *"And He hath on His vesture and on His thigh a name written, KING of kings, and LORD of lords."*

2. His <u>PLAN</u> of redemption 6/11/15

Revelation 1:5b – *"Unto Him that loved us, and washed us from our sins in <u>His own blood</u>."*

The past tense of the verbs *"loved"* and *"washed"* reminds us of the day our Lord Jesus died on the cross for our sins. <u>It was that moment in history</u> <u>when God demonstrated His love for us, and settled</u> <u>forever the problem of our sins.</u>

When the text says *"washed"* it uses the Greek word *"to loose"* and refreshes our minds with the great truth that we have been released from the slavery of sin, set free by the purchase price of the blood of Jesus Christ. I Corinthians 6:20 says: *"For ye are bought with a price: therefore glorify God in your body, and in your spirit, which are God's."* I Peter 1:18-19 reads: *"Forasmuch as ye know that ye were not redeemed with corruptible things, as silver and gold, from your vain conversation received by tradition from your fathers; But with the precious blood of Christ, as of a lamb without blemish and without spot."*

It was not the blood of an animal that atoned for our sins for Hebrews 10:4 says: *"For it is not possible that the blood of bulls and of goats should take away sins."* It was the blood of Jesus Christ that provided our redemption and salvation. Redemption is a primary theme throughout the Book of Revelation and the description of Jesus which continually emphasizes that fact that He is *"the Lamb"* which is mentioned 28 times.

3. His **PURPOSE** for the believer

Revelation 1:6a – *"And hath made us kings and priests unto God and His Father."*

What wonderful words of blessing! The Lord intends believers to be both *"kings"* and *"priests,"* and the goal of such authority and ministry is the Lord Himself – *"unto God and His Father."* Notice carefully that this statement is repeated often in the New Testament that the Father is the God and

Father of our Lord Jesus Christ – a mystery to us how God could be manifested as both Father and Son, and yet maintain a blessed relationship and distinction between one another so that the Son can refer to the Father as *"His God and Father."*

Some translations read that He has made us to be a *"kingdom"* rather than *"kings."* It is spiritual birth that we enter that kingdom according to John 3:3 – *"Verily, verily, I say unto thee, Except a man be born again, he cannot see the kingdom of God."* John 3:5 adds: *"Verily, verily, I say unto thee, Except a man be born of water and of the Spirit, he cannot enter the kingdom of God."* According to Colossians 1:13 we read: *"Who hath delivered us from the power of darkness, and hath translated us into the kingdom of His dear Son."*

The Apostle Peter makes it quite clear in I Peter 2:9 that all believers are *"priests."* The verse says *"But ye are a chosen generation, a royal priesthood, an holy nation, a peculiar people; that ye should shew forth the praises of Him Who hath called you out of darkness into His marvellous light."* Believers are *"a royal priesthood"* designed by God to proclaim His praise. We must always remember that the purpose of our priestly ministry and worship is to praise and worship the Lord, not ourselves!

4. His **PRAISE** for all eternity

Revelation 1:6b – *"to Him be glory and dominion forever and ever. Amen."* The Book of Revelation is

God's final message to the churches, and is intended to show us the ultimate objective of God in creating the world and humanity – that everything might praise and worship Him! This is a Book about worship. Often in the book we will read of creatures that God has made (both humans and angels) falling down and worshipping Him. The scene of heaven itself throughout the Book is one where the worship of God is the primary activity.

The *"Amen"* at the end of this section does not mean (of course!) that it is the end of what He has to say; it is a word of agreement, an outburst of praise (in a sense), proclaiming our joy at what was just said!

A SUMMARY OF THIS FINAL MESSAGE

Revelation 1:7-8 –*"Behold, He cometh with clouds; and every eye shall see Him, and they also which pierced Him; and all kindreds of the earth shall wail because of Him. Even so, Amen. I am Alpha and Omega, the beginning and the ending, saith the Lord, which is, and which was, and which is to come, the Almighty."*

These two verses give us an overview of the Book of Revelation. They reveal that it is a Book dealing with the coming of our Lord to this earth, and the character of our Lord himself. The Book unveils the event of His return and the glory of His Person – what it will be like when we see Him!

This overview includes two major issues of future events:

1. The Second <u>COMING</u> of Jesus Christ

Revelation 1:7 – *"Behold, He cometh with clouds; and every eye shall see Him, and they also which pierced Him; and all kindreds of the earth shall wail because of Him. Even so, Amen!"*

At least three things can be gleaned from this one glorious verse:

    (1)   The <u>ANTICIPATION</u> of the event
    (2)   The <u>ASSOCIATION</u> of clouds with His coming
    (3)   The <u>ATTITUDES</u> expressed when He comes

The <u>ANTICIPATION</u> of the event

The simple word *"Behold"* says it all! It is a simple and clear word asking for our attention, and is used 30 times in this Book of Revelation. It literally means "look for yourself." It suggests there is a responsibility that we all have in anticipating this great event of the return of Jesus Christ to planet earth. Are you looking for Him to come again? He said to His disciples in John 14:1-3:

"Let not your heart be troubled: ye believe in God, believe also in Me. In My Father's house are many mansions: if it were not so, I would have told you. I

go to prepare a place for you. And if I go and prepare a place for you, *I WILL COME AGAIN, and receive you unto Myself; there where I am, there ye may be also."*

When Jesus ascended back to heaven after His death, burial, and resurrection, we read in Acts 1:9-11:

"And when He had spoken these things, while they beheld, He was taken up; and a cloud received Him out of their sight. And while they looked stedfastly toward heaven as He went up, behold, two men stood by them in white apparel; Which also said, Ye men of Galilee, why stand ye gazing up into heaven? This same Jesus which is taken up from you into heaven, SHALL SO COME IN LIKE MANNER as ye have seen Him go into heaven."

Notice the simple word *"behold"* that introduces this amazing event – the ascension of our Lord back to heaven! The Bible does not say that the *"two"* who appeared unto them in white apparel were angels; that is a common belief among Christians. However, it is possible that these two, called *"two men"* were in fact, Moses and Elijah, who appeared with Him on the Mount of Transfiguration. Matthew 17:1-8 describes this amazing event:

"And after six days Jesus taketh Peter, James, and John his brother, and bringeth them up into an high mountain apart, and was transfigured before them: and His face did shine as the sun, and His

raiment was white as the light. And, behold, there appeared unto them Moses and Elias (Elijah) talking with Him. Then answered Peter, and said unto Jesus, Lord, it is good for us to be here: if Thou wilt, let us make here three tabernacles; one for Thee, and one for Moses, and one for Elias. While he yet spake, behold, a bright cloud overshadowed them: and behold a voice out of the cloud, which said, This is My beloved Son, in Whom I am well pleased; hear ye Him. And when the disciples heard it, they fell on their face, and were sore afraid. And Jesus came and touched them, and said, Arise, and be not afraid. And when they had lifted up their eyes, they saw no man, save Jesus only."

The Apostle John said in John 1:14: "And the Word was made flesh, and dwelt among us, (and we beheld His glory, the glory as of the only begotten of the Father), full of grace and truth." Yes, John was with Him at that glorious moment when His presence was exalted and manifested to Peter, James, and John. Also, the Apostle Peter said in II Peter 1:16-18: "For we have not followed cunningly devised fables, when we made known unto you the power and coming of our Lord Jesus Christ, but were eyewitnesses of His majesty. For He received from God the Father honor and glory, when there came such a voice to Him from the excellent glory, this is My beloved Son, in Whom I am well pleased. And this voice which came from heaven we heard, when we were with Him in the holy mount."

43

The **ASSOCIATION** of clouds with his coming

Revelation 1:7 – *"Behold, He cometh with clouds"*

Similar words are found in Matthew 24:30: *"And then shall appear the sign of the Son of man in heaven: and then shall all tribes of the earth mourn, and they shall see the Son of man coming in the clouds of heaven with power and great glory."*

These are not simply rain clouds, but clouds of glory that were prophesied in Daniel 7:13-14:

"I say in the night visions, and, behold, one like the Son of man came with the clouds of heaven, and came to the Ancient of days, and they brought Him near before Him. And there was given Him dominion, and glory, and a kingdom, that all people, nations, and languages, should serve Him: His dominion is an everlasting dominion, which shall not pass away, and His kingdom that which shall not be destroyed."

Luke 21:27 adds: *"And then shall they see the Son of man coming in a cloud with power and great glory."*

The Book of Revelation is focused upon the Second Coming of Jesus Christ that will occur at the end of the Great Tribulation, the coming Day of the Lord on planet earth. Previous to this event, the Bible speaks of an event in I Thessalonians 4:16-17:

"For the Lord Himself shall descend from heaven with a shout, with the voice of the archangel, and with the trump of God: and the dead in Christ shall rise first: Then we which are alive and remain shall be caught up together with them in the clouds, to meet the Lord in the air: and so shall we ever be with the Lord."

The words *"caught up"* come from the Greek word *harpazo* which in a Latin Bible becomes the word *rapturo* from which we get the English word *"rapture."* This is NOT the same event as described in the Book of Revelation. It occurs seven years (at least) previously. This event brings church age believers together *"in the clouds."* Old Testament believers, along with the believers of the Tribulation period (mentioned in Revelation 7), will be resurrected at the end of the Tribulation (Revelation 20).

Remember that it was a *"pillar of cloud"* that led the children of Israel through the wilderness by day. Exodus 13:21-22 says: *"And the LORD went before them by day in a pillar of a cloud, to lead them the way; and by night in a pillar of fire, to give them light; to go by day and night: He took not away the pillar of the cloud by day, nor the pillar of fire by night, from before the people."* This was a manifestation of the Divine presence. The glory of the Lord appeared *"in the cloud"* according to Exodus 16:10: *"And it came to pass, as Aaron spake unto the whole congregation of the children of Israel, that they looked toward the wilderness, and, behold, the glory of the LORD appeared in the cloud."*

It was also present when the tabernacle was built. In Exodus 40:34-38 we read:

"Then a cloud covered the tent of the congregation, and the glory of the LORD filled the tabernacle. And Moses was not able to enter into the tent of the congregation, because the cloud abode thereon, and the glory of the LORD filled the tabernacle. And when the cloud was taken up from over the tabernacle, the children of Israel went onward in all their journeys: but if the cloud were not taken up, then they journeyed not till the day that it was taken up. For the cloud of the LORD was upon the tabernacle by day, and fire was on it by night, in the sight of all the house of Israel, throughout all their journeys."

The *"clouds"* emphasize the Divine presence – Jewish people often speak of the *"Shekinah glory"* of the LORD that was dwelling with His people in both the cloud by day and the fire by night.

The **ATTITUDES** expressed when he comes

Revelation 1:7 says: *"and every eye shall see Him, and they also which pierced Him: and all kindreds of the earth shall wail because of Him. Even so. Amen."*

These words appear to be a clear reference to Zechariah 12:10-14:

"And I will pour upon the house of David, and upon the inhabitants of Jerusalem, the Spirit of grace and of supplications: and they shall look upon Me Whom they have pierced, and they shall mourn for Him, as one mourneth for his only son, and shall be in bitterness for Him, as one that is in bitterness for his firstborn.   In that day shall there be a great mourning in Jerusalem, as the mourning of Hadadrimmon in the valley of Megiddon.   And the land shall mourn, every family apart; the family of the house of David apart, and their wives apart; the family of the house of Nathan apart, and their wives apart; the family of the house of Levi apart, and their wives apart; the family of Shimei apart. and their wives apart; All the families that remain, every family apart, and their wives apart."

This prophecy speaks of the day when the inhabitants of Jerusalem will experience the outpouring of the Holy Spirit and they will *"look upon Me Whom they have pierced."*   They will *"mourn"* for Him as one mourns for his only son, and grieve for Him as one grieves for a firstborn.

Ezekiel 39:25-29 also confirms this event when it says:

"Therefore thus saith the Lord GOD; Now will I bring again the captivity of Jacob, and have mercy upon the whole house of Israel, and will be jealous

47

for My holy Name; After that they have borne their shame, and all their trespasses whereby they have trespassed against Me, when they dwelt safely in their land, and none made them afraid. When I have brought them again from the people, and gathered them out of their enemies' lands, and am sanctified in them in the sight of many nations; Then shall they know that I am the LORD their God, which caused them to be led into captivity among the heathen: but I have gathered them unto their own land, and have left none of them any more there. Neither will I hide My face any more from them: for I have poured out My Spirit upon the house of Israel, saith the Lord GOD."

Some believe that the word "spirit" in Zechariah 12:10 refers to the Holy Spirit, and many believe that it refers to the work of God in bringing His people to repentance. It is the spirit of conviction as well as the spirit of desire to seek God's forgiveness and restoration.

Ezekiel 39:29 seems to favor the view that it is the Holy Spirit that is poured out: *"for I have poured out My Spirit upon the house of Israel, saith the Lord GOD."* The prophecy of Joel 2:28-29 would also favor the view that it is the Holy Spirit that is poured out "upon all flesh" for once again it is called "My spirit" two times.

NOTE: The majority of Hebrew MSS read *"they will look to Me, the One they have pierced through."* Some, however, read *"they will look on Me in place of him whom they pierced.*" The result of this reading is that it is not Yahveh Who is pierced but someone else.

However, the Hebrew evidence overwhelmingly favors the traditional reading. Some will argue that it is not referring to a literal "piercing" as argued by Christian expositors, but rather an emotional "piercing."

The shift in pronouns is highly significant in the interpretation of this verse. In the first case, it is Yahveh Who is *"pierced"* by the usage of the pronoun *"Me"*; But, in the next phrase we read *"and they shall mourn for Him."*

If Yahveh is pierced through, who is the *"Him"* Who is being lamented? Why should the lament not be for Yahveh, the One Who has been pierced through? The most natural explanation is that the change in pronoun does not change the subject.

It is Yahveh Who is pierced and He is the One Whom His people, having come to their senses as to what they have done, mourn in repentance. From the standpoint of Yahveh, it is *"Me"* that is the focus; from the standpoint of the people it is *"Him."*

The verb *"to pierce"* (Hebrew: daqar) occurs 11 times; Here, in Zechariah, it appears twice – in 12:10 and in 13:3 where a false prophet is pierced through by his father and mother (cf. Deuteronomy 13:6-11).

The false prophet is *"pierced"* (slain) for his deception and lies; the true prophet is *"pierced"* for His holiness, righteousness and integrity. The New Testament clearly connects this passage to the death of our Lord Yeshua in John 19:33-37:

"But when they came to Jesus, and saw that He was dead already, they brake not His legs: But one of the soldiers with a spear pierced His side, and forthwith came there out blood and water. And he that saw it (the Apostle John) *bare record, and his record is true: and he knoweth that he saith true, that ye might believe. For those things were done, that the Scripture should be fulfilled, A bone of Him shall not be broken. And again another Scripture saith, They shall look on Him Whom they pierced."*

When the Bible says *"they shall mourn for Him as one mourneth for his only son"* – it is the Hebrew word *hayyachid* that is used. This is the same Hebrew word used in Genesis 22:2 when the LORD told Abraham: *"Take now thy son, thine only son Isaac."* Hebrews 11:17 translates it *"his only begotten son."*

Abraham had other sons, but this son, Isaac, was his unique son through whom the Messiah would come (cf. Hebrews 11:18). It is quite interesting to see that the LXX uses the Greek word *agapetos* to translate the Hebrew word – *"beloved."*

The words of Zechariah 12:10: *"and shall be in bitterness for Him, as one that is in bitterness for*

50

his firstborn" reminds us of the situation in ancient Egypt.

The word for *"firstborn"* (Hebrew: <u>bekor</u>) is rendered by the Greek Old Testament with the word <u>prototokos</u> which is used of our <u>Lord Yeshua</u> in Colossians 1:15: *"Who is the image of the invisible God, the <u>firstborn</u> of every creature."* Also, in Colossians 1:18 where we read: *"And He is the Head of the body, the church: Who is the beginning, the <u>firstborn</u> from the dead; that in all things He might have the preeminence."*

In <u>Zechariah 12:11</u> we read: *"In that day shall there be a great mourning in Jerusalem, as the mourning of Hadad-rimmon in the valley of Megiddon."*

The problem here is that we have no evidence whatsoever of any place or person by the name of Hadad-rimmon. Many Bible scholars connect this with the violent death of King Josiah at Megiddo.

II Kings 23:28-30 – *"Now the rest of the acts of Josiah, and all that he did, are they not written in the book of the chronicles of the kings of Judah? In his days Pharaoh-necho king of Egypt went up against the king of Assyria to the river Euphrates; and king Josiah went against him; and he slew him at Megiddo, when he had seen him. And his servants carried him in a chariot dead from Megiddo, and brought him to Jerusalem, and buried him in his own sepulcher. And the people of*

51

the land took Jehoahaz the son of Josiah, and anointed him king in his father's stead."

There is a passage in Jeremiah 22:10-12 that some connect with this reference in Zechariah 12:11:

"Weep ye not for the dead, neither bemoan him: but weep sore for him that goeth away: for he shall return no more, nor see his native country. For thus saith the LORD touching Shallum the son of Josiah king of Judah, which reigned instead of Josiah his father, which went forth out of this place; He shall not return thither anymore; But he shall die in the place whither they have led him captive, and shall see this land no more."

We also have a reference to an "ordinance" that involved mourning for Josiah in II Chronicles 35:20-27:

"After all this, when Josiah had prepared the temple, Necho king of Egypt came up to fight against Carchemish by Euphrates: and Josiah went out against him. But he sent ambassadors to him, saying, What have I to do with thee, thou king of Judah? I come not against thee this day, but against the house wherewith I have war: for God commanded me to make haste; forbear thee from meddling with God, Who is with me, that He destroy thee not. Nevertheless Josiah would not turn his face from him, but disguised himself, that he might fight with him, and hearkened not unto the words of Necho from the mouth of God, and

came to fight in the valley of Megiddo. And the archers shot at king Josiah; and the king said to his servants, Have me away; for I am sore wounded. His servants therefore took him out of that chariot, and put him in the second chariot that he had; and they brought him to Jerusalem, and he died, and was buried in one of the sepulchers of his fathers. And all Judah and Jerusalem mourned for Josiah. And Jeremiah lamented for Josiah: and all the singing men and the singing women spake of Josiah in their lamentations to this day, and made them an ordinance in Israel: and, behold, they are written in the lamentations. Now the rest of the acts of Josiah, and his goodness, according to that which was written in the law of the LORD, and his deeds, first and last, behold, they are written in the book of the kings of Israel and Judah."

The words of Zechariah 12:12 say: *"And the land shall mourn, every family apart."* The repentance is not a corporate or national one, but rather an individual one.

It is interesting that the royal house of David is not exempt from this repentance. The reference to the *"house of Nathan"* is no doubt the result of the curse placed upon Jechoniah (Coniah) mentioned in Jeremiah 22:28-30:

"Is this man Coniah a despised broken idol? Is he a vessel wherein is no pleasure? Wherefore are they cast out, he and his seed, and are cast into a land which they know not? O earth, earth, earth, hear

the word of the LORD. *Thus saith the LORD, Write ye this man childless, a man that shall not prosper in his days: for no man of his seed shall prosper, sitting upon the throne of David, and ruling any more in Judah.*"

The *"house of Levi"* also reveals that the religious leaders were not exempt either. Shimei was the grandson of Levi through Gershom and was not a priest (line traced through Kohath), and so all the Levites are also to mourn.

The verse that follows this amazing prophecy in Zechariah 12:10-14 clearly shows that cleansing is available for all who indeed repent!

Zechariah 13:1 – *"In that day there shall be a fountain opened to the house of David and to the inhabitants of Jerusalem for sin and for uncleanness."*

The first word refers to disobedience to God's revealed will, and the second refers to the defilement that will result from it.

If repentance occurs, there is forgiveness and cleansing – praise the Lord!

2. The glorious CHARACTER of the coming King

Revelation 1:8 – *"I am Alpha and Omega, the beginning and the ending, saith the Lord, which is,* and which was, and which is to come, the Almighty."

The word "Alpha" is referring to the first letter of the Greek alphabet, and the word "Omega" is the last letter. Our blessed Lord is everything that could ever be said and known! In Revelation 1:11 we read again: "I am Alpha and Omega, the first and the last" and in Revelation 1:17 – "Fear not; I am the first and the last." In Revelation 22:13 we read: "I am Alpha and Omega, the beginning and the end, the first and the last."

These words come from the prophecies of Isaiah. We read in Isaiah 44:6-8:

"Thus saith the LORD the King of Israel, and His Redeemer the LORD of hosts; I am the first, and I am the last; and beside Me there is no God. And who, as I, shall call, and declare it, and set it in order for Me, since I appointed the ancient people? and the things that are coming, and shall come, let them shew unto them. Fear ye not, neither be afraid: have not I told thee from that time, and have declared it? Ye are even My witnesses. Is there a God beside Me? Yea, there is no God; I know not any."

Isaiah 48:12 – "Hearken unto Me, O Jacob and Israel, My called; I am He; I am the first, I also am the last."

What a wonderful SUMMARY of the Book of Revelation is found in Revelation 1:7-8!

THE HISTORICAL SITUATION IN WHICH THE REVELATION WAS WRITTEN

Revelation 1:9-11 – *"I John, who also am your brother, and companion in tribulation, and in the kingdom and patience of Jesus Christ, was in the isle that is called Patmos, for the word of God, and for the testimony of Jesus Christ. I was in the spirit on the Lord's day, and heard behind me a great voice, as of a trumpet, saying, I am Alpha and Omega, the first and the last: and, What thou seest, write in a book, and send it unto the seven churches which are in Asia; unto Ephesus, and unto Smyrna, and unto Pergamos, and unto Thyatira, and unto Sardis, and unto Philadelphia, and unto Laodicea."*

Historical factors behind the Book of Revelation would include the following:

THE ROMAN EMPIRE
THE DESTRUCTION OF JERUSALEM
(70 AD problem)
THE ISLAND OF PATMOS
THE APOSTLE JOHN

THE ROMAN EMPIRE
The history behind the Roman Empire began in 705 BC as the Roman Republic. When Julius Caesar took the reins of leadership over 600 years later, it

was the beginning of the Empire. His nephew, Octavian, became Augustus Caesar, the first ruler of what was declared to be the Empire. Under his leadership the Pax Romana (Roman peace) was declared.

WHAT HAPPENED IN 70 AD, AND WAS THE BOOK OF REVELATION WRITTEN BEFORE THAT DATE?

The word "preterist" is from a Latin word meaning "past." Those who adhere to this viewpoint of Bible prophecy argue that the prophecies of the Olivet Discourse and the Book of Revelation were fulfilled in the events of the 70 AD destruction of Jerusalem and the Jewish Temple. Preterists believe that the Second Coming of Christ occurred in 70 AD in the sense of judgment, and that the result of this destruction of Jerusalem and the Jewish Temple is the replacement of the nation of Israel with the Church.

TWO IMPORTANT QUESTIONS:

1. Did the Second Coming of Jesus Christ occur in 70 AD in the sense of judgment upon the Nation of Israel?

2. Did the Church replace Israel in God's prophetic program for the future?

There are two primary proof texts which are used by those who believe the PRETERIST view of Bible prophecy:

PROOF TEXT #1

Matthew 16:28 – *"Verily I say unto you, There be some standing here, which shall not taste of death, till they see the Son of man coming in His kingdom."*

The connection with the Mount of Transfiguration is obvious – Matthew 17:1-2 (The conjunction *"and"* clearly establishes the connection between the two passages) The remark of Peter in II Peter 1:16-18 clearly points to the transfiguration and not the destruction of Jerusalem. The "some" is referring to Peter, James, & John.

PROOF TEXT #2

Matthew 24:34 – *"Verily I say unto you, This generation shall not pass, till all these things be fulfilled."*

The word *"generation"* from the Greek word *genos* is used 21 times; from the Greek word *genea* it is used another 42 times – a total of 63 times in the NT. The words *"this generation"* appear 16 of those times. Whatever the meaning of the word *"generation"* it is clear that it will exist until *"all these things"* are fulfilled. That cannot apply to the destruction of Jerusalem.

It is quite possible that the word *"generation"* refers not to a period of time as some suggest that Hebrews 3:9-10 teaches (40 years) but rather to the nation of Israel. The words *"this generation"* are more consistent when they are understood to be

Israel. It is a promise of the survival of the nation of Israel during the tribulation. (cf. Luke 11:50-51) Why would the words *"may be required of this generation"* apply to first century Jews who were not responsible for the death of the prophets mentioned? It would make sense if it applies to the nation of Israel. Also, in the chapter previous to Matthew 24-25 we have a clear connection of the words *"this generation"* that refer to Israel – Matthew 23:36.

SO, WHAT HAPPENED IN 70 AD?

1. The <u>PREDICTION</u> of Jesus was fulfilled
     Matthew 24:1-2; Luke 21:20-24

The destruction of the Second Jewish Temple happened in 70 AD!

2. The <u>PROPHECIES</u> of God about Israel were not cancelled nor fulfilled in the history of the Church!

The prophecy of God's everlasting and unconditional covenant to the children of Israel was not cancelled - Genesis 12:1-3; 17:7-8; Psalm 89:30-37

God has NOT forsaken them – Isa. 41:8-9, 17; 43:5-7; 45:25; 49:13-16; 54:6-8; Jer. 31:35-37; Romans 11:1-2

The prophecies of worldwide CALAMITIES did NOT occur in 70 AD – Matthew 24:4-28 (widespread deception, wars, plagues, famines, earthquakes, etc., and coming of Messiah, etc.)

The prophecy of Israel's COMING back to the land in the future did NOT happen – Isaiah 35:10; Jeremiah 30:3; 31:7-9; Ezekiel 36:24; Amos 9:13-15

The prophecy of a global CATASTROPHE called "The Great Tribulation" did NOT occur.

The prophecy of Israel's CONVERSION at the end of the tribulation did NOT happen – Isaiah 44:21-23; 59:20-21; 62:11-12; Zechariah 12:10; 13:1; Romans 11:25-27

The PROPHECIES in the Book of Revelation were NOT fulfilled in 70 AD!

The Preterists MUST argue for this book being written BEFORE the destruction of Jerusalem; However, history is clear that John was exiled to the island of Patmos during the reign of Domitian (81-96 AD) - long after the destruction of Jerusalem. All historical references to the date of the writing of the Book of Revelation state clearly that it happened in 95 AD during the reign of Domitian (81-96 AD).

The POPULATION of the world was NOT reduced by one half!

The PLANET was NOT affected as it will be by global disaster!

The **PLAGUE** of locusts did NOT occur in 70 AD!

The **PERSONS** known as the two witnesses did NOT appear in 70 AD!

The **PRESENCE** of the beast and the false prophet and their miracles NEVER happened in 70 AD!

The **PLACING** of a mark on people did NOT happen in 70 AD!

The **PREACHING** of 144,000 Jews NEVER happened in 70 AD!

The **POWER** of a worldwide earthquake did NOT happen in 70 AD!

The **PARTNERSHIP** of a ten-nation confederacy did NOT exist in 70 AD!

The **PUNISHMENT o**f Babylon the Great NEVER happened in 70 AD!

The **PERSON** of the Messiah did NOT return on a white horse!

The **PARTICULARS** of the 1000 year reign of Jesus Christ have NOT happened yet!

The final **PLACE** of judgment known as the Great White Throne did NOT happen!

The **PROMISE** of the heavenly city was NOT fulfilled in 70 AD!

In 70 AD Jerusalem and its Temple were destroyed – BUT, God did NOT cancel His everlasting covenant and today there is simply a partial blindness upon Israel that will soon be removed! Romans 11:25-27

Therefore: ISRAEL is NOT the Church and has never been forsaken by God!

Therefore: Bible Prophecies about the Tribulation have NEVER happened as yet!

Therefore: Our LORD YESHUA did NOT come again in 70 AD!

Therefore: Our BLESSED HOPE is still in the future!

ISLAND OF PATMOS

The island of Patmos is seldom mentioned by the ancient authors in their books. It is to be supposed that its prehistoric inhabitants were the Cariens. The name Patmos, as it is generally believed derives from the word Latmos. Patmos was at times colonized by the Doriens and thereafter followed the Ionians. It is said that the mythology hero Oreste pursued by the Erinnyes, because he killed his mother Clytemnestra, took shelter in Patmos, coming with the Argiens. The walls of the 6th and 4th centuries BC, of the ancient Acropole situated

situated over the hill Castelli, are evidencing the location of the ancient town.

From the well preserved until now relics, it is to be supposed that into the Acropolis ground existed at times the Apollon Temple, the Bacchus Temple and the Hippodrome. Old cemeteries, pottery fragments, carved works in bas-reliefs, inscriptions, sepulchral stones and other dispersed or framed into walls sculptures of the Christian orthodox churches, all said evidences are a proof of the flourishing and prosperous stand of the ancient Patmos.

At the former ancient age it was particularly adored in Patmos the goddess Diane, who was considered as the Patroness of the island. Under the domination of the Romans, the island continued to decline. It was abandoned and used as an exile place. In the year 95 AD, John the Apostle was banished to Patmos by the emperor Domitian for preaching the Gospel at Ephesus.

At the Emperor's death in 97 AD John returned to Ephesus where he lived to a ripe old age. A text entitled "Voyages and Miracles of St. John the Theologian" written by his disciple Prochoros was embraced by the Byzantine tradition and by the Christians in Patmos.

My (author) first visit to Patmos could easily understand why Rome made it a place of exile. It is a mountainous island with very little evidence of villages or cities of past history. High up on one of the mountains is the Greek monastery built over the supposed residence of John the Apostle and the place where he wrote the Book of Revelation.

The island is approximately ten miles long and six miles wide, covered with rocks and very little vegetation. A personal look at the island causes a person to see clearly why there was no escape from it – making a perfect place for exile.

According to Revelation 1:9 John was put on the island *"for the word of God, and for the testimony of Jesus Christ."*

The graves and tombstone markers of both John and the mother of Jesus are in the city of Ephesus to this day.

HOW DID THIS AMAZING APOCALYPSE COME TO JOHN?

Revelation 1:10-11 – *"I was in the Spirit on the Lord's day, and heard behind me a great voice, as of a trumpet, saying, I am Alpha and Omega, the first and the last: and, What thou seest, write in a book* (scroll), *and send it unto the seven churches which are in Asia; unto Ephesus, and unto Smyrna, and unto Pergamos, and unto Thyatira, and unto Sardis, and unto Philadelphia, and unto Laodicea."* One of the great Bible lands tours that believers can take today is a visit to the ancient sites of these seven churches and cities. The messages to these churches opens up to our minds and hearts when we see the places where they existed.

The word *"Asia"* is referring to the Roman province of today's western Turkey – Asia Minor.

The *"great voice"* is a "loud voice" like the sound of a trumpet (or Shofar). It reminds us of I Thessalonians 4:16 where the return of Jesus Christ is accompanied with a *"shout....and the trumpet of God."*

What is the meaning of the words *"I was in the Spirit on the Lord's day"*?

Some believe that this statement simply means that John was filled with the Spirit on Sunday! However, we do not believe that this is the point. First of all, *"the Lord's day"* is not referring to Sunday; This statement is referring to the important prophetic news about the coming *"Day of the LORD."* It is a phrase that refers to the seven years of the coming great tribulation! That's what most of the Book of Revelation is about!

The phrase *"in the Spirit"* is probably referring to the contrast between *"the flesh"* and *"the spirit."* A small *"s"* would be more appropriate in describing what is happening. John was being transferred by some spiritual understanding to the actual days of the future – Amazing indeed!

A VISION OF JESUS CHRIST
Revelation 1:12-20

A noticeable change has taken place from what the four gospels describe when they speak of Jesus Christ. This is a picture of what He is like now that He has risen from the dead. He is not pictured in the robe of humanity, but in the garments of royalty and deity. He is no longer the humble suffering Servant, willing to endure the agony and death of a Roman cross – He is now the KING of kings and LORD of lords! He has risen from the dead, and the glory He had before He came into the world in a manger in Bethlehem is now brilliantly displayed. It is a picture of glory and greatness.

HIS EXALTED POSITION

Revelation 1:12 – *"And I turned to see the voice that spake with me. And being turned, I saw seven golden candlesticks."*

The *"candlesticks"* or *"lampstands"* represent the seven churches (v. 20) and Jesus is standing in the midst of them. According to Revelation 2:1, He is the one Who *"walketh in the midst of the seven golden candlesticks."*

In Matthew 18:15-20 we read: *"Moreover if thy brother shall trespass against thee, go and tell him his fault between thee and him alone: if he shall hear thee, thou hast gained thy brother. But if he will not hear thee, then take with thee one or two more, that in the mouth of two or three witnesses every word may be established. And if he shall neglect to hear them, tell it unto the church: but if he neglect to hear the church, let him be unto thee as an heathen man and a publican* (tax-collector). *Verily I say unto you, whatsoever ye shall bind on earth shall be bound in heaven: and whatsoever ye shall loose on earth shall be loosed in heaven. Again I say unto you, That if two of you shall agree on earth as touching any thing that they shall ask, it shall be done for them of My Father which is in heaven. For where two or three are gathered together in My Name, there am I in the midst of them."*

The *"two or three"* are referring to being the witnesses as to what was said or done regarding the alleged transgression. If they are in agreement, it carries the force of our Lord's presence and authority.

To say that Jesus is *"in the midst of"* the churches is to recognize His central exalted position and place of authority. One of the greatest needs in our churches today is to see the exalted position of our Lord over all, and to submit to His authority. Too much attention and honor is paid to human leadership that often robs the Lord Jesus of His central position in the church. It is HE, not a board of elders or directors, or pastors, or congregation and its votes, that is the HEAD of the Church!

In Isaiah 6:1-4 we read: *"In the year that king Uzziah died I saw also the Lord sitting upon a throne, high and lifted up, and his train filled the temple. Above it stood the seraphims, each one had six wings; with twain he covered his face, and with twain he covered his feet, and with twain he did fly. And one cried unto another, and said, Holy, holy, holy, is the LORD of hosts: the whole earth is full of His glory. And the posts of the door moved at the voice of Him that cried, and the house was filled with smoke."*

We read again in Isaiah 57:15: *"For thus saith the high and lofty One that inhabiteth eternity, Whose Name is Holy; I dwell in the high and holy place, and with him also that is of a contrite and humble spirit, to revive the spirit of the humble, and to revive the heart of the contrite ones."* Psalm 92:8 says: *"But Thou, LORD, art most high for evermore."* Psalm 99:1-3 says: *"The LORD reigneth; let the people tremble: He sitteth between the cherubims; let the earth be moved. The LORD is great in Zion; and He is high above all the people. Let them praise Thy great and terrible Name; for it is holy."* Psalm 99:9 adds: *"Exalt the LORD our God, and worship at His holy hill; for the LORD our God is holy."*

HIS ETERNAL PRESENCE

Revelation 1:13 – *"And in the midst of the seven candlesticks one like unto the Son of man, clothed with a garment down to the foot, and gift about the paps with a golden girdle."*

The phrase *"Son of man"* is a Messianic term that was the favorite title of Jesus Himself. In Daniel 7:13-14 we read of its usage:

"I saw in the night visions, and, behold, one like the Son of man came with the clouds of heaven, and came to the Ancient of days, and they brought Him near before Him. And there was given Him dominion, and glory, and a kingdom, that all people, nations, and languages, should serve Him: His dominion is an everlasting dominion, which shall not pass away, and His kingdom that which shall not be destroyed."

The phrase *"the Son of man"* is the heart of the gospel message. God became man and brought salvation to us all. Because He is the God Who is always there, He can save us from our sins – He died and paid for them all. His humanity will be kept for all eternity. His resurrection is the guarantee to all believers of our future bodily resurrection as well as a blessing that we will have an everlasting revelation of God in human form. What an aid to our understanding and need!

His garment with which He is clothed, goes all the way down to His feet – it is the garment of royalty and reminds us that He is indeed the KING of kings and LORD of lords! The golden band around his chest pictures His majesty and authority. The garment is like the one worn by the Jewish High Priest of Exodus 39, and is a reminder that Jesus is our High Priest which is the message of Hebrews 3:1.

HIS EXCITING PICTURE

Revelation 1:14-16 – *"His head and His hairs were white like wool, as white as snow; and His eyes were as a flame of fire; and His feet like unto fine brass, as if they burned in a furnace; and His voice as the sound of many waters. And He had in His right hand seven stars: and out of His mouth went a sharp two-edged sword; and his countenance was as the sun shineth in his strength."*

This is no ordinary look at the man we know from the gospels in the Person of Jesus Christ. To say that His appearance is "exciting" and "unique" seems so inadequate in describing the picture of Him that is seen in the Book of Revelation. It is a glorious description that could be given to God alone!

Consider the following facts about the picture of our blessed resurrected Lord:

His **PURITY** – *"His head and His hairs were white like wool, as white as snow"*

Isaiah 1:18 says: *" Come now, and let us reason together, saith the LORD: though your sins be as scarlet, they shall be as white as snow; though they be red like crimson, they shall be as wool."*

The phrase *"white as snow"* speaks of cleansing and purity. There is no sin or evil in the Person of our blessed Lord, the Messiah of Israel. There never has been and never will be!

II Corinthians 5:21 states clearly: *"For He* (God the Father) *hath made Him* (God the Son) *to be sin for us, Who knew no sin; that we might be made the righteousness of God in Him."* Hebrews 4:12-16 makes this fact, the impeccability of the Messiah a clear message for all of us who come to the Father through the work and Person of the Son:

"For the word of God is quick, and powerful, and sharper than any two-edged sword, piercing even to the dividing asunder of soul and spirit, and of the joints and marrow, and is a discerner of the thoughts and intents of the heart. Neither is there any creature that is not manifest in His sight: but all things are naked and opened unto the eyes of Him with Whom we have to do. Seeing then that we have a great High Priest, that is passed into the heavens, Jesus the Son of God, let us hold fast our profession. For we have not an High Priest which cannot be touched with the feeling of our infirmities; but was in all points tempted like as we are, yet without sin. Let us therefore come boldly unto the throne of grace, that we may obtain mercy, and find grace to help in time of need."

He Who *"knew no sin"* and is totally *"without sin"* is able to be *"touched with the feeling of our infirmities."* What a Savior we have!

Hebrews 7:24-28 also declares: *"But this man, because He continueth ever, hath an unchangeable priesthood. Wherefore He is able also to save them to the uttermost that come unto God by Him, seeing He ever liveth to make intercession for them. For such an High Priest became us, Who is holy, harmless, <u>undefiled, separate from sinners</u>, and made higher than the heavens; Who needeth not daily, as those high priests, to offer up sacrifice, first for His own sins, and then for the people's; for this He did once, when He offered up Himself. For the law maketh men high priests which have infirmity; but the word of the oath, which was since the law, maketh the Son, <u>Who is consecrated for evermore</u>."*

The high priests (as important as they were and are) had to offer a sacrifice for their own sins, but our great High Priest did not need to do that since He was and is totally (in every way) without sin! Therefore He can bear our sins and pay the price of those sins with His own blood!

His <u>PENETRATION</u> – *"and His eyes were as a flame of fire"*

The *"eyes"* represent His knowledge of all things, for as Colossians 2:3 states: *"In Whom are hid all the treasures of wisdom and knowledge."* I John 3:20 says: *"For if our heart condemn us, God is greater than our heart, and <u>knoweth all things</u>."* As Hebrews 4:13 says: *"Neither is there any creature that is not manifest in His sight; but all* *things are naked and opened unto the <u>eyes</u> of Him with Whom we have to do."*

The words *"as a flame of fire"* suggest that He is indignant about what He sees. He intends to bring His judgment upon what He knows about this world and all humanity in it. The *"fire"* often represents judgment in the Bible. Hebrews 12:29 says: *"For our God is a consuming fire."* Hebrews 10:26-31 makes this fact so clear (as it relates to judgment):

"For if we sin wilfully after that we have received the knowledge of the truth, there remaineth no more sacrifice for sins, but a certain fearful looking for of judgment and <u>fiery indignation</u>, which shall devour the adversaries. He that despised Moses' law died without mercy under two or three witnesses: Of how much sorer punishment, suppose ye, shall he be thought worthy, who hath trodden under foot the Son of God, and counted the blood of the covenant, wherewith he was sanctified, an unholy thing, and hath done despite unto the Spirit of grace? For we know Him that hath said, Vengeance belongeth unto Me, I will recompense, saith the Lord. And again, The Lord shall judge His people. It is a fearful thing to fall into the hands of the living God."

It should be quite clear to all of us that we are accountable to Jesus Christ Who is the Judge of all the earth.

His **PUNISHMENT** – *"And His feet like unto fine brass, as if they burned in a furnace"*

The *"feet"* of our glorified Messiah also represent the issue of judgment. In Revelation 19:15 we read: *"and He treadeth the winepress of the fierceness and wrath of Almighty God."*

Isaiah 63:1-6 speaks of the future coming of our Messiah:

"Who is this that cometh from Edom, with dyed garments from Bozrah? This that is glorious in his apparel, travelling in the greatness of His strength? I that speak in righteousness, mighty to save. Wherefore art Thou red in Thine apparel, and Thy garments like him that <u>treadeth in the winevat</u>? I have <u>trodden the winepress alone</u>; and of the people there was none with Me: for I will <u>tread</u> them in Mine anger, and <u>trample</u> them in My fury; and their blood shall be sprinkled upon My garments, and I will stain all My raiment. For the day of vengeance is in Mine heart, and the year of My redeemed is come. And I looked, and there was none to help; and I wondered that there was none to uphold: therefore Mine own arm brought salvation unto Me; and My fury it upheld Me. And I will <u>tread down</u> the people in Mine anger, and make them drunk in My fury, and I will bring down their strength to the earth."

The Messiah's *"feet"* will one day trample/tread the winepress of the wrath of God. That *"winepress"* is mentioned also in Revelation 14:18-20:

"And another angel came out from the altar, which had power over fire; and cried with a loud cry to Him that had the sharp sickle, saying, Thrust in Thy sharp sickle, and gather the clusters of the vine of the earth; for her grapes are fully ripe. And the angel thrust in his sickle into the earth, and cast it into <u>the great winepress of the wrath of God.</u>" And <u>the winepress was trodden</u> without the city, and blood came out of the winepress, even unto the horse bridles, by the space of a thousand and six hundred furlongs."

It would appear that the distance of *"a thousand and six hundred furlongs"* (about 200 miles) is covering the entire land of Israel. Israel's land will be the coming *"winepress of the wrath of God."* The *"feet"* of the Messiah will trample those who thought they could attack God's people (Israel) and not pay a price for it. They are wrong! Zechariah 12:9 records the Messiah's words: *"And it shall come to pass in that day, that I will seek to destroy all the nations that come against Jerusalem."*

His <u>PROCLAMATION</u> — *"and His voice as the sound of many waters"*

We learn of the powerful voice of the Lord our Messiah in Psalm 29:3-11:

75

"The voice of the LORD is upon the waters: the God of glory thundereth: the LORD is upon many waters. The voice of the LORD is full of majesty. The voice of the LORD breaketh the cedars; yea, the LORD breaketh the cedars of Lebanon. He maketh them also to skip like a calf; Lebanon and Sirion like a young unicorn. The voice of the LORD divideth the flames of fire. The voice of the LORD shaketh the wilderness; the LORD shaketh the wilderness of Kadesh. The voice of the LORD maketh the hinds to calve, and discovereth the forests: and in His temple doth every one speak of His glory. The LORD sitteth upon the flood; yea, the LORD sitteth King forever. The LORD will give strength unto His people; the LORD will bless His people with peace."

Hebrews 12:25-29 speaks of the power of the Lord's voice:

"See that ye refuse not Him that speaketh. For if they escaped not who refused Him that spake on earth, much more shall not we escape, if we turn away from Him that speaketh from heaven: Whose voice then shook the earth: but now He hath promised, saying, Yet once more I shake not the earth only, but also heaven. And this word, Yet once more, signifieth the removing of those things that are shaken, as of things that are made, that those things which cannot be shaken may remain. Wherefore we receiving a kingdom which cannot be moved, let us have grace, whereby we may serve

God acceptably with reverence and godly fear: For our God is a consuming fire."

His <u>**POSITION**</u> – *"And He had in His right hand seven stars"*

The *"seven stars"* are referring to *"the angels of the seven churches"* (according to Revelation 1:20). In Revelation 2:1 we read: *"These things saith He that holdeth the seven stars in His right hand."*

His position and place of authority in heaven is pictured at the *"right hand"* of God the Father. It is the place where the Messiah is seated. Romans 8:34 says: *"Who is he that condemneth? It is Christ that died, yea rather, that is risen again, Who is even at the <u>right hand of God</u>, Who also maketh intercession for us."*

Hebrews 1:1-3 says: *"God, Who at sundry times and in divers manners spake in time past unto the fathers by the prophets, Hath in these last days (literally in Greek – "the last of these days") spoken unto us by His Son, Whom He hath appointed Heir of all things, by Whom also He made the worlds; Who being the brightness of His glory, and the express image of His Person, and upholding all things by the word of His power, when He had by Himself purged our sins, <u>sat down on the right hand of the Majesty on high.</u>"*

We also learn from Hebrews 1:6-7 the position of the Messiah in relationship to the angels of God:

"And again, when He bringeth in the first begotten into the world, He saith, And let all the angels of God worship Him. And of the angels He saith, Who maketh His angels spirits, and His ministers a flame of fire." Again, in Hebrew 1:14 we read: *"Are they not all ministering spirits, sent forth to minister for them who shall be heirs of salvation?"*

In addition to the *"seven stars in His right hand"* we have the statement of Revelation 5:1: *"And I saw in the right hand of Him that sat on the throne a book (scroll) written within and on the backside, sealed with seven seals."*

His <u>POWER</u> – *"And out of His mouth went a sharp two-edged sword"*

Revelation 19:15 – *"And out of His mouth goeth a sharp sword, that with it He should smite the nations: and He shall rule them with a rod of iron: and He treadeth the winepress of the fierceness and wrath of Almighty God."*

Hebrews 4:12 says: *"For the word of God is quick, and powerful, and sharper than any two-edged sword, piercing even to the dividing asunder of soul and spirit, and of the joints and marrow, and is a discerner of the thoughts and intents of the heart."*

God's Word comes out of the mouth of the Messiah and smites the nations and rules them with a rod of iron!

In John 1:1-3 we read: *"In the beginning was the Word (Greek: logos), and the Word was with God, and the Word was God. The same was in the beginning with God. All things were made by Him; and without Him was not any thing made that was made."* John 1:14 adds: *"And the Word was made flesh, and dwelt among us, (and we beheld His glory, the glory as of the only begotten of the Father,) full of grace and truth."*

The Greek word *logos* can be translated into the English word "revelation." Our Lord Messiah is the revelation of the eternal God! He became flesh to die for our sins!

But, our resurrected Lord Messiah is able to simply speak the words, and nations will fall! He is the KING of all kings, and the LORD of all lords! He is the Ruler over all the kingdoms of this world, and one day as Revelation 11:15 says: *"The kingdoms of this world are become the kingdoms of our Lord, and of His Christ; and He shall reign for ever and ever."*

In the Messianic Psalm 2, we read in verses 8-9: *"Ask of Me (the Father), and I shall give Thee the heathen for Thine inheritance, and the uttermost parts of the earth for Thy possession. Thou shalt break them with a rod of iron; Thou shalt dash them in pieces like a potter's vessel."*

The power of the Messiah's words are greater than all the armies and weapons of this world! It was His word that brought the universe and galaxies into existence. Hebrews 11:3 says: *"Through faith we understand that the worlds were framed by the word of God, so that things which are seen were not made of things which do appear."*

His <u>PICTURE</u> – *"and His countenance was as the sun shineth in his strength"*

Malachi 4:1-2 states: *"For, behold, the day cometh that shall burn as an oven; and all the proud, yea, and all that do wickedly, shall be stubble: and the day that cometh shall burn them up, saith the LORD of hosts, that it shall leave them neither root nor branch. But unto you that fear My Name shall the Sun of righteousness arise with healing in His wings..."*

When Peter, James, and John were with our Lord on the Mount of Transfiguration, Matthew 17:2 says that our Lord Yeshua *"was transfigured before them: and His face did shine as the sun, and His raiment was white as the light."* Mark 9:3 adds: *"And His raiment became shining, exceeding white as snow; so as no fuller on earth can white them."* Luke 9:29 adds: *"And as He prayed, the fashion of His countenance was altered, and His raiment was white and glistering."* Luke 9:32 says clearly – *"they saw His glory."*

Peter wrote in II Peter 1:16-18 – *"For we have not followed cunningly devised fables, when we made known unto you the power and coming of our Lord*

Jesus Christ, but were eyewitnesses of His majesty. For He received from God the Father honor and glory, when there came such a voice to Him from the excellent glory, This is My beloved Son, in Whom I am well pleased. And this voice which came from heaven we heard, when we were with Him in the holy mount."

When a person looks directly into the bright sunlight, he or she cannot see much else. May all of us understand that we are going to need resurrected eyes to behold the beauty, glory, and majesty of our risen Lord Messiah!

THE <u>IMPACT</u> OF THIS VISION UPON THE APOSTLE JOHN

Revelation 1:17-18 – *"And when I saw Him, I fell at His feet as dead. And He laid His right hand upon me, saying unto me, Fear not; I am the first and the last; I am He that liveth, and was dead; and, behold, I am alive forevermore, Amen; and have the keys of hell (Hades) and of death."*

1. His immediate <u>REACTION</u> – *"I fell at His feet as dead"*

According to Hebrews 1:6 we read: *"And again, when He bringeth in the first begotten into the world, He saith, And let all the angels of God worship Him."* In Revelation 22:8-9 it says: *"And I John saw these things, and heard them. And when I had heard and seen, I fell down to worship before the feet of the angel which shewed me these things. Then saith he unto me, See thou do it not: for I am thy fellow-servant, and of thy brethren the prophets, and of them which keep the sayings of this book: WORSHIP GOD!"*

When John fell at His feet, it was an immediate sign of worship. When Joshua met the *"Captain of the host of the LORD"* we read in Joshua 5:13-15 these words:

"And it came to pass, when Joshua was by Jericho, that he lifted up his eyes and looked, and, behold, there stood a man over against him with His sword drawn in His hand: and Joshua went unto Him, and said unto Him, Art Thou for us, or for our adversaries? And He said, Nay; but as captain of the host of the LORD am I now come. And Joshua fell on his face to the earth, and did worship, and said unto Him, What saith my lord unto His servant? And the captain of the LORD's host said unto Joshua, Loose thy shoe from off thy foot; for the place whereon thou standest is holy. And Joshua did so."

A similar incident occurred in the life of Moses, recorded in Exodus 3:2-6:

"And the angel of the LORD appeared unto him in a flame of fire out of the midst of a bush: and he looked, and, behold, the bush burned with fire, and the bush was not consumed. And Moses said, I will now turn aside, and see this great sight, why the bush is not burnt. And when the LORD saw that he

turned aside to see, God called unto him out of the midst of the bush, and said, Moses, Moses. And he said, Here am I. And He said, Draw not nigh hither: put off thy shoes from off thy feet, for the place whereon thou standest is holy ground. Moreover He said, I am the God of thy father, the God of Abraham, the God of Isaac, and the God of Jacob. And Moses hid his face; for he was afraid to look upon God."

In both cases (Joshua and Moses) the response was similar and reminds us of the *"holy ground"* that becomes such because of the mighty presence of the Lord Himself.

    2. The wonderful <u>RESPONSE</u> he heard!

"Fear not; I am the first and the last: I am He that liveth, and was dead; and, behold, I am alive forevermore, Amen; and have the keys of hell and of death."

        (1)   FEAR is not necessary!

<u>Remember</u> Who He is – *"the first and the last"* - (Revelation 1:11 and 22:13)
Isaiah 44:6 – *"Thus saith the LORD the King of Israel, and His Redeemer the LORD of hosts; I am the first, and I am the last; and beside Me there is no God."*

        (2)   FAITH is essential!

83

<u>Rejoice</u> in His death and resurrection – *"I am He that liveth, and was dead; and, behold, I am alive forevermore."*

(3)   FUTURE is under control!

<u>Rest</u> in His sovereign control over all – *"and have the keys of hell (Hades) and of death"*

THE <u>INSTRUCTION</u> AS TO WHAT HE SHOULD WRITE!

Revelation 1:19-20 – *"Write the things which thou hast seen, and the things which are, and the things which shall be hereafter; The mystery of the seven stars which thou sawest in My right hand, and the seven golden candlesticks. The seven stars are the angels of the seven churches: and the seven candlesticks which thou sawest are the seven churches."*

It is clear in examining the context of the Book of Revelation that its outline is given in these final verses of chapter one.

FIRST – *"Write the things which thou hast seen"*
These words refer to the marvelous vision of the resurrected Messiah that we have just examined.

SECOND – *"and the things which are"*

It would appear that this instruction is referring to the seven churches in chapters 2-3.

THIRD – *"and the things which shall be hereafter"*

The word *"hereafter"* in the Greek text is *meta tauta* – "after these things." The clue here is found in Revelation 4:1 – *"After this I looked, and, behold, a door was opened in heaven: and the first voice which I heard was as it were of a trumpet talking with me; which said, Come up hither, and I will shew thee things which must be hereafter."* Once again, the Greek text behind the word *"hereafter"* is *meta tauta* – the same words of Revelation 1:19. The majority of the words of the Book of Revelation are found in chapters 4-22, and are all future from the history and words to the seven churches in chapters 2-3.

BOOK OF REVELATION
Understanding the Future

THE LORD OF THE CHURCHES
Part I
Revelation 2-5

NEGLECTED PRIORITIES
The Church at EPHESUS
Revelation 2:1-7

"Unto the angel of the church of Ephesus write; These things saith He that holdeth the seven stars in His right hand, Who walketh in the midst of the seven golden candlesticks; I know thy works, and thy labor, and thy patience, and how thou canst not bear them which are evil: and thou hast tried them which say they are apostles, and are not, and hast found them liars; And hast borne, and hast patience, and for My Name's sake hast labored, and hast not fainted. Nevertheless I have somewhat against thee, because thou hast left thy first love. Remember therefore from whence thou art fallen, and repent, and do the first works; or else I will come unto thee quickly, and will remove thy candlestick out of his place, except thou repent. But this thou hast, that thou hatest the deeds of the Nicolaitans, which I also hate. He that hath an ear, let him hear what the Spirit saith unto the churches; To him that overcometh will I give to eat of the tree of life, which is in the midst of the paradise of God."

ABOUT EPHESUS

Ephesus, one of the 12 cities of the Ionian League during the classical Greek era. In the Roman period, it was for many years the second largest city of the Roman Empire, ranking behind Rome. It had a population of more than 250,000 in the 1st century BC which made it the second largest city in the world.

The city was famous for the Temple of Artemis (Diana), the multi-breasted idol goddess of sex and fertility, known as one of the "Seven Wonders of the Ancient World" - which was completed around 550 BC. Ten years earlier, the city was conquered by the Lydians under the mighty king Croesus who was instrumental in the reconstruction of the Temple of Artemis. The temple measured 425 feet long, 220 feet wide, and 60 feet high. The Persians under Cyrus the Great conquered the Ionians and made them a part of the Achaemenid Empire of ancient Persia.

In 356 BC, the temple of Artemis was burned down by a lunatic named Herostratus – it was the night Alexander the Great was born! The citizens of Ephesus began immediately the project of restoring the temple, greatly enlarging it. When Alexander defeated the Persians, the citizens of Ephesus warmly received him, and Alexander even offered to finish the restoration of the Temple if they would have his name inscribed on it. The Ephesians turned him down. After Alexander's death in 323 BC, Ephesus came under the rule of one of Alexander's generals, Lysimachus, in 290 BC. The Syrian king Seleucus I Nicator killed Lysimachus at the Battle of Corupedium in 281 BC, and Ephesus became a part of the Seleucid Empire. Soon the battle with the Ptolemaic Empire began, and the Egyptian fleet conquered Ephesus and brought it under Egyptian rule between 263-197 BC. In 190 BC, Ephesus came under the rule of the Attalid king of Pergamos, Eumenes II, who ruled Ephesus from 197-133 BC. After his grandson Attalus III died without any male heirs, the kingdom was taken over by the Roman Republic.

When Augustus became emperor in 27 BC, he made Ephesus (instead of Pergamos) the capital of proconsular Asia – the city became the seat of a Roman governor and grew into a major metropolis and center of commerce. Many archaeologists have estimated that Ephesus grew in population to 500,000 inhabitants.

The famous Roman theater was capable of holding over 25,000 spectators. In addition to drama, the theater was the scene in Roman times of many gladiatorial combats. The famous library of Celsus, containing over 15,000 scrolls, brought people from all over the world to Ephesus. The city had one of the most advanced aqueduct systems in the ancient world.

The city was partially destroyed in 263 AD by the Gothic barbarians, and found it difficult to restore itself to its former glory. It was finally destroyed in 401 AD by a mob led by John Chrysostom. Emperor Constantine I rebuilt much of the city and erected new public baths. The city was again destroyed by an earthquake in 614 AD.

The city enjoyed a wonderful harbor that made it an extremely important commercial city of the Roman Empire.

The city was also the final home and burial place of John the Apostle who wrote the Gospel of John, I, II, and III John, and the Book of Revelation when he was exiled to the Isle of Patmos. History confirms the date of 95 AD as the date of the Book of Revelation, and with the death of Diocletian in 96 AD, John was released and spent his final days in Ephesus. The burial place of the mother of Jesus, Miryam (Mary), is also found in Ephesus.

WHY SEVEN CHURCHES?

Some commentators have insisted that the number "seven" indicates completion, and that, therefore, the seven churches represent the total church throughout history. However, while there were seven actual churches by these names existing in John's day of 95 AD (the date of the writing of the Book of Revelation), there were more churches in existence than these seven. Also, what the Lord says to each church is a message that belongs to all the churches.

Some Bible teachers have placed these seven churches within historical time periods. While quite interesting, such a viewpoint cannot be conclusive or dependable. Church history has been marked by periods of revival and growth as well as periods of corruption, decline, and apostasy. The lessons of these seven churches must be carefully observed by Christians in every age of history, regardless of the brand name on a given church door or building.

In our opinion, the things said about each of these churches is a message intended for all churches. We have seven problems or descriptions to which all churches may at one time or another subscribe.

EPHESUS – *neglected priorities*
SMYRNA - *satanic opposition*
PERGAMOS – *religious compromise*
THYATIRA – *immoral practices*
SARDIS – *spiritual apathy*
PHILADELPHIA – *lost opportunities*
LAODICEA – *material prosperity*

These troubles affect all Christians and churches, not only when such matters specifically begin to influence us, but also when a given period of time is generally characterized by these problems.

WHAT ABOUT THE ANGEL OF EACH CHURCH?

Does each church have an *"angel"* over it? There are two viewpoints about these "angels":

1. The *"angel"* is the "PASTOR" of the church!

The idea behind this viewpoint centers on the broad meaning of the word *"angel"* as a "messenger."

According to this view, John was addressing the pastor of each church in order to impress upon them the message that Jesus Christ would have them deliver to their congregations.

2. The *"angel"* is a supernatural being, one of the angels mentioned throughout the Book of Revelation.

This appears to be a better answer. Revelation 1:20 emphasizes that the *"seven stars"* in our Lord's right hand are, in fact, the *"angels of the seven churches"* which Revelation 2:1 declares. This view does not require us to interpret symbolically, but literally. Angels are described in Hebrews 1:14 as *"ministering spirits"* sent forth to minister to those who will inherit salvation. These angels operate under the control and authority of our Lord Messiah.

The spiritual story behind the city of Ephesus is found in Acts 19.

1. The **BEGINNING** of this church came through the ministry of APOLLOS – Acts 18:24-28

"And a certain Jew named Apollos, born at Alexandria, an eloquent man, and mighty in the scriptures, came to Ephesus. This man was instructed in the way of the Lord; and being fervent in the spirit, he spake and taught diligently the

things of the Lord, knowing only the baptism of John. And he began to speak boldly in the synagogue: whom when Aquila and Priscilla had heard, they took him unto them, and expounded unto him the way of God more perfectly. And when he was disposed to pass into Achaia, the brethren wrote, exhorting the disciples to receive him: who, when he was come, helped them much which had believed through grace: For he mightily convinced the Jews, and that publicly, shewing by the scriptures that Jesus was Christ."

His **POWER** – *"eloquent man and mighty in the Scriptures"*

His **PASSION** – *"instructed in the way of the Lord; and being fervent in the Spirit"*

His **PERCEPTION** of Biblical truth – *"he spake and taught diligently the things of the Lord, knowing only the baptism of John"*

His **PRESENCE** in the synagogue – *"he began to speak boldly in the synagogue"*

His **PROGRESS** in the way of God – *"when Aquila and Priscilla...expounded unto him the way of God more perfectly"*

His **PREACHING** to other believers – *"helped them much which had believed through grace"*

His **PERSUASION** – *"he mightily convinced the Jews, and that publicly, by shewing by the scriptures that Jesus was Christ"*

2. The **BAPTISM** of 12 men who were disciples of John – Acts 19:1-7

"And it came to pass, that, while Apollos was at Corinth, Paul having passed through the upper coasts came to Ephesus: and finding certain disciples, He said unto them, Have ye received the Holy Ghost since ye believed? And they said unto him, We have not so much as heard whether there be any Holy Ghost. And he said unto them, Unto what then were ye baptized? And they said, Unto John's baptism. Then said Paul, John verily baptized with the baptism of repentance, saying unto the people that they should believe on Him which should come after him, that is, on Christ Jesus. When they heard this, they were baptized in the Name of the Lord Jesus. And when Paul had laid his hands upon them, the Holy Ghost came on them; and they spake with tongues, and prophesied. And all the men were about twelve."

Paul's **EXAMINATION** of certain disciples – Acts 19:1-5

1. As to **RECEIVING** the Holy Spirit

The Greek text of Acts 19:2 says *"Did you receive the Holy Spirit WHEN ye believed?"*

2. As to **RESPONDING** to water baptism

95

NOTE: Being baptized *"in the name of the Lord Jesus"* is not a formula, but rather a reference to His original command – Matthew 28:19 – comes to mean "upon the authority of."

Their EXPERIENCE of speaking with tongues and prophesying – Acts 19:6-7

In Acts we notice that the following people experienced speaking in tongues:

Acts 2 – Jews on the Day of Pentecost in the city of Jerusalem

Acts 8 – Samaritans in the city of Samaria

Acts 10 – Gentiles in the house of Cornelius

Acts 19 – Disciples of John the Baptist in the city of Ephesus

Speaking in *"tongues"* was the God-given ability to speak in the languages of the people that were not known by those doing the speaking. It was the evidence publicly that the promise of the Father had indeed arrived!

The EXPERIENCES that Paul had in the beginning of the church in Ephesus – Acts 19:8-20

1. As to the CIRCUMSTANCES in the synagogue
   Acts 19:8-10

"And he went into the synagogue, and spake boldly for the space of three months, disputing and persuading the things concerning the kingdom of God. But when divers were hardened, and believed not, but spake evil of that way before the multitude, he departed from them, and separated the disciples, disputing daily in the school of one Tyrannus. And this continued by the space of two years; so that all they which dwelt in Asia heard the word of the Lord Jesus, both Jews and Greeks."

NOTE: We have no historical record of a person named Tyrannus (Greek: "tyrant" – maybe a name his students gave him!) operating a school in Ephesus. One manuscript speaks of Paul teaching from 11:00 AM to 4:00 PM – five hours of instruction – however, there is no confirmation of this marginal note.

2. As to the <u>CONFRONTATION</u> with evil spirits
    Acts 19:11-16

"And God wrought special miracles by the hands of Paul: So that from his body were brought unto the sick handkerchiefs or aprons, and the diseases departed from them, and the evil spirits went out of them.   Then certain of the vagabond Jews, exorcists, took upon them to call over them which had evil spirits the Name of the Lord Jesus, saying, We adjure you by Jesus Whom Paul preacheth. And there were seven sons of one Sceva, a Jew, and chief of the priests, which did so. And the evil spirit answered and said, Jesus I know, and Paul I know;

but who are ye? And the man in whom the evil spirit was leaped on them, and overcame them, and prevailed against them, so that they fled out of that house naked and wounded."

3. As to the <u>CONSEQUENCES</u> of Paul's ministry
   Acts 19:17-20

"And this was known to all the Jews and Greeks also dwelling at Ephesus; and fear fell on them all, and the Name of the Lord Jesus was magnified. And many that believed came, and confessed, and shewed their deeds. Many of them also which used curious arts brought their books together, and burned them before all men: and they counted the price of them, and found it fifty thousand pieces of silver. So mightily grew the word of God and prevailed."

WHAT A START TO THE CHURCH OF EPHESUS!

NOTE: It is possible that places in Asia Minor province like Colosse and Hierapolis and even the remainder of the seven churches of Revelation were established at this time.

In personal visits to the amazing archaeological site of Ephesus, one is certainly impressed with the size of the ancient city and its location. The present estimation of the size of this city when the Apostle Paul came to it numbers from 300,000 to over 500,000 citizens. As the second largest city of the

Roman Empire, it was strategic as far as the gospel is concerned.

From the powerful words of Paul's letter to the Ephesians to the writing of the Book of Revelation by the Apostle John covered a period of time of just over 30 years. It did not take long for the message of Revelation 2:1-7 to be needed.

The <u>EXALTATION</u> of our Lord Yeshua Revelation 2:1-2a

"Unto the angel of the church of Ephesus write; These things saith He that holdeth the seven stars in His right hand, Who walketh in the midst of the seven golden candlesticks; I know thy works..."

1. His <u>CONTROL</u> – *"He that holdeth the seven stars in His right hand"*

One thing is quite clear in the Book of Revelation – our blessed Lord is in total control of the messages and events of this Book! These *"seven angels"* are doing what He bids them to do – they are His servants designed to serve Him in whatever ways He wants.

2. His <u>CENTRALITY</u> – *"Who walketh in the midst of the seven golden candlesticks"*

Our Lord Messiah is the central focus of all – He is at the center of the churches – He is the Head, and the church is His body!

Ephesians 4:15-16 makes it clear: *"But speaking the truth in love, may grow up into Him in all things, which is the <u>Head</u>, even Christ: From Whom the whole body fitly joined together and compacted by that which every joint supplieth, according to the effectual working in the measure of every part, maketh increase of the body unto the edifying of itself in love."*

Paul wrote in Colossians 2:9-10: *"For in Him dwelleth all the fullness of the Godhead bodily. And ye are complete in Him, which is the <u>Head</u> of all principality and power."*

3. His <u>COMPREHENSION</u> – *"I know thy works"*

This simple, yet powerful phrase, reveals that our Lord knows everything that is going on in all the churches. He makes this statement seven times to each of the churches – Revelation 2:2, 9, 13, 19; 3:1, 8, 15. Churches today are desperately in need of understanding this great truth – the Lord Who is HEAD of the church knows everything that we think, say, and do! Hebrews 4:13 confirms: *"Neither is there any creature that is not manifest in His sight: but all things are naked and opened unto the eyes of Him with Whom we have to do."*

Our <u>EFFORTS</u> cannot be substituted for love!

Revelation 2:2-4 – *"I know thy works, and thy labor, and thy patience, and how thou canst not bear them which are evil: and thou hast tried them which say they are apostles, and are not, and hast found them liars: and hast borne, and hast patience, and for My Name's sake hast labored, and hast not fainted. Nevertheless I have somewhat against thee, because thou hast left thy first love."*

There is no doubt about what the problem is – this church has neglected priorities – they have *"left"* their *"first love."* When this happens, other issues will come that will undermine the church's mission and purpose in this world.

It is commendable to have an abundance of gifts and abilities and to perform exemplary deeds: but without love, there is no real spiritual profit nor lasting effect upon people.

LABOR

The Lord knows all the work we have done for Him. Verse 2 adds *"for My Name's sake."* That is a special word of encouragement about all they were doing for the Lord. However, without love, it falls short of what the Lord wants from every church and person. The Greek word translated *"labor"* is *kopon* and refers to the weariness which our efforts can make upon us. Hebrews 6:10 uses it when it says:

"For God is not unrighteous to forget your work and <u>labor</u> of love, which ye have shewed toward his Name, in that ye have ministered to the saints, and do minister." The Lord sees it all, and knows why we do what we do, and is fully aware of how tired and weary we can be in serving Him faithfully.

PATIENCE

The Greek word *hupomonen* means to "bear up under a load." This word for "patience" is usually used for our ability to endure difficult circumstances. The word *"longsuffering"* is patience toward people. The Lord knows all the difficult tasks and circumstances of life that can test our ability to endure them. But, without love, it falls short of what the Lord wants from us.

Revelation 2:3 says *"And hast borne, and hast patience, and for My Name's sake hast labored, and hast not fainted."* It is evident that this church was being encouraged in their efforts to serve the Lord. But, one thing was still missing – LOVE!

DISCERNMENT

It is very clear that many churches and church leaders are lacking in spiritual discernment. They compromise with evil, and neglect the discipline that is necessary if we really love the Lord as we say we do.
Here's what we read in Revelation 2:2b – *"and how thou canst not bear them which are evil: and thou*

hast tried them which say they are apostles, and are not, and hast found them liars."

These folks at Ephesus were not tolerating that which is evil and deceitful. They were spiritually alert to deception and the lies of those in their day who claim to be the true apostles of the Lord. Such discernment is indeed rare. Today, too many churches tolerate such evil, and refuse to take a stand against the lies of the enemy.

II Corinthians 11:13-15 says: *"For such are false apostles, deceitful workers, transforming themselves into the apostles of Christ. and no marvel; for Satan himself is transformed into an angel of light. Therefore it is no great thing if his ministers also be transformed as the ministers of righteousness; whose end shall be according to their works."*

RESISTANCE

In verse 6 we find another matter which the Lord commends in this church – *"But this thou hast, that thou hatest the deeds of the Nicolaitans, which I also hate."*

It is important for churches and believers to love what God loves and to hate what God hates. We are not sure as to what is meant by the Nicolaitans. The word comes from two Greek words – the word for "victory" or "conquest" and the word for "laity" or "people." In Revelation 2:15, the Lord said to the church of Pergamos: *"So hast thou also them that hold the doctrine of the Nicolaitans, which thing I hate."* Apparently, the teaching of these people had now invaded the general life of the church, and was not being dealt with as it was in the church of Ephesus.

Some suggest that the Nicolaitans were those who dominated the lives of the average believer. Others speak of their heresy as being a part of the Gnostic movement which was prevalent in Asia Minor, the Roman province in which these seven churches were located. Some propose that (on the basis of Revelation 2:14-15) their teachings included the acceptance of fornication and idolatry. The fact is, we simply do not know.

The Lord's <u>EVALUATION</u> reveals the real problem – Revelation 2:4

"Nevertheless I have somewhat against thee, because thou hast left thy first love."

Possible views of the *"first love"*

1. Love for the Lord Himself
2. Love for other believers
3. Love for the Second Coming
4. Love for non-believers

All of the above views are possible, but with the usage of the *"first"* in front of the word *"love"* it would seem to narrow our choices.

In Matthew 22:35-40, a lawyer comes to Jesus with a question: *"Master, which is the greatest commandment in the law? Jesus said to him, Thou shalt love the Lord thy God with all thy heart, and with all thy soul, and with all thy mind. This is the <u>first</u> and great commandment. And the second is like unto it, Thou shalt love thy neighbor as thyself. On these two commandments hang all the law and the prophets."*

It would appear from the answer of Jesus to this lawyer that the *"first love"* is referring to our love for the Lord Himself! It is quite amazing how we can rationalize our lack of love by emphasizing our works. Churches can appear outwardly to be all that God wants them to be and do, but inwardly be cold and indifferent toward the Lord Himself!

Therefore, the most serious and often neglected priority of the church and its people is a sincere and intense love for the Lord. All else is secondary. It is fascinating to read the last verse of the Apostle Paul's letter to these same Ephesians, written some thirty years prior to this letter in Revelation:
"Grace be with all them that love our Lord Jesus Christ in sincerity."

Our Lord's <u>EXHORTATION</u> reveals how important love is – Revelation 2:5

"Remember therefore from whence thou are fallen, and repent, and do the first works; or else I will

come unto thee quickly, and will remove thy candlestick out of his place, except thou repent."

1. <u>REALIZE</u> that we have fallen from the place where He wants us to be!

2. <u>REPENT</u> of the fact of leaving our first love!

3. <u>RESPOND</u> by doing what should be first!

4. <u>REMEMBER</u> what may happen to your testimony and influence if you don't repent!

When the Lord says *"or else I will come unto thee quickly, and will remove thy candlestick out of his place, except thou repent"* it reveals how serious the matter of neglected priorities is!

His personal <u>ENCOURAGEMENT</u>
Revelation 2:7

"He that hath an ear, let him hear what the Spirit saith unto the churches; To him that overcometh will I give to eat of the tree of life, which is in the paradise of God."

The admonition to *"hear what the Spirit saith unto the churches"* is given in each church's letter. In other words, the message is not just for that one church, but for all churches!

The phrase *"To him that overcometh"* is used in Revelation 2:7, 11, 17, 26; 3:5, 12, 21 – all seven times. The apostle John reveals the meaning of this phrase in I John 5:4-5:

"For whatsoever is born of God overcometh the world: and this is the victory that overcometh the world, even our faith. Who is he that overcometh the world, but he that believeth that Jesus is the Son of God?"

Overcomers are, therefore, true believers; those who do not overcome are non-believers.

The *tree of life* was in the Garden of Eden, and according to Revelation 22:2 it will be found again in the heavenly city:

"In the midst of the street of it, and on either side of the river, was there the tree of life, which bare twelve manner of frits, and yielded her fruit every month: and the leaves of the tree were for the healing of the nations."

The *"tree of life"* is certainly the symbol of everlasting life and pictures our assurance as believers. The words *"paradise of God"* confirms that this is the meaning of this wonderful assurance and promise. It is certainly possible that our Lord's message to this church reveals how easy it is for a given church or individual believer to appear to be honoring the Lord and yet the heart be far from God. May we not forget the words of our Lord from

Mark 7:6-7 – *"Well have Isaiah prophesied of you hypocrites, as it is written, This people honoreth Me with their lips, but their heart is far from Me. Howbeit in vain do they worship Me, teaching for doctrines the commandments of men."*

SATANIC OPPOSITION
Church of Smyrna
Revelation 2:8-11

"And unto the angel of the church in Smyrna write; These things saith the first and the last, which was dead, and is alive; I know thy works, and tribulation, and poverty, (but thou art rich) and I know the blasphemy of them which say they are Jews, and are not, but are the synagogue of Satan. Fear none of those things which thou shalt suffer: behold, the devil shall cast some of you into prison, that ye may be tried; and ye shall have tribulation ten days: be thou faithful unto death, and I will give thee a crown of life. He that hath an ear, let him hear what the Spirit saith unto the churches; He that overcometh shall not be hurt of the second death."

HISTORICAL BACKGROUND

The Romans of Italy called this city "THE BEAUTY OF ASIA" and the "CITY OF LIFE AND STRENGTH" – located 35 miles north of Ephesus, a beautiful seaport, and still prospering today with over 200,000 people – its name today is Izmir. In 195 BC they erected a temple to the goddess of Rome and supported the Roman Republic which began in 705 BC. Smyrna became a seat of emperor worship and in 26 AD when several cities competed for the honor of building a temple to Emperor Tiberius, Smyrna was given that privilege.

The most famous street of Smyrna was called "THE GOLDEN STREET" which began at the seaside and ran the length of the city to the Acropolis on Mt. Pagus. At the sea was a temple to the goddess Cybele, and further up was the gorgeous temple of Apollo – a little higher was the temple to Aesculapius, the god of healing, and beyond that was a beautiful temple to the goddess Aphrodite – next was a monument to Homer and finally the temple to Zeus on the Acropolis. The theater seats more than 20,000 people.

Alexander the Great and his successors wanted to rebuild Smyrna as the model city, the most beautiful city in the world.

A large colony of Jews lived there with considerable influence upon civic authorities. Years later, Jews joined with Gentiles to form a mob and call for the death of the Bishop Polycarp, a disciple of the Apostle John. Tertullian and Irenaeus say that Polycarp was a bishop at the time of this letter and that John not only discipled him, but appointed him to that task.

On February 22, 166 AD, Polycarp was burned at the stake. It was reported that he said "86 years have I served Him and He has done me no wrong. How can I blaspheme my King Who saved me?" He spoke of serving the Lord for 86 years, which puts him in the church of Smyrna as a young man of 20-30 years old when John wrote this letter.

The name of the city is based on the word "myrrh" which gives off a sweet smell after it has been crushed – the root meaning is "bitter" and was used as an allegory, referring to the result of suffering and trials. It came from Balsam herb, spices, and medicine from the resin gum which was used as a drug to relieve pain. It was used as a drink that was given to Jesus on the cross according to Mark 15:23 – *"And they gave Him to drink wine mingled with myrrh: but He received it not."*

In John 19:38-40 it was used in the embalming of the body of Jesus:

"And after this Joseph of Arimathea, being a disciple of Jesus, but secretly for fear of the Jews, besought Pilate that he might take away the body of Jesus: and Pilate gave him leave. He came therefore, and took the body of Jesus. And there came also Nicodemus, which at the first came to Jesus by night, and brought a mixture of myrrh and aloes, about an hundred pound weight. Then took they the body of Jesus, and wound it in linen clothes with the spices, as the manner of the Jews is to bury."

If the first mark of a New Testament church is love, the second mark would be the ability to suffer and endure, which would be a demonstration of how effective and strong our love of the Lord really is. Jesus said in John 15:18-20:

"If the world hate you, ye know that it hated Me before it hated you. If ye were of the world, the world would love his own: but because ye are not of the world, but I have chosen you out of the world, therefore the world hateth you. Remember the word that I said unto you, The servant is not greater than his lord. If they have persecuted Me, they will also persecute you; if they have kept My saying, they will keep yours also."

As time went on, over 1500 were martyred, and later, another 800 on Mt. Pagus because these people refused to renounce their faith in Yeshua as Messiah. Tertullian, who witnessed many martyrdoms at Rome in his early twenties, wrote these words: "If the Tiber has overflowed its banks, if the Nile has remained in its bed, if the sky has been still, or the earth been in commotion, if death has made its devastations, or famine its afflictions, your cry immediately is 'This is the fault of the Christians.'"

NOTICE FOUR THINGS ABOUT YESHUA IN THESE FEW VERSES:

WHO He is – v. 8
WHAT He knows – v. 9
WHAT He commands – v. 10a
WHAT He promises – vv. 10b-11

WHO HE IS – Revelation 2:8

"And unto the angel of the church in Smyrna write; These things saith the first and the last, which was dead, and is alive"

1. He is the ETERNAL God – *"the first and the last"*

Isaiah 41:4 – *"Who hath wrought and done it, calling the generations from the beginning? I the LORD, the first, and with the last; I am He."*

Isaiah 44:6 – *"Thus saith the LORD the King of Israel, and His Redeemer the LORD of hosts; I am the first, and I am the last; and beside Me there is no God."*

Isaiah 48:12 – *"Hearken unto Me, O Jacob and Israel, My called; I am He; I am the first, I also am the last."*

Revelation 1:8 – *"I am Alpha and Omega, the beginning and the ending, saith the Lord, which is, and which was, and which is to come, the Almighty."*

Revelation 21:6 – *"And He said unto me, It is done. I am Alpha and Omega, the beginning and the end. I will give unto him that is athirst of the fountain of the water of life freely."*

Revelation 22:13 – *"I am Alpha and Omega, the beginning and the end, the first and the last."*

2. He is the RESURRECTED Lord – *"who was dead, and is alive"*

WHAT HE KNOWS – Revelation 2:9

"I know thy works, and tribulation, and poverty, (but thou art rich) and I know the blasphemy of them which say they are Jews, and are not, but are the synagogue of Satan."

1. Their **WORKS** – *"I know thy works"*

2. Their **TRIBULATION**

Matthew 5:10-12 – *"Blessed are they which are persecuted for righteousness' sake: for theirs is the kingdom of heaven. Blessed are ye, when men shall revile you, and persecute you, and shall say all manner of evil against you falsely, for My sake. Rejoice, and be exceeding glad: for great is your reward in heaven: for so persecuted they the prophets which were before you."*

II Timothy 3:11-12 – *"Persecutions, afflictions, which came unto me at Antioch, at Iconium, at Lystra: what persecutions I endured: but out of them all the Lord delivered me. Yea, and all that will live godly in Christ Jesus shall suffer persecution."*

3. Their **POVERTY** – *"but you are rich"*

Matthew 6:19-21 – *"Lay not up for yourselves treasures upon earth, where moth and rust doth corrupt, and where thieves break through and steal: But lay up for yourselves treasures in heaven, where neither moth, nor rust doth corrupt, and where thieves do not break through nor steal: For where your treasure is, there will your heart be also."*

4. The **<u>BLASPHEMY</u>** they endured – slander of others!

I Peter 2:19-23 – *"For this is thankworthy, if a man for conscience toward God endure grief, suffering wrongfully. For what glory is it, if, when ye be buffeted for your faults, ye take it patiently? But if, when ye do well, and suffer for it, ye take it patiently, this is acceptable with God. For even hereunto were ye called: because Christ also suffered for us, leaving us an example, that ye should follow His steps: Who did no sin, neither was guile found in His mouth: Who, when He was reviled, reviled not again; when He suffered, He threatened not; but committed Himself to Him that judgeth righteously."*

Their false CLAIM – *"who say they are Jews, and are not"*

Romans 2:28-29 – *"For he is not a Jew, which is one outwardly; neither is that circumcision, which is outward in the flesh: But he is a Jew, which is one inwardly; and circumcision is that of the heart, in the spirit, and not in the letter; whose praise is not of men, but of God."*

Their true CONNECTION – *"but are the synagogue of Satan"*

I Peter 5:8-11 – *"Be sober, be vigilant; because your adversary the devil, as a roaring lion, walketh about, seeking whom he may devour: Whom resist stedfast in the faith, knowing that the same afflictions are accomplished in your brethren that are in the world. But the God of all grace, Who hath called us unto His eternal glory by Christ Jesus, after that ye have suffered awhile, make you perfect, stablish, strengthen, settle you. To Him be glory and dominion forever and ever. Amen."*

WHAT HE COMMANDS – Revelation 2:10

"Fear none of those things which thou shalt suffer: behold, the devil shall cast some of you into prison, that ye may be tried; and ye shall have tribulation ten days: be thou faithful unto death, and I will give thee a crown of life."

As to FEAR – *"Fear none of these things which thou shalt suffer"*

1. The **PREDICTION** of suffering

   II Timothy 3:12 – *"Yea, and all that will live godly in Christ Jesus shall suffer persecution."*

2. The **PERSON** behind the persecution
   "the devil shall cast some of you into prison"

II Corinthians 11:13-15 – *"For such are false apostles, deceitful workers, transforming themselves into the apostles of Christ. And no marvel; for Satan himself is transformed into an angel of light. Therefore it is no great thing if his ministers also be transformed as the ministers of righteousness; whose end shall be according to their works."*

II Thessalonians 3:1-3 – *"Finally, brethren, pray for us, that the word of the Lord may have free course, and be glorified, even as it is with you: And that we may be delivered from unreasonable and wicked men: for all men have not faith. But the Lord is faithful, Who shall stablish you, and keep you from evil (the evil one)."*

Revelation 12:10 – *"And I heard a loud voice saying in heaven, Now is come salvation, and strength, and the kingdom of our God, and the power of His Christ: for the accuser of our brethren is cast down, which accused them before our God day and night."*

3. The **PURPOSE** of this suffering
   "that ye may be tried"

Job 23:10 – *"But He knoweth the way that I take: when He hath tried me, I shall come forth as gold."*

I Peter 1:6-7 – *"Wherein ye greatly rejoice, though now for a season, if need be, ye are in heaviness through manifold temptations: That the end of your faith, being much more precious than of gold that perisheth, though it be tried with fire, might be found unto praise and honor and glory at the appearing of Jesus Christ."*

    4. The <u>PERIOD</u> of suffering
       "ye shall have tribulation ten days"

NOTE: Three major viewpoints:

Ten general persecutions under Rome
(However, Nero's persecution preceded the date of this message, and the text indicates the "ten days" are future!)

Ten years of persecution under Emperor Diocletian (303-313 AD)

Simply, a short time!

As to <u>FAITHFULNESS</u> – *"be thou faithful unto death"*

Revelation 6:9 – *"And when He opened the fifth seal, I saw under the altar the souls of them that were slain for the word of God, and for the testimony which they held."*

Hebrews 11:32-40 – *"And what shall I more say? for the time would fail me to tell of Gideon, and of Barak, and of Samson, and of Jephthah; of David also, and Samuel, and of the prophets: Who through faith subdued kingdoms, wrought righteousness, obtained promises, stopped the mouths of lions, quenched the violence of fire, escaped the edge of the sword, out of weakness were made strong, waxed valiant in fight, turned to flight the armies of the aliens. Women received their dead raised to life again: and others were tortured, not accepting deliverance; that they might obtain a better resurrection: And others had trial of cruel mockings and scourgings, yea, moreover of bonds and imprisonment: They were stoned, they were sawn asunder, were tempted, were slain with the sword: they wandered about in sheepskins and goatskins; being destitute, afflicted, tormented; (Of whom the world was not worthy;) they wandered in deserts, and in mountains, and in dens and caves of the earth. And these all, having obtained a good report through faith, received not the promise: God having provided some better thing for us, that they without us should not be made perfect."*

Hebrews 12:1-2 – *"Wherefore seeing we also are compassed about with so great a cloud of witnesses, let us lay aside every weight, and the sin which doth so easily beset us, and let us run with patience the race that is set before us, Looking unto Jesus the Author and Finisher of our faith; Who for the joy that was set before Him endured the cross,*

119

despising the shame, and is set down at the right hand of the throne of God."

WHAT HE PROMISES – Revelation 2:10b-11

"I will give thee a crown of life. He that hath an ear, let him hear what the Spirit saith unto the churches; He that overcometh shall not be hurt of the second death."

1. A CROWN that makes it all worthwhile! *"crown of life"*

James 1:12 – *"Blessed is the man that endureth temptation: for when he is tried, he shall receive the crown of life, which the Lord hath promised to them that love Him."*

2. A CONSEQUENCE that will never be faced!
"shall not be hurt of the second death"

Revelation 20:6 – *"Blessed and holy is he that hath part in the first resurrection: on such the second death hath no power, but they shall be priests of God and of Christ, and shall reign with Him a thousand years."*

Revelation 20:14-15 – *"And death and hell were cast into the lake of fire. This is the second death. And whosoever was not found written in the book of life was cast into the lake of fire."*

There does not seem to be any particular condemnation of this church in Smyrna, but this city and the believers in it certainly faced serious death and persecution and tons of Satanic opposition.

WHO IS SATAN?

1. He was *"the anointed cherub"* who was created by God and because of pride has fallen from heaven!

Isaiah 14:12-15 – *"How are thou fallen from heaven, O Lucifer, son of the morning! How art thou cut down to the ground, which didst weaken the nations! For thou hast said in thine heart, I will ascend into heaven, I will exalt my throne above the stars of God: I will sit also upon the mount of the congregation, in the sides of the north: I will ascend above the heights of the clouds; I will be like the Most High. Yet thou shalt be brought down to hell, to the sides of the pit."*

Ezekiel 28:13-15 – *"Thou hast been in Eden the garden of God; every precious stone was thy covering, the sardius, topaz, and the diamond, the beryl, the onyx, and the jasper, the sapphire, the emerald, and the carbuncle, and gold: the workmanship of thy tabrets and of thy pipes was prepared in thee in the day that thou wast created. Thou are the anointed cherub that covereth; and I have set thee so: thou wast upon the holy mountain of God; thou hast walked up and down in the midst of the stones of fire. Thou wast perfect in thy ways from the day that thou wast created, till iniquity was found in thee."*

2. He is called *"an angel of light"*.

II Corinthians 11:14 – *"And no marvel; for Satan himself is transformed into an angel of light."*

3. He is called *"the devil"*.

I Peter 5:8 – *"Be sober, be vigilant; because your adversary the devil, as a roaring lion, walketh about, seeking whom he may devour."*

Revelation 12:9 – *"And the great dragon was cast out, that old serpent, called the Devil, and Satan, which deceiveth the whole world: he was cast out into the earth, and his angels were cast out with him."*

4. He is *"the angel of the bottomless pit"*.

Revelation 9:11 – *"And they had a king over them, which is the angel of the bottomless pit, whose name in the Hebrew tongue is Abaddon, but in the Greek tongue hath his name Apollyon."*

5. He is *"the father of lies"*.

John 8:44 – *"Ye are of your father the devil, and the lusts of your father ye will do. He was a murderer from the beginning, and abode not in the truth, because there is no truth in him. When he speaketh a lie, he speaketh of his own: for he is a liar, and the father of it."*

6. He is *"that wicked one"* who continues to sin.

I John 3:8 – *"He that committeth sin is of the devil; for the devil sinneth from the beginning. For this purpose the Son of God was manifested, that He might destroy the works of the devil."*

I John 5:18 – *"We know that whosoever is born of God sinneth not; but he that is begotten of God keepeth himself, and that wicked one toucheth him not."*

HOW DOES SATAN SEDUCE US?

II Corinthians 11:3 – *"But I fear, lest by any means, as the serpent beguiled Eve through his subtilty, so your minds should be corrupted from the simplicity that is in Christ."*

I Timothy 4:1 – *"Now the Spirit speaketh expressly, that in the latter times some shall depart from the faith, giving heed to seducing spirits, and doctrines of devils."*

1. He **CASTS** doubt on God's Word.

Genesis 3:1 – *"Now the serpent was more subtil than any beast of the field which the LORD God had made. And he said unto the woman, Yea, hath God said, Ye shall not eat of every tree of the garden?"*

2. He **CONTRADICTS** God's Word.

Genesis 3:4 – *"And the serpent said unto the woman, Ye shall not surely die."*

3. He **CHALLENGES** God's motives.

Genesis 3:5 – *"For God doth know that in the day ye eat thereof, then your eyes shall be opened, and ye shall be as gods, knowing good and evil."*

4. He **CONFUSES** people with miraculous deeds.

II Thessalonians 2:9 – *"Even him, whose coming is after the working of Satan with all power and signs and lying wonders."*

5. He **COUNTERFEITS** the work of God.

II Corinthians 11:13-15 – *"For such are false apostles, deceitful workers, transforming themselves into the apostles of Christ. And no marvel; for Satan himself is transformed into an angel of light. Therefore it is no great thing if his ministers also be transformed as the ministers of righteousness; whose end shall be according to their works."*

WHAT IS SATAN ABLE TO DO?

1. He deceives the whole world!

Revelation 12:9 – *"And the great dragon was cast out, that old serpent, called the Devil and Satan, which deceiveth the whole world; he was cast out into the earth, and his angels were cast out with him."*

2. He accuses the believers!

Revelation 12:10 – *"for the accuser of our brethren is cast down, which accused them before our God day and night."*

3. He tempts us to follow the lusts of the flesh!

John 8:44 – *"Ye are of your father the devil, and the lusts of your father ye will do. He was a murderer from the beginning, and abode not in the truth, because there is no truth in him. When he speaketh a lie, he speaketh of his own: for he is a liar, and the father of it."*

I Corinthians 7:5 – *"Defraud ye not one the other, except it be with consent for a time, that ye may give yourselves to fasting and prayer; and come together again, that Satan tempt you not for your incontinency."*

Ephesians 2:1-3 – *"And you hath He quickened, who were dead in trespasses and sins; Wherein in time past ye walked according to the course of this world, according to the prince of the power of the air, the spirit that now worketh in the children of disobedience: Among whom also we all had our conversation in times past in the lusts of our flesh and of the mind; and were by nature the children of wrath, even as others."*

4. He blinds the minds of unbelievers!

II Corinthians 4:3-4 – *"But if our gospel be hid, it is hid to them that are lost: In whom the god of this world hath blinded the minds of them which believe not, lest the light of the glorious gospel of Christ, Who is the image of God, should shine unto them."*

5. He hinders the work of believers!

I Thessalonians 2:18 – *"Wherefore we would have come unto you, even I Paul, once and again; but Satan hindered us."*

6. He devours your confidence in the Lord and His purposes, especially when you suffer!

I Peter 5:8 – *"Be sober, be vigilant; because your adversary the devil, as a roaring lion, walketh about, seeking whom he may devour."*

WHAT CAN WE DO ABOUT IT?

1. <u>REALIZE</u> the purpose of God in allowing Satanic attacks!

II Corinthians 12:7 – *"And lest I should be exalted above measure through the abundance of the revelations, there was given to me a thorn in the flesh, the messenger of Satan to buffet me, lest I should be exalted above measure."*

I Peter 5:8-11 – *"Be sober, be vigilant; because your adversary the devil, as a roaring lion, walketh about, seeking whom he may devour; Whom resist stedfast in the faith, knowing that the same afflictions are accomplished in your brethren that are in the world. But the God of all grace, Who hath called us unto His eternal glory by Christ Jesus, after that ye have suffered a while, make you perfect, stablish, strengthen, settle you. To Him be glory and dominion forever and ever. Amen!"*

2. <u>RELY</u> upon the prayer of Jesus Christ!

John 17:15 – *"I pray not that thou shouldest take them out of the world, but that thou shouldest keep them from the evil (one)."*

Romans 8:34 – *"Who is he that condemneth? It is Christ that died, yea rather, that is risen again, Who is even at the right hand of God, Who also maketh intercession for us."*

Hebrews 7:24-25 – *"But this Man, because He continueth ever, hath an unchangeable priesthood. Wherefore He is able also to save them to the uttermost that come unto God by Him, seeing He ever liveth to make intercession for them."*

3. <u>RECOGNIZE</u> the protection of God's armor!

Ephesians 6:11 – *"Put on the whole armor of God, that ye may be able to stand against the wiles of the devil."*

Ephesians 6:16 – *"Above all, taking the shield of faith, wherewith ye shall be able to quench all the fiery darts of the wicked (one)."*

4. <u>REMEMBER</u> the promise of God if we resist the devil!

James 4:7 – *"Submit yourselves therefore to God. Resist the devil, and he will flee from you."*

5. <u>RESPOND</u> to the presence and power of the Holy Spirit!

I John 4:4 – *"greater is He that is in you, than he that is in the world"*

RELIGIOUS COMPROMISE
Church in Pergamos
Revelation 1:12-17

*"And to the angel of the church in Pergamos write;
These things saith He which hath the sharp sword
with two edges; I know thy works and where thou
dwellest, even where Satan's seat is: and thou
holdest fast My Name, and hast not denied My
faith, even in those days wherein Antipas was My
faithful martyr, who was slain among you, where
Satan dwelleth. But I have a few things against
thee, because thou hast there them that hold the
doctrine of Balaam, who taught Balak to cast a
stumblingblock before the children of Israel, to eat
things sacrificed unto idols, and to commit
fornication. So hast thou also them hold the
doctrine of the Nicolaitans, which thing I hate.
Repent; or else I will come unto thee quickly, and
will fight against them with the sword of My
mouth. He that hath an ear, let him hear what the
Spirit saith unto the churches; To him that
overcometh will I give to eat of the hidden manna,
and will give him a white stone, and in the stone a
new name written, which no man knoweth saving
he that receiveth it."*

HISTORICAL BACKGROUND - PERGAMOS

Xenophon provides the earliest surviving
documentary mention of Pergamos. Captured by
Xenophon in 399 BC and immediately recaptured by
the Persians, it was severely punished in 362 BC

after a revolt. It did not become important until Lysimachus, King of Thrace, took possession, 301 BC, but soon after his lieutenant Philetaerus enlarged the town, the Kingdom of Thrace collapsed and it became the capital of the new kingdom of Pergamon which Philetaerus founded in 281 BC, beginning the Attalid dynasty. In 261 BC he bequeathed his possessions to his nephew Eumenes I (263-241 BC), who increased them greatly, leaving as heir his cousin Attalus I (241-197 BC).

The Attalids became some of the most loyal supporters of Rome in the Hellenistic world. Under Attalus I (241–197 BC), they allied with Rome against Philip V of Macedon, during the first and second Macedonian Wars, and again under Eumenes II (197–158 BC), against Perseus of Macedon, during the Third Macedonian War. For their support against the Seleucids, the Attalids were rewarded with all the former Seleucid domains in Asia Minor.

As a consequence of its rise to power, the city expanded greatly. Until 188 BC, it had not grown significantly since its founding by Philetaerus, and covered circa 21 hectares (52 acres). After this year, a massive new city wall was constructed, 4 kilometers (2.5 mi) long and enclosing an area of approximately 90 hectares (220 acres).

The Attalids ruled with intelligence and generosity. Many documents survive showing how the Attalids supported the growth of towns by sending in skilled artisans and by remitting taxes. They allowed the Greek cities in their domains to maintain nominal independence. They sent gifts to Greek cultural sites like Delphi, Delos, and Athens. They defeated the invading Celts. They remodeled the Acropolis of Pergamon after the Acropolis in Athens. When Attalus III (138–133 BC) died without an heir in 133 BC, he bequeathed the whole of Pergamon to Rome in order to prevent a civil war.

Not everyone in Pergamon accepted Rome's rule. Aristonicus, who claimed to be Attalus' brother as well as the son of Eumenes II, an earlier king, led a revolt among the lower classes with the help of Blossius. The revolt was put down in 129 BC, and Pergamon was divided among Rome, Pontus, and Cappadocia.

Pergamon was briefly the capital of the Roman province of Asia, before the capital was transferred to Ephesus.

After a slow decline, the city was favored by several imperial initiatives under Hadrian (117 – 138 AD). It was granted the title of metropolis and as a result of this an ambitious building program was carried out: massive temples, a stadium, a theatre, a huge forum and an amphitheatre were constructed. In addition, at the city limits the shrine to Asclepius (the god of healing) was expanded into a lavish spa.

The Sanctuary of Asclepius grew in fame and was considered one of the most famous therapeutic and healing centers of the Roman world. Galen, after Hippocrates, the most famous physician of antiquity, was born at Pergamon and received his early training at the Asclepeion.

Pergamon reached the height of its greatness under Roman Imperial rule and was home to about 200,000 inhabitants.

The Library of Pergamon was renowned, and second only to the Library of Alexandria, although not approaching Alexandria in scholarship.

The city was an early seat of Christianity and was granted a bishopric by the second century AD. Pergamon is mentioned in the Book of Revelation, as a dwelling place of Satan and a location of his throne, and that an early bishop named Antipas was martyred there.

The city suffered badly during the third century and was badly damaged by an earthquake in 262 AD and was sacked by the Goths shortly after.

Anatolia was invaded by the Persian Sassanid Empire in 620 AD and after the Persians were driven out by Byzantine forces, Pergamon was rebuilt on a much smaller scale by Emperor Constants II.

Pergamon was sacked by the armies of Maslama ibn Abd al-Malik on their way to the siege of Constantinople in 717 AD.

Pergamos was the chief city of Mysia, in Asia Minor. One of the "seven churches" was planted here (Rev. 1:11; 2:17). It was noted for its wickedness, insomuch that our Lord says "Satan's seat" was there. The church of Pergamos was rebuked for swerving from the truth and embracing the doctrines of Balaam and the Nicolaitans. Antipas, Christ's "faithful martyr," here sealed his testimony with his blood. This city stood on the banks of the river Caicus, about 20 miles from the sea. It is now called Bergama, and has a population of some twenty thousand, of whom about two thousand profess to be Christians. Parchment was first made here, and was called by the Greeks *pergamene*, from the name of the city.

Three kilometers south of the Acropolis down in the valley, there was the Sanctuary of Asclepius (also known as the Asclepium), the god of healing. The Ascelpium was approached along a 820 meter colonnaded sacred way. In this place people with health problems could bathe in the water of the sacred spring, and in the patients' dreams Asclepius would appear in a vision to tell them how to cure their illness. Archeology has found lots of gifts and dedications that people would make afterwards, such as small terracotta body parts, no doubt representing what had been healed. Galen, the most famous doctor in the ancient Roman Empire and personal physician of Emperor Marcus Aurelius, worked in the Ascelpium for many years.

Pergamon was a small settlement during the Archaic Period. Lysimachus, one of the generals of Alexander the Great and who had become the sovereign of Anatolia after 301 BC, delivered the war expenditures, at the amount of 9000 talents (1 talent is believed to be US $7,500 approx.), to Philetarios who was the commander of Pergamon, and the kingdom founded by Philetarios by using this sum of money following Lysimachus's death, flourished and became the most eminent center of culture of the Hellenistic period for 150 years. Eumenes I, Attalus I and Eumenes II were enthroned successively after Philetarios. Eumenes II took acropolis of Athens as an example and had the acropolis of Pergamon adorned with works of art which reflected fine taste, and Pergamon became one of the most graceful cities of the world. Attalus III who succeeded Attalus II, handed over his land to the Romans when he died in 133 BC.

In the Acropolis, the remains that you see on the left hand side while going in, are the monumental tombs or heroons built for the kings of Pergamon during the Hellenistic period. Shops are situated at their side. When you enter the Acropolis, the remains seen at your left side, are the foundations of Propylon (monumental gates) which were constructed by Eumenes II. When you pass to the square surrounded with three stoas of the Doric order you will notice the ruins of the temple of Athena, built during the time of Eumenes II in the 3rd century BC. It's just above the theater. The famous Library of Pergamon which contained

200,000 books, was situated north of the square. Antonius gave all the books of the library to Cleopatra as a wedding gift. The remains near the library, are some houses from the Hellenistic period. If you go up the stairs, you will see the remains of the palaces of Eumenes II and Attalus II. Inside the Acropolis there are houses, military barracks and military warehouses called "Arsenals". The building that has been restored at present is the Temple of Trajan. Trajan started it but after his death Emperor Hadrian (117-138 AD) finished the temple in Corinthian order and it was placed upon a terrace with dimensions of 68 m × 58 m (223.10 ft. × 190.29 ft.). Attempts have been continuing by the German archaeologists since 1976 to erect this temple which has 6 x 9 columns and a peripteros plan (one row of columns around the temple). It is completely marble.

The Theater of Pergamon, one of the steepest theaters in the world, has a capacity of 10,000 people and was constructed in the 3rd century BC. The theater underwent changes during the Roman period under the reign of Caracalla. There is a 246.5 m (808.73 ft) long and approximately 16 m (52.49 ft) wide stoa (portico) in front of the theater. The road in front of the theater leads to the Temple of Dionysus (known in Rome as Baccus, god of wine). The temple was constructed in the 2nd century BC and reconstructed in marble during Caracalla's period (211-217 AD). Its dimensions are 11.80 m × 20.22 m (38.71 ft. × 66.34 ft.). The temple, which arouses interest because of the staircase in front with a height of 4.5 m (14.76 ft.) and 25 steps, has an exquisite appearance.

The famous Altar of Zeus in Pergamon is on the south of the theater. Eumenes II (197-159 BC) constructed it as a memorial of the victory against the Galatians. This Altar has the shape of a horseshoe and its dimensions are 36.44 m × 34.20 m (119.55 ft × 112.20 ft). It is composed of four parts and the high relieves on it describe the war between the giants and the gods. The Altar which was taken away from Pergamon in 1871 and carried to Germany by the German engineer Carl Humann is exhibited at the Museum of Pergamum in Berlin, in a manner conforming to its original. Today the Turkish government is trying to get it back from Germany bringing the issue to the International Court of Justice in The Hague. On the south of the Altar, the Agora (market place) belonging to the 2nd century BC, is situated. In the middle of the Agora there is a small altar. Downwards in the Acropolis, the central city is placed. Inside Pergamon, there is the Temple of Serapis, built for the Egyptian Gods in the 2nd century AD. and called the Red Courtyard by locals. This is a basilica shaped building constructed under the reign of Hadrian, then, in the 4th century, it was converted into a church dedicated to St. John and became one of the Seven Churches of Christianity.

The museum is in Bergama and Asklepion (the ancient medical complex, hospital) is out of the city. It is believed that Asklepion, built in the name of

Aesculapius, the god of Health and Medicine, has existed since the 4th century BC. It contains premises such as a small theater with a capacity of 3,500 people, rooms where the patients were cured by the sound of water and music, the temple of Asklepion and the library. Here, the dreams of the patients were analyzed by their doctors (priests) 2000 years before Sigmund Freud did. One of the important personalities associated with the Asklepion was Galen (Galenus) from the 2nd century AD. It was under Eastern Roman rule except the Sassanid invasion in 620 AD. The Umayyad invasion in 715 AD and Sultanate of Rum rule between 1074 and 1097 AD. It was conquered by Karasids in 1302 AD. It was part of the Ottoman Empire in 1337 AD. During Ottoman rule, it was kaza centre in Karesi sanjak (Its centre was Balıkesir) between 1337 and 1868 AD, in Saruhan one (Its centre was Manisa) between 1868 and 1877 AD and finally in İzmir one. During the Turkish War of Independence, it was occupied by Greece in June 19, 1919, but was liberated in September 14, 1922.

Of course, much of the history since the first century AD is not important to the discussion of this letter that was sent by our Lord to the church that was established here. When the Apostle John wrote to the church at Pergamos, it was already a major city in Roman Empire days (95 AD).

A SERIOUS <u>EXPLANATION</u>
Revelation 2:12

"And to the angel of the church in Pergamos write; these things saith He which hath the sharp sword with two edges"

One simple but powerful description of our blessed Lord Jesus Christ begins this letter. The *"sharp sword with two edges"* is referring to *"the sword of My mouth"* mentioned in Revelation 1:16 and 19:15. It symbolizes the judgment which can come when He speaks the word. This is a church facing severe judgment if they do not repent. Christianity and paganism were opposites, but the Christians at Pergamos were trying to coexist. The result was **RELIGIOUS COMPROMISE** and sinful practices in the church and its members.

A DANGEROUS <u>ENVIRONMENT</u>
Revelation 2:13

"I know thy works and where thou dwellest, even where Satan's seat is: and thou holdest fast My Name, and hast not denied My faith, even in those days wherein Antipas was My faithful martyr, who was slain among you, where Satan dwelleth."

The emphasis on the problems at the church in Pergamos centers our attention on their environment – *"where Satan dwelleth."* It is where the gigantic altar existed in honor of the chief god of Grecian culture – Zeus. This altar was elevated about 800 feet above the city dwellings and buildings. It was visible for miles. The serpent god, Asklepios. the supposed god of healing, was a fitting symbol for the place where Satan's throne existed.

The American Medical Association still uses the serpent god in its graphics, monuments, and emblems.

The environment in which we live is often a test to our faith and our desire to live a godly life. Satan was not only present at Pergamos, He was ruling *("throne")*. Some cities in our present day have become "thrones of Satan." That's how strong his influence and control has been manifested and even tolerated by churches. This is a reminder to all believers that the pressures we face often come from the enemy of our souls, the devil himself. It is our profession of faith in the death and resurrection of our blessed Lord Messiah that is the special target of satanic attacks. That was true in Pergamos as well.

Their __COMMITMENT__ was evident even in the midst of the persecution.

Two things are brought to our attention that remind us that in spite of the pressures and persecution we may be experiencing, believers are able to maintain a strong commitment:

(1) Their __DEVOTION__ to the Name of the Lord
   "thou holdest fast My Name"

The issue here deals with the deity of our Lord. His *"Name"* is *"above every name"* – but a city devoted to emperor worship could not tolerate such loyalty from the believers to our Lord. It was a spiritual battle between Caesar and Christ - we must choose, regardless of the consequences we might face.

Matthew 10:32-33 makes it clear: *"Whosoever therefore shall confess Me before men, him will I confess before My Father which is in heaven. But whosoever shall deny Me before men, him will I also deny before My Father which is in heaven."*

(2)   Their <u>DENIAL</u> of the faith was absent from their loyalty to the Lord even though some lost their lives because of it
"and hast not denied My faith, even in those days wherein Antipas was My faithful martyr, who was slain among you, where Satan dwelleth."

It would appear that the issue deals with our public proclamation of faith, and it implies that this occurred under serious persecution. The name *"Antipas"* means "against all" – perhaps (whatever the circumstances might have been) he found himself all alone in standing for his faith. Situations such as this can exist in our places of employment as well as in the neighborhoods where we live. The church in Pergamos was commended for standing firm even when one of its members was killed for his faith.

A serious <u>EVALUATION</u> from the Lord!
Revelation 2:14-15

"But I have a few things against thee, because thou hast there them that hold the doctrine of Balaam, who taught Balak to cast a stumblingblock before the children of Israel, to eat things sacrificed unto idols, and to commit fornication. So hast thou also them that hold the doctrine of the Nicolaitans, which thing I hate."

The words that give us the title to this chapter seem appropriate – RELIGIOUS COMPROMISE! It can happen in the best of churches – the reasons may be varied, but the issue can creep up on us without us realizing what is happening. Two serious problems existed in the first century when the church was born, and they were the same issues that affected the nation of Israel in the past: IDOLATRY and IMMORALITY.

The <u>COMPROMISE</u> of Balaam the prophet

The details of this story are found in Numbers 22-25. Balaam was being seduced by Balak, the king of Moab who wanted Balaam to curse the children of Israel. To his credit, instead of cursing God's people he chose to bless them as God would want him to do.

However, the tactics of king Balak intensified and he offered Balaam financial gain if he would curse the people of Israel. According to Numbers 31:16 Balaam counselled the children of Israel to commit sin against the Lord, and there was a plague among the children of Israel that resulted from his bad counsel. His counsel to the children of Israel actually suggested the tactic of committing sexual sin with the Moabite women and participation in their pagan rituals. The facts are presented in Numbers 25:1-3:

"And Israel abode in Shittim, and the people began to commit whoredom with the daughters of Moab. And they called the people unto the sacrifices of their gods: and the people did eat, and bowed down to their gods. And Israel joined himself unto Baal-peor: and the anger of the LORD was kindled against Israel."

The teaching of Balaam might seem outwardly that it is loyal to God and His word; however, it was soft on sexual immorality and pagan worship. These things were tolerated. In II Peter 2:14-16 is a commentary on the story of Balaam:

"Having eyes full of adultery, and that cannot cease from sin; beguiling unstable souls: an heart they have exercised with covetous practices; cursed children: Which have forsaken the right way, and are gone astray, following the way of Balaam the son of Bosor, who loved the wages of unrighteousness; But was rebuked for his iniquity; the dumb ass speaking with man's voice forbad the madness of the prophet."

The <u>CORRUPTION</u> of the Nicolaitans

It is difficult to understand all that these people were doing and why the Lord hated them so. The meaning of their name is all we have to go on – it contains the word for "people" and the word to "conquer." They appear to be abusive to the common people of the church, trying to control things and to make things go the way they wanted rather than what the Lord wanted. But, we really don't know who they were and why the Lord hated their attitudes and actions. They appear to be a violation of spiritual leadership and servanthood.

A strong <u>EXHORTATION</u>
Revelation 2:16

"Repent; or else I will come unto thee quickly, and will fight against them with the sword of My mouth."

Five of the seven churches are told to *"repent."* The exceptions were Smyrna and Philadelphia. Unfortunately churches today do not focus on Biblical repentance. It is a word for believers as well as non-believers. It is a change of mind that leads to a change in conduct.

It is described in detail in II Corinthians 7:9-11 and involves seven kinds of attitudes and responses if it is really occurring in our hearts.

"Now I rejoice, not that ye were made sorry, but that ye sorrowed to repentance: for ye were made sorry after a godly manner, that ye might receive damage by us in nothing. For godly sorrow worketh repentance to salvation not to be repented of: but the sorrow of the world worketh death. For behold this selfsame thing, that ye sorrowed after a godly sort, what carefulness it wrought in you, yea, what clearing of yourselves, yea, what indignation, yea, what fear, yea, what vehement desire, yea, what zeal, yea, what revenge! In all things ye have approved yourselves to be clear in this matter."

A wonderful ENCOURAGEMENT
Revelation 2:17

"He that hath an ear, let him hear what the Spirit saith unto the churches; To him that overcometh will I give to eat of the hidden manna, and will give him a white stone, and in the stone a new name written, which no man knoweth saving he that receiveth it."

Once again, all believers are encouraged to listen to the Spirit's message to all the churches, not just the church in Pergamos. Encouragement is given *"to him that overcometh"* – a statement that refers to true believers, as we learned previously.

Two things are to be given to the overcomers by Jesus Christ as special rewards and encouragement:

144

Hidden manna to eat, and a white stone with a new name on it.

What is *"hidden manna"*?

The word *"hidden"* means that we do not know about it now, but the blessings of it will be revealed at a later time. *"Manna"* connects it with the special food God supplied for the people of Israel in the wilderness, and which John (in his gospel – John 6) used in symbolism of the life of the Lord Jesus Himself. He is the true Bread from heaven; if we eat of it, we shall live forever!

No doubt there is a connection with the pot of manna that was kept in the Ark in the tabernacle and later in the temple. It, of course, was *"hidden."* Revelation 11:19 reveals that the Ark is presently in heaven. It was believed in past history that Jeremiah hid the Ark before the destruction of Jerusalem. The point was that it would not be discovered until Israel is restored to its Messianic hope and glory. Perhaps several thoughts need to be associated with the phrase *"hidden manna."* John 6 makes it clear that Jesus Christ is the real *"manna"* from heaven of which the *"manna"* in the wilderness was merely a type. We now experience a personal relationship and fellowship with Him by faith, but the full expression of that experience will not be known until He comes again. Therefore, the spiritual *"manna"* the food which gives eternal life, is *"hidden"* at the present time, though real. But when Jesus Christ returns, it will no longer be *"hidden"* but fully enjoyed by believers forever. The symbolism of the pot of manna "hidden" inside the Ark of the Covenant relates well to this possible interpretation.

What is the *"white stone"* with a *"new name"* on it?

This is a very difficult symbolism and requires some careful research and investigation. Stones were used in ancient times to render a verdict, a white stone indicating acquittal, and a black stone that of condemnation. However, there is no mention or comparison of a white stone with a black stone in this passage.

Some choose to relate this stone to the stones on the breastplate of the High Priest in the Old Testament, representing the twelve tribes of Israel. However, not one of those stones was said to be a white stone or even a diamond, if that is what the white stone would look like.

Others choose to emphasize the ancient practice of using stones as counters in calculations. The idea here is that if you have been faithful to the Lord (overcomer), you will be counted among those who are saved. However, this does nothing to explain the whiteness of the stone or the new name written upon it.

One of the most interesting and plausible arguments about the use of stones in the ancient world comes from the practices of the Roman Empire. When the Roman Empire gave free doles of bread and free admission to entertainments, the tickets were often in the form of a white stone with a person's name on it. It was a well-established practice to reward the victors at the games with such a ticket to a special feast. Since the *"hidden manna"* probably implies eating at a feast in the future (namely – the "marriage supper of the Lamb" – Revelation 19) or enjoying the blessings of fellowship forever, it is quite possible that the white stone implies our entrance ticket to that heavenly feast.

The words *"new name"* do not imply "new from the standpoint of time" but rather "new in quality or its essential nature." The name may be referring to the Name of Jesus Christ, but rather to a special "new name" that reveals the eternal relationship of the overcomer to the promises of God.

Our Lord has so many wonderful promises to those who are true believers, the overcomers. I Corinthians 2:9 says: *"But as it is written, Eye hath not seen, nor ear heard, neither have entered into the heart of man, the things which God hath prepared for them that love Him."*

AMEN!

IMMORAL PRACTICES
Church in Thyatira
Revelation 2:18-29

"And unto the angel of the church in Thyatira write; These things saith the Son of God, Who hath His eyes like unto a flame of fire, and His feet are like fine grass; I know thy works, and charity, and service, and faith, and thy patience, and thy works; and the last to be more than the first. Notwithstanding I have a few things against thee, because thou sufferest that woman Jezebel, which calleth herself a prophetess, to teach and to seduce My servants to commit fornication, and to eat things sacrificed unto idols. And I gave her space to repent of her fornication; and she repented not. Behold, I will cast her into a bed, and them that commit adultery with her into great tribulation, except they repent of their deed. And I will kill her children with death; and all the churches shall know that I am He which searcheth the reins and hearts: and I will give unto every one of you according to your works. But unto you I say, and unto the rest in Thyatira, as many as have not this doctrine, and which have not known the depths of Satan, as they speak; I will put upon you none other burden. But that which ye have already hold fast till I come. And he that overcometh, and keepeth My works unto the end, to him will I give power over the nations: and he shall rule them with a rod of iron; as the vessels of a potter shall they be broken to shivers: even as I received of My Father. And I will give him the morning star. He

that hath an ear, let him hear what the Spirit sith unto the churches."

The name "Thyatira" means "the castle of Thya." Other names which it has borne are Pelopia and Semiramis. Before the time of Nicator the place was regarded as a holy city, for there stood the temple of the ancient Lydian sun-god, Tyrimnos; about it games were held in his honor. Upon the early coins of Thyatira this Asiatic god is represented as a horseman, bearing a double-headed battle-ax, similar to those represented on the sculptures of the Hittites. A goddess associated with him was Boreatene, a deity of less importance. Another temple at Thyatira was dedicated to Sambethe, and at this shrine was a prophetess, by some supposed to represent the Jezebel of Revelation 2:20, who uttered the sayings which this deity would impart to the worshippers.

Thyatira was specially noted for the trade guilds which were probably more completely organized there than in any other ancient city. Every artisan belonged to a guild, and every guild, which was an incorporated organization, possessed property in its own name, made contracts for great constructions, and wielded a wide influence. Powerful among them was the guild of coppersmiths; another was the guild of the dyers, who, it is believed, made use of the madder-root instead of shell-fish for making the purple dyestuffs. A member of this guild seems to have been Lydia of Thyatira, who, according to Acts 16:14, sold her dyes in Philippi. The color obtained by the use of this dye is now called Turkish red. The guilds were closely connected with the Asiatic religion of the place. Pagan feasts, with which immoral practices were associated, were held, and therefore the nature of the guilds was such that they were opposed to Christianity. According to Acts 19:10, Paul may have preached there while he was living at Ephesus, but this is uncertain; yet Christianity reached there at an early time. It was taught by many of the early church that no Christian might belong to one of the guilds, and thus the greatest opposition to Christianity was presented.

Thyatira is now represented by the modern town of Ak-Hissar on a branch line of the Manisa-Soma Railroad, and on the old Roman road 9 hours from Sardis. Ak-Hissar is Turkish for "white castle," and near the modern town may be seen the ruins of the castle from which the name was derived. The village is of considerable size; most of the houses are of mud, but several of the buildings erected by Caracalla are still standing, yet none of them are perfect. In the higher part of the town are the ruins of the pagan temples, and in the walls of the houses are broken columns and sarcophagi and inscribed stones. The population of 20,000 is largely Greek and Armenian, yet a few Jews live among them. Before the town is a large marsh, fever-laden, and especially unhealthful in the summer time, formed by the Lycus River, which the Turks now call Geurdeuk Chai. The chief modern industry is rug-making.

The city was known as "Pelopia" (Greek language: Πελοπία), but it was named Thyatira (Θυάτειρα) by king Seleucus I Nicator in 290 BC. He was at war with Lysimachus when he learned that his wife had given birth to a daughter. According to Stephanus of Byzantium, he called this city by the name that means "daughter", although it is likely that it is an older, Lydian name. In classical times, Thyatira stood on the border between Lydia and Mysia. It was famous for its dyeing and was a center of the indigo trade. Among the ancient ruins of the city, inscriptions have been found relating to the guild of dyers in the city. Indeed, more guilds are known in Thyatira than any other contemporary city in the Roman province of Asia (inscriptions mention the following: wool-workers, linen-workers, makers of outer garments, dyers, leather-workers, tanners, potters, bakers, slave-dealers, and bronze-smiths).

In early Christian times, Thyatira was home to a significant Christian church, mentioned as one of the seven Churches of the Book of Revelation in the Book of Revelation. According to Revelation, a woman named Jezebel (who called herself a prophetess) taught and seduced the Christians of Thyatira to commit sexual immorality and to eat things sacrificed to idols.

The Apostle Paul and Silas might have visited Thyatira during Paul's second or third journey, although the evidence is entirely circumstantial. They visited several small unnamed towns in the general vicinity during the second journey. While in

Philippi, Paul and Silas stayed with a woman named Lydia from Thyatira, who continued to help them even after they were jailed and released.

In 366 BC, a battle fought near Thyatira saw the army of Roman emperor Valens defeat Roman usurper Procopius.

In 1922 AD, the Patriarch of Constantinople appointed an Exarch for Western and Central Europe with the title Archbishop of Thyatira. The current Archbishop of Thyatira (since 1988) is Gregorios Theocharous. The Archbishop of Thyatira resides in London and has pastoral responsibility for the Greek Orthodox Church in the United Kingdom.

The __EXAMINATION__ of the church by Yeshua
Revelation 2:18

"And unto the angel of the church in Thyatira write: These things saith the Son of God, Who hath His eyes like unto a flame of fire, and His feet are like fine brass."

This is the only place in Revelation that uses the Name *"the Son of God"* even though it was used often by John in his writings. Two things are brought to our attention immediately by our Lord:

1. Yeshua (Jesus) is the Son of God!
2. Yeshua has eyes like a flame of fire, and feet like fine brass!

Some commentators see here a contrast between our Lord the Messiah and the Roman Emperor – a classic struggle especially in the first century AD. However, emperor worship was not prominent in Thyatira as it was in Pergamos.

A more likely connection is with the teaching of Psalm 2. One of its verses is quoted in the message to this church. We read in Psalm 2:8-9 these words:

"Ask of Me, and I shall give Thee the heathen for Thine inheritance, and the uttermost parts of the earth for Thy possession. Thou shalt break them with a rod of iron; Thou shalt dash them in pieces like a potter's vessel."

The promise to overcomers is indeed remarkable in the message to Thyatira. They will share in the powerful Messianic kingdom and rule and reign with the Messiah over the kingdoms of this world!

The deity, sovereignty, and authority of our Lord Yeshua must always be reestablished in the minds and hearts of believers if sinful practices are to be dealt with as God intends. It is not our authority that roots out evil, but our submission to His will. The issues are not merely temporary ones; they affect eternal destiny and reward.

The reference to His *"eyes"* and His *"feet"* reminds us of the vision of chapter one (verses 14-15) where we learned of His scrutiny, seeing all that we think, say, and do, and His severity, treading with His feet in the winepress of God's wrath against sin and unbelief. Revelation 2:23 confirms that this is the correct interpretation when it quotes from Jeremiah 17:9-10:

"The heart is deceitful above all things, and desperately wicked: who can know it? I the LORD search the heart, I try the reins, even to give every man according to the fruit of his doings." Verse 23 quotes *"and all the churches shall know that I am He which searcheth the reins and hearts; and I will give unto every one of you according to your works."*

May our churches and its leaders never forget the One to Whom we will all give account one day! We need to remember His authority, deity, and sovereignty over all, and His knowledge of all that is going on in our churches, and His role in judging us if we do not repent.

The __EVIDENCE__ of spiritual life
Revelation 2:19

"I know thy works, and charity, and service, and faith, and thy patience, and thy works; and the last to be more than the first."

In the midst of some very strong words of judgment concerning the sinful practices of this church, there is evidence of spiritual life as well. Appearances may deceive us, but God looks on the heart and knows the real truth behind the facade of our efforts to please Him.

In the examination of their *"works"* our Lord refers to four things worthy of commendation – love, service, faith, and patience.

1. A proper <u>MOTIVATION</u>

The church in Ephesus was rebuked for its lack of the *"first love,"* while folks in Thyatira are the only ones to receive this commendation for love.

A great lesson is revealed in mentioning the *"love"* of believers in Thyatira, a church that is strongly rebuked for compromising with sin. God's love does not mean we compromise with sin or justify sinful attitudes and practices because we have a measure of God's love in our midst. In the name of *"love"* many churches today are tolerant of sinful actions. The leadership often refuses to discipline such actions perhaps because they love the praise of men more than the approval of God. Often we are told that we have not right to tell people how to live their lives. Some say it is an invasion of privacy and even legally wrong to confront sinful practices (especially sexual ones) in the lives of church members. We have lost sight of what our Lord Yeshua thinks of the church, and have substituted our own insufficient and powerless viewpoints.

2. An effective <u>MINISTRY</u>

Their *"service"* was commended. But once again, our busyness for the Lord and His work is never a substitution for holiness and a godly lifestyle. The Greek word for *"service"* is our word for *"deacon."* It emphasizes voluntary ministry that focuses on the physical and material needs of people and often ignores their spiritual walk with the Lord.

Ephesians 4:12 reminds us that all believers are to be involved in the *"work of ministry"* and that includes using our spiritual gifts (I Peter 4:10-11).

This church in Thyatira was known for its love and service – most of us would be delighted to be a part of their fellowship.

3. A right <u>MESSAGE</u>

When their *"faith"* was commended, it brings up the importance of the right message. In Jude 3 we read:

"Beloved, when I gave all diligence to write unto you of the common salvation, it was needful for me to write unto you, and exhort you that ye should earnestly contend for the faith which was once delivered unto the saints."

Many churches proclaim their loyalty to a creed or statement of faith and yet tolerate sinful practices with no confrontation. When sinful practices are tolerated, it diminishes the strength of our beliefs – do we really believe what we teach?

4. A tough <u>MENTALITY</u>

The word *"patience"* refers to "bearing up under a load." It is certainly commendable that this church manifested such a quality in their life and ministry, but once again, it does not justify or defend a lack of holiness and a godly lifestyle. They had the patience that James speaks about that brings maturity and contentment. We read in James 1:2-4:

"My brethren, count it all joy when ye fall into divers temptations; Knowing this, that the trying of your faith worketh patience. But let patience have her perfect work, that ye may be perfect (mature) *and entire, wanting nothing."*

In this church there was also evidence of spiritual growth. Our Lord's remark *"and the last to be more than the first"* seems to reveal that a measure of growth was taking place and for that, we praise the Lord. But once again, it is no substitute for a life of holiness and godliness – sin must be confronted – the people must repent!

The <u>EXAMPLE</u> of moral decay
Revelation 2:20-21

"Notwithstanding, I have a few things against thee, because thou sufferest that woman Jezebel, which calleth herself a prophetess, to teach and to seduce My servants to commit fornication, and to eat things sacrificed unto idols. And I gave her space to repent of her fornication; and she repented not."

Who is JEZEBEL?

Here's what we know about her from the message to Thyatira:

1. She is a woman.
2. She calls herself a prophetess.
3. She teaches and seduces people to commit sexual sin and sacrifice to idols.
4. She is guilty of sexual sin herself.
5. She appears to be involved in occultic practices – *"depths of Satan."*
6. She is unrepentant.

In the Bible, Jezebel was the wife of Israel's king Ahab. The question is, is the references to Jezebel in the Old Testament merely symbolic of a woman affecting this church in the first century AD or is there a real woman named Jezebel in the church of Thyatira?

It would seem logical to argue that this is a real woman within the ministry of this church who indeed reflected the evil traits of the Old Testament Jezebel. There is parallel symbolism here, but no doubt an actual person affecting the people of this church.

Some say that an evil spirit (demon) was involved in the woman in Thyatira, producing through her life the same evil qualities of the wife of Ahab. That, of course, is possible. The context refers also to those who do not support *"this doctrine"* of Jezebel. That statement alone would argue for an actual person within the church of Thyatira. Her influence upon others appears to be quite strong. She claims a measure of spiritual authority, and teaches and seduces people to believe what she says. The two major issues of her teaching involve sexual immorality and a measure of idolatry, and at least, a compromise with food that was offered to idols. Often it involved festivals or feasts that were enjoyed by the pagan crowds and attended and somewhat supported by the believers in the church – attributed to the influential teaching of this woman.

Today we have many leaders who claim to be prophets or prophetesses, and say that God speaks directly to them and gives them special messages that are not found in the Bible. The danger of this should be obvious to all believers but unfortunately, many are deceived and following these people. A given teaching is right or wrong based upon the authority of the Bible, not the personality or claims of a given human leader!

Our Christian liberty does not allow us to violate the clear commands of the Bible. We are not free to sin!

The **EXPLANATION** of God's judgment
Revelation 2:22-23

"Behold, I will cast her into a bed, and them that commit adultery with her into great tribulation, except they repent of their deeds. And I will kill her

children with death; and all the churches shall know that I am He which searcheth the reins and hearts, and I will give unto every one of you according to your works."

1. The <u>DETERMINATION</u> of God to bring His judgment

Three times we read about God's coming judgment – *"I will."* Make no mistake about it – judgment will come upon all who refuse to repent!

The interesting fact in this passage, however, are the words of our Lord – *"and I gave her space to repent of her fornication; and she repented not."* This exalts the longsuffering of the Lord without removing the fact of His coming judgment.

2. The physical <u>DISEASE</u> upon Jezebel

The *"bed"* into which she is cast is a bed of serious illness. Her bed of sexual immorality will become a bed of serious illness. Perhaps this is a Biblical reference to the judgment of sexual sin that people experienced in this life – sexual sin brings sexual disease. This fact is indeed alarming as we see the awful consequences of sexual immorality in our culture today.

This fact is supported also by what the text says – *"and them that commit adultery with her."*

3. The great __DISTRESS__ upon her followers

Her followers will experience *"great tribulation"* if they do not repent of their sin. It is possible also to understand these words by making the meaning of the *"bed"* the same as the *"great tribulation."* It is possible that these words are referring to the coming *"Day of the Lord"* or the *"Day of God's Wrath"* that will soon be coming to planet earth!

4. The coming __DEATH__ for her children

It would seem logical to argue that *"her children"* are not the ones who *"commit adultery"* with her, but rather those who are influenced to do so by her teaching and deception, seducing believers to tolerate what she says. Perhaps the trade guilds of ancient Thyatira are a major part of the problem as they had parties (feasts and festivals) where gluttony, drunkenness, and sexual immorality took place. Christians who attended these parties, of course, would be tempted to participate.

The phrase *"her children"* would refer to future generations of those committed to her viewpoint and continue to propagate such teaching and sinful practices.

5. The clear __DESCRIPTION__ of God's coming judgment

It involves a simple point that we cannot escape the judgment of God – *"and all the churches shall know that I am He which searcheth the reins and hearts."* He knows all that we think, say, and do.

Everyone will be judged *"according to your works."* Even believers will be judged at the place called the Judgment Seat (Greek – *bema*) of Christ. Our *"works"* will be the basis for determining our rewards. II Corinthians 5:10 states: *"For we must all appear before the judgment seat of Christ; that every one may receive the things done in his body, according to that he hath done, whether it be good or bad."* In Revelation 22:12 it says: *"And, behold, I come quickly; and My reward is with Me, to give every man according as his work shall be."*

We are also told in Revelation 20:11-15 about the judgment that is coming upon all unbelievers!

"And I saw a great white throne, and Him that sat on it, from Whose face the earth and the heaven fled away; and there was found no place for them. And I saw the dead, small and great, stand before God; and the books were opened: and another book was opened, which is the book of life: and the dead were judged out of those things which were written in the books, according to their works. And the sea gave up the dead which were in it; and death and hell delivered up the dead which were in them: and they were judged every man according to their works. And death and hell were cast into the lake of fire. This is the second death. And whosoever

was not found written in the book of life was cast into the lake of fire."

The <u>EXHORTATION</u> to the faithful
Revelation 2:24-25

"But unto you I say, and unto the rest in Thyatira, as many as have not this doctrine, and which have not known the depths of Satan, as they speak; I will put upon you none other burden. But that which ye have already hold fast till I come."

It is not easy to stand for the Lord and remain faithful in the midst of a pagan environment that is filled with temptations and seduction. The Lord knows how difficult it is, and He places no other burden upon us except to *"hold fast"* what He has given to us until that sweet day when He comes again!

A great passage that deals with the problems which the believers in Thyatira were facing is the instruction which Paul gave the young believers in Thessalonica in I Thessalonians 4:1-8:

"Furthermore then we beseech you, brethren, and exhort you by the Lord Jesus, that as ye have received of us how ye ought to walk and to please God, so ye would abound more and more. For ye know what commandments we gave you by the Lord Jesus. For this is the will of God, even your sanctification, that ye should abstain from fornication: That every one of you should know

how to possess his vessel in sanctification and honor; Not in the lust of concupiscence, even as the Gentiles which know not God: That no man go beyond and defraud his brother in any matter; because that the Lord is the avenger of all such, as we also have forewarned you and testified. For God hath not called us unto uncleanness, but unto holiness. He therefore that despiseth, despiseth not man, but God, Who hath also given unto us His Holy Spirit."

It is clearly the will of God that believers stay away from sexual sin. Sex is a beautiful gift from the Lord to those who are married (husband and wife), and the sexual bed of married couples is undefiled – so says Hebrews 13:4. But, it violates the clear teaching of the Bible for us to be involved sexually with any person with whom we are not married.

The <u>ENCOURAGEMENT</u> to the overcomer
Revelation 2:26-28

"And he that overcometh, and keepeth My works unto the end, to him will I give power over the nations: And he shall rule them with a rod of iron; as the vessels of a potter shall they be broken to shivers: even as I received of My Father. And I will give him the morning star. He that hath an ear, let him hear what the Spirit saith unto the churches."

The important <u>PRINCIPLE</u> that leads to God's blessings – *"keepeth My works unto the end"*

The word *"keepeth"* is used 36 times in the writings of John. It is the phrase that speaks of our obedience to God and His Word. This evidence of the will of God in our lives is a clear evidence of our faith in our blessed Lord Yeshua!

The amazing __PROMISE__ of the Lord – *"to him will I give power over the nations"*

It would seem probable that this phrase refers to our ruling and reigning with the Lord in His coming kingdom. The quotation is from the Messianic passage in Psalm 2:8-9.

The wonderful __PRESENCE__ of the Messiah – *"And I will give him the morning star."*

Revelation 22:16 clearly points to our Lord Yeshua as the *"morning star."* Daniel 12:1-3 makes these statements about the future of His people:

"And at that time shall Michael stand up, the great prince which standeth for the children of thy people: and there shall be a time of trouble, such as never was since there was a nation even to that same time: and at that time thy people shall be delivered, every one that shall be found written in the book. And many of them that sleep in the dust of the earth shall awake, some to everlasting life, and some to shame and everlasting contempt. And they that be wise shall shine as the brightness of the firmament; and they that turn many to righteousness as the stars forever and ever."

The *"morning star"* is considered to be the brightest and the symbolism here would emphasize the glory that will be given to believers in the future. We will shine like the *"stars forever and ever."*

SPIRITUAL APATHY
Church in Sardis
Revelation 3:1-6

"And unto the angel of the church in Sardis write; These things saith He that hath the seven Spirits of God, and the seven stars; I know thy works, that thou hast a name that thou livest, and art dead. Be watchful, and strengthen the things which remain, that are ready to die: for I have not found thy works perfect before God. Remember therefore how thou hast received and heard, and hold fast, and repent. If therefore thou shalt not watch, I will come on thee as a thief, and thou shalt not know what hour I will come upon thee. Thou hast a few names even in Sardis which have not defiled their garments, and they shall walk with Me in white: for they are worthy. He that overcometh, the same shall be clothed in white raiment; and I will not blot out his name out of the book of life, but I will confess his name before My Father, and before His angels. He that hath an ear, let him hear what the Spirit saith unto the churches."

THE HISTORY OF SARDIS

Sardis was the capital of the ancient kingdom of Lydia, one of the important cities of the Persian Empire, the seat of a proconsul under the Roman Empire, and the metropolis of the province Lydia in later Roman and Byzantine times. As one of the seven churches of Asia, it was addressed by the author of the Book of Revelation in terms which seem to imply that its population was notoriously soft and fainthearted. Its importance was due, first to its military strength, secondly to its situation on an important highway leading from the interior to the Aegean coast, and thirdly to its commanding the wide and fertile plain of the Hermus.

The earliest reference to Sardis is in the "The Persians of Aeschylus (472 BC)" in the Iliad, the name Hyde seems to be given to the city of the Maeonian (i.e. Lydian) chiefs, and in later times Hyde was said to be the older name of Sardis, or the name of its citadel. It is, however, more probable that Sardis was not the original capital of the Maeonians, but that it became so amid the changes which produced the powerful Lydian empire of the 8th century BC.

The city was captured by the Cimmerians in the 7th century BC, by the Persians in the 6th, by the Athenians in the 5th, and by Antiochus III the Great at the end of the 3rd century BC. In the Persian era, Sardis was conquered by Cyrus the Great and formed the end station for the Persian Royal Road which began in Persepolis, capital of Persia. During the Ionian Revolt, the Athenians burnt down the city. Sardis remained under Persian domination until it surrendered to Alexander the Great in 334 BC.

The early Lydian kingdom was very advanced in the industrial arts and Sardis was the chief seat of its manufactures. The most important of these trades was the manufacture and dyeing of delicate woolen stuffs and carpets. The stream Pactolus which flowed through the market-place "carried golden sands" in early antiquity, which was in reality gold dust out of Mount Tumulus. It was during the reign of King Croesus that the metallurgists of Sardis discovered the secret of separating gold from silver, thereby producing both metals of a purity never known before. This was an economic revolution, for while gold nuggets panned or mined were used as currency, their purity was always suspect and a hindrance to trade. Such nuggets or coinage were naturally occurring alloys of gold and silver known as electrum and one could never know how much of it was gold and how much was silver. Sardis now could mint nearly pure silver and gold coins, the value of which could be (and was!) trusted throughout the known world. This revolution made Sardis rich and Croesus' name synonymous with wealth itself. For this reason, Sardis is famed in history as the place where modern currency was invented.

Disaster came to the great city under the reign of the emperor Tiberius, when in AD 17, Sardis was destroyed by an earthquake, but it was rebuilt. It was one of the great cities of western Asia Minor until the later Byzantine period.

Later, trade and the organization of commerce continued to be sources of great wealth. After Constantinople became the capital of the East, a new road system grew up connecting the provinces with the capital. Sardis then lay rather apart from the great lines of communication and lost some of its importance. It still, however, retained its titular supremacy and continued to be the seat of the metropolitan bishop of the province of Lydia, formed in AD 295. It was enumerated as third, after Ephesus and Smyrna, in the list of cities of the Thracesion thema given by Constantine Porphyrogenitus in the 10th century AD. However, over the next four centuries it was in the shadow of the provinces of Magnesia-upon-Sipylum and Philadelphia, which retained their importance in the region.

After 1071 AD the Hermus valley began to suffer from the inroads of the Seljuk Turks but the Byzantine general John Doukas reconquered the city in 1097 AD, the successes of the general Philokales in 1118 relieved the district from later Turkish pressure and the ability of the Comneni dynasty together with the gradual decay of the Seljuk Sultanate of Rum meant that it remained under Byzantine dominion. When Constantinople was taken by the Venetians and Franks in 1204 AD Sardis came under the rule of the Byzantine Empire of Nicea. However once the Byzantines retook Constantinople in 1261 AD, Sardis with the entire Asia Minor was neglected and the region eventually fell under the control of Ghazi emirs, the Cayster valleys and a fort on the citadel of Sardis was handed over to them by treaty in 1306 AD. The city continued its decline until its capture (and probable destruction) by the Mongol warlord Timur in 1402 AD.

By the 19th century AD, Sardis was in ruins, showing construction chiefly of the Roman period. The first large scale archaeological expedition in Sardis was directed by a Princeton University team led by Howard Crosby Butler between years 1910–1914 AD, unearthing a temple to Artemis, and more than a thousand Lydian tombs. The excavation campaign was halted by World War I, followed by the Turkish War of Independence, though it briefly resumed in 1922 AD. Some surviving artifacts from the Butler excavation were added to the collection of the Metropolitan Museum of Art in New York.

Since 2008 AD, the excavation has been under the directorship of Nicholas Cahill, professor at the University of Wisconsin–Madison. The laws governing archaeological expeditions in Turkey ensure that all archaeological artifacts remain in Turkey. Some of the important finds from the site of Sardis are housed in the Archaeological Museum of Manisa, including Late Roman mosaics and sculpture, a helmet from the mid-6th century BC, and pottery from various periods.

Since 1958 AD, both Harvard and Cornell Universities have sponsored annual archeological expeditions to Sardis. These excavations unearthed perhaps the most impressive synagogue in the western diaspora yet discovered from antiquity, yielding over eighty Greek and seven Hebrew inscriptions as well as numerous mosaic floors. The discovery of the Sardis synagogue has reversed previous assumptions about Judaism in the later Roman empire. Along with the discovery of the godfearers/*theosebeis* inscription from the Aphrodisias, it provides indisputable evidence for the continued presence of Jewish communities in Asia Minor and their integration into general Roman life at a time when many scholars previously assumed that Christianity had eclipsed Judaism.

The synagogue was a section of a large bath-gymnasium complex, that was in use for about 450 – 500 years. In the beginning, middle of the 2nd century AD, the rooms in which the synagogue is situated were used as changing rooms or resting rooms. The complex was destroyed in 616 AD by the Sassanian-Persians.

Sardis is located about 50 miles due east of Smyrna and about 30 miles south of Thyatira. It was the capital of the province of Lydia. The city was built on the acropolis and was thus able to defend itself quite well from possible invaders. Later in its history, a second city was built on the slopes of this 1500 hundred foot plateau for convenience and easier access.

The Lydian kingdom began around 1200 BC and was the center of opposition to European forces. Sardis, in particular, was the one great enemy of Ionian cities. In the great conflicts between Asia and Europe, Sardis stood as an impregnable fortress of defense for the cities of Asia. It was known as the "First Metropolis of Asia, and of Lydia, and of Hellenism." It was powerful in its influence, bolstered by an exceedingly wealthy and prosperous economy.

The conquest of Sardis by King Cyrus of Persia in the 6th century BC was a shock to the Greeks who had tried so often to conquer it. King Croesus of Saris and Lydia attacked Cyrus on the promise of victory by a Delphic oracle. but was soundly defeated. After Croesus returned to Sardis, Cyrus brought a surprise attack and caught the city unprepared. Three hundred years later, Antiochus the Great also captured the city and later it was taken by the Romans.

THE EARTHQUAKE

In 17 AD the city was devastated by an earthquake, but through the kindness of Emperor Tiberius, the city was able to recover. In appreciation, the city minted a special coin in honor of Tiberius and erected a temple as well.

THE ECONOMY

The economy of the city was affected by a fertile territory that was carefully cultivated, and by an active trade with other parts of the world. Its main industries dealt with the production of woolen goods and jewelry. Like Thyatira, Sardis was known for its special dyes and its ability to produce beautifully colored garments.

RELIGION

The religious background of Sardis is more difficult to ascertain. The evidence of emperor worship, pagan temples and idols, and occultic practices are present, but no particular influence stands out. Its coins have religious symbols, including the Greek god Zeus, and a specific temple was built by the city to the goddess Cybele who seems to be connected with nature in Greek mythology. From the 4th century BC there was a temple to Artemis, the multi-breasted goddess of sex and fertility so fervently worshipped by the Ephesians.

As in several cities of Asia province (western Turkey) healing powers were associated with pagan gods. The interesting point about Sardis is that such healing power was expanded to include restoring the dead. Perhaps this was connected with the hot springs which were located close to the city. One cannot help but connect this fact with the words of this letter – *"thou hast a name that thou livest, and art dead."* These words would remind the residents of Sardis of a glorious past which was now a meaningless present situation.

When John wrote the Book of Revelation, Sardis had already lost its former glory. The acropolis was no longer inhabited and the city was faced with a glorious past and no future!

Not much is known about the church prior to the writing of this letter. Neither its founding or development is referred to in the New Testament. One of its early bishops, Melito, wrote one of the first known commentaries on the Book of Revelation near the end of the second century AD.

In spite of the past wealth of the city, there is no boasting in this letter like that of Laodicea (Revelation 3:17). There does not seem to be a problem of persecution like other cities faced. There is no emphasis upon the impact of pagan religions or religious opposition. The church has a reputation and appears to be a normal congregation in the eyes of others. Herodotus, the Greek historian, said that the citizens of Sardis had a reputation for lax moral standards and open licentiousness which might explain the emphasis of verse four concerning a few people who had not *"defiled their garments."*

The general impression one gets when reading this letter is that the church is dying through apathy and indifference. The struggle against pagan influence and worldly viewpoints has been lost. The Christians have given up the fight and are not reaching their world for Jesus Christ. It's the problem so many fine churches of our day have experienced. They talk of the past and still have all the ingredients and message of former days, but they have lost their zeal, compromised with the world around them, and a terminal illness. If the present trend continues, the church will soon be a relic of the past, a reminder of how easily God's work can die when spiritual apathy sets in!

His <u>ASSESSMENT</u> of the church
Revelation 3:1

"And unto the angel of the church in Sardis write; These things saith He that hath the seven spirits of God, and the seven stars; I know thy works, that thou hast a name that thou livest, and art dead."

The reference to the *"seven spirits of God"* is referring to the seven angels mentioned throughout the Book of Revelation.

Some commentators of Revelation have argued that this phrase refers to the "sevenfold ministry of the Holy Spirit" quoting Isaiah 11:1-2:

"And there shall come forth a rod out of the stem of Jesse, and a Branch shall grow out of his roots: And the Spirit of the LORD shall rest upon Him, the spirit of wisdom and understanding, the spirit of counsel and might, the spirit of knowledge and of the fear of the LORD."

However, there are not seven traits in this passage describing the work of the Holy Spirit. The Hebrew text has three couplets making a total of six, not seven. Revelation 1:4 speaks of the *"seven spirits which are before His throne."* Revelation 8:2 says: *"And I saw the seven angels which stood before God; and to them were given seven trumpets."*

The main assessment of this church is the phrase *"thou hast a name that thou livest, and art dead."* It is possible that this is a play on the claims of certain occultists in Sardis who believed that the healing waters of their hot springs could raise the dead. Not only did that not happen, but their views about it were actually picturing the condition of the church in a dying culture.

We think we know what a church is like if we have been a member for a number of years. That may or may not be true. What we think and what the Lord knows are not always the same. This church had a reputation – the text says *"a name."* But our Lord Yeshua knows the real truth about the spiritual condition of the church. This church like this city is dying!

We should not be too quick to judge outward appearances or performance. The important questions deal with the inward man, the realm of the unseen, the heart of the individual. Are we really in a right relationship with the Lord in the innermost recesses of our hearts?

Many of us major in a good reputation. We want people to think well of us and to say nice things about us. However, our reputation is only what people think we are: our character is what God knows us to be.

We may want to hear the praises and commendations of others, but the one who walks with the Lord desires to hear his words (Matthew 25:21, 23): *"Well done, thou good and faithful servant – enter thou into the joy of the Lord."* It is His approval that we need, not the plaudits of men!

His <u>APPEAL</u> to this church
Revelation 2:2-3a

"Be watchful, and strengthen the things which remain, that are ready to die: for I have not found thy works perfect before God."

The words of our Lord reveal at least three things:

1. They were <u>UNCONCERNED</u> about their spiritual condition!

The words *"Be watchful"* literally means "to wake up"! The people of this church (like so many churches) are asleep spiritually, unconcerned, apathetic, and indifferent. The Apostle Paul writes in Ephesians 5:14: *"Awake thou that sleepest, and arise from the dead, and Christ shall give thee light."*

These words would have been especially meaningful to the people of Sardis. Their city had fallen on two previous occasions to surprise attacks (from Cyrus and Antiochus the Great) when they were asleep militarily.

However, there is a ray of hope here – even if the church suffers from spiritual apathy – it is not hopeless. The fact that our Lord challenges them to wake up shows that things can be different. The Lord has not given up on this church.

2. They were <u>UNAWARE</u> of how serious their spiritual condition was!

When our Lord says *"strengthen the things which remain, that are ready to die"* the people of this church must have been shocked to hear the truth. It appears to be a reference to their *"works"* which were not what the Lord wanted them to be. Their efforts had become (no doubt!) routine and very mechanical, lacking in real spiritual depth and vitality. If things don't change, their ministry and influence were about to be removed.

3. They were <u>UNRESPONSIVE</u> to what the Lord wanted in their lives!

The words *"for I have not found thy works perfect before God."* Too much concern about reputation and what others think can actually work against a life that seeks only the approval of the Lord.

The word *"perfect"* refers to that which is completed or fulfilled. Their works were not fulfilling the purpose of God – they were just performing without His Spirit controlling and fulfilling what God wanted to do with them.

It is also possible that their works were not *"perfect"* because they were not designed to glorify

the Lord and reach lost people with the true gospel;
They only wanted to build a good reputation!

The **ACTIONS** the Lord threatens to make if things do not change!
Revelation 3:3

"Remember therefore how thou hast received and heard, and hold fast, and repent. If therefore thou shalt not watch, I will come on thee as a thief, and thou shalt not know what hour I will come upon thee."

1. We must **REMEMBER** what the Bible teaches!

To *"remember therefore how thou hast received and heard"* is a reminder to all of us of the importance of God's Word. When the teaching of the Bible diminishes in any church ministry, the life and ministry of that people will deteriorate, and what replaces Biblical exposition is a poor substitute for the authority and power of the Word of God.

2. We must **REESTABLISH** our loyalty and obedience to the Word of God!

The words *"hold fast"* remind us of the essential nature of our obedience to the Word of God and our willingness to abide by what it teaches no matter what happens. When persecution comes, it is our loyalty to God and His Word that comforts, sustains, and gives us boldness to face the opposition.

3. We must <u>REPENT</u> of our wrong attitudes and practices!

To *"repent"* depends upon a "change of mind" that leads to an immediate "change of conduct." This church is dying and losing its place in a pagan world that desperately needs the message of our Lord Messiah brought to them on a daily basis.

The <u>ASSURANCE</u> our Lord gives to the faithful few who will respond!
Revelation 3:4-6

"Thou hast a few names even in Sardis which have not defiled their garments; and they shall walk with Me in white: for they are worthy. He that overcometh, the same shall be clothed in white raiment; and I will not blot out his name out of the book of life, but I will confess his name before My Father, and before His angels. He that hath an ear, let him hear what the Spirit saith unto the churches."

It is both sad and encouraging to read about the *"few names even in Sardis"* – apparently there was a small group of true believers who were loyal to the Lord and His Word.

1. Moral <u>PURITY</u> – *"which have not defiled their garments"*

The wickedness of a given generation does not justify the immorality among God's people! This church was in the middle of a moral mess, but praise the Lord there were some who maintained a purity of lifestyle and refused to get involved in the sexual immorality of their city that was often promoted by the "parties" of the trade guilds. Sexual sin can deeply affect our response to the Word of God. When we tolerate it in our midst and refuse to stand for holiness and a godly lifestyle, the disintegration of spiritual life will begin immediately.

2. Messiah's <u>PRESENCE</u> – *"they shall walk with Me in white for they are worthy"*

No doubt about it – this is a wonderful assurance to those who will live a godly lifestyle and honor the Lord's admonitions about moral purity and its importance. The presence of our Lord Messiah is established and the text says *"they shall walk with Me."*

The word *"worthy"* does not bypass our relationship to the Lord; it simply declares the basis for our relationship to Him is rooted in our moral purity and commitment to obey His Word.

3. Future <u>PROMISES</u> – *"clothed in white raiment; and I will not blot out his name out of the book of life, but I will confess his name before My Father, and before His angels."*

In spite of the declining influence of the church in Sardis, there were a few who maintained their walk with the Lord and did not compromise with the environment in which they lived every day. God promises some wonderful things for our faithfulness to Him:

> (1) <u>RESURRECTION</u> of their physical body – *"clothed in white raiment"*

Revelation 4:4 says that the 24 elders around the throne of God will be *"clothed in white raiment."* Revelation 19:8 says of the *"wife"* of the Lamb – *"to her was granted that she should be arrayed in fine linen, clean and white."*

> (2) <u>REMOVAL</u> of their name from the book of life – will not happen!

The words of assurance – *"I will not blot out his name out of the book of life"* – are not teaching that some names will be blotted out; It simply states the fact that those who are the faithful few in Sardis and loyal to the Lord and His Word – will never lose the promise of their eternal salvation!

> (3) <u>RECEPTION</u> in the presence of the Father and His angels!

No words are more encouraging than these: *"but I will confess his name before My Father, and before His angels"*

That is real assurance!

ETERNAL SECURITY
Church in Philadelphia
Revelation 3:7-13

"And to the angel of the church in Philadelphia write; These things saith He that is holy, He that is true, He that hath the key of David, He that openeth, and no man shutteth; and shutteth, and no man openeth; I know thy works: behold, I have set before thee an open door, and no man can shut it: for thou hast a little strength, and hast kept My word, and hast not denied My name. Behold, I will make them of the synagogue of Satan, which say they are Jews, and are not, but do lie; behold, I will make them to come and worship before thy feet, and to know that I have loved thee. Because thou hast kept the word of My patience, I also will keep thee from the hour of temptation, which shall come upon all the world, to try them that dwell upon the earth. Behold, I come quickly: hold that fast which thou hast, that no man take thy crown. Him that overcometh will I make a pillar in the temple of My God, and he shall go no more out: and I will write upon him the Name of My God, and the name of the city of My God, which is new Jerusalem, which cometh down out of heaven from My God: and I will write upon him My new Name. He that hath an ear, let him hear what the Spirit saith unto the churches."

THE HISTORY OF PHILADELPHIA

Philadelphia (modern Alaşehir) formed the see of one of the oldest dioceses of Asia Minor, established in the middle of the 1st century AD and was one of the Seven Churches of Asia mentioned in the New Testament Book of Revelation, by John the Apostle. From 325 AD it was the see of a bishop under the jurisdiction of the metropolitan of Sardis. The bishopric of Philadelphia was promoted to metropolis in ca. 1190, during the reign of Byzantine Emperor Isaac II Angelos (1185–1195).

As a result of the Turkish invasions in western Anatolia during the 14th century AD, the Christian population decreased dramatically and consequently several bishoprics and metropolises became inactive. However, Philadelphia managed to avoid the fate of the rest of the Byzantine domains in the region and remained an isolated Byzantine exclave surrounded by various Turkish states. At that time the local metropolitans played an essential role in the city's history, like Theoleptos (1293 AD – before 1326), who was also a scholar. Theoleptos was also in charge of the defense of Philadelphia, when it was besieged by the Turks in 1310 AD and is considered by contemporary chronicles as "savior of the city". In 1382 AD the local metropolis was expanded and included parts of the former metropolis of Lydia.

In 1390 AD the city came under Ottoman control in a peaceful way. In May 1394 AD a new metropolitan was appointed and the area of the local metropolis was further expanded over the nearby regions of

Kula and Kolis. The sacking of the city by the army of Timur, in 1402 AD, resulted in a substantial decline of the local Christian element. However, the latter did not disappear and the city remained the see of a metropolis. Probably due to the further decrease of the Christian population, the local metropolis became inactive; in 1577 AD the see of the metropolis was transferred to Venice and the title of the metropolitan was used by the prelate of the local Greek Orthodox community of the city until 1712 AD.

At the beginning of the 18th century, new prelates were sent to the Philadelphia diocese, mainly due to the demographic and financial revival of the Orthodox communities and in 1725 AD the metropolis of Philadelphia had been re-established. The population increase of the Christians continued until the 19th century AD. According to Greek estimates, published in 1905 AD, the metropolis of Philadelphia included 19 Orthodox communities, most of them Turkish-speaking Christians, consisting of 14,003 people, 25 parishes and 23 priests. The most numerous and active communities, apart from the one found in the city of Philadelphia itself, were in Kula region, Uşak, Denizli, Salihli and Afyon Karahisar.

Most of the metropolis became part of the Greek-controlled Smyrna Occupation Zone in 1919 AD. However, due to the developments of the Greco-Turkish War of 1919–1922 AD, the local Orthodox element evacuated the region entirely in the Greek-

Turkish population exchange of 1923 AD.

INFORMATION from the web site of Bible Gateway:

In 1681 AD, a London widow named Jane Lead took over the Philadelphian Society, a mystical, millenarian group that regarded itself as "the Germ of the commencement of the sole true Church, Virgin Bride of Jesus Christ, whose members, dispersed among the diverse Religions of the World, are soon to appear and unite with them, in order to form this pure and holy Church, such as the church of Philadelphia was at the birth of Christianity". Even today there are preachers who regard the seven churches in Revelation as a kind of chronological portrait of the Christian church through the centuries. They seize upon the church at Philadelphia as a model for the true church-- usually their own small but faithful congregation, in contrast to the mainstream but apostate "church at Laodicea"!

Philadelphia was a city of some importance founded in the second century B.C. by Attalus, king of Pergamum, in honor of his predecessor, Eumenes Philadelphus. The city was strategically situated in a fertile river valley on the main road from Sardis to Laodicea, directly east of Smyrna. The message to Philadelphia has captured the imagination of Christians through the centuries because no other message (not even the one to Smyrna) is so rich in promises. The Speaker's self-identification (v. 7) sets the stage for the first promise (v. 8), which is given unconditionally to the angel at Philadelphia and thus to the whole congregation. Like Eliakim, gatekeeper of the king's palace in Jerusalem (Isaiah 22:20-22), he holds the key of David, so that what he opens no one can shut, and what he shuts no one can open (v. 7). Consequently, he places before the angel an open door (v. 8).

Preachers who claim this promise for their congregations tend to interpret the open door as a door to mission or evangelism, as in Acts 14:27. W. M. Ramsay called Philadelphia a "missionary city" because of its strategic location for the spread of Greek culture eastward into Lydia and Phrygia. Yet the open door in the message to Philadelphia is more likely a door into heaven (see 4:1) or into the temple of God or into the new Jerusalem (see v. 12) than a door for evangelism. The open door is simply a guarantee of salvation or eternal life, like the promises to the "overcomers" in all seven messages. Another way of saying it is that I will also keep you from the hour of trial that is going to come upon the whole world to test those who live on the earth (v. 10). Like the *"two witnesses"* in Revelation 11:12 or the child born of the woman in 12:5, they will be "raptured," or taken up to God in heaven, before the wrath of God is poured out on the earth.

The problem here, as at Smyrna, is the presence of a *"synagogue of Satan,"* probably a group of Judaizing Gentiles who claim to be Jews though they are not, but are liars. Ignatius mentioned

Judaizing Gentiles in Philadelphia a few decades later and John's vision here is that Christ will make them come and fall down at your feet and acknowledge that I have loved you (v. 9). The promise echoes such biblical passages as Isaiah 45:14, 49:23 and 60:14, in which Gentile nations come to pay homage to Israel and Israel's God. The message is a reminder that the *synagogue of Satan* are Gentiles after all, and that their present allegiance to Judaism is no more than a lie and a pretense to avoid persecution. In the end, the angel and his congregation will be vindicated against these bogus Jews, for even with little strength they have kept my word and have not denied my name (v. 8).

Whatever the names may be, they represent to the angel at Philadelphia security, stability and divine protection. John may have remembered Eliakim again, who was *"like a peg into a firm place,"* and a *"seat of honor for the house of his father"* (Isaiah 22:23), but Eliakim turned out to be a peg that would not hold (Isaiah 22:25). Instead, the risen Jesus extends to whoever *"overcomes"* at Philadelphia the hope of becoming a pillar in the temple of My God. Never again will he leave it (v. 12). God's temple, or sanctuary, must be the temple in heaven, for there is no temple in the new Jerusalem (Revelation 21:22). The image of being fixed as a pillar in the heavenly temple will come to life later in a graphic description of those *"before the throne of God"* who *"serve him day and night in his temple"* (Revelation 7:15-17). In both passages, living in the temple of God becomes a metaphor for eternal salvation in the same way in which Christians have always understood the closing words of Psalm 23: *"and I will dwell in the house of the LORD forever."*

NOTES FROM J. VERNON MCGEE

Philadelphia is in an area that is subject to earthquakes. The great population that was in that area left primarily because of earthquakes and, of course, because of warfare. When Tamerlane and the other great pagan leaders came out of the East, it was a time when all those who were left were slaughtered. Therefore, today no descendants of the original population are there. However, this city has had continuous habitation from its very beginning.

This city was like a Greek island out in Lydia, out in the Anatolian country, an area which the Greeks considered to be heathen and pagan--the Greek word for it was "barbarian." In fact, anyone who was not a Greek was considered a barbarian in those days. The Lydian language was spoken there at first, but by the time of the apostles, the Greek language had taken over, and it was a typical Greek colony. This was the outpost of Greek culture in a truly Asiatic and Anatolian atmosphere. It was called a "little Athens" because of the fact that it was in this area and yet was truly Greek.

It was a fortress city used to waylay the enemy who would came in to destroy the greater cities like Ephesus and Smyrna and Pergamum--these were the three great cities. These other cities were largely fortress cities where garrisons were stationed either to stop the enemy or delay him as he marched toward the western coast.

Philadelphia is in a country where erosion is at work; the soil is quite alluvial, but it is very fertile soil. Beautiful laurel trees, many flowers, and was particularly celebrated for its excellent wine. Great vineyards cover the surrounding hills, and the head of Bacchus was imprinted on their coins.

The city did not get its name, as so many seem to think, from the Bible. Actually, the city got its name because of the love that Attalus II had for his brother Eumenes who was king of Pergamum. Attalus had a great love and loyalty for his brother, and because of that it is called "the city of brotherly love,"

In A.D. 17 a great earthquake struck this city and totally destroyed it. The same earthquake totally destroyed Sardis and many other Lydian cities throughout that area. Tiberius, the emperor at that time, allocated a vast sum of money for the rebuilding of these cities, and they were then restored.

This is the one church besides Smyrna for which our Lord had no word of condemnation, Why? Because it had turned to the Word of God. It is interesting concerning the two churches which He did not condemn that the places are still in existence, although the churches have disappeared. There are the remains of a Byzantine church, which reveals that Christianity was active there up until the twelfth or thirteenth century AD. The remains of that Byzantine church are still there, but that is not the pillar that is mentioned in verse 12, although many believe that it is, and that is where the guides take the tours. Why did the Turkish government get rid of that amphitheater? I'll tell you why: The Seljuk Turks brutally killed the Christians in Philadelphia, and they wanted to get rid of every vestige of that old civilization. Today they would rather that you and I forget about it. Philadelphia is the place where Christian and Saracen fought during the Crusades, and in 1922 AD Turkey and Greece fought in Philadelphia. There are apparently a few Christians there today, as I have suggested, but they are undercover because they would be severely persecuted. The church of Philadelphia continued into the thirteenth century AD. This church was in a very strategic area to be a missionary church, and that is actually what it was. I have labeled it the revived church because it returned to the Word of God and began to teach the Word of God.

A BRIEF SUMMARY OF WHAT WE KNOW ABOUT PHILADELPHIA

Philadelphia was located in a beautiful valley some 25 miles southeast of Sardis. It sat on a great trade route that in Byzantine times became the greatest trade route in the whole country. Philadelphia was connected vitally to the main communications line of Rome itself by which is maintained control and influence over much of the ancient world.

The name of the city (as mentioned earlier) comes from the loyalty which King Attalus of Pergamum, who sponsored the founding of the city, demonstrated to his brother King Eumenes. The original purpose behind this key city was to make it a center for spreading Greek language, culture, and manners throughout the Asian provinces such as Lydia and Phrygia. Its success is seen in that the Lydian language ceased to be used by 20 AD and was replaced by Greek.

While the evidence is sparse, it appears that the influence of Greek culture affected religious life in Philadelphia. Its coins reveal pagan gods such as Artemis and Asklepios, as well as pagan temples. Since grapes were one of its main crops, it's not surprising to learn that the pagan god, Dionysus, the god of wine and revelry, was worshipped here. In Byzantine and Medieval times, this church seemed to grow in influence as did the city itself.

When you visit the site of this ancient city, you are reminded of its vulnerability to natural disaster. It is located in a region where volcanoes have erupted producing large quantities of black lava. The earthquake of 17 AD that devastated Sardis also stuck Philadelphia, and the continual aftershocks caused a state of panic for several years.

Philadelphia is also known for its resistance to Moslem influence in the Middle Ages. While most of the surrounding cities fell early to the forces of Islam, Philadelphia remained Christian until the 14th century AD. The city today has a population of about 20,000 and even a Christian Bishop with five churches that claim about 1000 believers.

The **POWER** of Jesus Christ is behind it all!
Revelation 3:7-8

"And to the angel of the church in Philadelphia write; These things saith He that is holy, He that is true, He that hath the key of David, He that openeth, and no man shutteth; and shutteth, and no man openeth; I know thy works: behold, I have set before thee an open door, and no man can shut it: for thou hast a little strength, and hast kept My word, and hast not denied My Name."

His **CHARACTER** – *"He that is holy, He that is true"*

These two attributes of our Lord are in the words of the martyrs of Revelation 6:10 who cry with a loud voice: *"How long, O Lord, holy and true, does thou not judge and avenge our blood on them that dwell on the earth?"*

God's holiness demands that justice be done, and the fact that He is *"true"* makes what He says and does totally reliable. Justice will come in God's timing.

According to Hebrews 6:17-19 God's promises are based on the reliability of His character:

"Wherein God, willing more abundantly to shew unto the heirs of promise the immutability of His counsel, confirmed it by an oath: That by two immutable things, in which it was impossible for God to lie, we might have a strong consolation, who have fled for refuge to lay hold upon the hope set before us: which hope we have as an anchor of the soul, both sure and stedfast, and which entereth into that within the veil."

Because God is holy (will not lie) and true (totally reliable), we can trust Him to reward us when we respond to Him.

His __CONTROL__ – *"He that hath the key of David, He that openeth, and no man shutteth; and shutteth, and no man openeth."*

The *"key of David"* is discussed in Isaiah 22:20-25:

"And it shall come to pass in that day, that I will call My servant Eliakim the son of Hilkiah: And I will clothe him with thy robe, and strengthen him with thy girdle, and I will commit thy government into his hand: and he shall be a father to the

inhabitants of Jerusalem, and to the house of Judah. And the key of the house of David will I lay upon his shoulder; so he shall open, and none shall shut; and he shall shut, and none shall open. And I will fasten him as a nail in a sure place; and he shall be for a glorious throne to his father's house. And they shall hang upon him all the glory of his father's house, the offspring and the issue, all vessels of small quantity, from the vessels of cups, even to all the vessels of flagons. In that day, saith the LORD of hosts, shall the nail that is fastened in the sure place be removed, and be cut down, and fall: and the burden that was upon it shall be cut off: for the LORD hath spoken it."

The *"key of David"* was given to a man called Eliakim, a steward over King Hezekiah's household (descendant of King David). He was able to open and shut the doors that led into the treasures of the king. In that sense, he points to Jesus Christ Who also possesses the key of David, and opens and shuts the door into His Messianic kingdom. If the *"door"* is the symbol of opportunity and entrance as most Bible teaches argue, then the *"key"* is the symbol of authority and control.

Our Lord Yeshua has the control – He opens and shuts. That control is also obvious in the phrase repeated in each letter: *"I know thy words."* It is placed within this context to let us know that our Lord knows all about our efforts for Him, and He wants to encourage us by reminding us of His promises to those who are faithful to Him.

His **CHALLENGE** – *"behold, I have set before thee an open door, and no man can shut it: for thou hast a little strength, and hast kept My word, and hast not denied My Name."*

Some believe that this is a challenge to spread the gospel, speaking of expanded missionary opportunities. The Philadelphian believers were located in a strategic city, a gateway to many areas of the ancient world. It was a city dedicated to the spread of the Greek language and culture.

A more probable interpretation is that this *"open door"* speaks of entrance into the Messianic kingdom of our Lord Yeshua. The connection with the prophecy in Isaiah 22 supports this view. It also better fits the other letters – appeals to the faithful and promises to the overcomers, the true believers, our eternal hope. This view also relates better to what is said in verses 9-12. The challenge to *"hold fast"* in verse 11 is hard to connect with the view that this is a missionary challenge.

THREE THINGS ARE SAID OF THESE BELIEVERS IN PHILADELPHIA:

1. They **DEPENDED** upon the Lord's strength!
   "for thou hast a little strength"

This statement and the two that follow it are simply facts which the Lord knows about the believers in Philadelphia and the reasons why they are given such promises in the midst of what appears to be a difficult environment.

The truth about these believers is that they were not the strongest Christians in the Empire nor the most influential. They did not have great numbers of people when John writes to them, nor any outstanding leaders or unusual talents. But their *"little strength"* brought encouragement from the lips of our Lord – What wonderful assurance that brings to our own struggles!

2. They <u>DEDICATED</u> themselves to the Word of God – *"have kept My word"*

They guarded the Word of God in such a way as to warrant the commendation of the Lord. Their loyalty proves the validity of their faith and provides one of the reasons for the wonderful encouragement given in this letter. Obedience to God's Word is still the proof of our love for our blessed Lord Yeshua.

John 14:21 – *"He that hath My commandments, and keepeth them, he it is that loveth Me: and he that loveth Me shall be loved of My Father, and I will love him, and will manifest myself to him."*

James 1:22-25 – *"But be ye doers of the word, and not hearers only, deceiving your own selves. For if any be a hearer of the word, and not a doer, he is like unto a man beholding his natural face in a glass: For he beholdeth himself, and goeth his way,* and straightway forgetteth what manner of man he was. But whoso looketh into the perfect law of liberty, and continueth therein, he being not a forgetful hearer, but a doer of the work, this man shall be blessed in his deed."

3. They <u>DEVOTED</u> themselves to the Lord – *"and hast not denied My Name"*

These Philadelphian believers were loyal to the Name and character of our Lord Jesus Christ, as were some of those who lived in Pergamos (Revelation 2:13). They believed that He was (and is!) God in human flesh, and that to deny His true nature means that you are not a genuine believer and that you have the spirit of Antichrist!

I John 2:22-23 – *"Who is a liar but he that denieth that Jesus is the Christ? He is antichrist, that denieth the Father and the Son. Whosoever denieth the Son, the same hath not the Father; (but) he that acknowledgeth the Son hath the Father also."*

I John 4:2-3 – *"Hereby know ye that Spirit of God: Every spirit that confesseth that Jesus Christ is come in the flesh is of God: And every spirit that confesseth not that Jesus Christ is come in the flesh is not of God: and this is that spirit of antichrist, whereof ye have heard that it should come; and even now already is it in the world."*

The <u>PROTECTION</u> of Jesus Christ is all we need!

Revelation 3:9-10

"Behold, I will make them of the synagogue of Satan, which say they are Jews, and are not, but do lie; behold, I will make them to come and worship before thy feet, and to know that I have loved thee. Because thou hast kept the word of My patience, I also will keep thee from the hour of temptation, which shall come upon all the world, to try them that dwell upon the earth."

THE IMPORTANCE OF THIS PROMISE TO THE CHURCH OF PHILADELPHIA

Revelation 3:10- *"Because thou hast kept the word of My patience, I also will keep thee from the hour of temptation, which shall come upon all the world, to try them that dwell upon the earth."*

Christians throughout history have disagreed over the interpretation of this verse as to whether it is a promise of removal or one of immunity or protection during the coming "hour of temptation." It is, of course, a disagreement between Pre-tribulationalists and Post-tribulationalists.

The preposition translated *"from"* is not the Greek *apo*, but rather the Greek *ek* – meaning "out of". Post-tribulationalists are right when they argue that there will be believers who live on earth during the coming tribulation (cf. Revelation 7). Pre-tribulationalists agree but insist that they are not church-age believers, but rather a multitude of Gentile believers who are saved during the tribulation.

Post-tribulationalists use John 17:15 to support their belief that Revelation 3:10 is a promise of protection or immunity from the coming tribulation. Yeshua said in His prayer to His Father in heaven: *"I pray not that thou shouldest take them out of the world, but that thou shouldest keep them from the evil (one)."* Pre-tribulationalists argue that these words are referring to those living in the church age, and not those living in the tribulation time.

The definite article *("the")* appears before the word *"hour"* and before the word *"temptation"* in the Greek text of Revelation 3:10. Its usage confirms that it is a specific trial that is coming upon the entire world. The purpose of this coming trial is to test those who *"dwell on the earth."* In Revelation, the earth-dwellers are all non-believers.

This verse given to the church in Philadelphia is a wonderful promise to all church-age believers that we will not be going through the coming tribulation but rather be rescued (raptured) and delivered by our blessed Lord!

ARGUMENTS ABOUT BELIEVERS IN THE TRIBULATION

Believers who have died will obviously not go through the coming tribulation!

Revelation 6;9-11 – *"And when He had opened the fifth seal, I saw under the altar the souls of them that were slain for the word of God, and for the testimony which they held: And they cried with a loud voice, saying, How long, O Lord, holy and true, dost thou not judge and avenge our blood on them that dwell on the earth? And white robes were given unto every one of them; and it was said unto them, that they should rest yet for a little season, until their fellow-servants also and their brethren, that should be killed as why were, should be fulfilled."*

A great multitude of Gentiles will become believers during the tribulation and many will be martyred for their faith!

Revelation 6:11 – *"that should be killed as they were, should be fulfilled"*

Revelation 7:14 – *"These are they which came out of great tribulation, and have washed their robes, and made them white in the blood of the Lamb."*

Revelation 11:7 – *"the beast that ascendeth out of the bottomless pit shall make war against them, and shall overcome them, and kill them."*

Revelation 13:7 – *"And it was given unto him to make war with the saints, and to overcome them."*

Revelation 20:4 – *"and I saw the souls of them that were beheaded for the witness of Jesus, and for the word of God, and which had not worshipped the beast, neither his image, neither had received his mark upon their foreheads, or in their hands; and they lived and reigned with Christ a thousand years."*

All believers who are alive on earth at the time of the Rapture, along with church-age believers who have died and are resurrected at the Rapture, will NOT go through the tribulation!

NOTE: One of the arguments people use against the pre-tribulational rapture of the church is the lack of evidence in church history (the same could be said for the church's attitude toward Israel).

In the book THE INCREDIBLE COVER-UP by Dave MacPherson, he states that this pre-trib view can be traced back to a Scottish lady named Margaret MacDonald who had a private, questionable revelation on this matter in Port Glasgow, Scotland.

Robert Norton, an MD, preserved her handwritten account in two of his books and said that it was the first time in church history that anyone ever split the second coming of Jesus Christ into two distinct parts or stages.

Through the visits of John Darby of the Plymouth Brethren, her views were then spread. It appeared in the September, 1830, edition of "The Morning Watch", a Plymouth Brethren publication.
The promotion of this view was primarily the result of the Scofield Reference Bible of 1909 AD.

This whole argument is exposed for being a "shame" and a "distorted" presentation in Tim LaHaye's book entitled "The Rapture" – published by Harvest House.

However, in the document called "The Shepherd of Hermes", Book I, the 4th vision, chapter 2, there is a description of the vision of this shepherd who meets a wild beast but is not harmed by the beast. The shepherd reports his encounter with the wild animal to a heavenly interpreter:

"I was met by a beast of such a size that it coulddestroy peoples, but through the power of the Lord and His great mercy, I escaped from it."

The heavenly interpreter explains to the shepherd that his escape from the beast means that the elect of God will escape the Great Tribulation:

"You have escaped from great tribulation on account of your faith, and because you did not doubt in the presence of such a beast. Go, therefore, and tell the elect of the Lord His mighty deeds, and say to them that the beast is a type of the great tribulation that is coming."

In the document, "Against Heresies" by Irenaeus, in Book V, chapter 19, he says:

"And therefore, when in the end the church shall be

suddenly caught up from this evil age, it is said, *There shall be tribulation such as has not been 60since the beginning, neither shall be.'"*

The <u>HOUSE</u> of Satan – *"Behold, I will make them of the synagogue of Satan, which say they are Jews, and are not, but do lie"*

The *"synagogue of Satan"* was mentioned in our discussion of the church at Smyrna – Revelation 2:9 says: *"and I know the blasphemy of them which say they are Jews, and are not, but are the synagogue of Satan."* In the message to Smyrna we read of their *"blasphemy"* but now in the message to Philadelphia we read that they *"do lie."* In both cases we read that they *"say they are Jews, and are not."* The possibilities of interpretation include:

1. Literal view – they are not Jews at all, not even racially or physically – they are Gentiles who are acting like they are Jews.

2. Spiritual view – they are physical Jews, but not true believers in the Bible (Jewish Tanakh or Old Testament).

3. Occultic view – they are involved in loyalty to Satan – practicing demonic rituals.

The <u>HONOR</u> of true believers – *"behold, I will make them to come and worship before thy feet, and to know that I have loved thee"*

They are unbelievers who will acknowledge one day that the believers of the church at Philadelphia are for real! In Isaiah 45:14 we read:

"Thus saith the LORD, The labor of Egypt, and merchandise of Ethiopia and of the Sabeans, men of stature, shall come over unto thee, and they shall be thine; they shall come after thee; in chains they shall come over, and they shall fall down unto thee, they shall make supplication unto thee, saying, surely God is in thee; and there is none else, there is no God."

These words are not mentioned to reflect on all Jewish people. It is quite clear in this text that these people are lying when they say they are Jews; they are not true Jews at all. A true Jew is one who has expressed his faith and confidence in the promise of God to Abraham, Isaac, and Jacob, and has come to believe in God's Messiah, Who alone can offer redemption and salvation as the prophets of old clearly taught. Such Jews know that the salvation of Gentiles is a part of that promise. Galatians 3:6-9 says:

"Even as Abraham believed God, and it was accounted to him for righteousness. Know ye therefore that they which are of faith, the same are the children of Abraham. And the scripture, foreseeing that God would justify the heathen through faith, preached before the gospel unto Abraham, saying, In thee shall all nations (Gentiles) be blessed. So then they which be of faith are blessed with faithful Abraham."

Those who do not have faith in the promises of God may claim to be part of God's chosen and beloved people (Israel), but because of their unbelief they

206

become tools in the hands of the devil himself to persecute both Jewish and Gentile Christians. That's why their religious meetings are described as a *"synagogue of Satan."* He is using them to further his attacks on true believers, whether they be Jew or Gentile.

The believers in Philadelphia are likened to the believers in Israel who will one day see that all those who have opposed and resisted them and their message will in the end acknowledge that they are deeply loved by the Lord!

The **HOUR** of temptation – *"I also will keep thee from the hour of temptation, which shall come upon all the world, to try them that dwell upon the earth."*

As we pointed out earlier in the discussion of the message to the church of Philadelphia, this is a promise by the Lord to REMOVE the true believers from the coming tribulation, not simply the issue of IMMUNITY or protection while they go through the tribulation.

The **PURPOSE** behind this message
Revelation 3:11 – *"Behold, I come quickly; hold that which thou hast, that no man take thy crown"*

This is not referring to a special coming to judge a particular church and remove their testimony and influence, but it is a reference to the overall teaching of the Book - the Second Coming of Jesus Christ! Our Lord uses these exact words three times in the last chapter of the Book of Revelation (22:7, 12, 20).

His coming in the future will be sudden, a surprise to many, and a shock to the world that has ignored and denied that it will ever happen! The challenge is to *"hold fast"* what you have. Our word today might be the word "commitment." In I John 2:28 the apostle John spoke these words of warning:

"And now, little children, abide in Him; that, when He shall appear, we may have confidence, and not be ashamed before Him at His coming."

When our Lord said *"that no man take thy crown"* He did not use the plural *"crowns."* He is referring to one *"crown"* namely, the *"crown of righteousness"* that is promised to all true believers in II Timothy 4:8:

"Henceforth there is laid up for me a crown of righteousness, which the Lord, the righteous judge, shall give me at that day: and not to me only, but unto all them also that love His appearing."

The <u>PROMISES</u> to overcomers
Revelation 3:12

"Him that overcometh will I make a pillar in the temple of My God, and he shall go no more out; and I will write upon him the Name of My God, and the name of the city of My God, which is new

Jerusalem, which cometh down out of heaven from My God: and I will write upon him My new Name."

The issues of these promises involved security, permanence, and future identity. We have first of all, the promise of an eternal PLACE – *"a pillar in the temple of My God."* But, there is no temple in the eternal city (Revelation 21:22). The phrase is to be taken figuratively, not literally. The *"temple of My God"* refers to the dwelling place of God, and the fact of describing the believers as a *"pillar"* indicates a permanent place with the Lord forever and ever.

It was a custom in Roman times for a religious leader of the imperial cult of emperor worship to build a statute or monument near the entrance of a temple with an inscription that included his name, his father's name, his place of birth, and the year of his office as the official priest of the Roman Empire.

We are reminded of Isaiah 56:5 – *"Even unto them will I give in Mine house and within My walls a place and a name better than of sons and of daughters: I will give them an everlasting name, that shall not be cut off."*

We also have a promise of not only an eternal PLACE but a new NAME. Three things are said here about our future identity:

(1)   The NAME of my God
(2)   The NAME of the city of My God

(3)   My new Name!

In Revelation 14:1 we read of the 144,000 Jewish evangelists that they have their *"Father's Name written in their foreheads."* In Revelation 22:4 we read: *"and His Name shall be in their foreheads."*

What a wonderful assurance – we belong to the Lord! An old song by Norman J. Clayton (from 1938) gave us these sweet words:

> *Jesus my Lord, will love me forever; From Him no pow'r of evil can sever; He gave His life to ransom my soul; Now I belong to Him!*

> *Once I was lost in sin's degradation; Jesus came down to bring me salvation; Lifted me up from sorrow and shame; Now I belong to Him!*

> *Joy floods my soul, for Jesus has saved me, freed me from sin that long had enslaved me; His precious blood He gave to redeem, Now I belong to Him!*

> CHORUS
> *Now I belong to Jesus, Jesus belongs to me; Not for the years of time alone, but for eternity!*

The <u>PRIORITY</u> of this message
Revelation 2:13 – *"He that hath an ear, let him hear what the Spirit saith unto the churches."*

Are we listening to the words of the Spirit to all the churches, including the church at Philadelphia?

There is an underlying thought behind these words that appear at the end of each of the seven letters – the messages are directly to all the believers in all the churches. You might live in California or Canada or Europe, Africa, or South America – but the messages of these churches are for each person who claims to be a follower of our Lord Yeshua!

One more church message is left – LAODICEA!

MATERIAL PROSPERITY
Church of Laodicea
Revelation 3:14-22

"And unto the angel of the church of the Laodiceans write: These things saith the Amen, the faithful and true witness, the beginning of the creation of God; I know thy works, that thou art neither cold nor hot: I would thou wert cold or hot. So then because thou art lukewarm, and neither cold nor hot, I will spue thee out of My mouth. Because thou sayest, I am rich, and increased with goods, and have need of nothing; and knowest not that thou art wretched, and miserable, and poor, and blind, and naked: I counsel thee to buy of Me gold tried in the fire, that thou mayest be rich; and white raiment, that thou mayest be clothed, and that the shame of thy nakedness do not appear; and anoint thine eyes with eye-salve, that thou mayest see. As many as I love, I rebuke and chasten: be zealous therefore, and repent. Behold, I stand at the door and knock: If any man hear My voice, and open the door, I will come in to him, and will sup with him, and he with Me. To him that overcometh will I grant to sit with Me in My throne, even as I also overcame, and am set down with My Father in His throne. He that hath an ear, let him hear what the Spirit saith unto the churches."

THE HISTORY OF LAODICEA

If the angel at Philadelphia was given an *"open door"* (3:8), individuals at Laodicea are told of another door, one that they must open: Here I am! *I stand at the door and knock. If anyone hears my voice and opens the door, I will come in and eat with him, and he with me* (v. 20). These words have often been romanticized in popular religious art, in pictures of Jesus "knocking at the heart's door." What is wrong is that Jesus is standing outside the door, excluded from the banquet like the homeless stranger. The poignant plea, though directed first to the church at Laodicea, is strategically placed near the end of the series of messages as Christ's last appeal to any congregation that has shut him out. The beautiful "invitation" is at the same time a severe indictment of a church that is self-sufficient, complacent and only marginally Christian.

Laodicea was situated southeast of Philadelphia in the Lycus River valley. Its congregation was the only one of the seven, with the possible exception of Ephesus, to receive communications both from the apostle Paul and from John of Patmos. This congregation formed a cluster with two others (mentioned by Paul, but not by the book of Revelation) at Colossae and Hierapolis, and possibly with certain other house churches in the same general area. Paul in Colossians speaks of his strenuous efforts for them and for those at Laodicea, and for all who had not met him personally (Colossians 2:1). He mentions his coworker Epaphras, who had brought the Christian message to the region (1:7) and was still working hard for you and for those at Laodicea and Hierapolis" (4:13). He sends greetings "to the brothers at Laodicea, and to Nympha and the church in her house (4:15), requesting that after this letter has been read to you, see that it is also read in the church of the Laodiceans and that you in turn read the letter from Laodicea (4:16).

From this we learn that the letter to the Colossians was intended for Laodicea as well (including a house church there in the home of a woman called Nympha) and that Paul sent yet another letter to Laodicea, possibly a letter now lost, possibly the one known as "Ephesians" or possibly "Philemon," which was addressed to a house church in the same general area in the home of a certain Philemon, Apphia and Archippus (Philemon 1-2). If Revelation, like Paul's letters, was meant to be shared with other congregations beyond the seven named, the message to Laodicea may have included congregations at Colossae and Hierapolis as well (Papias, for example, bishop of Hierapolis in the second century AD, was apparently quite familiar with the book of Revelation).

By the time Revelation was written, the Christian community in Laodicea and vicinity seems to have prospered. The church at Laodicea is described as boasting, I am rich; I have acquired wealth and do not need a thing. But in contrast to the church at Smyrna, which was materially poor but rich in God's sight (2:9), this church is wretched, miserable, poor, blind and naked. Their works are compared to tepid water, neither cold nor hot. I wish you were either one or the other! So, because you are lukewarm--neither hot nor cold--I am about to spit you out of my mouth (vv. 15-16).

The site where Laodicea once stood includes an elaborate fountain and a water tower supplied by an aqueduct from hot springs at the site of modern Denizli, four miles south. Not surprisingly, many have suggested a possible local reference here, a play on words, contrasting what may have been the tepid water of the aqueduct at Laodicea with the possibly fresher and colder water at Colossae and with the very hot water of the cascades at Hierapolis. Yet readers in any of the Asian cities, no matter how close or how far away their water supply, would have understood the metaphor. Either cold or hot water is good for something, but lukewarm water is not. The point of the rebuke is not lack of zeal or enthusiasm. If it were, "lukewarm" would at least have been better than "cold"! The point is rather the utter worthlessness of what the congregation has done and is doing. The metaphor is a more blunt and colorful way of saying what was said to the church at Sardis: *"for I have not found thy works perfect before God* (3:2)."

SOME ADDITIONAL FACTS

Laodicea was the chief city of the Lycus River Valley region. The full name of the city was Laodicea ad Lyceum (Laodicea on the Lycus). The city was originally known as Diospolis ("the City of Zeus").

The Greek deity considered to be the greatest of the Olympian gods. Homer, the Greek poet, often called Zeus "the father of gods and men," the ruler and protector of all.

The city was founded between 261 and 253 B.C. by Antiochus II Theos, king of Syria, and named in honor of his wife, Laodice (Laodike). The early population of the city probably consisted of natives of the area, Hellenized Greeks and veteran soldiers in the army of Antiochus II.

The city became part of the kingdom of Pergamon and later passed into Roman hands in 133 B.C. Cicero, the famous Roman orator and statesman, served as governor of the province, residing mostly in Laodicea.

Laodicea was a great center of banking and finance. It was one of the wealthiest cities of the ancient world! When Laodicea was destroyed by an earthquake in 60 A.D., they refused aid from the Roman empire and rebuilt the city from their own wealth. "One of the most famous cities of Asia, Laodicea, was in the same year overthrown by an earthquake and without any relief from us recovered itself by its own resources" (Tacitus, Annals, 14:27).

"The city was at the crossroads of north-south traffic between Sardis and Perga and east-west from the Euphrates to Ephesus. Laodicea quickly became a rich city, rich enough to be able to rebuild itself without outside help after the destructive earthquake of 60 A.D. In common with many of the Hellenistic cities there was a prosperous Jewish colony established there well before the Christian era. The city's reputation was for its money transactions and the good quality of raven-black wool grown in the area.

Laodicea was a great center for the manufacturing of clothing -- the sheep which grazed around Laodicea were famous for the soft, black wool they produced. Laodicea was well known for its school of medicine.

One of the principles of medicine at that time was that compound diseases required compound medicines. One of the compounds used for strengthening the ears was made from the spice nard (spikenard? an aromatic plant). Galen says that it was originally made only in Laodicea, although by the second century AD it was made in other places also. Galen also described a medicine for the eyes made of Phrygian stone. Aristotle spoke of it as a Phrygian powder. The term used by John in Revelation is the same that Galen uses to describe the preparation of the Phrygian stone. Would not these medicinal concoctions be a reason why John cautions the Laodiceans to buy ointment for your eyes so that you may see (Revelation 3:18)?

The principal deity worshipped in Laodicea was the Phrygian god Men Karou, the Carian Men. In connection with this god's temple there grew up a famous school of medicine, which followed the teachings of Herophilus (330-250 BC) who began administering compound mixtures to his patients on the principle that compound diseases require compound medicines.

Two of the doctors from Laodicea were so famous that their names appear on the coins of the city (Zeuxis and Alexander Philalethes).

The hot springs at Hierapolis, just six miles across the Lycus River valley and to the south, are probably what John had in mind when he spoke of lukewarm water (Revelation 3:15-17). No other city on the Lycus Valley was as dependent on external water supplies as Laodicea. Water was also piped in through an aqueduct from Colosse.

The lukewarmness for which, thanks to this letter, the name of Laodicea has become proverbial may reflect the condition of the city's water supply. The water supplied by the spring ... was tepid and nauseous by the time it was piped to Laodicea, unlike the therapeutic hot water of Hierapolis or the refreshing cold water of Colossae.

Water piped into Laodicea by aqueduct from the south was so concentrated with minerals that the Roman engineers designed vents, capped by removable stones, so the aqueduct pipes could periodically be cleared of deposits.

Our Lord did not accuse the brethren in Laodicea of apostasy, nor with following some false prophet or engaging in emperor worship. The church is accused of being "lukewarm" -- this is the only congregation about which the Lord had nothing good to say!

The remains of the city are basically unexcavated, so most of what we know about the history of the city comes from written sources. The remains of two theaters, one Greek and one Roman, are on the northeastern slope of the plateau. A large stadium which also served as an amphitheater, dedicated by a wealthy citizen to the Roman emperor Vespasian in 79 AD, can be found on the opposite end of the plateau. The stadium was used for both athletic contests and gladiatorial shows. Archaeologists discovered a life-sized statue of the goddess Isis in the ancient nymphaeum, or monumental fountain.

The Gate to Ephesus, triple-arched and flanked by towers, was devoted to the Emperor Domitian (81-96 AD). On the south-west side stand a number of buildings built under Vespasian (69-79 AD). An aqueduct bringing water into the city ended in a 16 foot tall water tower which distributed water throughout the city.

An inscription erected by a freed slave from Laodicea was dedicated to Marcus Sestius Philemon. It will be recalled that a Philemon who owned the slave Onesimus (Philemon 10) was a leader in the church of Colossae. We cannot identify this Philemon with the slaveholder to whom Paul wrote, but the coincidence of the inscription from the same area is intriguing, especially since it refers to the manumission of a slave.

A BRIEF SUMMARY OF LAODICEA

Laodicea was located about 40 miles SE of Philadelphia. It was a part of a tri-cities area, including Colosse and Hierapolis. It was the chief city of the province of Phyrgia. According to Colossians 4:16, Paul wrote them a letter at the same time he wrote to Colosse. Epaphras might have been the founder (cf. Col. 1:7; 4:12-13) or Archippus (Col. 4:17).

Laodicea was destroyed by a terrible earthquake in 60 ad, but was rebuilt without any help from Rome. It was a great banking center with a famous medical school dedicated to the serpent god, Asklepios. They had a special powder which they claimed could cure eye diseases. They also manufactured cloth, garments and carpets from wool of local sheep that were very soft in texture and glossy black in color.

The word "Laodicea" comes from two Greek words: the word "to rule" and the word for "people." It suggested not only a democracy, but an attitude of self-confidence.

The ruins of the city reveal a Roman stadium which was dedicated to the Emperor Vespasian who ordered the destruction of Jerusalem in 70 ad.

One of the most fascinating facts about the city which was built on a plateau 100 feet above the Lycus river, was its limestone cliffs and waterfalls of "lukewarm, sulfur-like, tasting water."

FOUR THINGS ABOUT OUR LORD THAT REMIND US OF THE NEED TO REPENT:

HIS IDENTITY REMINDS US THAT WE ARE TOTALLY DEPENDENT UPON HIM!

Revelation 3:14 – *"And unto the angel of the church of the Laodiceans write; These things saith the Amen, the faithful and true witness, the beginning of the creation of God."*

1. It involves His **IMMUTABILITY** - *"the Amen"*

The Hebrew word carries the idea of that which is fixed and unchangeable.

II Corinthians 1:18-22 – *"But as God is true, our word toward you was not yea and nay. For the Son of God, Jesus Christ, Who was preached among you by us, even by me and Silvanus and Timotheus, was not yea and nay; but in Him was yea. For all the promises of God in Him are yea, and in Him Amen, unto the glory of God by us. Now He which stablisheth us with you in Christ, and hath anointed us, is God; Who hath also sealed us, and given the earnest of the Spirit in our hearts."*

2. It involves His <u>RELIABILITY</u> - *"the faithful and true witness"*

Revelation 1:5 – *"And from Jesus Christ, Who is the faithful witness, and the first begotten of the dead, and the prince of the kings of the earth"*

John 3:11-12 – *"Verily, verily, I say unto thee, We speak that we do know, and testify that we have seen; and ye receive not our witness. If I have told you earthly things, and ye believe not, how shall ye believe, if I tell you of heavenly things?"*

John 3:32-33 – *"And what He hath seen and heard, that He testifieth; and no man receiveth His testimony. He that hath received His testimony hath set to His seal that God is true."*

Psalm 89:34-37 – *"My covenant will I not break, nor alter the thing that is gone out of My lips. Once have I sworn by My holiness that I will not lie unto David. His seed shall endure forever, and his throne as the sun before Me. It shall be established forever as the moon, and as a faithful witness in heaven."*

3. It involves His <u>PREEMINENCE</u> – *"the beginning of the creation of God"*

Revelation 1:8 – *"I am Alpha and Omega, the beginning and the ending, saith the Lord, which is,* *and which was, and which is to come, the Almighty."*

Colossians 1:15-18 – *"Who is the image of the invisible God, the firstborn of every creature: For by Him were all things created, that are in heaven, and that are in earth, visible and invisible, whether they be thrones, or dominions, or principalities, or powers: all things were created by Him, and for Him: And He is before all things, and by Him all things consist. And He is the Head of the body, the church: Who is the beginning, the firstborn from the dead; that in all things He might have the preeminence."*

HIS <u>INSIGHT</u> REMINDS US THAT WE CANNOT HIDE FROM GOD!

Revelation 3:15-17 – *"I know thy works, that thou art neither cold nor hot: I would thou wert cold or hot. So then because thou art lukewarm, and neither cold nor hot, I will spue thee out of My mouth. Because thou sayest, I am rich, and increased with goods, and have need of nothing; and knowest not that thou art wretched, and miserable, and poor, and blind, and naked."*

"I know thy works" - 2:2, 9, 13, 19; 3:1, 8, 15

1. **They were INDIFFERENT to the work of the Lord!**
   "lukewarm" – merely professing believers

Matthew 7:21-23 – *"Not every one that saith unto Me, Lord, Lord, shall enter into the kingdom of heaven; but he that doeth the will of My Father which is in heaven. Many will say to Me in that day, Lord, Lord, have we not prophesied in Thy Name? and in Thy Name have cast out devils? And in Thy Name done many wonderful works? And then will I profess unto them, I never knew you: depart from Me, ye that work iniquity."*

2. They were INSENSITIVE to their own spiritual need!

The BASIC <u>REASON</u> - *"because thou sayest, I am rich, and increased with goods, and have need of nothing"*

The BAD <u>RESULTS</u> - five descriptions:

> *"wretched"*
> *"miserable"*
> *"poor"* - destitute, totally lacking in
>   spiritual wealth - used 35 times
> *"blind"* - used 54 times
> *"naked"* - used 15 times
> (salvation is pictured like a garment)

HIS <u>INSTRUCTION</u> REMINDS US OF THE SERIOUSNESS OF OUR SPIRITUAL CONDITION!

Revelation 3:18-19 – *"I counsel thee to buy of Me gold tried in the fire, that thou mayest be rich; and white raiment, that thou mayest be clothed, and that the shame of thy nakedness do not appear; and anoint thine eyes with eye-salve, that thou mayest see. As many as I love, I rebuke and chasten: be zealous therefore, and repent."*

1. We must <u>RECOGNIZE</u> our spiritual need and that only Jesus Christ can meet that need!

    It is a need of **spiritual riches** - *"I counsel thee to buy of me gold tried in the fire, that, thou mayest be rich"*

    It is a need of **spiritual clothing** - *"and white raiment, that thou mayest be clothed"* - *"that the shame of thy nakedness do not appear"*

    It is a need of **spiritual vision** - *"and anoint thine eyes with eye-salve, that thou mayest see"*

2. We must <u>REALIZE</u> why He rebukes and chastens us!   *"as many as I love"*

3. We must RESPOND with repentance! *"be zealous therefore and repent"*

HIS <u>INVITATION</u> REMINDS US THAT IT IS A PERSONAL DECISION THAT WE MUST MAKE!

Revelation 3:20-22 – *"Behold, I stand at the door and knock: if any man hear My voice, and open the door, I will come in to him, will sup with him, and he with Me."*

Notice four things:

1. His <u>PLACE</u> - *"Behold, I stand at the door"*
    He is outside the door of the church!

2. His <u>PLEA </u>- *"and knock"* - continues to do so!

3. Our <u>PART</u> - *"if any man hear my voice, and open the door"* - the invitation is to any individual within this church!

What is the "door"?

1. The door of the church

2. The door through which Jesus Christ will come again

3. The door of a believer's heart - the issue under this view is that of fellowship with the Lord

4. The door of an unbeliever's heart - they

were merely professing believers without
a genuine relationship to the Lord!

4. His **<u>PROMISES</u>**

His abiding **<u>presence</u>** - *"I will come in to
him, and will sup with him, and he with Me"*

Our eternal **<u>position</u>** - *"will I grant to sit
with Me in My throne, even as I also
overcame, and am set down with My
Father in His throne"*

THE THRONE OF GOD
Revelation 4:1-11

The <u>WORD</u> which invited John to come up to the third heaven!
Revelation 4:1

"After this I looked, and, behold, a door was opened in heaven: and the first voice which I heard was as it were of a trumpet talking with me; which said, Come up hither, and I will shew thee things which must be hereafter."

There are 186 usages of the word *"throne"* in the King James Version of the Bible. There are 14 usages in Revelation 4.

No chapters of the Bible are so inviting, thrilling, and worshipful as chapters 4 and 5 of the Book of Revelation. The Lord welcomes us to heaven itself, giving us a brief look at what takes place there and what we can anticipate for ourselves in the future.

In chapter 4, the primary focus is on God the Father, sitting upon His throne, enjoying the worship of His creatures. In chapter 5, the focus is on God the Son, the Messiah of Israel, our Lord Jesus Christ, Who is also the One Whom all heaven adores and worships. What tremendous insights are to be found in these two chapters about the unique relationship of the Father and the Son.

The central feature of chapter 4 is the throne of God. Forty-five times the Book of Revelation refers to thrones, and only 15 times in the rest of the New Testament. Here is the throne book of the Bible!

THE THRONE OF GOD in the Psalms

In addition to specific passages that mention the throne of God, we also have a few passages in the Psalms that speak of the LORD GOD *"sitting in the heavens."* Here is what we learn:

Psalm 2:4 – *"He that <u>sitteth</u> in the heavens shall laugh"*

Psalm 9:7 – *"But the LORD shall endure forever: He hath prepared His <u>throne</u> for judgment."*

Psalm 11:4 – *"The LORD is in His holy temple, the LORD's <u>throne</u> is in heaven..."*

Psalm 29:10 – *"The LORD <u>sitteth</u> upon the flood; yea, the LORD <u>sitteth</u> King forever."*

Psalm 45:6 – *"Thy <u>throne</u> O God, is forever and ever; the sceptre of Thy kingdom is a right sceptre."*

Psalm 47:8 – *"God reigneth over the heathen; God <u>sitteth</u> upon the <u>throne</u> of His holiness"*

Psalm 89:14 – *"Justice and judgment are the habitation of Thy <u>throne</u>..."*

Psalm 93:2 – *"Thy <u>throne</u> is established of old: Thou art from everlasting."*

Psalm 97:2 – *"Clouds and darkness are round about Him: righteousness and judgment are the habitation of His <u>throne</u>."*

Psalm 99:1 – *"The LORD reigneth; let the people tremble: He <u>sitteth</u> between the cherubims; let the earth be moved."*

Psalm 103:19 – *"The LORD hath prepared His <u>throne</u> in the heavens; and His kingdom ruleth over all."*

The <u>MEANING</u> of the door in heaven
Revelation 4:1

"After this I looked, and, behold, a door was opened in heaven: and the first voice which I heard was as it were of a trumpet talking with me; which said, Come up hither, and I will shew thee things which must be hereafter."

When people speak of a *"door"* through which one enters heaven, they are speaking accurately. You may have heard people speak of Peter being at the gates of heaven and checking people before they enter. While that is stretching things a bit, it is interesting that it was to Peter that our Lord Yeshua gave the *"keys"* to the kingdom of heaven to make sure that everyone entering really belongs; it refers to his introducing the gospel to the Gentiles (Acts

230

10) at the house of Cornelius and, in general, to all who will believe in Jesus Christ as Lord and Savior.

According to Revelation 4:1 (listed above), this *"door"* was *"opened in heaven."* This is the only place where such a picture is given except when John saw the Second coming of Jesus Christ on a white horse and said in Revelation 19:11: *"And I saw heaven opened."* It is possible that this indicates that the *"door"* was closed during the period of time preceding His return.

We also remember from Revelation 3:20 that there is another *"door"* that we can open. That verse says (quoting Jesus): *"Behold, I stand at the door, and knock: If any man hear My voice, and open the door, I will come in to him, and will sup with him, and he with Me."*

Of course, this *"door"* is not the *"door"* in heaven, but rather refers to the *"door"* of the church in Laodicea. Interesting that Jesus is outside of the church knocking at the door. Because it seems to teach that a person can open that door in order to have Jesus come in and have a meal together, many have suggested that the invitation is extended to individuals within the church. Therefore, many have suggested that this *"door"* is referring to the *"door"* of a person's heart.

The <u>MESSAGE</u> of the trumpet

Revelation 4:1 says *"and the first voice which I heard was as it were of a trumpet talking with me; which said, Come up hither, and I will shew thee things which must be hereafter."*

This voice *"of a trumpet talking"* appears to be the same voice that John heard when he says in Revelation 1:10 – *"I was in the Spirit* (simply "in spirit") *on the Lord's day* (or "the day of the Lord"), *and heard behind me a great voice, as of a trumpet."* The voice identifies itself and says in Revelation 1:11: *"I am Alpha and Omega, the first and the last."* Yes, it is the voice of the Lord Jesus Himself!

The **MANIFESTATION** of the future

The latter part of Revelation 4:1 tells us what the voice was going to show John – *"Come up hither, and I will shew thee things which must be hereafter."* That last word is the same that is in Revelation 1:19, a Greek term, *meta tauta, "after these things"* – in other words, after the *"things which are"* – the seven churches of Revelation 2-3.

The **MAJESTY** of what John saw in heaven

Revelation 4:2-6 – *"And immediately I was in the spirit; and behold, a throne was set in heaven, and one sat on the throne. And He that sat was to look upon like a jasper and a sardine stone: and there was a rainbow round about the throne, in sight like unto an emerald. And round about the throne were four and twenty seats: and upon the seats I saw four and twenty elders sitting, clothed in white raiment; and they had on their heads crowns of gold. And out of the throne preceded lightnings and thunderings and voices: and there were seven lamps of fire burning before the throne, which are the seven spirits of God. And before the throne there was a sea of glass like unto crystal: and in the midst of the throne, and round about the throne, were four beasts full of eyes before and behind."*

What an amazing sight that must have been! As we read it today, we are still amazed at the description of this throne of God in heaven. Human words are inadequate, but they will have to do for now. They are our only means of understanding what God wants to convey to us about heaven. The word *"behold"* suggests the need to pay special heed to what is being said and described. It deserves our alertness and attention.

Please notice that this passage is organized around four phrases concerning the throne of God:

"on the throne"
> *"One sat on the throne"*

"round about the throne"
> *"a rainbow round about the throne"*
> *"four and twenty seats (thrones)"*
> *"four beasts full of eyes before and behind"*

"out of the throne"
> *"lightnings and thunderings and voices"*

"before the throne
> *"a sea of glass like unto crystal"*
> *"seven lamps of fire burning"*

WHO WAS "ON THE THRONE"?

The One Who was *"on the throne"* is called *"Lord God Almighty* (Revelation 4:8), *"which was, and is, and is to come."* Revelation 4:11 says of this One Who is *"on the throne"* – *"for Thou hast created all things"* – He is the CREATOR of everything!

John describes this One in His appearance as *"like a jasper and a sardine stone."* The word *"like"* (used throughout Revelation) emphasizes a simile, that is, a likeness in some way, but not the same as! God is not a stone, obviously! His appearance, however, seemed *"like"* two precious stones: *"jasper and a sardine stone."*

The *"jasper"* stone is mentioned in Revelation 21:11 when the heavenly city, the new Jerusalem, is being described: *"Having the glory of God: and her light was like unto a stone most precious, even like a jasper stone, clear as crystal."* Revelation 21:18 speaks of *"the building of the wall of it was of jasper."* Verse 19 says that the first foundation of the wall was *"jasper."* Many argue that it is like a diamond – when light shines through it, there is usually a beautiful spectrum of colors!

Our heavenly Father is brilliant light and in terms of His appearance it is like the colors of a diamond through which light comes!

The *"sardine"* stone is named after the city of Sardis where beautiful red stones have been found. Most likely it is in color like a blood-red ruby. Combined with the rainbow, we have a dazzling impression of transcendent glory – the glory of God the Father on his throne!

WHAT WAS "ROUND THE THRONE?

Three things are mentioned: *"a rainbow"* and *"four and twenty thrones"* and *"four beasts full of eyes before and behind."*

Why *"a rainbow"*?

Genesis 9:8-17 gives us the needed background:

"And God spake unto Noah, and to his sons with him, saying, And I, behold, I establish My covenant with you, and with your seed after you; And with every living creature that is with you, of the fowl, of the cattle, and of every beast of the earth with you; from all that go out of the ark, to every beast of the earth. And I will establish My covenant with you; neither shall all flesh be cut off any more by the waters of a flood; neither shall there any more be a flood to destroy the earth. And God said, This is the token of the covenant which I make between Me and you and every living creature that is with

you, for perpetual generations: I do set My bow in the cloud, and it shall be for a token of a covenant between Me and the earth. And it shall come to pass, when I bring a cloud over the earth, that the bow shall be seen in the cloud: And I will remember My covenant, which is between Me and you and every living creature of all flesh; and the waters shall no more become a flood to destroy all flesh. And the bow shall be in the cloud; and I will look upon it, that I may remember the everlasting covenant between God and every living creature of all flesh that is upon the earth. And God said unto Noah, This is the token of the covenant, which I have established between Me and all flesh that is upon the earth."

Each covenant of God contains a "sign" of that covenant which causes us to remember what God has said. Behind the "rainbow" is the faithful promise of our God. The world will never again experience a global disaster like the Genesis flood! However, the future will bring a global disaster by fire (II Peter 3). The *"rainbow"* that is around about the throne of God, *"in sight like unto an emerald"* is a picture of the faithfulness of God!

Who are the 24 elders?

Revelation 4:4 – *"And round about the throne were four and twenty seats: and upon the seats I saw four and twenty elders sitting, clothed in white raiment; and they had on their heads crowns of gold."*

Revelation 4:10 – *"The four and twenty elders fall down before Him that sat on the throne, and worship Him that liveth forever and ever, and cast their crowns before the throne..."*

The term "elders" is used in the Book of Revelation 11 times: Revelation 4:4, 10; 5:6, 8, 11, 14; 7:11, 13; 11:16; 14:3; 19:4; Out of these 11 times, 6 use the number "24" in front of the word "elders."

There is no doubt that the issue of the 24 elders is critical to the whole argument of Pre-tribulationalism. George Eldon Ladd, a Post-tribulationalist, admits that very fact in his commentary on the Book of Revelation.

Here are the facts about the 24 elders:

1. They sit on thrones around the throne of God in heaven – Revelation 4:4a

2. They are clothed in white raiment – Revelation 4:4b

3. They have crowns of gold on their heads – Revelation 4:4c

4. They are pictured as ones who fall down before God and worship Him, casting their crowns at His feet – Revelation 4:10-11; 5:14.

5. They are also pictured as falling down before the Lamb, and have harps and bowls of

incense representing the prayers of the saints
Revelation 5:8

6. They sing a new song about the worthiness of
the Lamb – Revelation 5:9-10

The very fact that the 24 elders are seen in heaven,
NOT on earth during the judgments of the
Tribulation forces us to connect them with the
following possibilities:

They refer to angels.

They refer to all believers who have died and are
now in heaven.

They refer to Gentile believers who are saved during
the Tribulation and are martyred.

They refer to the Nation of Israel.

They refer to church-age believers only.

The 24 elders cannot refer to angels because they
are identified separately from them in Revelation
5:11 and 7:11. They cannot refer to the Gentile
multitude that is saved during the tribulation on the
basis of the discussion of Revelation 7:13-14.

The description of these 24 elders in Revelation 4:4
connects them with the promises to church-age
believers in Revelation 2 and 3. The words about
them sitting on thrones remind us of Revelation

3:21; the reference to them being clothed in white raiment connects us with the words of Revelation 3:5; the picture of them with crowns of gold on their heads reminds us of Revelation 2:10 and 3:11.

These 24 elders are not called "priests" or "saints" but rather "elders." That is a specific description of church leaders as well as the "elders" who acted as judges and administrators of justice among the children of Israel.

However, the "elders" of the Sanhedrin who are often connected with the priests and the scribes are not treated as genuine believers in the New Testament. They are the ones who condemned our Lord to death and delivered Him to the Romans for crucifixion.

The use of the number "24" is also very instructive. There have been many attempts by Bible teachers to divide this number into the 12 tribes of Israel and the 12 apostles of the Church. But, there is no Biblical warrant for that kind of exegesis. The number is found in I Chronicles 24 and 25 and refers to 24 divisions of priests and musicians for the Nation of Israel. But, these are not called "priests" or "musicians" but rather "elders."

It would appear that the best answer to the identity of the 24 elders would be that this is a reference to church-age believers only.

An important footnote to the identity of the *"elders"* is the remark in Revelation 7. One of the elders inquires as to the identity of the great multitude who will come out of the tribulation. Obviously, the great multitude of believers in the tribulation period are not to be identified with the 24 elders. In addition, *"all the angels"* of God are distinguished from the elders in Revelation 7:11, so the elders cannot refer to either the great multitude who come out of the tribulation or to angels.

It is also difficult to see how the 24 elders could represent the completed Nation of Israel, since Revelation 7 speaks of 144,000 Jews on earth during the tribulation, and Revelation 12 speaks of the nation's persecution by Satan during the tribulation period (as do many of the prophets in the Old Testament).

The only completed group of God's creatures left (excluding Israel, angels, and the great multitude who come out of the tribulation) is the church. They are not mentioned as being on earth during the tribulation. It was to the Church in Philadelphia that the Lord promised (3:10): *"Because thou hast kept the word of My patience, I also will keep thee from* (literally – "out of") *the hour of temptation, which shall come upon all the world, to try them that dwell upon the earth."*

The number *"24"* when used of the priests and musicians represents the whole nation of Israel. It is not speculation, therefore, to suggest that the 24 elders represent a completed body of people in heaven while the tribulation is happening on earth.

It is also very convincing that the 24 elders represent the church of Jesus Christ in heaven during the tribulation when the Bible gives three "church" descriptions of them in Revelation 4:4: *"and upon the seats* (thrones) *I saw four and twenty elders sitting, clothed in white raiment; and they had on their heads crowns of gold."* Back in chapters 2-3 we learned the following about church overcomers (true believers):

> *"sitting on thrones"* – Revelation 3:21
> *"clothed in white robes"* – Revelation 3:5
> *"wearing crowns of gold:* - Revelation 2:10

What about the *"four beasts full of eyes before and behind"* that were *"round about the throne"*?

The Greek word translated as *"beasts"* is not the same word as used in Revelation 13 – that passage speaks of a "wild, untamed, ferocious" beast. Here it is the word for "living creatures." They are mentioned several times and appear to be involved with the worship of God – cf. Revelation 4:9; 5:8, 11, and 14. They also speak to John about the first four seal judgments – Revelation 6:2-8. These living creatures are mentioned in the Book of Ezekiel 12 times in the first 10 chapters. Ezekiel 10:20 clearly identifies them as "cherubims" (angels).

The appearance of these four living creatures is likened to a lion, a calf (ox), a man, and an eagle. The word *"like"* expresses a similarity in appearance but should not be regarded literally. These four characterizations are the same as those in Ezekiel 1:10, and it is difficult to decipher their meaning. Some of the viewpoints by various scholars include:

1. All angels have the characteristics of these four creatures.

2. Jesus Christ is pictured as seen in the four gospels (very difficult to prove!).

3. It illustrates the attributes of God (majesty, strength, intelligence, sovereignty).

4. It reminds us of Israel's encampment around the tabernacle.

Their tents were pitched in the order which placed Judah (lion), the first of three tribes on one side: Ephraim (ox) on one side: Reuben (man) on one side; and Dan (eagle) on one side. This view is interesting, but once again difficult to prove.

The first view seems the most likely. There is a sense in which these angels represent all the angels of God. They hold a unique position in relation to the throne of God. While all the angels are *"around* the throne" (Revelation 5:11), the four living creatures are said to be *"in the midst of the throne"* as well as *"around the throne."* Because of what they say (Revelation 4:8) in praising God's holiness, we are reminded of the angels of Isaiah 6 that are called *"seraphims."* It is fascinating to read in the Isaiah account that these angels were standing above the throne of God, constantly praising God for His holiness, power, and preeminence. In one sense, we can describe these four living creatures as the worship leaders of heaven, inspiring by their words and actions all of heaven's residents to pour out their worship toward the One Who sits on the throne!

The statement that these creatures are *"full of eyes before and behind"* is suggestive of the omniscience of the One who sits on the throne. They do His bidding with a deep awareness of His desire and plan. They also *"do not rest day or night"* which is a reminder that God never sleeps or slumbers; He is constantly working out His plan, making decisions in heaven and earth that will bring all things to a grand climax and fulfillment, demonstrating that He is to be worshipped and praised forever and ever!

What was *"out of the throne"*?

The lightnings, thunder, and voices that proceed from the throne are the way God announces a coming storm of His judgment falling upon planet earth. These sights and sound introduce a mighty display of God's presence, power, and wrath.

Job 37:2-5 – *"Hear attentively the noise of His voice, and the sound that goeth out of His mouth. He directeth it under the whole heaven, and His lightning unto the ends of the earth. After it a voice roareth: He thundereth with the voice of His excellency; and He will not stay them when His voice is heard. God thundereth marvelously with His voice; great things doeth He, which we cannot comprehend."*

Psalm 18:13-15 – *"The LORD also thundered in the heavens, and the Highest gave His voice, hail stones and coals of fire. Yea, He sent out His arrows, and scattered them; and He shot out lightnings, and discomfited them. Then the channels of waters were seen, and the foundations of the world were discovered at Thy rebuke, O LORD, at the blast of the breath of Thy nostrils."*

What was *"before the throne"*?

1. Seven lamps of fire

These seven lamps of fire before the throne *"are the seven spirits of God"* mentioned previously in Revelation 1:4 and 3:1 and 5:6. They are the seven angels who stand before God, ready to do His bidding. We see them again in Revelation 8:2 where John says *"And I saw the seven angels which stood before God; and to them were given seven trumpets."*

2. A sea of glass

We read in Revelation 15:2 – *"And I saw as it were a sea of glass mingled with fire: and them that had gotten the victory over the beast, and over his image, and over his mark, and over the number of his name, stand on the sea of glass, having the harps of God."*

In Exodus 24:10, Moses, Aaron, Nadab, Abihu, and 70 elders of Israel received a similar manifestation of the presence of the Lord: *"And they saw the God of Israel: and there was under His feet as it were a paved work of a sapphire stone, and as it were the body of heaven in his clearness."*

It is a well discovered fact that ancient monarchs created something similar in front of their thrones, an area paved in a way to indicate the separation between the king and his subjects. It emphasized their majesty and greatness over all. Perhaps the primary point of the sea of glass before the throne of God is to picture the holiness, majesty, and purity of God Himself, and that He is separate from His creation. The transparency or clearness of that sea of glass might emphasize God's penetrating gaze into all things that take place on earth.

The <u>WORSHIP</u> of all those in heaven

Revelation 4:8-11 – *"And the four beasts had each of them six wings about him; and they were full of eyes within: and they rest not day and night, saying, Holy, holy, holy, Lord God Almighty, which was, and is, and is to come. And when those beasts give glory and honor and thanks to Him that sat on the throne, Who liveth forever and ever, The four and twenty elders fall down before Him that sat on the throne, and worship Him that liveth forever and ever, and cast their crowns before the throne, saying, Thou art worthy, O Lord, to receive glory and honor and power: for Thou hast created all things, and for Thy pleasure they are and were created."*

Fourteen times in this one chapter the word *"throne"* appears. Not only in the Book of Revelation the *"throne book of the Bible,"* but Revelation 4 is the *"throne chapter of the Bible."* It centers in the exaltation of God the Father and climaxes with the worship of all heavenly creatures. It clearly reveals the primary objective of all believers and all creation – the glory, praise, and worship of Almighty God!

1. The continual <u>RESPONSE</u> of the four living creatures

Verse 8 says that they *"rest not day and night"* in their praise and worship of the LORD. It is a continual response and reminds us of what heaven will be like!

Their words *"Holy, holy, holy, Lord God Almighty, which was, and is, and is to come"* worship the LORD for three basic things: His holiness, His power, and His eternal nature and plan. The repetition of the word *"holy"* might be for added emphasis or it may suggest the tri-unity of God. He is our God, but appears from the Biblical record to exist as three Persons – Father, Son, and Holy Spirit.

God is holy in two primary ways: He is separate from all that He created and is not to be identified with the physical and material universe; and, He is separate from sin. The holiness of God emphasizes both His transcendence as well as His moral purity.

These cherubim worship leaders of heaven are praising God for His eternal nature and plan by calling Him the One *"which was, and is, and is to come."* He is the eternal God, living, governing, in past, present, and future history. These same words are applied to Jesus Christ, God's Son, in Revelation 1:8.

The basic response of these cherubims remind all creatures that we should praise the Lord continually for He alone is worthy.

The worship of these angels also reveals what believers should be doing as a habit of life! Their actions help all of us to know how we should respond to the Lord – by giving Him glory, honor, thanks, and praise for all that He is and does!

2. The immediate <u>REACTION</u> of the elders

Whenever the four living creatures give worship to God, the 24 elders *"fall down before Him that sat on the throne, and worship Him that liveth forever and ever, and cast their crowns before the throne, saying, Thou art worthy, O Lord, to receive glory and honor and power: for Thou hast created all things, and for Thy pleasure they are and were created."*

The <u>WAY</u> they react to the worship of the cherubim angels – *"fall down"* - clearly an act of recognizing the Lord's greatness and the need of complete submission to His authority and control of all things.

In Ephesians 3:14-15 we read of the kind of response we should give to the Lord because we now have *"access"* into His presence by the redemption of His Son, our Savior (Ephesians 2:18 and 3:12): *"For this cause* (because we now have *"access"*) *I bow my knees unto the Father of our Lord Jesus Christ, of Whom the whole family in heaven and earth is named."* Then, we read these final words in the Apostle Paul's prayer (Ephesians 3:20-21):

"Now unto Him that is able to do exceeding abundantly above all that we ask or think, according to the power that worketh in us, Unto Him be glory in the church by Christ Jesus throughout all ages, world without end, Amen."

We also read about <u>WHAT</u> these 24 elders do in the presence of Almighty God – *"cast their crowns before the throne."* This reveals the deep adoration and worthiness of the One on the throne when compared with their accomplishments in serving the Lord. The rewards given to the believers fade into insignificance in the worship of our God!

Their <u>WORDS</u> of praise emphasize His worthiness in terms of creation and His *"pleasure"*: *"Thou art worthy, O Lord, to receive glory and honor and power: for Thou hast created all things, and for Thy pleasure they are and were created."*

They are praising the Lord for two basic things: His power in creating all things, and His purpose in bringing all into existence – *"for Thy pleasure."*

WHY ARE WE HERE ON PLANET EARTH? What is the real meaning of our lives? What are our goals and objectives? What are we trying to accomplish?

Revelation 4 is a clear testimony of what heaven is going to be like and gives us fresh and concise information on Who and what is behind all the events and circumstances of our lives. Our heavenly Father, the Creator of everything, deserves and desires our worship and praise. It is time that we recognize His ultimate purpose for our lives – to honor, glorify, and thank Him every day of our lives because He is Creator, and has a purpose in human history and events even though to us it seems that things are often confusing and very chaotic!

LET'S JUST PRAISE THE LORD!

WORTHY IS THE LAMB!
Revelation 5:1-14

The scene in heaven begins with the One Who sat on the throne – our heavenly Father! It now continues by focusing on the Person and work of His Son, our Savior and Redeemer, the One Who sits at the right hand of His Father. He is the LAMB of God!

The Apostle John begins this chapter with the familiar and often used words – *"I saw."* They are repeated in verses 2, 6, and 11. He also says that he *"heard"* voices in heaven in verse 11. One of the 24 elders spoke with him (verse 5). What an amazing and thrilling opportunity for this first century AD believer and apostle! He was there, in heaven, seeing and hearing these wonderful things as an eyewitness. It reminds us that the apostles of our Lord received direct and marvelous revelations from God that are now written for us to read and understand.

There are two basic things discussed in Revelation 5: One deals with the SCROLL with seven seals (verses 1-7), and the other with the SONG to the Lamb (verses 8-14).

The <u>SCROLL</u> with seven seals
Revelation 5:1-7

"And I saw in the right hand of Him that sat on the throne a book (scroll) *written within and on the*

backside, sealed with seven seals. And I saw a strong angel proclaiming with a loud voice, Who is worthy to open the book, and to loose the seals thereof? And no man in heaven, nor in earth, neither under the earth, was able to open the book, neither to look thereon. And I wept much, because no man was found worthy to open and to read the book neither to look thereon. And one of the elders saith unto me, Weep not; behold, the Lion of the tribe of Judah, the Root of David, hath prevailed to open the book, and to loose the seven seals thereof. And I beheld, and, lo, in the midst of the throne and of the four beasts, and in the midst of the elders, stood a Lamb as it had been slain, having seven horns and seven eyes, which are the seven spirits of God sent forth into all the earth. And he came and took the book out of the right hand of Him that sat upon the throne."

A certain degree of drama is connected with this scroll. The emphasis on it shows its importance as it relates to the events of the tribulation that are described so graphically in the Book of Revelation. The scroll appears to be a summary of what God intends to do in bringing world history to a grand finale!

The <u>IDENTITY</u> of the scroll
Revelation 5:1

"And I saw in the right hand of Him that sat on the throne a book written within and on the backside, sealed with seven seals."

1. The <u>PLACE</u> where it is located – *"the right hand of Him that sat on the throne"*

It emphasizes not only the source from which the scroll comes, but also the authority and control of God behind everything that the scroll reveals. God is in control of the events of planet earth and is working out His eternal plan.

2. The <u>PARTICULARS</u> of the design – *"written within and on the backside, sealed with seven seals"*

One of the first and obvious conclusions that we can draw about this scroll is that the seals need to be broken in order to read their message. The fact that it is written on both sides no doubt indicates the extensiveness of its message, and symbolically reveals that it contains a great deal about the future.

A Roman law required that a will was to be sealed seven times. The wills of Caesar Augustus and Emperor Vespasian were sealed in this way. Some see this scroll, therefore, as the "last testament" of the one who died. This scroll contains a message of His wrath upon those who reject His love and His sacrificial death – He is the Lamb that was slain!

It is of great interest to prophecy students that the Book of Daniel predicts much of what is recorded in the Book of Revelation. In Daniel 12:4 we read:

"But thou, O Daniel, shut up the words, and seal the book, even to the time of the end: many shall run to and fro, and knowledge shall be increased."

In Daniel 12:8-9 we read these words: *"And I heard, but I understood not; then said I, O my Lord, what shall be the end of these things? And He said, Go thy way, Daniel: for the words are closed up and sealed till the time of the end."*

But, here in Revelation, the scroll with its seven seals is going to be open for all of us to read and hear its messages.

The IMPORTANCE of the scroll
Revelation 5:2-4

"And I saw a strong angel proclaiming with a loud voice, Who is worthy to open the book, and to loose the seals thereof? And no man in heaven, nor in earth, neither under the earth, was able to open the book, neither to look thereon. And I wept much, because no man was found worthy to open and to read the book, neither to look thereon."

1. The PROCLAMATION of a strong angel

The word *"strong'* could emphasize the importance of the angel and his message, but it could also be a clue as to which angel is involved. Some Bible teachers hold that it refers to the angel Gabriel whose name means "strength of God." It was the angel Gabriel who communicated to Daniel about future events (Daniel 8:10).

The text uses a Greek word for *"proclaiming"* that speaks of a herald, one who simply proclaimed a message without any added commentary or explanation. A herald spoke with urgency and was under orders to proclaim it in behalf of a higher authority. When the Bible says the angel spoke with a *"loud voice"* we are reminded that this message is one of great concern and urgency. Loud voices are mentioned frequently in the Book of Revelation to denote the importance of what is being said. A person who is *"worthy"* is sought in order to break the seals and open the scroll.

2. The <u>PROBLEM</u> John faced – *"because no man was found worthy to open the book, and to read the book, neither to look thereon."*

If we read this outburst of tears correctly, it is possible that John is heartbroken because no redeemer can be found!

The <u>INTRODUCTION</u> of the One Who is worthy – Revelation 5:5-7

"And one of the elders saith unto me, Weep not: behold, the Lion of the tribe of Judah, the Root of David, hath prevailed to open the book, and to loose the seven seals thereof. And I beheld, and, lo, in the midst of the elders, stood a Lamb as it had been slain, having seven horns and seven eyes,

which are the seven spirits of God sent forth into all the earth. And he came and took the book out of the right hand of Him that sat upon the throne.”

1. He is the <u>LION</u> of the tribe of Judah!

The word *“lion”* is used 155 times in the Old Testament in its various forms, but only 9 times in the New Testament of which 6 usages are in the Book of Revelation. They are symbols of strength and boldness.

Judges 14:18 – *“And the men of the city said unto him on the seventh day before the sun went down, What is sweeter than honey? And what is stronger than a lion? And he (Samson) said unto them, If ye had not plowed with my heifer, ye had not found out my riddle.”*

Proverbs 28:1 – *“The wicked flee when no man pursueth: but the righteous are bold as a lion.”*

The Lord describes Himself as a *“lion”* in Hosea 5:14: *“For I will be unto Ephraim as a lion, and as a young lion to the house of Judah: I, even I, will tear and go away; I will take away, and none shall rescue him.”*

Most of us can identify with the lion who *“roars”* and the Lord says in Joel 3:16: *“The LORD also shall roar out of Zion, and utter His voice from Jerusalem; and the heavens and the earth shall shake: but the LORD will be the hope of His people, and the strength of the children of Israel."*

The phrase *"the Lion of the tribe of Judah"* is referring to Genesis 49:9-10 as Jacob blesses his children:

"Judah is a lion's whelp: from the prey, my son, thou art gone up: he stooped down, he couched as a lion, and as an old lion; who shall rouse him up? The sceptre shall not depart from Judah, nor a lawgiver from between his feet, until Shiloh come: and unto Him shall the gathering of the people be."

The Messiah must come from the line of Judah, the 4th son of Jacob's wife, Leah. His name means "praise." Jesus Christ is the Messianic Lion Who will rule and reign over all the earth!

2. He is the <u>LINE</u> of David!

The Messiah will not only come from Judah, but also from a specific family within that tribe – the family of Jesse, for Isaiah 11:1 says: *"and there shall come forth a rod out of the stem of Jesse, and a Branch shall grow out of his roots."*

Jeremiah 23:5-6 prophesies: *"Behold, the days come, saith the LORD, that I will raise unto David a righteous Branch, and a King shall reign and prosper, and shall execute judgment and justice in the earth. In His days Judah shall be saved, and Israel shall dwell safely: and this is His Name whereby He shall be called, THE LORD OUR RIGHTEOUSNESS."*

In Revelation 22:16 Jesus Himself says:

"I Jesus have sent Mine angel to testify unto you these things in the churches. I am the root and the offspring of David, and the bright and morning star."

Psalm 132:11 teaches: *"The LORD hath sworn in truth unto David; He will not turn from it: Of the fruit of thy body will I set upon thy throne."* Miryam (Mary) was a direct descendant of King David through his son Nathan. Yes, the Messiah came out of the womb of a woman in David's line!

When Joseph married Mary after the birth of Jesus, he then adopts Jesus as his legal son, thus the promise of God that the Messiah will be also in the line of David through his son Solomon was fulfilled.

II Samuel 7:12-13: *"And when thy days (King David) be fulfilled, and thou shalt sleep with thy fathers, I will set up thy seed after thee, which shall proceed out of thy bowels, and I will establish His kingdom. He shall build an house for My Name, and I will stablish the throne of his kingdom forever."*

In discussing the issue of the priesthood and the relationship of our Lord to the king and priest named Melchizedek (Genesis 14), we read these words from Hebrews 7:14-17 – *"For it is evident that* our Lord sprang out of Judah; of which tribe Moses spake nothing concerning priesthood. And it is yet far more evident: for that after the similitude of Melchizedec there ariseth another priest, Who is made, not after the law of a carnal commandment, but after the power of an endless life. For He testifieth, Thou art a priest forever after the order of Melchizedec."

3. He is the <u>LAMB</u> to Whom all heaven gives its worship and praise!

Revelation 5:6-7 – "And I beheld, and, lo, in the midst of the throne and of the four beasts, and in the midst of the elders, stood a Lamb as it had been slain, having seven horns and seven eyes, which are the seven spirits of God sent forth into all the earth. And He came and took the book out of the right hand of Him that sat upon the throne."

(1) His <u>CENTRALITY</u> – "in the midst of the elders"

In Revelation 1:13 we saw a picture of the risen Christ "in the midst of the seven candlesticks." In Revelation 2:1 He is the One "Who walketh in the midst of the seven golden candlesticks" which is picturing the seven churches. Our Lord Yeshua is the central Person, the One Who has "first place" in the hearts of His believing disciples!

An interesting fact is that the Messiah is now "standing" and no longer seated at the right hand of the throne of God the Father.

   (2)   His <u>CONDITION</u> – *"a Lamb as it had been slain"*

The Greek verb is in the perfect tense which indicates a past event with results that continue into the present. He died over 1900 years ago, but the effects of what He did at the cross continue to this present hour.

The symbolism of a slain lamb reminds us all of the sacrificial system of the Jewish people. A sacrifice for sin must be provided in order for redemption to take place. When John the Baptist introduced Jesus in John 1:29, he said: *"Behold, the Lamb of God, which taketh away the sin of the world."*

The Apostle Peter wrote in I Peter 1:18-19:

"Forasmuch as ye know that ye were not redeemed with corruptible things, as silver and gold, from your vain conversation received by tradition from your fathers; But with the precious blood of Christ, as of a lamb without blemish and without spot"

The Apostle Paul wrote in Romans 3:24-26:

"Being justified freely by His grace through the redemption that is in Christ Jesus: Whom God hath set forth to be a propitiation through faith in His

blood, to declare His righteousness for the remission of sins that are past, through the forbearance of God; To declare, I say, at this time His righteousness: that He might be just, and the justifier of him which believeth in Jesus."

Paul added these words in Romans 5:8-11:

"But God commandeth His love toward us, in that, while we were yet sinners, Christ died for us. Much more then, being now justified by His blood, we shall be saved from wrath through Him. For if, when we were enemies, we were reconciled to God by the death of His Son, much more, being reconciled, we shall be saved by His life. And not only so, but we also joy in God through our Lord Jesus Christ, by Whom we have now received the atonement (Greek: reconciliation)."

The picture of this slain Lamb of God is not of an animal lying on the altar of sacrifice; the Lamb *"stood"* in the midst of heaven's audience reminding us all that He arose from the dead!

The picture of the Lamb of God is used 28 times in the Book of Revelation. Interestingly, the motto of the Moravian church is "OUR LAMB HAS CONQUERED!"

(3)   His <u>CHARACTERISTICS</u> – *"having seven horns and seven eyes"*

The *"horns"* are used as symbols of authority and power, sometimes representing individual rulers and at other time representing nations (Daniel 7). It is possible that the *"seven horns"* represent the fullness of the slain Lamb's power and authority to rule and reign.

The *"seven eyes"* of the Lamb of God are said to be *"the seven spirits"* that are sent out into all the earth to do the Lord's bidding and will. These *"seven spirits"* are mentioned in Revelation 3:1 and stated to be the *"seven stars"* which according to Revelation 1:20 are the *"seven angels"*. They appear often in the Book of Revelation and carry out the wishes of our Lord.

In Zechariah 4:10 we read: *"For who hath despised the day of small things? For they shall rejoice and shall see the plummet in the hand of Zerubbabel with those seven; they are the eyes of the LORD, which run to and fro through the whole earth."*

The *"eyes of the Lord"* see everything at all times – They represent the omniscience of our Lord.

The <u>SONG</u> to the Lamb
Revelation 5:8-14

"And when he had taken the book, the four beasts and four and twenty elders fell down before the Lamb, having every one of them harps, and golden vials full of odors, which are the prayers of saints. And they sung a new song, saying, Thou art

worthy to take the book, and to open the seals thereof: for Thou wast slain, and hast redeemed us to God by Thy blood out of every kindred, and tongue, and people, and nation; And hast made us unto our God kings and priests: and we shall reign on the earth. And I beheld, and I heard the voice of many angels round about the throne and the beasts and the elders: and the number of them was ten thousand times ten thousand, and thousands of thousands; Saying with a loud voice, Worthy is the Lamb that was slain to receive power, and riches, and wisdom, and strength, and honor, and glory, and blessing.   And every creature which is in heaven, and on the earth, and under the earth, and such as are in the sea, and all that are in them, heard I saying, Blessing, and honor, and glory, and power, be unto Him that sitteth upon the throne, and unto the lamb forever and ever. And the four beasts said, Amen. And the four and twenty elders fell down and worshipped Him that liveth forever and ever."

The above passage is one of the most remarkable of all the Book of Revelation! We see clearly what the motive and purpose of God is for all the creatures that He has made – it is the WORSHIP of the One Who sits on the throne, and the Lamb that was slain! 28 times in the Book of Revelation, the apostle John calls our blessed Lord Yeshua – THE LAMB OF GOD!

The <u>REACTION</u> of heaven to the taking of the scroll by the Lamb of God

Revelation 5:8-10

1. They reacted with <u>SUBMISSION</u>, recognizing the <u>SOVEREIGNTY</u> of the Lamb of God!

"And when He had taken the book, the four beasts and four and twenty elders fell down before the Lamb, having every one of them harps, and golden vials full of odors, which are the prayers of the saints."

At the moment when the Lamb of God takes the scroll out of the right hand of God the Father Who sits on the throne, heaven responds. The worship leaders (*"four beasts"* – cherubim angels) and the 24 elders *"fell down before the Lamb."*

(1) They play music on their *"harps"* – *"having every one of them harps"*

The *"harp"* is a traditional instrument of worship according to Psalm 33:1-3:

"Rejoice in the LORD, O ye righteous: for praise is comely for the upright. Praise the LORD with harp: sing unto Him with the psaltery and an instrument of ten strings. Sing unto Him a new song; play skilfully with a loud noise."

Psalm 98:5-6 – *"Sing unto the LORD with the harp; with the harp, and the voice of a psalm. With trumpets and sound of cornet make a joyful noise before the LORD, the King."*

Psalm 147:7 – *"Sing unto the LORD with thanksgiving; sing praise upon the harp unto our God."*

(2)　They offer incense in *"golden vials"* *"golden vials full of odors, which are the prayers of saints"*

We have a specific reference to this "incense" in Revelation 8:3-5:

"And another angel came and stood at the altar, having a golden censer; and there was given unto him much incense, that he should offer it with the prayers of all saints upon the golden altar which was before the throne. And the smoke of the incense, which came with the prayers of the saints, ascended up before God out of the angel's hand. And the angel took the censer, and filled it with fire of the altar, and cast it into the earth: and there were voices, and thunderings, and lightnings, and an earthquake."

The *"altar of incense"* in the earthly tabernacle and temple was sitting right in front of the second veil behind which was the *"Holy of holies"* and the place where the *"Ark of the covenant"* was sitting. The *"incense"* that is offered always speaks of the prayers of priest and people rising up to the nostrils and attention of God Himself. We read in Psalm 141:2 – *"Let my prayer be set forth before Thee as incense; and the lifting up of my hands as the evening sacrifice."*

It is possible that the *"prayers"* mentioned here in chapter 5 is a reminder that the church in heaven (24 elders – explained below) will be interceding for those who become believers during the tribulation as well as for the Nation of Israel. It is also possible that these *"prayers"* represent the prayer of God's people which our Lord instructed us to pray in Matthew 6:9-10:

"After this manner therefore pray ye: Our Father which art in heaven, Hallowed by Thy Name. Thy kingdom come. Thy will be done in earth, as it is in heaven."

    2. They reacted with <u>SINGING</u> recognizing His wonderful SALVATION!

Revelation 5:9-10 – *"And they sung a new song, saying, Thou art worthy to take the book, and to open the seals thereof: for Thou wast slain, and hast redeemed us to God by Thy blood out of every kindred, and tongue, and people, and nation; And hast made us unto our God kings and priests: and we shall reign on the earth."*

What is the *"new song"*?

The Greek word for *"new"* (*kainen*) that is used in verse 9 does not mean "new from the standpoint of time"; it refers to that which is new in quality, or fresh, or unique. The Psalms often speak of singing a *"new song"* – consider the following:

Psalm 33:3 – *"Sing unto Him a new song"*

Psalm 96:1 – *"O sing unto the LORD a new song; sing unto the LORD, all the earth."*

Psalm 98:1 – *"O sing unto the LORD a new song; for He hath done marvellous things: His right hand, and His holy arm, hath gotten Him the victory."*

Psalm 144:9 – *"I will sing a new song unto Thee, O God: upon a psaltery and an instrument of ten strings will I sing praises unto Thee."*

Psalm 149:1 – *"Praise ye the LORD. Sing unto the LORD a new song, and His praise in the congregation of saints."*

Also, Isaiah 42:10 says: *"Sing unto the LORD a new song, and His praise from the end of the earth, ye that go down to the sea, and all that is therein; the isles, and inhabitants thereof."*

In Revelation 14:1-3 we read of the 144,000 Jews in the tribulation:

"And I looked, and, lo, a Lamb stood on the mount Zion, and with Him an hundred forty and four thousands, having His Father's Name written in their foreheads. And I heard a voice from heaven, as the voice of many waters, and as the voice of a great thunder: and I heard the voice of harpers harping with their harps: And they sung as it were a new song before the throne, and before the four

beasts, and the elders: and no man could learn that song but the hundred and forty and four thousand, which were redeemed from the earth."

In Revelation 5:9-10 we learn the words of this *"new song"* – "THOU ART WORTHY"

(1)   It tells us why the Lamb is worthy to take the scroll and to open its seals!

(2)   His worthiness is based on His death!

(3)   His blood was the price of our redemption!

(4)   The 24 elders represent every tribe, tongue, people and nation!

(5)   Our relationship to God as kings and priests has been made possible by His redemption and guarantees that we shall reign on the earth!

BUT, WHO ARE THE 24 ELDERS?

Revelation 4:4 states – *"And round about the throne were four and twenty seats: and upon the seats I saw four and twenty elders sitting, clothed in white raiment; and they had on their heads crowns of gold."*

Revelation 4:10 adds – *"The four and twenty elders fall down before Him that sat on the throne, and worship Him that liveth forever and ever, and cast their crowns before the throne..."*

The term "elders" is used in the Book of Revelation 11 times: Revelation 4:4, 10; 5:6, 8, 11, 14; 7:11, 13; 11:16; 14:3; 19:4. Out of these 11 times, 6 use the number "24" in front of the word "elders."

There is no doubt that the issue of the 24 elders is critical to the whole argument of Pre-tribulationalism. The late George Eldon Ladd, a Post-tribulationalist, admits that very fact in his commentary on the Book of Revelation.

Here are the facts about the 24 elders:

1. They sit on thrones around the throne of God in heaven – Revelation 4:4a

2. They are clothed in white raiment – Revelation 4:4b

3. They have crowns of gold on their heads – Revelation 4:4c

4. They are pictured as ones who fall down before God and worship Him, casting their crowns at His feet – Revelation 4:10-11; 5:14.

5. They are also pictured as falling down before the Lamb, and have harps and bowls of incense representing the prayers of the saints Revelation 5:8

6. They sing a new song about the worthiness of
   the Lamb – Revelation 5:9-10

The very fact that the 24 elders are seen in heaven,
NOT on earth during the judgments of the
Tribulation forces us to connect them with the
following possibilities:

1. They refer to angels.

2. They refer to all believers who have died and
    are now in heaven.

3. They refer to Gentile believers who are saved
    during the Tribulation and are martyred.

4. They refer to church-age believers only.

The 24 elders cannot refer to angels because they
are identified separately from them in Revelation
5:11 and 7:11. They cannot refer to the Gentile
multitude that is saved during the tribulation on the
basis of the discussion of Revelation 7:13-14.

The description of these 24 elders in Revelation 4:4
connects them with the promises to church-age
believers in Revelation 2 and 3. The words about
them sitting on thrones remind us of Revelation
3:21; the reference to them being clothed in white
raiment connects us with the words of Revelation
3:5; the picture of them with crowns of gold on their
heads reminds us of Revelation 2:10 and 3:11.

These 24 elders are not called "priests" or "saints" but rather "elders." That is a specific description of church leaders in addition to the "elders" who acted as judges and administrators of justice among the children of Israel.

However, the "elders" of the Sanhedrin who are often connected with the priests and the scribes are not treated as genuine believers in the New Testament. They are the ones who condemned our Lord to death and delivered Him to the Romans for crucifixion.

The use of the number "24" is also very instructive. There have been many attempts by Bible teachers to divide this number into the 12 tribes of Israel and the 12 apostles of the Church. But, there is no Biblical warrant for that kind of exegesis. The number "24" is found in I Chronicles 24 and 25 and refers to 24 divisions of priests and musicians for the Nation of Israel. But, these are not called "priests" or "musicians" but rather "elders."

THE PROBLEM OF BIBLE TRANSLATIONS
Revelation 5:9-10

In the King James version of the Bible, we read – *"And they sung a new song, saying, Thou art worthy to take the book, and to open the seals thereof; for Thou wast slain, and hast redeemed US to God by Thy blood out of every kindred, and tongue, and people, and nation; And hast made US unto OUR God kings and priests: and WE shall reign on the earth."*

First of all, in relation to the differences in verse 10 between the King James Version (and New King James and the Geneva Bible) and other English translations, the Greek text shows a number of variant readings. If the third person plural is preferred, it still does not prove anything because it can simply refer to those mentioned in verse 9.

It is interesting that we have in Revelation 1:6 these words: *"And hath made US kings and priests unto God"* – and there is no variation in the manuscripts supporting another reading. It would appear that the King James Version of Revelation 5:10 is supported by the reading of Revelation 1:6.

Secondly, the real problem depends upon the manuscript evidence behind Revelation 5:9. Does the evidence support the word "US" or a reading of "THEM" or "MEN" or "PEOPLE" etc.? The Greek manuscripts (that we have today) of the passage in Revelation 5:9 are 24 in number, and 23 of them read "US" – only Codex Alexandrinus differs in this regard. We also have many Latin manuscripts of this verse and all of them read "US." Even the primary languages into which the Greek version was soon translated – all read "US." The issue is critical to the argument – are the 24 elders singing a song of redemption about themselves or about others who would be redeemed during the Tribulation? It appears that the evidence is overwhelming and that the King James translation is the correct one of Revelation 5:9.

NOTE: It is fascinating to read all the arguments concerning the Greek manuscripts of Revelation 5:9. In the arguments of those opposed to the King James Version of this verse, we read such things as appear on the web site Sola Scriptura and then is quoted by other sites:

"The use of the word 'us' in Revelation 5:9-10 and 'we' in verse 10 are found only in the King James Version of 1611 (not true!). When the King James Version was translated, only a small number of printed Greek texts were available to the translators. They include the 1567 edition of Theodore Beza and the third edition of Stephanus which was printed in 1550. These editions were the primary texts for the well-known 'Textus Receptus' which was actually printed in 1633 and was the dominant Greek text until the nineteenth century. Since that time, older and more textually credible (an opinion, not a fact!) Greek manuscripts than the ones available to Stephanus and Beza have been found. Two well-attested and authoritative uncial manuscripts (Sinaiticus and Alexandrinus) are among these finds."

The opening statement is quite misleading since there are thousands of manuscripts previous to 1611 that read "us." In reference to Greek texts, it is fascinating to see the admission that the Textus Receptus was "the dominant Greek text until the nineteenth century." The statement that certain manuscripts are "older and more textually credible" and are, therefore, "well-attested and authoritative" is almost amusing in its credibility! The ONLY Greek text of Revelation 5:9 that omits the word "us" is Codex Alexandrinus (about 240 Greek fragments are available on the Book of Revelation, but only 24 contain the reading of Revelation 5:9.).

Their mention of Sinaiticus does not help them, since it reads "us" as well. Since half of its New Testament leaves are missing, and the Shepherd of Hermes and the Epistle of Barnabas inserted into the text, it hardly represents that which is more credible. Codex Vaticanus, along with Sinaiticus, are the favorite Greek manuscripts of modern English translations. Interestingly, Codex Vaticanus ends at Hebrews 9:14 and there is nothing the rest of the way (including Revelation 5:9-10!). It also contains the Jewish Apocryphal books, not as a separate section, but woven throughout the text of the Biblical books. Also, Codex Basilianus (in the Vatican) reads "us." The word "us" is also in ALL Latin manuscripts as well as Coptic and Armenian.

WHAT ABOUT THE "TEXTUS RECEPTUS"?
(The Greek text behind the King James Bible)

The first edition of the Greek text to be published was that of Desiderius Erasmus in 1516 AD, followed by his edition in 1519 AD which was used by Martin Luther for his German translation of the Bible. Erasmus also published editions in 1522, 1527, and

1535 AD, the last two of which contained some changes from the Complutensian Polyglot printed in 1514 AD, but not circulated until 1522 AD. This Complutensian Greek text was reprinted with only a few changes in 1571, 1572, 1573, 1574, 1583, 1584 AD, and in Geneva, editions were put out from 1609 to 1628 AD.

Simon Colinaeus, a printer in Paris, published an edition of the Greek text in 1534 AD based upon those of Erasmus and the Complutensian Greek NT. It was superseded by the famous editions of his step-son, Robert Stephens, who printed editions in 1546, 1549, and 1550 AD, the last one known as the "royal edition." This was the primary Greek text used by the King James translators, along with additions by Theodore Beza, especially the one of 1598 AD.

The Elzevir partners, Bonaventure and Abraham, published editions of the Greek text in 1624, 1633, and 1641, following primarily the 1565 edition by Theodore Beza. The preface to the 1633 edition gave the name to this historical tradition of manuscript evidence and called it "Textus Receptus." In the course of time, it was applied to the Stephens text of 1550 AD and those which followed. The primary edition behind this Greek text is that of F.H.A. Scrivener that was published by Cambridge University Press in 1894 and 1902 AD.

About two-thirds of the NT Greek text was discovered in the 20th century AD – manuscripts that preceded 300 AD and the famous Codex Sinaiticus and Codex Vaticanus, and Codex Alexandrinus.

Codex Vaticanus differs greatly from the Textus Receptus throughout the NT. The great Greek scholar Dean Burgon published in 1881 that in the gospels alone, Codex Vaticanus omits 2877 words, adds 536, substitutes 935, transposes 2098, and modifies 1132 – making 7578 total changes! Codex Sinaiticus has 8972 changes from the Textus Receptus.

The popular Greek texts of today are dependent upon two ecumenical institutes in Germany. To illustrate, the 26th edition of the Nestle Greek text was done according to Kurt Aland "in cooperation with the appropriate agencies of the Roman Catholic Church."

Codex Vaticanus is the Greek text used by the Emphatic Diaglot which is behind the Watchtower Bible of the Jehovah Witnesses.

Codex Vaticanus ends at Hebrews 9:14 and excludes the Pastoral Epistles and the Book of Revelation. It contains all 14 Apocryphal books – contains 7579 changes from the Textus Receptus.

Codex Sinaiticus has one-half of its NT leaves missing, and contains the Epistle of Barnabas and the Shepherd of Hermes. It has 9000 changes from the Textus Receptus.

Tischendorf, the one who found Codex Sinaiticus, made 3369 changes in his 8th edition from his 7th edition.

In English, the above two MSS make over 30,000 changes.

Today we have over 5500 Greek MSS, over 10,000 Latin MSS, and over 4000 in other primary languages. We also have over 86,000 separate references in the writings of early church leaders.

The King James Bible was translated by 54 men who labored from 1607 to 1610 AD – spent hours in prayer and insisted on unanimous decisions on the readings of the text. It was indeed a remarkable effort and has been the Bible of the English speaking world for over 350 years.

It is our conclusion that the 24 elders are singing a song of redemption about themselves and that the King James Version of the Bible (along with the New King James and the Geneva Bible) is the correct translation of the new song recorded in Revelation 5:9-10.

You may be asking – "What difference does it make, and why go to all the trouble that is listed above?"

The answer is quite important: The King James reading of the text clearly teaches that church-age believers (represented by the 24 elders in heaven) are singing a song about their own redemption, and since these 24 elders are in heaven all during the tribulation period – the correct view of Bible prophecy as to the Rapture of the church-age believers (Jew and Gentile) is that they are removed BEFORE the tribulation begins! Our response is simple – PRAISE THE LORD!

The <u>RESPONSE</u> of all creation
Revelation 5:11-14

"And I beheld, and I heard the voice of many angels round about the throne and the beasts and the elders: and the number of them was ten thousand times ten thousand, and thousands of thousands; Saying with a loud voice, Worthy is the Lamb that was slain to receive power, and riches, and wisdom, and strength, and honor, and glory, and blessing. And every creature which is in heaven, and on the earth, and under the earth, and such as are in the sea, and all that are in them, heard I saying, Blessing, and honor, and glory, and power, be unto Him that sitteth upon the throne, and unto the Lamb forever and ever. And the four beasts said, Amen. And the four and twenty elders fell down and worshipped Him that liveth forever and ever."

Every time the above passage is read, we need to hear the music of Handel's MESSIAH!

This is a heavenly praise gathering, a worship service par excellence. May we never forget the marvelous scene depicted for us in these verses. How we need to understand the ultimate objective of God for all His creation!

The <u>MULTITUDE</u> that is involved

This multitude in heaven includes the four worship leaders (*"beasts"* or "living creatures" or "cherubim angels") and the 24 elders representing the church-age believers, and the number is simply astounding! It is given as *"ten thousand times ten thousand, and thousands or thousands."* In other words – too many to count – they are innumerable. The highest number in the Greek mathematical system of ancient times was "ten thousand" – and this passage multiplies it and then adds *"thousands of thousands"* – as if to say, it was more than anyone could ever count!

In verse 13 we are told that *"every creature which is in heaven, and on the earth....and such as are in the sea, and all that are in them"* – they were all involved in the praise of our Lord.

Romans 8:19-23 teaches us: *"For the earnest expectation of the creature waiteth for the manifestation of the sons of God. For the creature was made subject to vanity, not willingly, but by reason of Him Who hath subjected the same in hope, Because the creature itself also shall be delivered from the bondage of corruption into the glorious liberty of the children of God. For we know that the whole creation groaneth and travaileth in pain together unto now, and not only they, but ourselves also, which have the firstfruits of the Spirit, even we ourselves groan within ourselves, waiting for the adoption, to wit, the redemption of our body."*

When Revelation 5:13 mentions those *"under the earth"* it is probably referring to demonic creatures, fallen angels, or unclean spirits. They also will one day acknowledge the sovereignty and greatness of our Lord, the Lamb of God.

The <u>MESSAGE</u> which all creation proclaims

"Worthy is the Lamb that was slain to receive power, and riches, and wisdom, and strength, and honor, and glory, and blessing." Four of these seven characteristics are given to the One Who sits on the throne as well as to the Lamb forever and ever!

There is no higher joy or responsibility for the believer that the praise and adoration of Almighty God and His Messiah, the Lamb of God!

The <u>MANNER</u> in which the four beasts and the 24 elders respond

The *"four beasts"* (cherubim angels) are like the "Amen corner" of heaven. The Greek text indicates that they keep on saying *"Amen."* The 24 elders do what they usually do – *"fell down and worshipped Him that liveth forever and ever."*

What a remarkable passage of worship, praise, and adoration of God the Father and His Son, our Savior, Jesus Christ our Lord, the Messiah Who will rule and reign on earth for 1000 years in His special kingdom!

May the Lord fill our hearts with praise for Who He is and for all that He has done!

BOOK OF REVELATION
Understanding the Future

THE LION OVER THE NATIONS
Part II
Revelation 6-20

THE FOUR HORSEMEN
Revelation 6:1-8

"And I saw when the Lamb opened one of the seals, and I heard, as it were the noise of thunder, one of the four beasts saying, Come and see. And I saw, and behold a white horse: and he that sat on him had a bow; and a crown was given unto him: and he went forth conquering, and to conquer. And when He had opened the second seal, I heard the second beast say, Come and see. And there went out another horse that was red: and power was given to him that sat thereon to take peace from the earth, and that they should kill one another: and there was given unto him a great sword. And when He had opened the third seal, I heard the third beast say, Come and see. And I beheld, and lo a black horse; and he that sat on him had a pair of balances in his hand. And I heard a voice in the midst of the four beast say, A measure of wheat for a penny, and three measures of barley for a penny; and see thou hurt not the oil and the wine. And when He had opened the fourth seal, I heard the voice of the fourth beast say, Come and see. And I looked, and behold a pale horse: and his name that sat on him was Death, and Hell followed with him. And power was given unto them over the fourth part of the earth, to kill with sword, and with hunger, and with death, and with the beasts of the earth."

The scene now shifts from the wonderful praise of heaven to the tragic judgments upon planet earth.

Many Bible teachers point out the relationship between the judgments of Revelation and the teaching of Daniel. In Revelation 6:17 there is a remark about what is happening on the earth as the sixth seal was opened by the Lord. It says *"For the great day of His wrath is come; and who shall be able to stand?"*

Daniel 9:24-27 reveals a serious connection with the teachings of the Book of Revelation:

"Seventy weeks are determined upon Thy people and upon Thy holy city, to finish the transgression, and to make an end of sins, and to make reconciliation for iniquity, and to bring in everlasting righteousness, and to seal up the vision and prophecy, and to anoint the most Holy. Know therefore and understand, that from the going forth of the commandment to restore and to build Jerusalem unto the Messiah the Prince shall be seven weeks, and threescore and two weeks: the street shall be built again, and the wall, even in troublous times. And after threescore and two weeks shall Messiah be cut off, but not for Himself: and the people of the prince that shall come shall destroy the city and the sanctuary; and the end thereof shall be with a flood, and unto the end of the war desolations are determined. And he shall confirm the covenant with many for one week: and in the midst of the week he shall cause the sacrifice

and the oblation to cease, and for the overspreading of abominations he shall make it desolate, even until the consummation, and that determined shall be poured upon the desolate."

THE <u>CAUSES</u> BEHIND THIS PROPHECY

1. The <u>SOVEREIGNTY</u> of God – *"Seventy weeks are determined"* – nobody is going to change that fact!

2. The <u>SINS</u> of God's people (three things are predicted)

The REBELLION will be no more – *"to finish the transgression"* – the definite article is referring to a particular rebellion – the apostasy of Israel will end!

The REFINING of Israel will be accomplished – *"make an end of sins"* (statement refers to God's judgment – Ezekiel 20:33-38; Zechariah 13:8-9)

The RECONCILIATION will take place - *"to make reconciliation for iniquity"* Isaiah 53:1-6; II Corinthians 5:19

3. The <u>SETTING UP</u> of God's kingdom

The COMING of everlasting righteousness – Isaiah 11:1-5; Jeremiah 23:5-6

The CONCLUSION of vision and prophecy – *"seal up"* – same Hebrew word as *"make an end"* – Revelation 22:18-19 cf. Hebrews 1:1-3

The CONSECRATION of the HOLY of Holies – *"to anoint the most Holy"* – Ezekiel 43:12; Zechariah 14:16-21

THE <u>COMMAND</u> THAT BEGINS THE PROPHECY

1. It involves the <u>BUILDING</u> of Jerusalem's wall – there were four commands concerning Jerusalem's restoration:

    (1) CYRUS – II Chronicles 36; Ezra 1:1-4; 6:1-5 – 538 BC – rebuild the temple!
    (2) DARIUS – Ezra 6:6-12 – 519 BC
    (3) ARTAXERXES – Ezra 7:11-26 – 458 BC
    (4) ARTAXERXES LONGIMANUS – March 14, 445 BC – it was finished in 52 days – Nehemiah 6:15

2. It involves the <u>BLESSING</u> of the coming Messiah - *"unto the Messiah the Prince"* – an event about the fact that the Messiah has come!

3. It involves the <u>BELIEF</u> that the *"weeks"* represent *"years"* NOT *"days"* (the Hebrew word is "seven"

NOTE: By multiplying 483 years (69 "sevens") by 360 days (prophetic year) = 173,880 days! From March 14, 445 BC, we come out to April 6, 32 AD, the day of His triumphal entry into Jerusalem!

NOTE: Luke 3:1 mentions the *"fifteenth year of the reign of Tiberias Caesar"* – he began his reign in 14 AD – that brings us to 28 AD. Epiphanius said that Jesus was baptized in the fall of 28 AD, and that He died in the spring of 32 AD.

Herod the Great died on January 14, 1 BC – he was alive when Jesus was born.

Tertullian: Jesus was born 41 years after Augustus began his reign in 43 BC. Jesus was born 15 years before Augustus died on August 19, 14 AD.

Tertullian: Jesus was born 28 years after the death of Cleopatra (30 BC)

Irenaeus: Jesus was born in the 41st reign of Augustus (began in 43 BC)

John the Baptist was born 280 days after the 8th division of Abia which ended on July 13, 3 BC – it was Passover – April 19-20, 2 BC. Jesus was born six months after John was born – possibly on Rosh HaShana in 2 BC. April 6, 32 AD was the day of His triumphal entry into Jerusalem.

This prophecy of Daniel also reveals that there is a connection between Rome's destruction of Jerusalem and the Second Temple (Herod) and the coming of a world leader who will enforce a peace agreement upon the people of Israel. In the middle of its terms, he will break that covenant and will go into a rebuilt temple of the Jews in Jerusalem and demand that he be worshipped. It would appear that this *"coming prince"* is the Antichrist!

OPENING THE SEALS DESCRIBES THE START OF THE GREAT TRIBULATION!

Our Lord Yeshua predicted in Matthew 24:21-22: *"For then shall be great tribulation, such as was not since the beginning of the world to this time, no, nor ever shall be. And except those days should be shortened, there should no flesh be saved: but for the elect's sake* (Israel) *those days shall be shortened."*

When the sixth seal is opened we read these words in Revelation 6:17 – *"For the great day of His wrath is come; and who shall be able to stand?"*

THE DAY OF GOD'S WRATH IS COMING!
(details in next chapter)

The Apostle Paul wrote to the young church at Thessalonica and said (I Thessalonians 5:1-3: *"But of the times and the seasons, brethren, ye have no need that I write unto you. For yourselves know perfectly that the day of the Lord so cometh as a thief in the night. For when they shall say, Peace and safety; then sudden destruction cometh*

287

upon them, as travail upon a woman with child; and they shall not escape."

The term "THE DAY OF THE LORD" appears 25 times in the Bible and is referring to the coming Great Tribulation. It is the worst holocaust of terror and destruction that has ever come upon planet earth.

THREE SETS OF JUDGMENTS

In trying to understand what the Book of Revelation predicts about the future of planet earth, we have three sets of judgments presented to us:

> SEVEN SEALS
> SEVEN TRUMPETS
> SEVEN BOWLS OF WRATH

The text indicates that these three sets of judgments will happen in order, one following the other.

SEAL #1 – a rider on a white horse
Revelation 6:1-2

"And I saw when the Lamb opened one of the seals, and I heard, as it were the noise of thunder, one of the four beasts saying, Come and see. And I saw, and behold a white horse: and he that sat on him had a bow; and a crown was given unto him: and he went forth conquering, and to conquer."

Some teachers of prophecy have asserted that this first seal is the Second Coming of Jesus Christ. It is true that when our Lord does come, we are told in Revelation 19:11 – *"And I saw heaven opened, and behold a white horse; and He that sat upon him was called Faithful and True, and in righteousness He doth judge and make war."*

Others have said that this seal represents the gospel and its conquest of human hearts.

Why do we believe that neither of the above views are correct about the rider on a white horse:

1. Jesus Christ in NOT the rider, but is the One Who opens the first seal.

His worthiness to open the seals seems to place Him outside and above the messages that are written on the scroll.

2. The remaining seals deal with judgment and tragedy.

This fact causes us to question why the first seal would depart from the overall scheme of things contained in these seal judgments.

3. The *"crown"* is not the same as that stated in Revelation 19.

Revelation 19:12 says: *"His eyes were as a flame of fire, and on His head were many crowns; and He* had a Name written, that no man knew, but He Himself.”

In the Greek text, we have two different words for the word *“crown.”* In Revelation 6:2 the word is *“stephanos”* - the simple crown of one who won a victory in the games of stadium times. In Revelation 19:12, the Greek word is *“diademata”* – our English word “diadems” comes directly from this word. The text of Revelation 19:12 also says *“many”* diadems! It is the crown of royalty and majesty.

WHO IS THE “RIDER ON A WHITE HORSE”?

This is a “counterfeit” Christ, a false Messiah, namely, the Antichrist. In Matthew 24:4-5 our Lord Yeshua taught His disciples: *“Take heed that no man deceive you. For many shall come in My Name, saying, I am Christ; and shall deceive many.”*

In being careful with the words of this text, we notice that the *“crown”* was *“given unto him.”* He also had *“a bow”* depicting military conquest. The words *“he went forth conquering, and to conquer.”* That is his motive – *“to conquer”* and his efforts were continual – *“conquering.”*

The Great Tribulation will begin with a new ruler rising to power on the scene of world history. Daniel the prophet predicted the coming of such a leader. II Thessalonians 2 describes him as *“the man of sin"* and *"the son of perdition"* and *"the lawless one."*

Our present world desires such a leader – we are gripped with a "messiah syndrome" believing that such a leader can bring peace to this world. It is not difficult to see how allegiance could be given by the world's populations to such a leader. He will deceive them and be energized by the power of Satan himself.

SEAL #2 – the rider on a red horse
Revelation 6:3-4

"And when He (the Lamb of God) *had opened the second seal, I heard the second beast say, Come and see. And there went out another horse that was red: and power was given to him that sat thereon to take peace from the earth, and that they should kill one another: and there was given unto him a great sword."*

The picture of a *"fiery red horse"* has always been a portrait of war and bloodshed. It is possible that this rider is the same as the first seal. The coming world leader will arise in an atmosphere of proclaiming peace, but he will soon take it from the earth.

Our Lord Yeshua told us that there was coming a time of *"wars and rumors of wars."* The 20th century was the most violent and the loss of lives the greatest in human history! Things are not getting better. The world is filled with violence, and senseless murder is now commonplace.

The description of this *"horse"* reminds us of the description of Satan in Revelation 12:3 – *"a great red dragon."*
What happens when the *"red horse"* comes?

1. World <u>PEACE</u> is ended!
   "power was given to him...to take peace from the earth"

2. Many <u>PEOPLE</u> are killed!
   "that they should kill one another"

3. Military <u>POWER</u> in the hands of one man!
   "there was given unto him a great sword"

"Peace on earth" will not come to this planet until the Prince of Peace, the Messiah of Israel, our blessed Lord Yeshua comes again! Isaiah 9:6-7 makes it very clear:

"For unto us a child is born, unto us a son is given: and the government shall be upon His shoulder; and His Name shall be called Wonderful, Counsellor, The mighty God, The everlasting Father, The Prince of peace. Of the increase of His government and peace there shall be no end, upon the throne of David and upon His kingdom, to order it, and to establish it with judgment and with justice from henceforth even forever. The zeal of the LORD of hosts will perform this."

Giving this *"great sword"* to this coming world leader is a picture of unusual authority and power. Revelation 13:7 says that *"power was given unto him to continue forty and two months."* That is a statement dealing with half of the Great Tribulation!

SEAL #3 – the rider on a black horse
Revelation 6:5-6

"And when He had opened the third seal, I heard the third beast say, Come and see. And I beheld, and lo a black horse; and he that sat on him had a pair of balances in his hand. And I heard a voice in the midst of the four beasts say, a measure of wheat for a penny, and three measures of barley for a penny; and see thou hurt not the oil and the wine."

Black is a picture of death resulting from famine and starvation. Lamentations 4:8-9 says: *"Their visage is blacker than a coal: they are not known in the streets: their skin cleaveth to their bones; it is withered, it is become like a stick. They that be slain with the sword are better than they that be slain with hunger: for these pine away, stricken through for want of the fruits of the field."*

Famine usually follows war and bloodshed. Any person who has witnessed the serious famine that has spread across Africa is aware of the terrible tragedy that literally devastates whole populations and destroys the will and strength of any people.

The tragic conditions that this horseman represents:

1. <u>INFLATION</u> will take place!

The *"pair of balances"* in the hand of the black horse rider suggests that the economic balance of things is going to be severely altered.

2. <u>INCREASES</u> in food prices will occur!

A Roman "denarius" (the word translated as *"penny"*) was equal to a day's wages. In the coming tribulation, food prices will rise so high that it will take a whole day's earnings to purchase enough wheat for one meal for an average family. Barley is the food used for animals. Families will be forced to turn to this kind of food in order to survive.

3. <u>ITEMS</u> of luxury will not be affected!

The end of verse 6 says *"see thou hurt not the oil and the wine."* These are items that the rich enjoy, and are used for pleasure and leisure times.

SEAL #4 – *the rider on a pale horse*

Revelation 6:7-8 – *"And when He had opened the fourth seal, I heard the voice of the fourth beast say, Come and see. And I looked, and behold a pale horse: and his name that sat on him was Death, and Hell (Hades) followed with him. And power was given unto them over the fourth part of the earth, to kill with sword, and with hunger, and with death, and with the beasts of the earth.”*

This horse is the color of a corpse and goes well with the name of its rider – *“Death.”* This rider is followed by *“Hell”* which is the Greek word *“Hades”* the place of the wicked dead, a place of awful torment.

It is remarkable indeed to read that this rider of the pale horse will have *“power...over the fourth part of the earth.”* If the population of the world stands at 8 billion people soon, that means that 2 billion people will be killed! And, the tribulation period is just beginning!

This is not talking about those who die from old age or bad health; The text lists four methods by which the residents of planet earth will be killed:
SWORD
HUNGER
DEATH
BEASTS

The word *“death”* is a separate category by which people will be killed. Most believe that this is no doubt referring to plagues and diseases (which are already running rampant and many out of control).

The word *“beasts”* suggests that the animals will be radically changed and become threats to human life and suffering.

Ezekiel 14:21 says: *"For thus saith the Lord GOD; How much more when I send My four sore judgments upon Jerusalem, the sword, and the famine, and the noisome beast, and the pestilence, to cut off from it man and beast?"*

These four horsemen of the Apocalypse are enough to reveal the horror and catastrophe of the coming days of the tribulation. These judgments appear to be the beginning of the tragedies that will afflict this planet and its people.

Is there any hope? That is a very important question! The hope is found in our faith and commitment to our Lord Jesus Christ, the Messiah of Israel, and the coming KING of kings, and LORD of lords! All other solutions will be to no avail – the tragedies will strike all nations, and the disaster will be unbelievable and impossible to stop!

During the tribulation there will be 144,000 Jews who will become strong and loyal believers in the Messiah and take His message all over the world! According to Revelation 7 there will also be a great multitude of Gentiles (that no one can number!) from every nation, language, and people, who will become believers in the middle of all the tragedies that are taking place!

The issue for all of us is to make sure of our relationship to the Messiah, our blessed Lord Yeshua before it is too late!

THE DAY OF GOD'S WRATH
Revelation 6:9-17

"And when He had opened the fifth seal, I saw under the altar the souls of them that were slain for the word of God, and for the testimony which they held: And they cried with a loud voice, saying, How long, O Lord, holy and true, dost Thou not judge and avenge our blood on them that dwell on the earth? And white robes were given unto every one of them; and it was said unto them, that they should rest yet for a little season, unto their fellow-servants also and their brethren, that should be killed as they were, should be fulfilled. And I beheld when He had opened the sixth seal, and, lo, there was a great earthquake; and the sun became black as sackcloth of hair, and the moon became as blood; And the stars of heaven fell unto the earth, even as a fig tree casteth her untimely figs, when she is shaken of a mighty wind. And the heaven departed as a scroll when it is rolled together; and every mountain and island were moved out of their places. And the kings of the earth, and the great men, and the rich men, and the chief captains, and the mighty men, and every bondman, and every free man, hid themselves in the dens and in the rocks of the mountains; And said to the mountains and rocks, Fall on us, and hide us from the face of Him that sitteth on the throne, and from the wrath of the Lamb: For the great day of His wrath is come; and who shall be able to stand?"

There is a day coming to planet earth that will make all previous days seem insignificant by comparison! It will not be a pleasant day; It is a day filled with terror and panic such as the people of earth have never experienced!

Disasters have come to earth on many occasions and those who have been a part of them and have survived will find it hard to believe that a worst scenario is soon to come, the consequences of which have never been seen in previous history!

The Bible warns of this coming day in many passages of its pages. The Apostle Paul who wrote 14 of the 27 books in the New Testament, wrote these words in I Thessalonians 5:1-3:

"But of the times and the season, brethren, ye have no need that I write unto you. For yourselves know perfectly that the day of the Lord so cometh as a thief in the night. For when they shall say 'Peace and safety' – then sudden destruction cometh upon them as travail upon a woman with child; and they shall not escape."

Some folks want to believe that he was referring to what happened in 70 AD when Rome destroyed Jerusalem and the Second Temple of the Jews. That was indeed a terrible day in human history, a day that Jesus predicted would come. But, a worse day was prophesied frequently by the Bible that would surprise the world and plunge it into an incredible chaos with millions losing their lives in the horrible disasters that are coming.

Perhaps you are among those who have questioned these prophecies and you doubt seriously that such disasters will come to planet earth. Maybe you have thrown such thinking into a general category of "conspiracy theories" or some wild ravings of religious people who use such talk to convince people of their particular religious viewpoint.

Hollywood has produced movies showing enormous disasters to hit planet earth. Perhaps, you say, these are just movies that have nothing to do with reality. But, many people, including some brilliant scientists, have already concluded that the planet is headed for disaster and serious trouble in the near future.

The Bible speaks of a coming day that is certainly longer than 24 hours in length. It appears that these prophecies speak of a period of time that could last for several years. The very term "THE DAY OF THE LORD" is found 25 times in the Bible and is not the only description used of a coming time of great disaster upon planet earth. Other phrases include:

    DAY OF GOD'S VENGEANCE
    DAY OF GOD'S WRATH

We also find in our studies of Bible prophecy a phrase that corresponds often to this coming "DAY OF THE LORD." It is the simple wording "IN THAT

DAY." Sometimes it refers to an historical time and even that has already transpired. But, many times, what it describes can only refer to a future time that we know to be the Great Tribulation.

Books in the Bible like Isaiah, Jeremiah, Ezekiel, and Daniel – they speak of this coming day of tragedy and disaster. They are called "Major Prophets" because of their size and content. There is also a group of books often called "The Twelve" – they seem to be an integrated system and they speak frequently of future times of coming disaster.

Zephaniah 1:14-18 is an example that speaks of the coming day of God's wrath:

"The great day of the LORD is near, it is near, and hasteth greatly, even the voice of the day of the LORD: the mighty man shall cry there bitterly. That day is a day of wrath, a day of trouble and distress, a day of wasteness and desolation, a day of darkness and gloominess, a day of clouds and thick darkness, A day of the trumpet and alarm against the fenced cities, and against the high towers. And I will bring distress upon men, because they have sinned against the LORD: and their blood shall be poured out as dust, and their flesh as the dung. Neither their silver nor their gold shall be able to deliver them in the day of the LORD's wrath; but the whole land shall be devoured by the fire of His jealousy: for He shall make a speedy riddance of all them that dwell in the land."

SEAL #5 – *souls under the altar that were killed for their faith and confidence in the Word of God!*

Millions of God's people have been slaughtered throughout history. Hebrews 11:35 speaks of those in the past who were *"tortured"* and in the verses that follow we read of *"mockings and scourgings, yea, moreover of bonds and imprisonment: They were stoned, they were sawn asunder...slain with the sword"* and the total number has been astronomical especially in the so-called "modern history" of this planet. Under the regime of Adolph Hitler, millions were killed simply because they were Jews or Christians who refused to support "The Third Reich" and its diabolical plans. Under Communism, millions were slaughtered under Russian leaders like Joseph Stalin and others. Today, we see the unbelievable happening all over the world as Islam exercises its beliefs and practices of killing those who will not renounce their faith in Jesus Christ as Lord and Savior. The truth that Islam refuses to acknowledge is that thousands of Muslims are renouncing their commitment to Islam and are turning their lives over to Jesus Christ as Lord and Savior! As a result, Islam continues to kill its own people by the thousands in many countries of the world.

The opening of the fifth seal gives us a clear picture of what these martyred souls are saying and what the Lord is doing to comfort their hearts and minds.

1. The <u>CRIES</u> of the martyrs

Revelation 6:10 – *"and they cried with a loud voice, saying, How long, O Lord, holy and true, dost Thou not judge and avenge our blood on them that dwell on the earth?"*

It is obvious that those believers who have died are conscious and able to communicate. They are also interested in Bible prophecy. A day is coming when the Lord God will do exactly what they are asking – He will *"judge and avenge"* the blood of those who have been killed for their faith.

2. The <u>COMFORT</u> which the Lord brings

Revelation 6:11 – *"and white robes were given unto every one of them; and it was said unto them, that they should rest yet for a little season, until their fellow-servants also and their brethren, that should be killed as they were, should be fulfilled."*

The placing of *"white robes"* on each of them reveals that there must be a temporary physical body for those who died and are with the Lord as they wait for their resurrection body.

II Corinthians 5:1-8 teaches: *"For we know that if our earthly house of this tabernacle were dissolved, we have a building of God, an house not made with hands, eternal in the heavens. For in this we groan, earnestly desiring to be clothed upon with our house which is from heaven: If so be that being clothed we shall not be found naked. For we that are in this tabernacle do groan, being burdened: not for that we would be unclothed, but clothed upon, that mortality might be swallowed up of life. Now He that hath wrought us for the selfsame thing is God, Who also hath given unto us the earnest of the Spirit. Therefore we are always confident, knowing that, whilst we are at home in the body, we are absent from the Lord: (For we walk by faith, not by sight:) We are confident, I say, and willing rather to be absent from the body, and to be present with the Lord."*

3. The <u>CONDITION</u> of these martyrs

Verse 11 says *"that they should rest yet for a little season."* Revelation 14:13 adds: *"Blessed are the dead which die in the Lord from henceforth: Yea, saith the Spirit, that they may rest from their labors; and their works do follow them."*

It is comforting to all of us who have lost family and friends through death – to know that these who are believers in our Lord Jesus are "resting" – Praise the Lord!

4. The <u>COMING</u> of additional martyrs

Verse 11 also says that they should rest *"until their fellow-servants also and their brethren, that should be killed as they were, should be fulfilled."*

It is comforting to know that the plan of God is operating on planet earth even when fellow believers are killed (as they continue to be so!).

SEAL #6 – the great earthquake and serious disasters in the heavens and on the earth

1. The <u>EARTHQUAKE</u> that hits planet earth!

Revelation 6:12 – *"And I beheld when He had opened the sixth seal, and, lo, there was a <u>great earthquake</u>..."*

At the time of the death of Yeshua on a Roman cross we read in Matthew 17:50-54: *"Jesus, when He had cried again with a loud voice, yielded up the ghost. And, behold, the veil of the temple was rent in twain from the top to the bottom; and the earth did quake, and the rocks rent; And the graves were opened; and many bodies of the saints which slept arose, and came out of the graves after His resurrection, and went into the holy city, and appeared unto many. Now when the centurion, and they that were with him, watching Jesus, saw the <u>earthquake</u>, and those things that were done, they feared greatly, saying, Truly this was the Son of God."*

In Matthew 28:2 we read: *"And, behold, there was a <u>great earthquake</u>: for the angel of the Lord descended from heaven, and came and rolled back the stone from the door, and sat upon it."*

We also read in Revelation 8:5 that when the angel cast the censor's ingredients to the earth, there were "*voices, and thunderings, and lightnings, and an earthquake.*"

Revelation 11:13 speaks of another earthquake: "*And the same hour was there a <u>great earthquake</u>, and the tenth part of the city fell, and in the <u>earthquake</u> were slain of men seven thousand: and the remnant were affrighted, and gave glory to the God of heaven.*"

Revelation 11:19 adds: "*And the temple of God was opened in heaven, and there was opened in heaven, and there was seen in His temple the ark of His testament: and there were lightnings, and voices, and thunderings, and an <u>earthquake</u>, and great hail.*"

Revelation 16:18 – "*And there were voices, and thunders, and lightnings; and there was a <u>great earthquake</u>, so mighty an <u>earthquake</u>, and so great.*"

2. The <u>EVENTS</u> in the heaven and earth!

Revelation 6:12b-14 – "*and the sun became black as sackcloth of hair, and the moon became as blood; And the stars of heaven fell unto the earth, even as a fig tree casteth her untimely figs, when she is shaken of a mighty wind. And the heaven departed as a scroll when it is rolled together; and every* mountain and island were moved out of their places."

SUN – *"became black as sackcloth of hair"*

MOON – *"became as blood"*

STARS – *"fell unto the earth"*

HEAVEN – *"departed as a scroll when it is rolled together"*

MOUNTAIN and ISLAND – *"moved out of their places"*

Joel 2:30-31 teaches: *"And I will shew wonders in the heavens and in the earth, blood, and fire, and pillars of smoke. The sun shall be turned into darkness, and the moon into blood, before the great and the terrible day of the LORD come."* Joel 3:15 adds: *"The sun and the moon shall be darkened, and the stars shall withdraw their shining."*

Isaiah 13:10-13 – *"For the stars of heaven and the constellations thereof shall not give their light: the sun shall be darkened in his going forth, and the moon shall not cause her light to shine. And I will punish the world for their evil, and the wicked for their iniquity; and I will cause the arrogancy of the proud to cease, and will lay low the haughtiness of the terrible. I will make a man more precious than fine gold; even a man that the golden wedge of Ophir. Therefore I will shake the heavens, and the*

306

earth shall remove out of her place, in the wrath of the LORD of hosts, and in the day of His fierce anger."

Amos 8:9-10 – *"And it shall come to pass in that day, saith the Lord GOD, that I will cause the sun to go down at noon, and I will darken the earth in the clear day: and I will turn your feasts into mourning, and all your songs into lamentations; and I will bring up sackcloth upon all lions, and baldness upon every head; and I will make it as the mourning of an only son, and the end thereof as a bitter day."*

Some prophecy teachers take the above passages and make them allegorical, depicting social and political upheaval.   However, such a view takes liberties with the plain sense of God's Word and tries to reinterpret events of the future in the context of present understanding and situations.

Many teachers believe these events are literal and will take place as described, but they disagree as to when they will occur.   Among pre-millennialists there are three major viewpoints about the catastrophic events of the sixth seal judgment of planet earth:

(1)   They refer to the earthquake that will occur at the Second Coming of Jesus Christ at the end of the Tribulation.

Those who hold this view usually point out that a great earthquake does happen at the pouring out of the seventh bowl of wrath described as the final plague on the earth (Revelation 16:17-21). Yet, though they see the similarities between chapters 6 and 16, they fail to expound on the differences. This is not the same event. In chapter 6, the great day of God's wrath "has come"; in chapter 16 and verse 17 we read *"It is done!"* The one begins the judgments of God, and the other ends it.

(2) They refer to the earthquake that was predicted in Ezekiel 38:19-20:

"For in My jealousy and in the fire of My wrath have I spoken, Surely in that day there shall be a great shaking in the land of Israel; So that the fishes of the sea, and the fowls of the haven, and the beasts of the field, and all creeping things that creep upon the earth, and all the men that are upon the face of the earth, shall shake at My presence, and the mountains shall be thrown down, and the steep places shall fall, and every wall shall fall to the ground."

In speaking about a future earthquake, the prophet Ezekiel speaks of an invasion into Israel by a northern power/coalition in the end time. Is this the earthquake of Revelation 6? Probably not – the one in Ezekiel happens only in the land of Israel whereas the one in Revelation 6 declares: *"every mountain and island were moved out of their places."*

(3)   They refer to a particular earthquake that will happen at the beginning of the tribulation.

From the words of Revelation 6 it would seem that this is the best view and the correct one. Verse 17 says *"For the great day of His wrath is come; and who shall be able to stand?"* It is the great disaster that will announce as it were that God's wrath coming to planet earth is here!

3. The <u>EXPERIENCE</u> to which the people of earth will react in panic!

Revelation 6:15-17 – *"And the kings of the earth, and the great men, and the rich men, and the chief captains, and the mighty men, and every bondman, and every free man, hid themselves in the dens and in the rocks of the mountains; And said to the mountains and rocks, Fall on us, and hide us from the face of Him that sitteth on the throne, and from the wrath of the Lamb: For the great day of His wrath is come; and who shall be able to stand?"*

The entire population of planet earth is in a panic! World leaders and rulers have no answers but are filled with fear along with the rest of the population. The panic causes them to run and hide.   This attempt to hide and to appeal to the mountains and rocks to fall on them demonstrates how severe and intense this state of panic really is. They are aware that this judgment is unusual and not a normal earthquake!   They realize that this disaster is coming directly from God the Father and God the Son, the Lamb of God!

The cry of verse 17 is *"Who shall be able to stand?"* In Malachi 3:1-3 we read these similar words:

"Behold, I will send My Messenger, and He shall prepare the way before Me: and the Lord, Whom ye seek, shall suddenly come to His temple, even the Messenger of the covenant, Whom ye delight in: behold, He shall come, saith the LORD of hosts. But who may abide the day of His coming? And who shall stand when He appeareth? For He is like a refiner's fire, and like fullers' soap: And He shall sit as a refiner and purifier of silver: and He shall purify the sons of Levi, and purge them as gold and silver, that they may offer unto the LORD an offering in righteousness."

Our Lord Yeshua predicted in Luke 21:25-26:
"And there shall be signs in the sun, and in the moon, and in the stars; and upon the earth distress of nations, with perplexity; the sea and the waves roaring; Men's hearts failing them for fear, and for looking after these things which are coming on the earth: for the powers of heaven shall be shaken."

There is no greater issue to face than eternal life, and escaping the coming wrath of God. God's wrath will be poured out upon this planet during the coming tribulation period, but as awful as that will be, it is nothing compared to the wrath of God that executes the judgment of Hell upon those who refuse to put their faith and trust in the death and resurrection of our blessed Lord Yeshua!

Our present generation has no desire to hear of these things or to believe them. We want to be happy and reminded of our self-worth and potential for success. The real issue has not changed – it is HEAVEN or HELL! It is life or death!
Where will you spend eternity?

TRIBULATION BELIEVERS
Revelation 7:1-17

Although church-age believers (represented by the 24 elders in heaven during the tribulation period on earth) are in heaven in the presence of the Lord Himself, there will be two groups of believers who will come out of the Great Tribulation. One group consists of 144,000 Jewish people who are supernaturally protected by God from the judgments and tragedies of the coming tribulation. The other group is an innumerable multitude who come from every nation and language, and become believers during the tribulation. They are Gentiles from all over the world.

The SEALED SERVANTS of our God
Revelation 7:1-8

"And after these things I saw four angels standing on the four corners of the earth, holding the four winds of the earth, that the wind should not blow on the earth, nor on the sea, nor on any tree. And I saw another angel ascending from the east, having the seal of the living God: and he cried with a loud voice to the four angels, to whom it was given to hurt the earth and the sea, Saying, Hurt not the earth, neither the sea, nor the trees, till we have sealed the servants of our God in their foreheads. And I heard the number of them which were sealed: and there were sealed an hundred and forty and four thousand of all the tribes of the children of Israel. Of the tribe of Judah were sealed twelve

thousand. Of the tribe of Reuben were sealed twelve thousand. Of the tribe of Gad were sealed twelve thousand. Of the tribe of Asher were sealed twelve thousand. Of the tribe of Nepthalim were sealed twelve thousand. Of the tribe of Manasseh were sealed twelve thousand. Of the tribe of Simeon were sealed twelve thousand. Of the tribe of Levi were sealed twelve thousand. Of the tribe of Issachar were sealed twelve thousand. Of the tribe of Zebulon were sealed twelve thousand. Of the tribe of Joseph were sealed twelve thousand. Of the tribe of Benjamin were sealed twelve thousand."

Out of the many attempts to identify this group of 144,000 Jews, 12,000 from each tribe listed, there are basically two viewpoints: One is the symbolical view, and the other is the literal view. Unless there are some obvious reasons in the text to make this passage symbolical, it is better to take the words literally.

The <u>PURPOSE</u> of the four angels
Revelation 7:1-3

"And after these things I saw four angels standing on the four corners of the earth, holding the four winds of the earth, that the wind should not blow on the earth, nor on the sea, nor on any tree. And I saw another angel ascending from the east, having the seal of the living God: and he cried with a loud voice to the four angels, to whom it was given to hurt the earth and the sea, Saying, Hurt not the

earth, neither the sea, nor the trees, till we have sealed the servants of our God in their foreheads."

The basic command that these four angels received was to withhold judgment upon the earth, sea, and trees until the 144,000 servants of God are sealed or protected. When we look ahead to chapter 8, we observe that great harm was done on a wide scale to the earth, sea, and trees.

These angels are the ones that God uses to bring His judgments and wrath upon the earth. God gives them authority and power to carry out this *"harm,"* but does not allow them to do so until the 144,000 persons are sealed. These servants are not to be touched or harmed and they appear to be the only ones during the tribulation that are so protected by God.

The Bible contains 29 lists of the tribes of Israel. This particular one is not the final list in the chronology of the nation. After the tribulation comes, the kingdom of the Messiah will be set up on earth. In the list of Ezekiel 48, Dan (a tribe which is absent from this list in Revelation 7) is listed first, and Ephraim appears again in the place of Joseph, his father. Levi is not listed in the land divisions, but is honored with a special place and area immediately around the temple.

According to Ezekiel 48:30-34, the gates of the Messianic city, the new Jerusalem, will have the names of the twelve tribes of Israel. In that list, we find Reuben, Judah, Levi, Joseph, Benjamin, Dan, Simeon, Issachar, Zebulun, Gad, Asher, and Naphtali. Once again, like the list in Revelation 7, Ephraim is dropped out and his father Joseph appears in the list. Ephraim's brother, Manasseh, is also missing, and is replaced by the priestly tribe of Levi. The interesting thing about this final listing is that it represents the original listing in Genesis 35:22-26 where only the sons of Jacob are listed, not the two sons of Joseph (Ephraim and Manasseh).

Because of God's promises of land to these twelve tribes, He keeps His Word and mentions those to whom He originally promised such an inheritance. However, in the role the 144,000 play during the tribulation and in the honor God bestows upon His people in the new Jerusalem, changes are made. The question is, WHY?

In the case of the 144,000, the absence of the tribe of Dan might be the result of Dan's involvement in idolatry in Israel's past. Judges 18:30 states that it was the children of Dan who set up the carved image and that it was the descendants of Manasseh who performed the role of priests for this pagan system. The tribe of Dan continued this idolatry until the time of the captivity. Dan did not represent religious loyalty and commitment, and the predictions of Deuteronomy 29:14-29 may be the reason for Dan's removal.

This could be the reason why Ephraim is not mentioned. According to I Kings 12:28-29, King

Jeroboam set up two golden calves for worship, one in Dan, and the other in Bethel, which is in the land of Ephraim. Hosea 4:17 says *"Ephraim is joined to idols."*

The number of each tribe, the listing of the tribes, and the specific statement that they are *"tribes of the children of Israel"* point to a literal interpretation. The absence of symbolical language is also a strong reason for avoiding any unusual speculation or interpretations of this group of 144,000. The listing of these twelve tribes helps refute the contention by some that certain tribes of Israel are "lost." They are obviously not lost in the mind and plan of God.

It is best to interpret this passage as it is written. It is speaking of 144,000 Jews who will be divinely protected from the judgments of the tribulation to carry on God's purposes and plan. Attention is given to these Jews again in Revelation 14:1-5.

The SAVED SAINTS who come out of the Great Tribulation
Revelation 7:9-17

1. The PEOPLE who are described
Revelation 7:9-10

"After this I beheld, and, lo, a great multitude, which no man could number, of all nations, and kindreds, and people, and tongues, stood before the throne, and before the Lamb, clothed with white

robes, and palm in their hands; and cried with a loud voice, saying, Salvation to our God which sitteth upon the throne, and unto the Lamb."

(1)   Their <u>COUNTRIES</u> and <u>CULTURES</u>

The phrase *"after these things"* or *"after this"* appears several times in Revelation. It is possible that this is a connection with the 144,000. Maybe these Jews are the ones used by God to bring this great innumerable multitude to believe in Yeshua as their Messiah and Lord.

The multitude is huge and cannot be numbered and they come from all nations of the world. Our Lord Yeshua gave the command to His disciples to *"teach all nations"* (Matthew 28:19 account) and to *"preach the gospel to every creature"* (Mark 16:15).

It appears that all *"tongues"* will be represented. That fact alone is amazing in light of the hundreds of languages that have yet to receive one verse of the Bible in their own language! We are not sure how it is going to happen, but one thought is that the 144,000 Jews will be able to speak in all languages of the world (like on the Day of Pentecost in Acts 2), communicating the gospel of Jesus Christ in the language and culture of thousands of people groups in this world presently who have never heard the true gospel of our Lord.

(2)   Their <u>CLOTHING</u> – *"clothed with white robes"*

The *"white"* clothing speaks of the garments of salvation. Revelation 19:7-8 says: *"Let us be glad and rejoice, and give honor to Him: for the marriage of the Lamb is come, and His wife hath made herself ready. And to her was granted that she should be arrayed in fine linen, clean and white: for the fine linen is the righteousness of saints."*

(3) Their CRIES – *"Salvation to our God which sitteth upon the throne, and unto the Lamb"*

According to Joel 2:28-32 (quoted by Peter on the Day of Pentecost in Acts 2) God will one day pour out His Spirit on all flesh. That includes a multitude of Gentiles as well as Jews. Since Joel's prophecy contains predictions about the coming tribulation events (Joel 2:30-31), it is possible that the complete fulfillment of these facts will happen when the 144,000 Jews preach the gospel of the Messiah in all the languages of the world during the tribulation period. Our Lord Yeshua said in Matthew 24:14: *"And this gospel of the kingdom shall be preached in all the world for a witness unto all nations; and then shall the end come."*

(4) Their CONDITION – *"stood before the throne, and before the Lamb, clothed with white robes, and palms in their hands"*

This statement that says they *"stood before the throne and before the Lamb"* might possibly indicate that they may have died as martyrs and may be the ones mentioned in Revelation 6:11 – *"until their fellow-servants also and their brethren, that should be killed as they were, should be fulfilled."*

The palm branches in their hands picture a common Jewish practice of victory and rejoicing. A similar event was done at the triumphal entrance of our Lord into Jerusalem according to John 12:12-13:

"On the next day much people that were come to the feast, when they heard that Jesus was coming to Jerusalem, Took branches of palm trees, and went forth to meet Him, and cried, Hosanna: Blessed is the King of Israel that cometh in the Name of the Lord."

The **PRAISE** of heaven
Revelation 7:11-12

"And all the angels stood round about the throne, and about the elders and the four beasts, and fell before the throne on their faces, and worshipped God, Saying, Amen: Blessing, and glory, and wisdom, and thanksgiving, and honor, and power, and might, be unto our God forever and ever. Amen."

The statement that *"all the angels"* were standing around the throne with *"the elders"* – clearly determines that the 24 elders cannot be angels.

The <u>PROBLEM</u> with their identity
Revelation 7:13-14

"And one of the elders answered, saying unto me, What are these which are arrayed in white robes? And whence came they? And I said unto him, Sir, thou knowest. And he said to me, These are they which came out of great tribulation, and have washed their robes, and made them white in the blood of the Lamb."

The words *"which came out of great tribulation"* clearly separates these believers from any other group of saved people throughout human history. They are unique to the tribulation period. Yet, salvation is the same in the tribulation as it is today! They are in heaven because their robes have been washed and made white in the blood of the Lamb. Hebrews 9:22 says that *"without the shedding of blood there is no remission* (forgiveness)*."* We are saved by the blood of Jesus Christ which paid for our sins – all of them! There is only one gospel – the gospel of the death and resurrection of our Lord Yeshua!

Does this passage teach that people who do not receive the gospel in this life will have a "second chance" to believe it in the tribulation? Many Bible teachers hold this view, however, before we agree, we need to read carefully the words of II Thessalonians 2:10-12:

"And with all deceivableness of unrighteousness in them that perish; because they received not the love of the truth, that they might be saved. And for this cause God shall send them strong delusion, that they should believe a lie: That they all might be damned who believed not the truth, but had pleasure in unrighteousness."

The passage is speaking about the deception of the Antichrist, the lawless one, who will work miracles through the efforts and power of Satan. The ones who will be deceived are *"them that perish."* The reason given is *"because they received not the love of the truth, that they might be saved."* It appears that those who hear the gospel now, but do not respond to it are not going to receive it during the tribulation period either. God will see to it. He will send them *"strong delusion"* that they should believe the list of the Antichrist.

This seems to imply that the multitude of believers who come out of every nation are those who have never heard the gospel of Jesus Christ or been given a chance to respond to it.

The **PROMISES** of God to this multitude
Revelation 7:15-17

"Therefore are they before the throne of God, and serve Him day and night in His temple: and He that sitteth on the throne shall dwell among them. They shall hunger no more, neither thirst any more; neither shall the sun light on them, nor any heat.

For the Lamb which is in the midst of the throne shall feed them, and shall lead them unto living fountains of waters: and God shall wipe away all tears from their eyes."

WHAT A WONDERFUL DAY THAT WILL BE!

1. God promises them a special **PLACE**!

They will be *"before the throne of God."* What wonderful assurance of God's very presence – *"He that sitteth on the throne shall dwell among them."*

This is not only a place of God's presence, but it is a place of service – *"serve Him day and night in His temple."* The new city, the holy Jerusalem, has no temple according to Revelation 21:22. This temple could be a symbolic term for the worship of heaven or a literal temple in heaven or the one that will be set up on earth during the millennial reign of Jesus Christ!

We also learn in Revelation 21:25 that there is no night in the new Jerusalem. But, we read that they serve the Lord *"day and night."* That is simply written for our benefit and means "unending service" or it could refer to their service for the Messiah during the millennium on earth, which, of course, follows the tribulation period out of which they will come.

2. God promises them complete **PROTECTION**!

Revelation 7:16 – *"They shall hunger no more, neither thirst any more; neither shall the sun light on them, nor any heat."*

This promise is found in Isaiah 49:10: *"They shall not hunger nor thirst; neither shall the heat nor sun smite them: for He that hath mercy on them shall lead them, even by the springs of water shall He guide them."*

Psalm 121:1-8 adds wonderful words of God's future protection: *"I will lift up mine eyes unto the hills, from whence cometh my help. My help cometh from the LORD, which made heaven and earth. He will not suffer thy foot to be moved: He that keepeth thee shall not slumber, Behold, He that keepeth Israel shall neither slumber nor sleep. The LORD is thy keeper: the LORD is thy shade upon thy right hand. The sun shall not smite thee by day, nor the moon by night. The LORD shall preserve thee from all evil: He shall preserve thy soul. The LORD shall preserve thy going out and thy coming in from this time forth, and ever for evermore."*

3. God promises them eternal <u>PEACE</u>!

Revelation 7:17 – *"For the Lamb which is in the midst of the throne shall feed them, and shall lead them unto living fountains of waters: and God shall wipe away all tears from their eyes."*

These words remind us of the beautiful and peaceful message of the Shepherd of Israel, our blessed Lord!

Psalm 23:1-6 – *"The LORD is my Shepherd; I shall not want. He maketh me to lie down in green pastures: He leadeth me beside the still waters. He restoreth my soul: He leadeth me in the paths of righteousness for His Name's sake. Yea, though I walk through the valley of the shadow of death, I will fear no evil: for Thou art with me; Thy rod and Thy staff they comfort me. Thou preparest a table before me in the presence of mine enemies: Thou anointest my head with oil; my cup runneth over. Surely goodness and mercy shall follow me all the days of my life: and I will dwell in the house of the LORD forever."*

The final words of chapter 17 say it all – *"and God shall wipe away all tears from their eyes."* Again, in Revelation 21:4 we read: *"And God shall wipe away all tears from their eyes; and there shall be no more death, neither sorrow, nor crying, neither shall there be any more pain: for the former things are passed away."*

This wonderful promise comes from Isaiah 25:8: *"He will swallow up death in victory; and the Lord GOD will wipe away tears from off all faces; and the rebuke of His people shall He take away from off all the earth: for the LORD hath spoken it."*

The presence of *"tears"* does not mean that they were shed in heaven and were then wiped away. It reflects back on our lives here on earth where we inevitably experience many tears and sorrows. The promise is that those tears will never again be present – God shall wipe all of that away forever, including death itself! HALLELUJAH!

Yes, there will be believers in the tribulation period. They will come to know the Lord during that period of time and will represent all nations and language groups of the world. They will suffer a great deal for their faith in the Lord and will be killed. But the Lord will fulfil His promises to them and to all of us who come to believe in our blessed Messiah – YESHUA HAMASHIACH!

FOUR TERRIBLE TRUMPETS
Revelation 8:1-13

The judgments of the tribulation period are found written in the scroll with seven seals which the Lamb of God took from the right hand of God the Father. The Lamb is the only one who is *"worthy"* to open the scroll and loose its seals. There are seven seals, six of which have already been opened. The seventh seal contains a rather extended message and reveals seven angels with seven trumpets. These trumpet judgments are found in the scroll after the seventh seal is broken.

The **PRELUDE** to judgment
Revelation 8:1-5

"And when He had opened the seventh seal, there was silence in heaven about the space of half an hour. And I saw the seven angels which stood before God; and to them were given seven trumpets. And another angel came and stood at the altar, having a golden censer; and there was given unto him much incense, that he should offer it with the prayers of all saints upon the golden altar which was before the throne. And the smoke of the incense, which came with the prayers of the saints, ascended up before God out of the angel's hand. And the angel took the censer, and filled it with fire of the altar, and cast it into the earth: and there were thunderings, and lightnings, and an earthquake."

1. The <u>SILENCE</u> in heaven

Revelation 8:1 – *"And when He had opened the seventh seal, there was silence in heaven about the space of half an hour."*

The silence of heaven is like the "calm before the storm." After seeing and hearing all the praise and worship of heaven, this silence is a dramatic pause and prelude to the events that would soon follow. The silence is in direct contrast to the loud voices of the great multitudes of heaven. Something unusual is about to take place – something of enormous importance.

2. The <u>SOUNDING</u> of trumpets

Revelation 8:2 – *"And I saw the seven angels which stood before God; and to them were given seven trumpets."*

Trumpets have been used often in the life of Israel. A loud trumpet was blown at Mount Sinai at the giving of the law – Exodus 19:19: *"And when the voice of the trumpet sounded long, and waxed louder and louder, Moses spake, and God answered him by a voice."*

At the celebration of the *"feasts of the LORD"* in Leviticus 23:23-25 we had the blowing of trumpets: *"And the LORD spake unto Moses, saying, Speak unto the children of Israel, saying, In the seventh month, in the first day of the month, shall ye have a*

Sabbath, a memorial of blowing of trumpets, an holy convocation. Ye shall do no servile work therein: but ye shall offer an offering made by fire unto the LORD."

We call it the "Feast of Trumpets" and also it is known as Rosh Hashanah, meaning "the beginning of the year."

Ten days after Rosh Hashanah is the celebration of Yom Kippur, the Day of Atonement. In Leviticus 25:9 we learn that a trumpet was blown on the Day of Atonement at the time of the Year of Jubilee:
"Then shalt thou cause the trumpet of the jubilee to sound on the tenth day of the seventh month, in the day of atonement shall ye make the trumpet sound throughout all your land."

According to Numbers 10:1-8 we learn of the practice in Israel of blowing the trumpets:

"And the LORD spake unto Moses, saying, Make thee two trumpets of silver; of a whole piece shalt thou make them: that thou mayest use them for the calling of the assembly, and for the journeying of the camps. And when they shall blow with them, all the assembly shall assemble themselves to thee at the door of the tabernacles of the congregation. And if they blow but with one trumpet, then the princes, which are heads of the thousands of Israel shall gather themselves unto thee. When ye blow an alarm, then the camps that lie on the east parts shall go forward. When ye blow an alarm the

second time, then the camps that lie on the south side shall take their journey: they shall blow an alarm for their journeys.   But when the congregation is to be gathered together, ye shall blow, but ye shall not sound an alarm.   And the sons of Aaron, the priests, shall blow with the trumpets; and they shall be to you for an ordinance forever throughout your generations."

The prophet Joel speaks of a trumpet being blown to sound an alarm concerning the coming of the Day of the LORD – Joel 2:1 – *"Blow ye that trumpet in Zion, and sound an alarm in My holy mountain: let all the inhabitants of the land tremble: for the day of the LORD cometh, for it is nigh at hand."*   We also read in Joel 2:15 these words: *"Blow the trumpet in Zion, sanctify a fast, call a solemn assembly."*

3.   The <u>SMOKE</u> of incense from the altar

"And another angel came and stood at the altar, having a golden censer; and there was given unto him much incense, that he should offer it with the prayers of all saints upon the golden altar which was before the throne.   And the smoke of the incense, which came with the prayers of the saints, ascended up before God out of the angel's hand. And the angel took the censer, and filled it with fire of the altar, and cast it into the earth: and there were voices, and thunderings, and lightnings, and an earthquake."

IS THIS ANGEL A PICTURE OF JESUS CHRIST?
While some prophecy teachers say so, it would appear to us that this is impossible for the following reasons:

(1)   Jesus Christ as the Lamb of God is the One who opens the scroll.

(2)   John is rebuked in Revelation 22:8-9 for trying to worship an angel; Hebrews 1:6 says of Jesus Christ: *"Let all the angels of God worship Him."*

(3)   The mention of the seven angels in verse 2 seems to govern the mention of *"another angel"* in verse 3.   The Greek word for *"another"* means "another of the same kind" and is a strong grammatical factor for concluding the this is an angel just like the seven mentioned in verse 2.

(4)   While the phrase *"the Angel of the LORD"* seems to be a description of the Messiah in the Old Testament, there is no evidence in the New Testament that the word *"angel"* ever refers to Jesus Christ.   In fact, the exact opposite is implied.

WHAT IS MEANT BY THE "OFFERING OF INCENSE" ON A HEAVENLY GOLDEN ALTAR?

It is a beautiful reminder of an Old Testament practice. Every morning and evening the priests would use a golden censer to put incense on the altar of incense in front of the second veil of the tabernacle or temple. Behind this veil was the Holy of Holies into which only the High Priest could go once a year on the Day of Atonement. The Lord told Moses in Exodus 30:6: *"And thou shalt put it before the veil that is by the ark of the testimony before the mercy seat that is over the testimony, where I will meet with thee."*

The role of the priest is to offer the prayers of the people to God. The smoke of the incense burning on the altar was a picture of prayer rising to God. According to Revelation 8:3, this incense represents the *"prayers of all the saints upon the golden altar which was before the throne."*

The altar here is described as being *"the golden altar which was before the throne."* It seems unlikely that this special altar and its special place would be an altar of sacrifice. More likely, it is a beautiful fulfillment of the altar of incense which God commanded the Jews to build for worship in the tabernacle and temple. An altar in heaven is mentioned seven times in Revelation 6:9; 8:3 (twice); 8:5; 9:13; 14:18; 16:7.

Revelation 8:4 says of the incense that represented the *"prayers of the saints"* – it *"ascended up before God out of the angel's hand."* The angel then *"filled it* (the censer) *with fire of the altar, and cast it into the earth; and there were voices, and thunderings, and lightnings, and an earthquake."* God's authority and power is behind these trumpet judgments. When the earthquake happens (after the one in Revelation 6:12-17) the inhabitants of earth would be filled with fear and anxiety as another one comes, causing them to wonder that terrible judgments must be on the verge of happening again!

The **PUNISHMENT** of the four trumpets
Revelation 8:6-12

"And the seven angels which had the seven trumpets prepare themselves to sound. The first angel sounded, and there followed hail and fire mingled with blood, and they were cast upon the earth: and the third part of trees was burnt up, and all green grass was burnt up. And the second angel sounded, and as it were a great mountain burning with fire was cast into the sea: and the third part of the sea became blood; and the third part of the creatures which were in the sea, and had life, died; and the third part of the ships were destroyed. And the third angel sounded, and there fell a great star from heaven, burning as it were a lamp, and it fell upon the third part of the rivers, and upon the fountains of waters; And the name of the star is called Wormwood: and the third part of the waters became wormwood; and many men died of the waters, because they were made bitter. And the fourth angel sounded, and the third part of the sun was smitten, and the third part of the moon, and

the third part of the stars; so as the third part of them was darkened, and the day shone not for a third part of it, and the night likewise."

TRUMPET JUDGMENT #1 – trees and grass burned up!

Revelation 8:7 – *"The first angel sounded, and there followed hail and fire mingled with blood, and they were cast upon the earth: and the third part of trees were burnt up, and all green grass was burnt up."*

A judgment such as this would have enormous effect upon the quality of life and available food supplies. Trees not only produce food, they are essential protection from violent storms and flooding. This verse predicts that one-third of all trees on the planet are destroyed by this judgment. It is difficult to imagine what this might mean for human life and survival!

This judgment is similar to what happened to Egypt at the time of Moses. Exodus 9:22-26:

"And the LORD said unto Moses, Stretch forth thine hand toward heaven, that there may hail in all the land of Egypt, upon man, and upon beast, and upon every herb of the field, throughout the land of Egypt. And Moses stretched forth his rod toward heaven: and the LORD sent thunder and hail, and the fire ran along upon the ground; and the LORD rained hail upon the land of Egypt. So there was

hail, and fire mingled with the hail, very grievous, such as there was none like it in all the land of Egypt since it became a nation. And the hail smote throughout all the land of Egypt all that was in the field, both man and beast; and the hail smote every herb of the field, and brake every tree of the field. Only in the land of Goshen, where the children of Israel were, was there no hail."

TRUMPET JUDGMENT #2 – sea life and ships destroyed!

At the beginning of the plagues in Egypt, the water of the Nile River was turned into blood. Something similar is happening in this future judgment.

1. One-third of the Sea becomes blood!

Revelation 8:8-9 – *"And the second angel sounded, and as it were a great mountain burning with fire was cast into the sea: and the third part of the sea became blood. And the third part of the creatures which were in the sea, and had life, died; and the third part of the ships were destroyed."*

What did John see when he spoke of *"a great mountain burning with fire was cast into the sea"*? Some suggest a giant meteor and others suggest a nuclear or atomic explosion. The words *"the sea"* include the definite article, and therefore, it probably refers to the Mediterranean Sea. The fact that the entire Mediterranean Sea becomes blood, one can only imagine what will happen to animal life as well as human life.

2. One-third of sea life is killed!

The Mediterranean Sea is filled with fish, and supplies the food needs of many countries and people. This particular disaster will have a serious effect upon the people of the world, especially those who live in countries dependent upon the fishing industry in the Mediterranean Sea.

Hosea 4:3 predicts: *"Therefore shall the land mourn, and every one that dwelleth therein shall languish, with the beasts of the field, and with the fowls of heaven; yea, the fishes of the sea also shall be taken away."*

Zephaniah 1:2-3 adds: *"I will utterly consume all things from off the land, saith the LORD. I will consume man and beast; I will consume the fowls of the heaven, and the fishes of the sea, and the stumbling blocks with the wicked: and I will cut off man from off the land, saith the LORD."*

3. One-third of the ships are destroyed!

This particular tragedy becomes more significant when a person studies the presence of naval vessels in the Mediterranean Sea. Flying over this area, one can see from the plane the multitude of naval and shipping vessels that locate themselves in this Sea. It is covered with ships including many cruise ships carrying thousands of people. As a result of this disaster, many people will be killed.

TRUMPET JUDGMENT #3 – rivers and springs made bitter!

Revelation 8:10-11 – *"And the third angel sounded, and there fell a great star from heaven, burning as it were a lamp, and it fell upon the third part of the rivers, and upon the fountains of waters; And the name of the star is called Wormwood: and the third part of the waters became wormwood; and many men died of the waters, because they were made bitter."*

Most Bible prophecy teachers believe that this *"great star"* is a giant meteor. That may be the truth, but the consequence of it is certainly unusual. The name *"Wormwood"* is associated in the Bible with bitterness. Lamentations 3:15 says: *"He hath filled me with bitterness, he hath made me drunken with wormwood."* Amos 5:7 also mentions it – *"Ye who turn judgment to wormwood, and leave off righteousness in the earth."*

It is connected strongly with the LORD's judgment in Jeremiah 9:13-16:

"And the LORD saith, Because they have forsaken My law which I set before them, and have not obeyed My voice, neither walked therein; But have walked after the imagination of their own heart, and after Baalim, which their fathers taught them:

Therefore thus saith the LORD of hosts, the God of Israel; Behold, I will feed them, even this people, with wormwood, and give them water of gall to drink. I will scatter them also among the heathen, whom neither they nor their fathers have known: and I will send a sword after them, till I have consumed them."

Again, in Jeremiah 23:15: *"Therefore thus saith the LORD of hosts concerning the prophets; Behold, I will feed them with wormwood, and make them drink the water of gall: for from the prophets of Jerusalem is profaneness gone forth into all the land."*

Wormwood is God's judgment upon those who disobey Him. Its bitter taste suggests death. This terrible disaster will affect the water supply of the planet and bring about the death of many people. We all need water; it is basic to human survival. One can only imagine what sort of additional tragedies will occur because of the terrible pollution caused by this third trumpet judgment.

TRUMPET JUDGMENT #4 – sun, moon, and stars darkened

Revelation 8:12 – *"And the fourth angel sounded, and the third part of the sun was smitten, and the third part of the moon, and the third part of the stars; so as the third part of them was darkened, and the day shone not for a third part of it, and the night likewise."*

The problems arising from this judgment extend to many areas of life that we take for granted. One needs only to experience darkness over an extended period of time in order to appreciate the light. Several years ago my wife was confined to a darkened room for about ten weeks due to an infection of her face and eyes. Her appreciation of light, especially the light of the sun on a clear day, became very important to her.

The sources of light in this universe are all struck by this judgment. God clearly shows us that they are also dependent upon His power and control. The sun, moon, and stars have consistently been used in pagan religions as objects of worship. This judgment will reveal that only God Himself is to be worshipped. This judgment reminds us of what happened in Egypt long ago. We read in Exodus 10:21-23 the following:

"And the LORD said unto Moses, Stretch out thine hand toward heaven, that there may be darkness over the land of Egypt, even darkness which may be felt. And Moses stretched forth his hand toward heaven; and there was a thick darkness in all the land of Egypt three days: They saw not one another, neither rose any from his place for three days: but all the children of Israel had light in their dwellings."

The **PROCLAMATION** of a flying angel
Revelation 8:13

"And I beheld, and heard an angel flying through the midst of heaven, saying with a loud voice, Woe, woe, woe, to the inhabiters of the earth by reason of the other voices of the trumpet of the three angels, which are yet to sound!

Some expositors believe that the translation here should read *"eagle"* instead of *"flying angel."* There are manuscript variations on this verse. However, the evidence supports the reading of the King James Version of the Bible. After all, the Bible supports the use of angels in announcing God's plans – why do we need an exception here?

The word *"woe"* (mentioned 3 times describing three more trumpet judgments) is one of those unique words whose sound indicates its meaning. It is a warning of what is to come. The last three trumpet judgments are more severe than the first four.

These judgments will fall upon *"the inhabitants of the earth"* – a term that often refers to unbelievers who take the mark of the beast and do not repent of their deeds.

DEMONIC ATTACK
Revelation 9:1-21

TRUMPET JUDGMENT #5 – locusts that come out of Hell!
Revelation 9:1-11

"And the fifth angel sounded, and I saw a star fall from heaven unto the earth: and to him was given the key of the bottomless pit. And he opened the bottomless pit; and there arose a smoke out of the pit, as the smoke of a great furnace; and the sun and the air were darkened by reason of the smoke of the pit. And there came out of the smoke locusts upon the earth: and unto them was given power, as the scorpions of the earth have power. And it was commanded them that they should not hurt the grass of the earth, neither any green thing, neither any tree; but only those men which have not the seal of God in their foreheads. And to them it was given that they should not kill them, but that they should be tormented five months: and their torment was as the torment of a scorpion, when he striketh a man. And in those days shall men seek death, and shall not find it; and shall desire to die, and death shall flee from them. And the shapes of the locusts were like unto horses prepared unto battle; and on their heads were as it were crowns like gold, and their faces were as the faces of men. And they had hair as the hair of women, and their teeth were as the teeth of lions. And they had breastplates, as it were breastplates of iron; and

the sound of their wings was as the sound of chariots of many horses running to battle. And they had tails like unto scorpions, and there were stings in their tails: and their power was to hurt men five months. And they had a king over them, which is the angel of the bottomless pit, whose name in the Hebrew tongue is Abaddon, but in the Greek tongue hath his name Apollyon."

It is possible that the Apostle John, writing in the first century AD, uses symbols and illustrations from his knowledge and experiences in describing the terrible judgments that would come on planet earth in the future. As a Jewish leader, and well acquainted with the history of Israel and the messages of the prophets, he, no doubt, thought of the prophet Joel's predictions. In Joel 1:1-6 we read of a locust plague that is coming in the future:

"The word of the LORD that came to Joel the son of Pethuel. Hear this, ye old men, and give ear, all ye inhabitants of the land. Hath this been in your days, or even in the days of your fathers? Tell ye your children of it, and let your children tell their children, and their children another generation. That which the palmerworm hath left hath the locust eaten; and that which the locust hath left hath the cankerworm eaten; and that which the cankerworm hath left hath the caterpillar eaten. Awake, ye drunkards, and weep; and howl, all ye drinkers of wine, because of the new wine, for it is cut off from your mouth. For a nation is come up upon My land, strong, and without number, whose *teeth are the teeth of a lion, and he hath the cheek teeth of a great lion."*

The <u>LEADER</u> of the locusts
Revelation 9:1-2, 11

"And the fifth angel sounded, and I saw a star fall from heaven unto the earth: and to him was given the key of the bottomless pit. And he opened the bottomless pit; and there arose a smoke out of the pit, as the smoke of a great furnace; and the sun and the air were darkened by reason of the smoke of the pit.

"And they had a king over them, which is the angel of the bottomless pit, whose name in the Hebrew tongue is Abaddon, but in the Greek tongue hath his name Apollyon."

His <u>POSITION</u>

1. He is the star that fell from heaven to the earth!

2. He is the angel of the bottomless pit!
   Revelation 9:11

3. He is the king of the locusts!
   Revelation 9:11

4. He loses his access to heaven!
Revelation 9:1 – *"I saw a star fall from heaven unto the earth"*

His removal from access to heaven where he has been accusing believers day and night – Revelation 12:7-10 gives the details:

"And there was war in heaven: Michael and his angels fought against the dragon; and the dragon fought and his angels, and prevailed not; neither was their place found any more in heaven. And the great dragon was cast out, that old serpent, called the Devil, and Satan, which deceiveth the whole world: he was cast out into the earth, and his angels were cast out with him. And I heard a loud voice saying in heaven, Now is come salvation, and strength, and the kingdom of ur God, and the power of His Christ: for the accuser of our brethren is cast down, which accused them before our God day and night."

According to Job 1:6-7 Satan has had access to God in heaven where he continues to accuse believers throughout history: *"Now there was a day when the sons of God* (fallen angels) *came to present themselves before the LORD, and Satan came also among them. And the LORD said unto Satan, Whence comest thou? Then Satan answered the LORD, and said, From going to and fro in the earth, and from walking up and down in it."* That day of his access will come to an end during the tribulation. Remember that Satan is not the king of

Hell, but rather its chief prisoner. Matthew 25:41 quotes our Lord Yeshua as saying: *"Depart from Me, ye cursed, into everlasting fire, prepared for the devil and his angels."*

His <u>POWER</u>

The power of Satan is definitely limited. He is not omnipresent – he cannot be everywhere at once, but through the angels that sinned and morally fell with him, it appears that his kingdom is quite extensive on planet earth.

1. A key was given to him!

This clearly shows that his power is limited and controlled by Almighty God. According to Revelation 1:18 our Lord Yeshua has *"the keys of Hell and death."* However, the key that unlocks the chains of those demonic spirits in the bottomless pit (literally – the abyss) was given to Satan. He obviously did not have it in his control. God is using Satan to accomplish His purposes on planet earth.

Luke 16:22-26 tells a few details about the place we call "Hell" (Greek term – Hades):

"And it came to pass, that the beggar (Lazarus) died, and was carried by the angels into Abraham's bosom: the rich man also died, and was buried; and in Hell (Hades) he lift up his eyes, being in torments, and seeth Abraham afar off, and Lazarus in his bosom. And he cried and said, Father Abraham, have mercy on me, and send Lazarus,

that he may dip the tip of his finger in water, and cool my tongue; for I am tormented in this flame. But Abraham said, Son, remember that thou in thy lifetime receivedst thy good things, and likewise Lazarus evil things: but now he is comforted, and thou art tormented. And beside all this, between us and you there is a great gulf fixed: so that they which would pass from hence to you cannot; neither can they pass to us, that would come from thence."

II Peter 2:4 tells us: *"For if God spared not the angels that sinned, but cast them down to hell (Greek word: Tartaros), and delivered them into chains of darkness, to be reserved unto judgment."*

It is fascinating to notice what Revelation 11:7 says about the coming *"beast"* (Antichrist): *"And when they shall have finished their testimony, the beast that ascendeth out of the bottomless pit shall make war against them, and shall overcome them, and kill them."* The Antichrist comes out of the Abyss, the bottomless pit, a place of eternal torment!

2. He is the king of the locusts!

Revelation 9:11 says: *"And they had a king over them, which is the angel of the bottomless pit, whose name in the Hebrew tongue is Abaddon, but in the Greek tongue hath his name Apollyon."*

One of the reasons for believing that this locust plague is not referring to actual locusts is that they have a king over them. Proverbs 30:27 says: *"The locusts have no king, yet go they forth all of them by bands."* Scientists tell us that what drives them is no locust leader, but the wind currents.

We need to be careful, however, not to underestimate the power of Satan. He controls a vast empire of wicked spirits and through them affects the lives of millions of people. We don't know how many demons there are. The word *"legion"* is used in one case where a man was possessed by demons. That word refers to at least 6000 evil spirits! Revelation 12:4 speaks of the *"tail"* of Satan that he used to draw a third of all the angels of heaven with him when he was cast to the earth."

His <u>PURPOSE</u>

Revelation 9:11 gives a clue to what his motives are as the Bible tells us that his name in Hebrew is Abaddon, and in Greek it is Apollyon. These words refer to "the destroyer." Satan is out to ruin people's lives! I Peter 5:8 says: *"Be sober, be vigilant; because your adversary the devil, as a roaring lion, walketh about, seeking whom he may devour."*

The <u>LOOK</u> of the locusts
Revelation 9:3-10

    1. Their <u>AUTHORITY</u>

In Revelation 9:3 we read: *"and unto them was given power, as the scorpions of the earth have power."*

Revelation 9:5 adds: *"And to them it was given that they should not kill them, but that they should be tormented five months: and their torment was as the torment of a scorpion, when he striketh a man."*

Revelation 9:10 says: *"And they had tails like unto scorpions, and there were stings in their tails: and their power was to hurt men five months."*

(1) As to <u>TIME</u> – they had *"five months"* to torment humanity!

(2) As to the <u>TARGETS</u> – they are not allowed to *"hurt the grass of the earth, neither any green thing, neither any tree; but only those men which have not the seal of God in their foreheads."*

(3) As to <u>TORMENT</u> – *"their torment was as the torment of a scorpion, when he striketh a man"*

While a scorpion sting is usually not fatal (though children often die from such a sting!), it is very painful. The venom affects the veins and the nervous system. Normally such pain and discomfort last for several days. This plague will be far more intense and serious. Revelation 9:6 says: *"and in those days shall men seek death, and shall* not find it; and shall desire to die, and death shall flee from them."

2. Their <u>APPEARANCE</u>

Needless to say, their appearance is unlike that of normal locusts. Revelation 9:7-9 describes them:

"And the shapes of the locusts were like unto horses prepared unto battle; and on their heads were as it were crowns like gold, and their faces were as the faces of men. And they had hair as the hair of women, and their teeth were as the teeth of lions. And they had breastplates, as it were breastplates of iron; and the sound of their wings was as the sound of chariots of many horses running to battle."

Joel 2:4-11 gives a bit of background on this awful attack by demonic forces:

"The appearance of them is as the appearance of horses; and as horsemen, so shall they run. Like the noise of chariots on the tops of mountains shall they leap, like the noise of a flame of fire that devoureth the stubble, as a strong people set in battle array. Before their face the people shall be much pained: all faces shall gather blackness. They shall run like mighty men; they shall climb the wall like men of war; and they shall march every one on his ways, and they shall not break their ranks: Neither shall one thrust another; they shall walk every one in his path: and when they fall

upon the sword, they shall not be wounded. They shall run to and fro in the city; they shall run upon the wall, they shall climb up upon the houses; they shall enter in at the windows like a thief. The earth shall quake before them; the heavens shall tremble: the sun and the moon shall be dark, and the stars shall withdraw their shining: And the LORD shall utter His voice before His army: for His camp is very great and very terrible; and who can abide it?"

Incredible – giving us a greater idea of this demonic plague of Revelation 9 that is coming upon planet earth!

THIS IS ONLY THE BEGINNING!
Revelation 9:12

"One woe is past; and, behold, there come two woes more hereafter."

TRUMPET JUDGMENT #6 – the army that will kill one-third of the world's population!
Revelation 9:13-21

Many Bible scholars and prophecy teachers believe that Trumpet Judgments #5 and #6 are describing the same event. However, verse 12 suggests the opposite. The sixth trumpet judgment is another "woe" like the 5th judgment, but distinct from it. The verse ends with the words – *"two woes more hereafter"* of *"after these things."*

In the 5th trumpet judgment humanity is being tormented for five months;   in the 6th trumpet judgment one-third of the world's population is killed – quite a difference!

The **CONTROL** of this army
Revelation 9:13-15

"And the sixth angel sounded, and I heard a voice from the four horns of the golden altar which is before God, Saying to the sixth angel which had the trumpet, Loose the four angels which are bound in the great river Euphrates.   And the four angels were loosed, which were prepared for an hour, and a day, and a month, and a year, for to slay the third part of men."

The fallen angels (also called *"evil spirits"* and/or *"demons"*) are under the control of God Himself. Consider at least three things that reveal this control:

1. The **PRONOUNCEMENT** that is made!

"and I heard a voice from the four horns of the golden altar which is before God." Some Bible teachers believe that this is the same angel as Revelation 8:3 where we read: *"And another angel came and stood at the altar, having a golden censer."* Some believe that it is one of the four "cherubim" angels who are the worship leaders of heaven. But, it is also possible that this is the voice of God Himself.   Revelation 9:13 says that the

"voice" came from the *"four horns of the golden altar which is before God."* If it was simply another angel we would probably read *"before God's throne."* Without that wording, it leaves us with a strong belief that it is the voice of God Himself in this pronouncement.

2. The <u>PLACE</u> where the army is bound!

Revelation 9:14 reads: *"Loose the four angels which are bound in the great river Euphrates."* The fact that this army is *"bound"* emphasizes the authority and control of God over them. These *"four angels"* are not the four worship leaders of heaven or any of God's holy angels, for they are not *"bound."* According to the Bible it is the *"wicked angels"* or *"demons"* that are bound (II Peter 2:4; Jude 6-7).

The river Euphrates was one of the four rivers which came out of the Garden of Eden. Since it was the place of Satan's original deception of Adam and Eve, it is possible that God has kept these demons in check there as a reminder of the original evil that Satan brought into the world.

Another possibility is its connection with Babylon and the symbolism of Revelation 17:5 – *"And upon her forehead was a name written, MYSTERY, BABYLON THE GREAT, THE MOTHER OF HARLOTS AND ABOMINATIONS OF THE EARTH."* According to Revelation 18:2: *"Babylon the great is fallen, is fallen, and is become the habitation of devils, and the hold of every foul spirit, and a cage of every unclean and hateful bird."*

The Euphrates River is also the natural boundary between the lands of the Far East and the Middle East, Europe, and the western nations. Perhaps this is the connection to the killing of one-third of the world's population by this demonic army. The size of the army might indicate the nations of the Far East in this number. We simply do not know, nor do we have any additional information.

3. The **PREPARATION** of this army!

Verse 15 says: *"And the four angels were loosed, which were prepared for an hour, and a day, and a month, and a year, for to slay the third part of men."*

Demons operate under God's authority and time schedules. These demonic forces are prepared by God at some point in past history and are now being used by God to fulfil His purposes in the judgment of planet earth. Again, God's timing and providential control of all things, including Satan and the world of demons, is clearly indicated.

At the 4th seal judgment in Revelation 6:8 we learned that the *"fourth part of the earth"* would be killed. We also read in Revelation 8:11 that *"many men died of the waters, because they were made bitter."* Now we read that this demonic army will be responsible for killing one-third of the world.

Putting this all together, if the world's population stands at eight billion people, then one-fourth is killed (that would be about 2 billion people) and then many more (no number given) by the bitter waters – now one-third more are killed by the demonic army – (another 2 billion people) – that means that even though there are more plagues to come on planet earth, already by the sixth trumpet judgment over one half of the world's population is killed (could be four billion people – incredible!).

The **CHARACTERISTICS** of this army
Revelation 9:16-17

"And the number of the army of the horsemen were two hundred thousand thousand; and I heard the number of them. And thus I saw the horses in the vision, and them that sat on them, having breastplates of fire, and of jacinth, and brimstone: and the heads of the horses were as the heads of lions; and out of their mouths issued fire and smoke and brimstone."

1. The **SIZE** of this army

Revelation 9:16 – *"and the number of the army of the horsemen were two hundred thousand thousand: and I heard the number of them."*

The size of this army is incredible – 200,000,000! It is possible that the number is not to be taken literally but simply suggests an army that is impossible to count and is greater than anything humanity has ever seen! However, there is no reason to take any other viewpoint than this is a literal army of that size!

2. The <u>SYMBOLISM</u> of this army

Revelation 9:17 – *"And thus I saw the horses in the vision, and them that sat on them, having breastplates of fire, and of jacinth, and brimstone: and the heads of the horses were as the heads of lions; and out of their mouths issued fire and smoke and brimstone."*

This description does not say *"like horses."* It says *"I saw the horses in the vision."* There are no symbolic words either when describing their *"breastplates"* of *"mouths."* However, it does say that the *"heads of the horses were <u>as</u> the heads of lions."* Also, in verse 19 we read that *"their tails were <u>like</u> unto serpents."*

So, what is being described – we simply do not know; Many Bible teachers believe that the passage is describing military machines or weapons of war. After all, verse 17 says that out of their *"mouths, issue fire and smoke and brimstone."*

The <u>CONSEQUENCES</u> of this demonic attack
Revelation 9:18-21

"By these three was the third part of men killed, by the fire, and by the smoke, and by the brimstone, which issued out of their mouths. For their power

is in their mouth, and in their tails: for their tails were like unto serpents, and had heads, and with them they do hurt. And the rest of the men which were not killed by these plagues yet repented not of the works of their hands, that they should not worship devils, and idols of gold, and silver, and brass, and stone, and of wood: which neither can see, nor hear, nor walk; neither repented they of their murders, nor of their sorceries, nor of their fornication, nor of their thefts."

Needless to say, these consequences reveal the enormity of this attack – planet earth will be devastated by it and millions will die!

1. The **PLAGUES** bring death to one-third of the population of planet earth!

Three things come out of their *"mouths"* – *"fire"* and *"smoke"* and *"brimstone."* It is highly possible that we are looking at military weapons of war. All peace attempts that may be promoted in our world and may be prevalent at the beginning of the tribulation period, will not last! It is not money or treaties that need to be signed; the problem is in the human heart – that must be changed, and that takes the power of the gospel of Jesus Christ!

2. The **POWER** of this attack will result in unbelievable human death and tragedy!

Verse 19 says *"For their power is in their mouth, and in their tails, for their tails were like unto serpents, and had heads, and with them they do hurt.*

It appears that in addition to the death of millions, there will be serious hurt upon humanity because of their power.

    3. Their wicked <u>PRACTICES</u> do not stop or change!

Revelation 9:20-21 – *"And the rest of the men which were not killed by these plagues yet repented not of the works of their hands, that they should not worship devils, and idols of gold, and silver, and brass, and stone, and of wood: which neither can see, nor hear, nor walk; Neither repented they of their murders, nor of their sorceries, nor of their fornication, nor of their thefts."*

What an indictment of human belief and behavior! Two things are brought to our attention:

    (1)   The <u>WORSHIP</u> of demons and idols

Humanity was designed by the Creator to worship Him and His Messiah, the Lamb of God. If we don't do that, we will invent our own forms of worship – demons and idols.

Romans 1:18-23 speaks clearly of what will happen if we ignore and turn away from the worship of Almighty God:

"For the wrath of God is revealed from heaven against all ungodliness and unrighteousness of men, who hold (suppress) the truth in unrighteousness; Because that which may be known of God is manifest in them; for God hath shewed it unto them. For the invisible things of Him from the creation of the world are clearly seen, being understood by the things that are made, even His eternal power and Godhead; so that they are without excuse: Because that, when they knew God, they glorified Him not as God, neither were thankful; but became vain in their imaginations, and their foolish heart was darkened. Professing themselves to be wise, they became fools, and changed the glory of the uncorruptible God into an image made like to corruptible man, and to birds, and to fourfooted beasts, and creeping things."

The above passage clearly reveals the problem – when we don't worship God, we will substitute the worship of what our own minds and hands have designed!

(2)   The <u>WICKEDNESS</u> that results from the lack of repentance!

Verse 21 says: *"Neither repented they of their murders, nor of their sorceries, nor of their fornication, nor of their thefts."*

MURDERS – Violent crime continues to be portrayed and promoted in movies, television,

Internet, books, magazines and newspapers. It almost seems that the producers of such media have decided that this is what the public wants to see and hear. They are appealing to the depravity of the human heart. The random killing of people without reason appears to be dominating our culture. Ideas as to the causes behind all this violence continue to be discussed and debated, but nothing seems to stop it.

In addition of the killing of people on our streets and in our schools, our culture tolerates the most terrible of all such crimes – the murder of the unborn!

The horrible sin of abortion has taken the lives of millions of children before they ever had the chance to see life outside of their mothers' wombs. The blood of such innocent children is on the hands of an unrepentant generation.

SORCERIES – This is not referring simply to fascination and involvement with occultic practices, although that is certainly a part of it. Horoscopes, palm reading, astrology, tarot cards, etc. are certainly forms of sorcery. However, the Greek word indicates the use of drugs which has become a worldwide tragedy. In spite of law enforcement efforts and agencies designed to combat the spread and use of drugs in our society, drugs continue to destroy the lives of millions, to the profit of the few who market and distribute them.

FORNICATION – the Greek word is referring to sexual sin, and refers to all kinds of sex outside of the marriage of husband and wife. Hebrews 13:4 says: *"Marriage is honorable in all, and the bed (coitus) undefiled: but whoremongers and adulterers God will judge."*

No sin so captures and controls our lives as that of sexual immorality. It is treated so lightly today in spite of the danger of sexually-transmitted diseases. We continue to encourage and tolerate the display of immorality, and our children and young people are often the targets of such promotion.

THEFTS – Stealing is a national and international problem that is literally out of control. Police must often look the other way because they cannot handle all of the reported cases. We now talk of serious theft versus harmless or petty theft. Is there really a difference? Of course not.

Stealing is wrong even if involves a pencil or pen that does not belong to you. Stealing a bicycle is the same sin as stealing a car. It is just as wrong for a child to steal a few coins or dollars from his parents as it is for an executive to embezzle funds from the company for which he works.

The clear fact of a culture heading for disaster and the judgment of God is our lack repentance before God for what we have done. May God open our eyes before it is too late!

THE LITTLE BOOK
Revelation 10:1-11

After describing six terrible trumpet judgments which result in millions of people being killed, John is given a vision of a mighty angel with a little book that prepares him for what is yet ahead. The seventh trumpet is sounded apparently at the middle of the tribulation period and its message contains all the events that remain.

The original scroll (Revelation 5:1) was sealed with seven seals. Each of those seals had now been broken by Jesus Christ and the message unveiled for all to read. The seventh seal introduced us to seven trumpets (Revelation 8:1-2), and we are now looking at the seventh trumpet which contains the longest message of all. It will cover the last three and a half years of the tribulation period, the most awful holocaust of terror, suffering, violence, and catastrophe the world has ever seen!

Matthew 24:21 quotes the words of our Lord Yeshua when He said: *"For then shall be great tribulation, such as was not since the beginning of the world to this time, no, nor ever shall be."*

The <u>APPEARANCE</u> of a mighty angel
Revelation 10:1-4

"And I saw another mighty angel come down from heaven, clothed with a cloud: and a rainbow was upon his head, and his face was as it were the sun,

and his feet as pillars of fire: And he had in his hand a little book (scroll) open: and he set his right foot upon the sea, and his left foot on the earth, and cried with a loud voice, as when a lion roareth: and when he had cried, seven thunders uttered their voices. And when the seven thunders had uttered their voices, I was about to write: and I heard a voice from heaven saying unto me, Seal up those things which the seven thunders uttered, and write them not."

1. The <u>IDENTITY</u> of this angel

In the Book of Revelation, angels are angels, not symbols of events, things, places, or other persons. Some Bible teachers argue that this *"mighty angel"* is none other than Jesus Christ. Jehovah Witnesses teach that Jesus Christ is Michael the Archangel, but that cannot be true. All the angels of God are told to worship Jesus Christ in Hebrews 1:6: *"And again, when He bringeth in the first begotten into the world, He saith, And let all the angels of God worship Him."*

We are strictly forbidden to worship angels in Revelation 22:8-9: *"And I John saw these things and heard them. And when I had heard and seen, I fell down to worship before the feet of the angel which shewed me these things. Then saith he unto me, See thou do it not: for I am thy fellow-servant, and of thy brethren the prophets, and of them which keep the sayings to this book: worship God."*

This angel is identified with the following unusual characteristics:

(1)　He came down *"from heaven"*

(2)　He was *"clothed with a cloud"*

(3)　A *"rainbow was upon his head"*

(4)　His *"face was as it were the sun"*

(5)　His *"feet as pillars of fire"*

It is quite understandable that people would believe that this is none other than our Lord Jesus Christ Himself. There are similarities between the above descriptions and the ones of our Savior in Revelation 1. But, is this Jesus Christ? Our answer is an emphatic "NO!"

Jesus Christ is never described as an *"angel"* in the Book of Revelation.　In dealing with His preincarnate presence in the Old Testament, the Messiah is identified as *"the angel of the LORD."* and is even called the *"LORD."*

Also, in Revelation 10:1, this *"angel"* is called *"another mighty angel."* The word *"another"* is the Greek word *allon* which means "another of the same kind." In Revelation 5:2 John say *"a strong angel proclaiming with a loud voice, Who is worthy to open the book, and to loose its seals thereof?"* And, of course, the only One Who was worthy is the Lamb of God, our blessed Lord Jesus, the Messiah of Israel. The angel of Revelation 10:1 is simply *"another mighty angel"* – like the one back in Revelation 5:2.

There are two main possibilities as to the identity of this *"mighty angel"*: One, would be Gabriel whose name means "strength of God." Another possibility would be Michael, the Archangel. Both Gabriel and Michael are involved in the Book of Daniel with future prophetic events. Michael's name means "Who is like God!"

What about the *"little book"* in the angel's hand?

The description of this scroll in terms of size makes its message smaller than the seven-sealed scroll. The size could also mean that most of the message has already been explained, leaving a smaller part to reveal. We notice some very strong signs of the importance of this *"little book."*

1. Its <u>PRESENCE</u> in the angel's hand

In addition to that fact, we have its strategic location in the unraveling of the seven seals – it is associated with the seventh trumpet judgment which seems to connect with what remains in the Book of Revelation. In other words, the 7th trumpet covers all of the events and predictions of Revelation 11-22.

2. The <u>PLACE</u> where the angel is standing.

Once again we have a dramatic fact about this *"little book"* or the remainder of the seven-sealed scroll. Verse 2 says that this angel *"set his right foot upon the sea, and his left foot on the earth."* It is a picture of His authority and control over the events and message of the *"little book."*

3. The <u>POWER</u> of the angel's voice

Revelation 10:3 says that the angel *"cried with a loud voice, as when a lion roareth: and when he had cried, seven thunders uttered their voices."* It appears that the power of God's voice is behind this angel's cries. Several passages of the Bible connect the power of God's voice with the roaring of a lion.

Job 4:9-10 – *"By the blast of God they perish (the wicked), and by the breath of His nostrils are they consumed. The roaring of the lion, and the voice of the fierce lion, and the teeth of the young lions, are broken."*

Isaiah 31:4 – *"For thus hath the LORD spoken unto me, Like as the lion and the young lion roaring on his prey when a multitude of shepherds is called forth against him, he will not be afraid of their voice, nor abase himself for the noise of them: so shall the LORD of hosts come down to fight for mount Zion, and for the hill thereof."*

Hosea 5:14 – *"For I will be unto Ephraim as a lion, and as a young lion to the house of Judah: I, even I, will tear and go away; I will take away, and none shall rescue him."*

Hosea 11:10 – *"They shall walk after the LORD: He shall roar like a lion: when He shall roar, then the children shall tremble from the west."*

Joel 3:16 – *"The LORD also shall roar (as a lion) out of Zion, and utter His voice from Jerusalem; and the heavens and the earth shall shake: but the LORD will be the hope of His people, and the strength of the children of Israel."*

Amos 3:8 – *"The lion hath roared, who will not fear? the Lord GOD hath spoken, who can but prophesy?"*

2. The <u>INSTRUCTION</u> of the seven thunders

Revelation 10:4 – *"And when the seven thunders had uttered their voices, I was about to write: and I heard a voice from heaven saying unto me, Seal up those things which the seven thunders uttered, and write them not."*

These *"thunders"* come from the throne of God. Revelation 4:5 says *"And out of the throne proceeded lightnings and thunderings and voices"* We also remember that in Revelation 8:5 that when the angel cast the fire of his censer to the earth, we read: *"and there were voices, and thunderings, and lightnings, and an earthquake."*

This dramatic scene emphasizes clearly the great importance of the message of the *"little book."*
Psalm 29:3-4 says: *"The voice of the LORD is upon the waters: the God of glory thundereth: The LORD is upon many waters. The voice of the LORD is powerful; the voice of the LORD is full of majesty."*

As John prepares to write what he heard, the voice from heaven stopped him and said: *"Seal up those things which the seven thunders uttered, and write them not."* This is very unusual since the Book of Revelation is intended to reveal the events of the future, not seal them up!

While it is difficult to understand why John was not allowed to write about what the seven thunders said, many Bible teachers speculate that the coming message and what has already been revealed – speaks of the terrible suffering that God's people will endure during the tribulation, and especially the last half of it.

The <u>ANNOUNCEMENT</u> of the mighty angel
Revelation 10:5-7

"And the angel which I saw stand upon the sea and upon the earth lifted up his hand to haven, and sware by Him that liveth forever and ever, Who created heaven, and the things that therein are, and the earth, and the things that therein are, and

the sea, and the things which are therein, that there should be time no longer: But in the days of the voice of the seventh angel, when he shall begin to sound, the mystery of God should be finished, as He hath declared to His servants the prophets."

1. The announcement is based on God's authority!

The angel *"swears"* by God Who created all things. The importance of God's character and promises are being illustrated here. God will not lie. The end is coming: God's purposes will be fulfilled on this planet!

2. The announcement is based on God's timing!

Revelation 10:6 – the angel declares *"that there should be time no longer."* The time has come for God's plans to be fulfilled in terms of His judgment upon planet earth. It is the answer that the martyred saints were asking back in Revelation 6:9-11. Human history is operated by God according to His plans, not ours! Psalm 135:5-6 says: *"For I know that the LORD is great, and that our Lord is above all gods. Whatsoever the LORD pleased, that did He in heaven, and in earth, in the seas, and all deep places."*

We are told in Revelation 10:7: *"But in the days of the voice of the seventh angel, when he shall begin to sound, the mystery of God should be finished, as He hath declared to His servants the prophets."*

Even though Revelation 11:15 speaks of the *"seventh angel sounded"* the words *"It is done"* do not come until Revelation 16:17 at the time of the final plague.

3. The announcement is based on God's promises!

The promise of God is described as *"the mystery of God,"* – that which He declared to His servants the prophets. The long standing promise of God is about to be fulfilled. No longer mysterious and hidden, God now reveals what He will do!

Although the prophets were used by God to speak of many future events, much of what they predicted they did not understand in its complete terms of fulfillment.

The **APPLICATION** of the angel's message
Revelation 10:8-11

"And the voice which I heard from heaven spake unto me again, and said, Go and take the little book which is open in the hand of the angel which standeth upon the sea and upon the earth. And I went unto the angel, and said unto him, Give me the little book. And he said unto me, Take it, and eat it up; and it shall make thy belly bitter, but it shall be in thy mouth sweet as honey. And I took the little book out of the angel's hand, and ate it up; and it was in my mouth sweet as honey: and as soon as I had eaten it, my belly was bitter. And he said unto me, Thou must prophesy again before

many peoples, and nations, and tongues, and kings."

    1. The message <u>**ILLUSTRATES**</u> a previous revelation!

What John did was similar to the experience of the prophet Ezekiel. Ezekiel 2:3-3:3:

"And He said unto me, Son of man, I send thee to the children of Israel, to a rebellious nation that hath rebelled against Me: they and their fathers have transgressed against Me, even unto this very day. For they are impudent children and stiffhearted. I do send thee unto them; and thou shalt say unto them, Thus saith the Lord GOD. and they, whether they will hear, or whether they will forbear, (for they are a rebellious house,) yet shall they know that there hath been a prophet among them. And thou, son of man, be not afraid of them, neither be afraid of their words, though briers and thorns be with thee, and thou dost dwell among scorpions: be not afraid of their words, nor be dismayed at their looks, though they be a rebellious house. And thou shalt speak My words unto them, whether they will hear, or whether they will forbear: for they are most rebellious. But thou, son of man, hear what I say unto thee; Be not thou rebellious like that rebellious house: open thy mouth, and eat that I give thee. And when I looked, behold, a hand was sent unto me; and, lo, a roll of a book was therein; And He spread it before me; and it was written within and without: and there was

written therein lamentations, and mourning, and woe. *Moreover He said unto me, Son of man, eat that thou findest; eat this roll, and go speak unto the house of Israel. So I opened my mouth, and He caused me to eat that roll. And He said unto me, Son of man, cause thy belly to eat, and fill thy bowels with this roll that I give thee. Then did I eat it; and it was in my mouth as honey for sweetness.*"

Then, in Ezekiel 3:14 we read: "*So the Spirit lifted me up, and took me away, and I went in bitterness, in the heat of my spirit; but the hand of the LORD was strong upon me.*"

The situation in the life of Ezekiel in the above passages reveals clearly what John was also going to experience in Revelation 10. In Ezekiel's day, God's judgment fell upon the people of Israel. Babylon destroyed Jerusalem and the temple of Solomon in 586 BC. The symbol of eating the scroll pictures the complete assimilation of the message of the Lord. The prophet who proclaims the message is not unrelated to its impact. It becomes a part of him.

2. The message <u>INVOLVES</u> a twofold response.

John experiences both sweetness and bitterness. To hear God's Word and to know that He will fulfil His promises and judge this sinful world is sweet news to the believer's heart and ears. But the longer we contemplate what God will do, the more we see that the bitter is mixed with the sweet. God's people will suffer greatly during the tribulation period. We rejoice that God's plan is fulfilled and His righteous judgment executed, but we also grieve to see what His people will suffer.

Perhaps the full impact of what John experienced is a reminder to all who proclaim God's wonderful Word, and speak of His coming judgment and wrath. We must speak it with a measure of sorrow and bitterness. A broken heart is a prerequisite to the proclamation of God's judgment and wrath.

3. The message **INDICATES** a special responsibility!

The Apostle John is told that he *"must prophesy again before many peoples, and nations, and tongues, and kings."* His hesitation no doubt came from his bitter stomach as he realized the awful suffering the tribulation will bring. But the angel orders him to continue.

To all preachers of the Word of God, God's Word must be proclaimed no matter how it affects or offends people. We should speak God's truth in love, of course, but there is too much compromise in the pulpits of our churches. The Bible's message about God's wrath and judgment is rarely heard or understood by today's culture. There is no message more important for our world than that which the Book of Revelation clearly presents. May God help us to be faithful to it, and to heed what it says!

THE TWO WITNESSES
AND THE TEMPLE
Revelation 11:1-19

The <u>MEASURING</u> of the Temple of God
Revelation 11:1-2

"And there was given me a reed like unto a rod: and the angel stood, saying, Rise, and measure the temple of God, and the altar, and them that worship therein. But the court which is without the temple leave out, and measure it not; for it is given unto the Gentiles: and the holy city shall they tread under foot forty and two months."

Will a Jewish temple be rebuilt in Jerusalem during the tribulation?

Apparently so. John is told to *"measure the temple of God."* Notice that it is not called just *"a temple."* It is called *"the temple of God."* Also, in II Thessalonians 2:4 we read of the coming *"man of sin"* or the *"son of perdition"* that *"he as God sitteth in the temple of God, shewing himself that he is God."* In Matthew 24:15 we read: *"When ye therefore shall see the abomination of desolation, spoken of by Daniel the prophet, stand in the holy place, (whoso readeth, let him understand:)*

The word for *"temple"* in this passage in the Greek language is *naon* which is referring to the holy place where only the priests could go. It does not refer to the entire temple complex.

The *"altar"* might refer to the brazen altar where sacrifices would take place, or to the altar of incense mentioned previously in the Book of Revelation, and the only altar inside of the Holy Place of the Temple.

In Jerusalem today we have the Temple Institute, led by Rabbi Chaim Richman. They are dedicated to the rebuilding of the Jewish Temple. Any tour group that visits their facility becomes aware quickly of the plans to rebuild the Temple. Most all of the items essential for worship have already been built or made.

Daniel 12:11 says: *"And from the time that the daily sacrifice shall be taken away, and the abomination that maketh desolate set up, there shall be a thousand two hundred and ninety days."*

In Daniel 9:27 we read of a covenant that will be enforced upon the people of Israel by a coming world leader known by most people as the Antichrist and the restoration of the Jewish temple and its sacrificial system will be possible once again. However, this covenant which appears to be seven years in length will be broken by the Antichrist and he will cause the sacrifice and the oblation (offerings) to cease.

WHY MEASURE THE TEMPLE?

Good question! It is possible that the instruction to measure the temple suggests what the last part of Revelation 11:2 reveals – that the Gentiles will *"tread under foot forty and two months"* or 3½ years. Apparently the Gentiles will take control of Jerusalem and its holy sites. Because of the reference to the temple worshipers, the measurement might indicate God's protection of His people during such a Gentile takeover. As Israel was separated from the Egyptians who were suffering the consequences of God's judgment and plagues, so the Jews of the tribulation period will be set apart by God and divinely protected. The act of measuring the temple circumscribes an area that uniquely belongs to God.

Our Lord Yeshua predicted that Jerusalem would be in Gentile hands until the *"times of the Gentiles"* were fulfilled. We read in Luke 21:24: *"And they shall fall by the edge of the sword, and shall be led away captive into all nations; and Jerusalem shall be trodden down of the Gentiles, until the times of the Gentiles be fulfilled."*

Even though Israel today supposedly controls the Temple Mount, yet in the 1967 war, when the Temple Mount was captured by Israel, General Moshe Dayan gave the control of this sacred place to the Great Muslim Council. That problem remains to this day and causes great grief to the Jewish people who cannot even pray on that Temple Mount without raising the wrath of the Muslim people.

The *"forty and two months"* of Gentile control of Jerusalem and its Temple Mount will be achieved in the last half of the tribulation period.

The <u>MESSAGE</u> of the Two Witnesses
Revelation 11:3

"And I will give power unto My two witnesses, and they shall prophesy a thousand two hundred and threescore days, clothed in sackcloth."

When we examine the powerful preaching of these two witnesses in the tribulation period, we must conclude that this is a ministry unlike anything we have ever seen! They are able to do things that we normally cannot do, and the whole world becomes much aware of their abilities and the seriousness of their message. In unbelief, the world will rejoice when they are dead, no longer troubling them with their message and miracles.

According to Revelation 11:3 they will preach for 1260 days or 42 months. Their preaching will take place, no doubt, in the first half of the tribulation period. We are not told much about people's response to their message, but we do know that 144,000 Jews will put their faith in the Messiah, and as a result, be protected by God during the days of the tribulation, and proclaim this message to the entire world. It is possible that the 144,000 Jews will come to faith in the Messiah of Israel through the powerful preaching of the two witnesses.

Their message is a message of repentance. They are clothed in sackcloth, the garment worn by the prophets of God who preached repentance. It is the garment that suggests the need to mourn and lament over our sins and to get right with God. John the Baptist and Jesus Himself preached a message of repentance saying: *"Repent! For the kingdom of heaven is at hand."*

The <u>MEANING</u> of the Two Witnesses
Revelation 11:4

"These are the two olive trees, and the two candlesticks standing before the God of the earth."

The above words remind us of the teaching of Zechariah 4. The prophet Zechariah preached a message of repentance of the people of Israel during the days of the Babylonian captivity. His inspired proclamation and visions encouraged the people to return to the land of Israel and to rebuild the temple that was destroyed by Babylon in 586 BC. In his vision recorded in Zechariah 4, he saw a lampstand of solid gold with a bowl on top of it. There were seven lamps with seven pipes connected to the bowl of oil. On either side of the lampstand were two olive trees from which two gold pipes carried oil to the bowl on top of the lampstand.

John's reference to the *"two olive trees, and the two candlesticks"* is an allusion to two leaders in Jewish history named Joshua (the High Priest) and Zerubbabel (governor) who were motivated to lead the people of Israel to rebuild the temple. Zerubbabel would lay the foundation of the temple and also finish it according to Zechariah 4:9: *"The hands of Zerubbabel have laid the foundation of this house; his hands shall also finish it; and thou shalt know that the LORD of hosts hath sent me unto you."*

Then we read in Zechariah 4:11-14 these words:

"Then answered I, and said unto him, what are these two olive trees upon the right side of the candlestick and upon the left side thereof? And I answered again, and said unto him, What be these two olive branches which through the two golden pipes empty the golden oil out of themselves? And he answered me and said, Knowest thou not what these be? And I said, No, my lord. Then said he, These are the two anointed ones, that stand by the Lord of the whole earth."

Zechariah was shown a candlestick (lampstand) of pure gold. It had seven lamps arranged on the same level under a bowl which served as a reservoir for olive oil. The oil would flow from the bowl to keep the lamps full. This particular candlestick was similar to the one placed in the tabernacles and in Solomon's temple with one major difference: the tabernacle and temple candlesticks had to be filled with oil by the priests. The one Zechariah saw was automatically filled with an endless supply of oil that was not dependent upon anyone attending it.

When the vision is interpreted correctly, it represents God's people giving fullness of light to the world because of the abundant flow of the Holy Spirit. Zechariah 4:6 is a wonderful reminder to all of God's people when it says: *"This is the word of the LORD unto Zerubbabel, saying, Not by might, nor by power, but by My Spirit, saith the LORD of hosts."*

Zechariah 4:10 states a serious question: *"For who hath despised the day of small things? For they shall rejoice, and shall see the plummet in the hand of Zerubbabel with those seven; they are the eyes of the LORD, which run to and fro through the whole earth."*

Those who *"despised the day of small things"* may have been older Jews who thought this temple was insignificant compared with the magnificence of the former temple. However, no work that God directs is unimportant or insignificant but has eternal value and importance. The reference to the *"plummet"* in Zerubbabel's hand was confirmation that God had ordained this work.

The two olive trees, with their oil-supplying branches represent the *"two anointed ones"* that stand by the Lord of the whole earth. The idea of their standing by the Lord is that of "serving" the Lord. This refers to the anointing of priests and kings, and in this case to Joshua and Zerubbabel who served as types of the Messiah Who is both Priest and King. The candlestick, therefore, represents Israel as a light to the nations. While this applied partially to Zechariah's time, the complete fulfillment will come during the millennial reign of our blessed Lord Yeshua, the Messiah of Israel. Another partial fulfillment is found in these two witnesses in the tribulation period.

In Zechariah's vision and prophecy there was only one lampstand, whereas there are two lampstands in Revelation 11:4. This distinction reveals that we are not to make the two passages identical, but rather to see that the one illustrates the other.

Who are the *"two witnesses"*?

Attempts to identify them have led to a wide variety of interpretations. Some see a symbolical view of referring to Israel and the Church. Others say it refers to Israel and the Word of God. Many speak of the connection of Zerubbabel and Joshua coming back as the two witnesses. Others in some frustration argue that these *"two witnesses"* are two unique individuals who have never before existed.

Some of the more popular interpretations refer to Enoch and Elijah (two men who were taken to heaven by unusual circumstances); The most probable interpretation refers them to Moses and Elijah. A strong case can be made for Moses, the one representing the law, and for Elijah, the one representing the prophets. The miraculous powers mentioned in Revelation 11:6 certainly point to these two men. They were the two men who appeared with our Lord Yeshua on the Mount of Transfiguration (probably Mount Hermon). Two men in white apparel appeared to the disciples at the ascension of Jesus into heaven, reminding them of His Second Coming. We read in Acts 1:9-11 these words: *"And when He had spoken these things, while they beheld, He was taken up; and a cloud received Him out of their sight. And while they looked stedfastly toward heaven as He went up, behold, two men stood by them in white apparel; which also said, Ye men of Galilee, why stand ye gazing up into heaven? This same Jesus which is taken up from you into heaven, shall so come in like manner as ye have seen Him go into heaven."*

According to Malachi 4:5-6, Elijah the prophet is to appear on the earth before the Messiah returns:

"Behold, I will send you "Elijah the prophet before the coming of the great and dreadful day of the LORD: And he shall turn the heart of the fathers to the children, and the heart of the children to their fathers, lest I come and smite the earth with a curse."

1. The **PROTECTION** of the two witnesses

Revelation 11:5 – *"And if any man will hurt them, fire proceedeth out of their mouth, and devoureth their enemies: and if any man will hurt them, he must in this manner be killed."*

God supernaturally protects them by giving them awesome power. Death will come to anyone who even wants to harm them. Here is another reason for believing that these two witnesses are Moses and Elijah. A similar fate befell their enemies in the Old Testament. In the case of Moses we read in Numbers 16:35: *"And there came out a fire from the LORD, and consumed the two hundred and fifty men that offered incense."* And in the case of Elijah we read in II Kings 1:10-14:

"And Elijah answered and said to the captain of fifty, If I be a man of God, then let fire come down from heaven, and consume thee and thy fifty. And there came down fire from heaven, and consumed him and his fifty. Again also he sent unto him another captain of fifty with his fifty. And he answered and said unto him, O man of God, thus hath the king said, Come down quickly. And Elijah answered and said unto them, If I be a man of God, let fire come down from heaven, and consume thee and thy fifty. And the fire of God came down from heaven, and consumed him and his fifty. And he sent again a captain of the third fifty with his fifty, and the third captain of fifty went up, and came and fell on his knees before Elijah, and besought him, and said unto him, O man of God, I pray thee, let my life, and life of these fifty thy servants, be precious in thy sight. Behold, there came fire down from heaven, and burnt up the two captains of the former fifties with their fifties: therefore let my life now be precious in thy sight."

2. The <u>POWER</u> of the two witnesses

Revelation 11:6 – *"These have power to shut heaven, that it rain not in the days of their prophecy: and have power over waters to turn them to blood, and to smite the earth with all plagues, as often as they will."*

One cannot help but associate these demonstrations of power with the work of Elijah and Moses. We read in James 5:16-17: *"Elias was a man subject to like passions as we are, and he prayed earnestly that it might not rain: and it rained not on the earth by the space of three years and six months. And he prayed again, and the heaven gave rain, and the earth brought forth her fruit."*

And, of course, it was Moses who struck the waters of Egypt so that they turned to blood (Exodus 7:20). Moses was involved in the plagues of ancient Egypt, and the words of verse 6 remind us of him.

The <u>MURDER</u> of the two witnesses
Revelation 11:7-10

"And when they shall have finished their testimony, the beast that ascendeth out of the bottomless pit shall make war against them, and shall overcome them, and kill them. And their dead bodies shall lie in the street of the great city, which spiritually is called Sodom and Egypt, where also our Lord was crucified. And they of the people and kindreds and tongues and nations shall see their

dead bodies three days and an half, and shall not suffer their dead bodies to be put in graves. And they that dwell upon the earth shall rejoice over them, and make merry, and shall send gifts one to another; because these two prophets tormented them that dwelt on the earth."

This is the first of 36 references to the *"beast."* There are three kinds of *"beasts"* in Revelation:

1. SATAN – the beast out of the bottomless pit
    Revelation 11:7

2. ANTICHRIST – the beast out of the sea
    Revelation 13:1

3. FALSE PROPHET – the beast coming up out of the earth
    Revelation 13:11

    (1)   The <u>PLACE</u> where their bodies are displayed!

The term *"great city"* appears 10 times in the Book of Revelation. It is used of the new Jerusalem, the heavenly city (Revelation 21:10) as well as the city of Babylon (Revelation 14:8; 16:19; 17:18; 18:10, 16, 18, 19, 21). However, the city depicted here is the earthly Jerusalem, the place *"where also our Lord was crucified."* How interesting that this city of Jerusalem as become like Sodom and Egypt! The word *"spiritually"* indicates that the spiritual condition of the city is like that of ancient Sodom that was destroyed by God for all its wickedness and immorality. Egypt is a symbol reminding us of oppression and slavery.

(2)   The <u>PUBLICITY</u> that the two witnesses receive!

For three and a half days all the peoples, tribes, tongues, and nations of the world will see the dead bodies of the two witnesses. Before television and satellites, this prediction seemed impossible. People will be so thrilled to see them dead no burial will be allowed.

The reason for all this celebration is simply stated – these two witnesses tormented those who dwell on the earth. Unbelievers are "tormented" by a message of repentance. The prophets of God have been killed throughout history. The world is no friend to God or to His messengers. Hebrews 11:35-38 speaks of this hostility and danger:

"Women received their dead raised to life again: and others were tortured, not accepting deliverance; that they might obtain a better resurrection: And others had trial of cruel mockings and scourgings, yea, moreover of bonds and imprisonment: They were stoned, they were sawn asunder, were tempted, were slain with the sword: they wandered about in sheepskins and goatskins; being destitute, afflicted, tormented; (Of whom the world was not worthy:) they wandered

in deserts, and in mountains, and in dens and caves of the earth."

The <u>MANNER</u> in which God revealed His power
Revelation 11:11-13

"And after three days and an half the Spirit of life from God entered into them, and they stood upon their feet; and great fear fell upon them which saw them. And they heard a great voice from heaven saying unto them, Come up hither. And they ascended up to heaven in a cloud; and their enemies beheld them. And the same hour was there a great earthquake, and the tenth part of the city fell, and in the earthquake were slain of men seven thousand: and the remnant were affrighted, and gave glory to the God of heaven."

1. Their <u>RESURRECTION</u> – *"the Spirit of life from God entered into them, and they stood upon their feet."*

2. The <u>REVELATION</u> of God's power – *"they ascended up to heaven in a cloud: and their enemies beheld them."*

3. The <u>RESULTS</u> from this event

    (1)   Great fear
    (2)   Great Earthquake
    (3)   Death of 7000 men
    (4)   Remnant gave glory to God

The results were indeed amazing and shocking to the world who celebrated the death of these two prophets of God. It is interesting to observe that a great earthquake occurs at the 6th seal judgment, and at the 6th trumpet judgment, and at the last plague judgment.

The phrase about the *"remnant"* who give *"glory to the God of heaven"* probably indicates their conversion to faith in the Messiah of Israel, and could very well be referring to the salvation of the 144,000 Jews.

In the midst of the world's celebrations of their deaths, God miraculously intervenes as the *"Spirit of life from God entered into them."* What a wonderful encouragement to all of us today. We too shall rise; resurrection day is coming. Romans 8:11 states: *"But if the Spirit of Him that raised up Jesus from the dead dwell in you, He that raised up Christ from the dead shall also quicken your mortal bodies by His Spirit that dwelleth in you."*

THE THIRD WOE IS COMING!
Revelation 11:14

"The second woe is past; and, behold, the third woe cometh quickly."

In Revelation 10:7 we read: *"But in the days of the voice of the seventh angel, when he shall begin to sound, the mystery of God should be finished, as He hath declared to His servants the prophets."*

The first woe refers to the locust plague at the 5th trumpet judgment.

The second woe refers to the demonic attack at the 6th trumpet judgment.

The third woe refers to the sounding of the 7th trumpet judgment.

The <u>MAJESTY</u> of God and His plan
Revelation 11:15-19

"And the seventh angel sounded; and there were great voices in heaven, saying, The kingdoms of this world are become the kingdoms of our Lord, and of His Christ; and He shall reign forever and ever. And the four and twenty elders, which sat before God on their seats (thrones), *fell upon their faces and worshipped God, Saying, We give Thee thanks, O Lord God Almighty, which art, and wast, and art to come; because Thou hast taken to Thee thy great power, and hast reigned. And the nations were angry and Thy wrath is come, and the time of the dead, that they should be judged, and that Thou shouldest give reward unto Thy servants the prophets, and to the saints, and them that fear Thy Name, small and great; and shouldest destroy them which destroy the earth. And the temple of God was opened in heaven, and there was seen in His temple the ark of His testament: and there were lightnings, and voices, and thunderings, and an earthquake, and great hail."*

The sounding of the 7th trumpet continues over the last three and a half years of the tribulation period. Its message covers all that transpires during the last half of the tribulation, right up to the great and long-awaited event of the Second Coming of Jesus Christ.

1. The <u>EXTENT</u> of His Majesty

Revelation 11:15 – *"And the seventh angel sounded; and there were great voices in heaven, saying, The kingdoms of this world are become the kingdoms of our Lord, and of His Christ; and He shall reign forever and ever."*

God announces that He is taking over!

Daniel 2:44 – *"And in the days of these kings shall the God of heaven set up a kingdom, which shall never be destroyed: and the kingdom shall not be left to other people, but it shall break in pieces and consume all these kingdoms, and it shall stand forever."*

Daniel 7:14 – *"And there was given Him dominion, and glory, and a kingdom, that all people, nations, and languages, should serve Him: His dominion is an everlasting dominion, which shall not pass away, and His kingdom that which shall not be destroyed."*

Zechariah 14:9 – *"And the LORD shall be king over all the earth: in that day shall there be one LORD, and His Name one."*

I Corinthians 15:20-28 tells us the details:

"But now is Christ risen from the dead, and become the firstfruits of them that slept. For since by man came death, by man came also the resurrection of the dead. For as in Adam all die, even so in Christ shall all be made alive. But every man in his own order: Christ the firstfruits; afterward they that are Christ's at His coming. Then cometh the end, when He shall have delivered up the kingdom to God, even the Father; when He shall have put down all rule and all authority and power. For He must reign, till He hath put all enemies under His feet. The last enemy that shall be destroyed is death. For He hath put all things under His feet. But when He saith all things are put under Him, it is manifest that He is excepted, which did put all things under Him. And when all things shall be subdued unto Him, then shall the Son also Himself be subject unto Him that put all things under Him, that God may be all in all."

2. The <u>EVALUATION</u> of His Majesty

Revelation 11:16-18 – *"And the four and twenty elders, which sat before God on their seats (thrones), fell upon their faces, and worshipped God, Saying, We give Thee thanks, O Lord God Almighty, which art, and wast, and art to come,*

389

because Thou hast taken to Thee Thy great power, and hast reigned. And the nations were angry and Thy wrath is come, and the time of the dead, that they should be judged, and that "Thou shouldest give reward unto Thy servants the prophets, and to the saints, small and great; and shouldest destroy them which destroy the earth."

(1)   The <u>RESPONSE</u> that is given.

Upon hearing the *"great voices in heaven"* that announce the coming of the kingdoms of our Lord, and of His Christ, the 24 elders *"fell upon their faces and worshipped God."*

The number one priority of every believer should be the worship and praise of Almighty God. We were created to worship the God Who made us. The action of falling down on their faces demonstrates a clear understanding of God's greatness and the believer's humility before God. The worship they expressed was a giving of thanks. Thanksgiving is the sacrifice that God wants from our lips. Hebrews 13:15-16 says: *"By Him therefore let us offer the sacrifice of praise to God continually, that is, the fruit of our lips giving thanks to His Name. But to do good and to communicate forget not: for with such sacrifices God is well pleased."* We need more of this attitude and response in our lives today. God is to be glorified, not humanity which God created for His pleasure and glory!

(2)   The <u>REASONS</u> for their exaltation.

The reasons for praising and worshiping God are clearly given here and serve as a constant reminder to all believers of what God wants from us.

Reason #1 – God's <u>POWER</u> is being proclaimed!
Revelation 11:17b – *"because Thou hast taken to Thee Thy great power, and hast reigned."*

Reason #2 – God's <u>PLAN</u> is bring accomplished!
Revelation 11:18b – *"the time of the dead, that they should be judged,"*

Reason #3 – God's <u>PROMISE</u> is being fulfilled!
Revelation 11:18c – *"and that Thou shouldest give reward unto Thy servants the prophets, and to the saints, and them that fear Thy Name, small and great:*

Reason #4 – God's <u>PUNISHMENT</u> is being declared!
Revelation 11:18d – *"and shouldest destroy them which destroy the earth."*

The <u>EXPRESSION</u> of His Majesty
Revelation 11:19

"And the temple of God was opened in heaven, and there was seen in His temple the ark of the testament: and there were lightnings, and voices, and thunderings, and an earthquake, and great hail."

Revelation 11 begins with a temple on earth, and ends with the temple in heaven. When people inquire about the location of the Ark of the

Covenant, they usually forget about this verse. Yes, there is a temple in heaven, and the Ark of the Covenant is there!

In chapter 4 there were *"lightnings, thunderings, and voices"* that came from the throne of God the Father. In chapter 8 there were *"noises, thunderings, lightnings, and an earthquake"* that preceded the seven trumpet judgments. And, now in Revelation 11:19 there were *"lightnings, and voices, and thunderings, and an earthquake, and great hail."* These remarkable displays of the forces of nature are clear signs that God's judgment has come.

Revelation 11 is a crucial chapter that marks a dividing point between the first half and the second half of the tribulation period. It reminds us all that God is in absolute control and that all the kingdoms of this world are under His direction. The remaining chapters of this Book of Revelation will reveal how God is going to bring His final judgments upon planet earth and set up a kingdom that will never be destroyed! Praise the Lord!

SATAN'S WAR AGAINST ISRAEL
Revelation 12:1-17

The <u>WONDERS</u> in heaven
Revelation 12:1-6

"And there appeared a great wonder in heaven; a woman clothed with the sun, and the moon under her feet, and upon her head a crown of twelve stars. And she being with child cried, travailing in birth, and pained to be delivered. And there appeared another wonder in heaven; and behold a great red dragon, having seven heads and ten horns, and seven crowns upon his heads. And his tail drew the third part of the stars of heaven, and did cast them to the earth: and the dragon stood before the woman which was ready to be delivered, for to devour her child as soon as it was born. And she brought forth a man child, who was to rule all nations with a rod of iron: and her child was caught up unto God, and to His throne. And the woman fled into the wilderness, where she hath a place prepared of God, that they should feed her there a thousand two hundred and threescore days."

The Nation of Israel has a prominent place in God's plan for human history. In one respect, all human history is vitally related to the history and destiny of the people of Israel. God's promise to Abraham in Genesis 12:1-3 reveals that all nations of the world will be blessed through the descendants of Abraham.

393

According to the Bible, Satan has a deep hatred of the Jewish people and has sought by many means to destroy them. God has never allowed that to happen, though some political leaders have dedicated themselves to eliminating Israel from the face of the earth. These leaders have perished as will all who curse Abraham's descendants. God is committed to their survival and future glory. He will one day restore the kingdom to Israel, and a Jewish Messiah will rule from Jerusalem over the entire world. Naturally, many Gentiles do not appreciate such words nor do they believe that such a prophecy will ever be fulfilled.

In Revelation 12, details about Israel's troubles and survival during the tribulation period are given. The nation is represented by a woman with a special child, who is none other than the Messiah Himself.

1. The <u>SIGN</u> of the woman

Revelation 12:1-2 – *"And there appeared a great wonder in heaven; a woman clothed with the sun, and the moon under her feet, and upon her head a crown of twelve stars: And she being with child cried, travailing in birth, and pained to be delivered.*

Revelation 12:5-6 – *"And she brought forth a man child, who was to rule all nations with a rod of iron: and her child was caught up unto God, and to His throne. And the woman fled into the wilderness, where she hath a place prepared of God, that they should feed her there a thousand two hundred and threescore days."*

(1) Her <u>CONNECTION</u> with religion.

A woman is often used to symbolize a religious system or set of beliefs. In Revelation 2, a woman named Jezebel is used to picture false teaching and sexual immorality. In Revelation 17 *"the great harlot"* is used to picture the false religious system that will dominate the world in end times. Believers in Jesus Christ are referred to as the *"wife"* of the Lamb in Revelation 19:7, and the heavenly city, the new Jerusalem, is described as *"the bride, the Lamb's wife"* in Revelation 21.

Likewise Israel is described as the wife of the Lord and often as a wife who has departed from her husband (Like Jeremiah 3). It is, therefore, quite reasonable for this woman to refer to Israel or at least to stand as a symbol of some religious system or group of people.

Revelation 12:1 says this is *"a great wonder* (sign) *in heaven."* It is the first of seven "signs" that occur in the Book of Revelation:

12:1 – a woman clothed with the sun
12:3 – a great red dragon
13:1 – the beast
13:13-14 – the false prophet
15:1 – seven angels with the seven last plagues
16:14 – unclean spirits working miracles

19:20 – beast and false prophet cast into the lake of fire

(2)   Her <u>CLOTHING</u>

Unusual attempts have been made in the past to identify this woman. The Roman Catholic church has stated that the woman represents the Virgin Mary. Also, Mary Baker Eddy, founder of Christian Science, claimed that she was the woman of Revelation 12, and that the child was the religious system of Christian Science.

However, the description of the sun, moon, and twelve stars makes the identification clear. It is a reference to Joseph's dream in which the sun, moon, and twelve stars represent Joseph's father, mother, and brothers, bowing down to him.

Genesis 37:9-11 – *"And he* (Joseph) *dreamed yet another dream, and told it his brethren, and said, Behold, I have dreamed a dream more; and, behold, the sun and the moon and the eleven stars made obeisance to me. And he told it to his father, and to his brethren: and his father rebuked him, and said unto him, What is this dream that thou hast dreamed? Shall I and thy mother and thy brethren indeed come to bow down ourselves to thee to the earth? And his brethren envied him; but his father observed the saying."*

Jacob had 12 sons, including Joseph, representing the heads of the 12 tribes of Israel. The woman of Revelation 12 is the Nation of Israel.

(3) Her <u>CRIES</u> of labor pains

Revelation 12:2 – *"And she being with child cried, travailing in birth, and pained to be delivered."*

At the time of the birth of Jesus Christ, Israel was in a great deal of pain. They were under the heel of Rome, and they suffered much under Rome's rule. It is understandable why some consider the woman to be the Virgin Mary in that she indeed did give birth to the Messiah. But this refers to the nation's travail, not to Mary's. The Messiah is the child of the nation of Israel as well as the child of Mary.

(4) Her <u>CHILD</u>

Revelation 12:5 – *"And she brought forth a man child, who was to rule all nations with a rod of iron: and her child was caught up unto God, and to His throne."*

> The Child's <u>AUTHORITY</u> – *"rule all nations with a rod of iron"*

Psalm 2:7-9 – *"I will declare the decree: the LORD hath said unto Me, Thou art My Son; this day have I begotten Thee. Ask of Me, and I shall give Thee the heathen for Thine inheritance, and the uttermost parts of the earth for Thy possession.*

Thou shalt break them with a rod of iron; Thou shalt dash them in pieces like a potter's vessel."

Revelation 19:15 says specifically: *"And out of His mouth goeth a sharp sword, that with it He should smite the nations: and He shall rule them with a rod of iron: and He treadeth the winepress of the fierceness and wrath of Almighty God."*

Psalm 23:4 speaks of the Good Shepherd Who carries a rod and a staff – one for correction (rod) and the other for protection (staff). When God judges Israel (Ezekiel 20:37), He makes them pass *'under the rod"* – the *"rod"* is the symbol of judgment and correction.

> The Child's <u>ASCENSION</u> – *"and her Child was caught up unto God, and to His throne"*

The words *"caught up"* come from the Greek word *"harpazo"* – the same word used for the rapture of church age believers in I Thessalonians 4:17. It is also used of the Apostle Paul in II Corinthians 12:2, 4 as the text says that he was *"caught up"* to the third heaven (Paradise).

> (5) Her <u>CARE</u> by God during the tribulation

Revelation 12:5 – *"And the woman fled into the wilderness, where she hath a place prepared of God, that they should feed her there a thousand two hundred and threescore days."*

Jesus said in John 14:1-3 – *"Let not your heart be troubled: ye believe in God, believe also in Me. In My Father's house are many mansions: if it were not so, I would have told you. I go to prepare a place for you. And if I go and prepare a place for you, I will come again, and receive you unto Myself; that where I am, there ye may be also."*

How wonderful to realize that God has also prepared a place for His people Israel during the tribulation period! Somewhere in *"the wilderness"* God has a special place. It will provide protection as well as provision for their physical needs.

2. The <u>SYMBOLISM</u> of the dragon

Revelation 12:3-4 – *"And there appeared another wonder in heaven; and behold a great red dragon, having seven heads and ten horns, and seven crowns upon his heads. And his tail drew the third part of the stars of heaven, and did cast them to the earth: and the dragon stood before the woman which was ready to be delivered, for to devour her child as soon as it was born."*

(1)   The <u>IDENTITY</u> of the dragon

The context of this chapter leaves no doubt as to the true identity of the dragon. Verse 9 says: *"and the great dragon was cast out, that old serpent, called the Devil, and Satan, which deceiveth the whole world: he was cast out into the earth, and his angels were cast out with him."*

Yes, this is Satan, the adversary of God's people, the hater of Israel and the Jewish people. The phrase *"that old serpent"* leaves no questions in our minds as to his identity – he is the serpent of Genesis 3 who tempted Eve to disobey God.

The color of the dragon is fascinating – a fiery red! This is clearly a picture of his murderous motivations. In John 8:44 we read the words of our Lord Yeshua to the religious leaders of His day: *"Ye are of your father the devil, and the lusts of your father ye will do. He was a murderer from the beginning, and abode not in the truth, because there is no truth in him. When he speaketh a lie, he speaketh of his own: for he is a liar, and the father of it."* These two things capture his intent and motives toward God's people:

 He is a MURDERER!
 He is the FATHER of LIES!

The Dragon and the Beast

Revelation 12:3 – *"And there appeared another wonder in heaven; and behold, a great red dragon, having seven heads and ten horns, and seven crowns upon his heads."*

In Revelation 13:1 we read: *"And I stood upon the sand of the sea, and saw a beast rise up out of the sea, having seven heads and ten horns, and upon his horns ten crowns, and upon his heads the name of blasphemy."*

The above two verses show a serious connection between the dragon and the beast. II Corinthians 4:4 says that the dragon (Satan) is *"the god of this world"* who has *"blinded the minds of them which believe not, lest the light of the glorious gospel of Christ, Who is the image of God, should shine unto them."* Ephesians 2:2-3 adds about the dragon:

"Wherein in time past ye walked according to the course of this world, according to the prince of the power of the air, the spirit that now worketh in the children of disobedience: Among whom also we all had our conversation in times past in the lusts of our flesh, fulfilling the desires of the flesh and of the mind; and were by nature the children of wrath, even as others."

In saying that the beast has *"seven heads and ten horns"* it reveals Satan's involvement in the nations and governments of this world. Revelation 13:2 says that *"the dragon gave him* (the beast) *his power, and his seat, and great authority."*

The *"crowns upon his heads"* show Satan's power and authority over the major empires of the world. These *"heads"* represent the empires of the world's history as we shall learn later in chapters 13, 17, and 18.

The Stars and the Dragon

Revelation 12:4 says *"and his* (Satan) *tail drew the third part of the stars of heaven, and did cast them* to the earth." Verse 9 adds *"he was cast out into the earth, and his angels were cast out with him."*

So, the stars are angels. Apparently, one-third of all the angels God created joined Satan in his rebellion and conspiracy against God Himself. Up until the time of this chapter, the devil has had access into the presence of God (like a prosecuting attorney in a courtroom) where he has been accusing believers *"before our God day and night (v.10)."* There are millions of angels, and one-third of them associated themselves with Satan, *"the anointed cherub"* who fell into his sin and rebellion which we learn in Isaiah 14:12-15:

"How art thou fallen from heaven, O Lucifer, son of the morning! How art thou cut down to the ground, which didst weaken the nations! For thou hast said in thine heart, I will ascend into heaven, I will exalt my throne above the stars of God: I will sit also upon the mount of the congregation, in the sides of the north: I will ascend above the heights of the clouds; I will be like the Most High. Yet thou shalt be brought down to hell, to the sides of the pit."

These *"stars"* which are definitely called *"angels"* are the ones of Jude 6 – *"the angels which kept not their first estate, but left their own habitation, He hath reserved in everlasting chains under darkness unto the judgment of the great day."* They are also the ones mentioned in II Peter 2:4: *"For if God spared not the angels that sinned, but cast them* down to hell, and delivered them into chains of darkness, to be reserved unto judgment."

Revelation 12:4b says: "and the dragon stood before the woman which was ready to be delivered, for to devour her child as soon as it was born."

Herod's murder of all the male babies of Bethlehem who were two years old and younger was a fulfillment of this prophecy.

This conflict was predicted in Genesis 3:15: "And I will put enmity between thee (serpent) and the woman, and between thy seed and her seed (the Messiah); it shall bruise thy head, and thou shalt bruise His heel."

The above prophecy points to the death of the Messiah which Satan thought was his victory, but turned out to be his ultimate defeat. Our Lord's death on the cross struck the fatal blow since all of our sins were paid for by His substitutionary atonement, a fact assured by our Lord's resurrection. What a wonderful salvation!

The WAR in heaven
Revelation 12:7-9

"And there was war in heaven: Michael and his angels fought against the dragon; and the dragon fought and his angels, and prevailed not; neither was their place found any more in heaven. And the great dragon was cast out, that old serpent, called *the Devil, and Satan, which deceiveth the whole world: he was cast out into the earth, and his angels were cast out with him."*

Angels at war! It seems so incredible, and yet it makes sense if you know the teaching of the Bible regarding good and evil spirits. Evil angels or unclean spirits (demons) are trying to defeat and destroy believers while good angels are defending and protecting them. In the tribulation, one great final battle settles the issue forever!

This war in heaven is a part of the prophecy of Daniel 12:1-2:

"And at that time shall Michael stand up, the great prince which standeth for the children of Thy people: and there shall be a time of trouble, such as never was since there was a nation even to that same time: and at that time Thy people shall be delivered, every one that shall be found written in the book. And many of them that sleep in the dust of the earth shall awake, some to everlasting life, and some to shame and everlasting contempt."

Michael is the Archangel (there are no others!) and his special mission is the defense and protection of the children of Israel. Revelation 12, as we shall soon see, is the story of the devil's hatred of Israel. Michael and his angels are their defense!

Two things happen in this war in heaven – Satan and his angels lost, and also were *"cast out"* of heaven, shutting up any further access to the throne of God in order to accuse believers.

Satan is a conquered enemy! Our Lord Yeshua said in John 12:31 – *"Now is the judgment of this world: now shall the prince of this world be cast out."* Romans 16:20 says: *"And the God of peace shall bruise Satan under your feet shortly."* Hebrews 2:14 says: *"that through death He might destroy him that had the power of death, that is, the devil."* I John 4:4 reminds us: *"Ye are of God, little children, and have overcome them: because greater is He that is in you, than he that is in the world."*

Satan fell morally and spiritually long ago, but his being cast out of heaven with no more access to God for his accusations will not happen until the middle of the tribulation period.

Revelation 12:9 reveals three things about Satan:

(1)　He was directly involved in the temptation of Adam and Eve!
　　　"that old serpent"

(2)　He is a slanderer and an adversary!
　　　"called the Devil, and Satan"

(3)　He deceives the whole world!
　　　"which deceiveth the whole world"

The <u>WAY</u> believers have overcome Satan!
Revelation 12:10-12

"And I heard a loud voice saying in heaven, Now is come salvation, and strength, and the kingdom of our God, and the power of His Christ: for the accuser of our brethren is cast down, which accused them before our God day and night. And they overcame him by the blood of the Lamb, and by the word of their testimony, and they loved not their lives unto the death. Therefore rejoice, ye heavens, and ye that dwell in them. Woe to the inhabiters of the earth and of the sea! For the devil is come down unto you, having great wrath, because he knoweth that he hath but a short time."

The coming kingdom of the Messiah is the stone that crushes and destroys all the kingdoms of this world. Daniel 2:44-45 makes it abundantly clear:

"And in the days of these kings shall the God of heaven set up a kingdom, which shall never be destroyed: and the kingdom shall not be left to other people, but it shall break in pieces and consume all these kingdoms, and it shall stand forever. Forasmuch as thou sawest that the stone was cut out of the mountain, without hands, and that it brake in pieces the iron, the brass, the clay, the silver, and the gold; the great God hath made known to the king what shall come to pass hereafter: and the dream is certain, and the interpretation thereof sure."

His kingdom is an everlasting kingdom that shall never be destroyed! Satan will be bound for a thousand years during the reign of our Lord Yeshua as the Messiah of Israel!

Victory for the believer is based on the blood of Jesus Christ – *"And they overcame him by the blood of the Lamb, and by the word of their testimony; and they loved not their lives unto the death."* Yes, many believers will come to faith in the Lord during the tribulation but will also be killed for it. However, all of these martyrs will be resurrected at the end of the tribulation along with all Old Testament saints!

The **WRATH** of Satan against Israel
Revelation 12:13-17

"And when the dragon saw that he was cast unto the earth, he persecuted the woman which brought forth the man child. And to the woman were given two wings of a great eagle, that she might fly into the wilderness, into her place, where she is nourished for a time, and times, and half a time, from the face of the serpent. And the serpent cast out of his mouth water as a flood after the woman, that he might cause her to be carried away of the flood. And the earth helped the woman, and the earth opened her mouth, and swallowed up the flood which the dragon cast out of his mouth. And the dragon was wroth with the woman, and went to make war with the remnant of her seed, which keep the commandments of God, and have the testimony of Jesus Christ."

The **PERSECUTION** is connected to the Messiah!

Revelation 12:13 – *"And when the dragon saw that he was cast unto the earth, he persecuted the woman which brought forth the man child."*

The hostility between the serpent and the woman and her Seed was predicted in Genesis 3:15, and has continued throughout history. It is at the root of the devil's fury against the Jewish people.

The **PROTECTION** of the Lord will be given to the Jewish people!

Revelation 12:14-16 – *"And to the woman were given two wings of a great eagle, that she might fly into the wilderness, into her place, where she is nourished for a time, and times, and half a time, from the face of the serpent. And the serpent cast out of his mouth water as a flood after the woman, that he might cause her to be carried away of the flood. And the earth helped the woman, and the earth opened her mouth, and swallowed up the flood which the dragon cast out of his mouth."*

God is going to protect His people just as He cared for them through their wilderness wanderings in the past.

   1. The **EAGLE** of God's protection.

This beautiful picture of the *"wings of a great eagle"* reminds us of the protection and care of the Lord in the past. We read in Exodus 19:4: *"Ye have seen what I did unto the Egyptians, and how I bare you on eagles' wings, and brought you unto Myself."*

Deuteronomy 32:10-12 – *"He found him in a desert land, and in the waste howling wilderness; He led him about, He instructed him, He kept him as the apple of His eye. As an eagle stirreth up her nest, fluttereth over her young, spreadeth abroad her wings, taketh them, beareth them on her wings: So the LORD alone did lead him, and there was no strange god with him.."*

Yes, like the eagle who cares for his young ones, so the Lord provides for His people.

The reference to the *"wilderness"* reminds us of the words of Daniel 11:41: *"He (the "king" who "shall do according to his will") shall enter also into the glorious land, and many countries shall be overthrown: but these shall escape out of his hand, even Edom, and Moab, and the chief of the children of Ammon."* Perhaps it is for this reason (God's protection) that the people of Israel will hide in these regions from the terrible persecution that is coming.

2. The <u>EXTENT</u> of God's protection.

The children of Israel will be *"nourished for a time, and times, and half a time, from the face of the serpent."* According to Revelation 12:6, the Lord will *"feed her there a thousand two hundred and threescore days."* In other words, Israel will be divinely protected from the devil's attacks in the last half of the tribulation period.

3. The <u>EXAMPLE</u> of God's protection.

In Revelation 12:15-16 we learn of the Devil's attempt to destroy Israel with a *"flood."* Can Satan cause a literal flood? Under God's permission and plan the answer is "yes" as it was in the days of Job. Some see a literal flood and others view this as a symbolic act. But, there is no symbolic language here using words like "as" or "like." This is apparently a literal attempt by Satan to destroy the children of Israel.

The <u>PURPOSES</u> of Satan against Israel
Revelation 12:17

"And the dragon was wroth with the woman, and went to make war with the remnant of her seed, which keep the commandments of God, and have the testimony of Jesus Christ."

While it may be a reference to Jewish believers only there is no reason why it could also refer to Gentile believers in the tribulation – they are also *"the remnant of her seed."* The *"martyrs"* mentioned in Revelation 6:9 were *"slain for the word of God, and for the testimony which they held."* Also, in Revelation 14:12 we read: *"Here is the patience of the saints: here are they that keep the commandments of God, and the faith of Jesus."* The descriptions are indeed similar!

Satan's war with Israel is described in the next few chapters explaining how he will unleash his anger toward Israel and his diabolical plans to destroy the very people God says will never cease to exist!

COMING GLOBAL LEADERS
Revelation 13:1-18

In Revelation 12, the dragon was described as having *"seven heads and ten horns."* That description is a prelude to what we discover in chapter 13. It is Satan himself who brings two world leaders to power, one political and the other religious. Both are called *"beasts,"* one *"rising out of the sea"* and the other *"coming up out of the earth."* This unholy trinity includes the following:

> First beast out of the bottomless pit: SATAN
> Second beast out of the sea: ANTICHRIST
> Third beast out of the earth: FALSE PROPHET

Revelation 17:8 declares that the second beast with seven heads and ten horns will also come out of the *"bottomless pit."* They (Antichrist and False Prophet) originate from the *"bottomless pit"* (the Abyss) and as "demons of hell" they are energized by Satan himself.

THE WORLD POLITICAL LEADER
Revelation 13:1-10

The <u>IDENTITY</u> of this global leader
Revelation 13:1-3

"And I stood upon the sand of the sea, and saw a beast rise up out of the sea, having seven heads, and ten horns, and upon his horns ten crowns, and his heads the name of blasphemy. And the beast

which I saw was like unto a leopard, and his feet were as the feet of a bear, and his mouth as the mouth of a lion: and the dragon gave him his power, and his seat, and great authority. And I saw one of his heads as it were wounded to death; and his deadly wound was healed: and all the world wondered after the beast."

In Revelation 17:15 the word *"waters"* represents the sea of humanity, the nations of the world. If it is symbolic language for the origin of this beast, then the Antichrist, coming up out of the nations of the world, would be Gentile, and not Jewish. However, the language describing this beast in Revelation 13:2 more accurately reflects Daniel's dream and visions in Daniel 7. He saw *"four great beasts"* coming up from the sea, each one distinct and different from the others. Daniel 7:4-8 describes this remarkable vision of the future:

"The first was like a lion, and had eagle's wings: I beheld till the wings thereof were plucked, and it was lifted up from the earth, and made stand upon the feet as a man, and a man's heart was given to it. And behold another beast, a second, like to a bear, and it raised up itself on one side, and it had three ribs in the mouth of it between the teeth of it: and they said thus unto it, Arise, devour much flesh. After this I beheld, and lo another, like a leopard, which had upon the back of it four wings of a fowl; the beast had also four heads; and dominion was given to it. After this I saw in the night visions, and behold a fourth beast, dreadful and terrible, and

strong exceedingly; and it had great iron teeth: it devoured and brake in pieces, and stamped the residue with the feet of it: and it was diverse from all the beasts that were before it; and it had ten horns. I considered the horns, and, behold, there came up among them another little horn, before whom there were three of the first horns plucked up by the roots: and, behold, in this horn were eyes like the eyes of man, and a mouth speaking great things."

In Daniel 7:2 his dream spoke of *"the great sea"* out of which the *"beasts"* in his vision came up. The imagery probably refers to the Mediterranean Sea. On the basis of the information in the Book of Revelation we might also conclude that the *"great sea"* is a symbolic look at the abyss itself, out of which comes the demonic creatures.

1. The <u>ASSOCIATION</u> of the beast with the dragon

Both creatures are described as having *"seven heads and ten horns."* The only difference is that the dragon had crowns on his heads whereas the beast has crowns on his horns. In Revelation 17 we read of a harlot who rides on the beast. The woman represents *"that great city"* which reigns over the *"kings of the earth."* It would seem, therefore, that the *"beast"* represents the *"kings of the earth."* It is a picture of world history, the nations and leaders of the past and present. The *"heads"* are referring to seven world empires, and the horns (on the 7th head) represent the final kingdom on earth that will produce the Antichrist – also known from Daniel 7 as the *"little horn."* Further details will be given when we examine carefully the details and descriptions in chapters 17 and 18.

2. The <u>AUTHORITY</u> of this coming global leader

We are told in Revelation 13:2b that *"the dragon gave him his power, and his seat, and great authority."* If our view of the *"seven heads"* is correct that they are, in fact, seven world empires, then Satan has been the dominating power behind them all – after all he is (as the Bible teaches) *"the god of this world."*

3. The <u>APPEARANCE</u> of this coming leader

Revelation 13:2 clearly connects with the dream and vision of the prophet Daniel as we have mentioned previously. The imagery of a lion, bear, and leopard is similar to the words of Revelation 13:2: *"And the beast which I saw was like unto a leopard, and his feet were as the feet of a bear, and his mouth as the mouth of a lion."*

We believe that the symbolism of Daniel's dream and vision refers to world empires as well as that of the Book of Revelation.

> **THE LION = The empire of BABYLON**
> **THE BEAR = The empire of MEDO-PERSIA**

THE LEOPARD = The empire of GREECE

The *"four wings"* on the back of the leopard reminds us of the four divisions of Alexander the Great's empire after his death:

> LYSIMACHUS
> CASSANDER
> SELEUCUS
> PTOLEMY

Daniel's dream is looking from the standpoint of the empire of Babylon in which he was a major player and prophet. In John's vision in the Book of Revelation he is looking back from the advantage of the fifth world empire – ROME!

4. The <u>ATTRACTION</u> of the coming leader

Revelation 13:3 – *"And I saw one of his heads as it were wounded to death; and his deadly wound was healed: and all the world wondered after the beast."*

It was not one of his *"horns"* that received the *"deadly wound"* but rather one of his *"heads."* This death is referring to the demise of the 6th world empire – ROME! It would come back to life as a 10 nation confederacy (*"ten horns"*).

Two major viewpoints are expressed by Bible scholars and teachers concerning this wound of the beast that was healed.

1. **It refers to a particular PERSON!**

This view has always had numerous supporters, and it, of course, fascinates the proponents as they try to convince the reader of who it might be. The attempts have been numerous, such as:
> JUDAS ISCARIOT
> NERO
> MUSSOLINI
> HITLER
> STALIN
> EUROPEAN LEADER
> ISLAMIC LEADER

While interesting to surmise and develop a logical reason for a given person, it would seem more likely that if one of the *"seven heads"* was wounded to death, then it would refer to one of the world empires or governments.

2. **It refers to a world EMPIRE!**

It would seem logical if the 6th world empire was ROME that it is the *"head"* that died, but would come back to life again as a ten-nation or ten-division empire (*"ten horns"*). There have been six world empires in the history of the world:
> EGYPT
> ASSYRIA
> BABYLON
> MEDO-PERSIA
> GREECE
> ROME

There is still one to come. It appears to be a confederacy that would include the entire world of the end times. The Antichrist would come to power within the structure of the 7th world empire – a ten-division empire, he being an outsider at first, but comes to power quickly and powerfully (more in chapter 17 and 18).

The **INFLUENCE** of this coming leader
Revelation 13:4-8

"And they worshipped the dragon which gave power unto the beast: and they worshipped the beast, saying, Who is like unto the beast? Who is able to make war with him? And there was given unto him a mouth speaking great things and blasphemies; and power was given unto him to continue forty and two months. And he opened his mouth in blasphemy against God, to blaspheme His Name, and His tabernacle, and them that dwell in heaven. And it was given unto him to make war with the saints, and to overcome them: and power was given him over all kindreds, and tongues, and nations. And all that dwell upon the earth shall worship him, whose names are not written in the book of life of the Lamb slain from the foundation of the world."

1. The **ADORATION** he will receive.

Revelation 13:4 teaches that *"all the world"* (v. 3) will worship the dragon and the beast. It is not simply the worship of a world empire that would come back to life, but the individual known as the *"little horn"* (Daniel 7:8) or "the Antichrist."

A series of military victories over hostile forces would certainly endear this future government to the peoples of the world.

2. The <u>ARROGANCE</u> this coming leader will manifest.

Revelation 13:5-6 – *"And there was given unto him a mouth speaking great things and blasphemies; and power was given unto him to continue forty and two months. And he opened his mouth in blasphemy against God, to blaspheme His Name, and His tabernacle, and them that dwell in heaven."*

Daniel 7:8 says that this coming leader has a *"mouth speaking great things."* Daniel 7:25 adds: *"And he shall speak great words against the Most High, and shall wear out the saints of the Most High, and think to change times and laws: and they shall be given into his hand until a time and times and the dividing of time.* Daniel 11:36 says of a coming willful king: *"and he shall exalt himself, and magnify himself above every god, and shall speak marvellous things against the God of gods, and shall prosper till the indignation be accomplished; for that that is determined shall be done.*

In II Thessalonians 2:4 we read that this coming leader (called *"the man of sin...the son of perdition"*) *"opposeth and exalteth himself above all that is called God, or that is worshipped; so that he as God sitteth in the temple of God, shewing himself that he is God."*

3. The <u>ANGER</u> he will display toward the saints.

Revelation 13:6 says that he will *"blaspheme"* God, His Name, His tabernacle, and *"them that dwell in heaven."* It is possible that his anger is focused on those who will be raptured (*"them that dwell in heaven"*) – perhaps denying that this was the reason so many people are missing!

Daniel 7:25 says of this coming leader: *"And he shall speak great words against the Most High, and shall wear out the saints of the Most High, and think to change times and laws: and they shall be given into his hand until a time and times and the dividing of time* (3½ years or 1260 days or 42 months). Revelation 13:7 states: *"And it was given unto him to make war with the saints, and to overcome them; and power was given him over all kindreds, and tongues, and nations."*

One thing is very clear: No true believers will be worshiping the coming world leader, the Antichrist. He will be worshiped by those whose names are not written in the Book of Life, and those who will one day be cast into the lake of fire, according to Revelation 20:15.

The <u>INSTRUCTION</u> to believers today

Revelation 13:9-10

"If any man have an ear, let him hear. He that leadeth into captivity shall go into captivity: He that killeth with the sword must be killed with the sword. Here is the patience and the faith of the saints."

The opening words of verse 9 remind us of the messages to the seven churches. It is a challenge to all of us who read these remarkable prophecies. Are they having any effect upon us now? Are we listening carefully? Have we committed all to Jesus Christ, or are we tempted to follow the ways of this world of unbelievers?

The words *"he that leadeth into captivity shall go into captivity"* and *"he that killeth with the sword must be killed with the sword"* speak of Divine retribution and revenge. Sin will be paid for; no one gets away with anything. Judgment day is coming. It is also an encouragement to believers who will be taken into captivity and killed. There will be a future resurrection for all who suffer like this!

The words *"Here is the patience and the faith of the saints"* can be understood as an exhortation not to take revenge or seek to retaliate. Patience refers to bearing up under a load or a burden, and faith would emphasize the importance of confidence in God and His purposes. Both will be greatly needed in the tribulation by believers as well as in any period of history before that awful time of persecution.

THE WORLD RELIGIOUS LEADER
Revelation 13:11-18

Two leaders are prominent in the tribulation period: one is political and the other is religious. World government is represented by the *"beast"* and the religious system of the end times is controlled by the *"false prophet"* who is described in verses 11 and 12.

The DESCRIPTION of the religious leader
Revelation 13:11-12

"And I beheld another beast coming up out of the earth; and he had two horns like a lamb, and he spake as a dragon. And he exerciseth all the power of the first beast before him, and causeth the earth and them that dwell therein to worship the first beast, whose deadly wound was healed."

1. His ASSOCIATION with the first beast

The word *"another"* means in Greek grammar "another of the same kind." The word *"beast"* is the same word used of the first leader. This religious leader has the same "beastlike" character and attitudes of the world political leader. They are two of a kind. This second beast comes *"out of the earth"* in contrast to heaven. The first beast came out of the sea.

2. His <u>APPEARANCE</u>

The lamb is always a religious symbol and is used in sacrifices. This second beast is like a lamb that has *"two horns."* Interesting that our Lord Yeshua is the Lamb of God and has *"seven horns"* not two! Since lambs do not have *"horns"* the *"horns"* are symbols of authority. The *"two horns"* of this second beast might indicate that he exercises authority in two realms (political and religious) or as we sometimes say "he wears two hats."

3. His <u>ATTITUDE</u>

This beast (according to verse 11) *"spake as a dragon."* The primary communication of the dragon is deception (Revelation 12:9). It is important to realize that the devil is not against religion. He uses it for his own end and purposes. He deceives us with religion as surely as with any other method or device. This religious leader, the false prophet, will speak as the dragon does, deceiving people with his brand of false religion.

II Corinthians 11:3 warns us: *"But I fear, lest by any means, as the serpent beguiled Eve through his subtilty, so your minds should be corrupted from the simplicity that is in Christ."*

4. His <u>AUTHORITY</u>

It appears by the way things are presented in this passage that world government has control over world religion. The dragon gave the first beast his authority; now, satanic authority is given by the first beast to the second beast, the false prophet. This religious leader does nothing without the approval from the political leader. He exercises his authority *"before him"* meaning "in his presence," the presence of the first beast, the political leader.

5. His <u>AIM</u>

The religious leader will promote the worship of world government. His purpose is to get people to support and follow world government and its special leader, the Antichrist. We should be hesitant about all attempts to promote a global government, either through economics, politics, or religion. According to Bible prophecy, it is satanic. Without the rule of the Messiah, world government is doomed to failure. It is Satan's plan and will result in the persecution and death of believers!

The <u>DECEPTION</u> of this religious leader
Revelation 13: 13-15

"And he doeth great wonders, so that he maketh fire come down from heaven on the earth in the sight of men, and deceiveth them that dwell on the earth by the means of those miracles which he had power to do in the sight of the first beast; saying to them that dwell on the earth, that they should make an image to the beast, which had the wound by a sword, and did live. And he had power to give life unto the image of the beast, that the image of

the beast should both speak, and cause that as many as would not worship the image of the beast should be killed."

1. The <u>PERFORMANCE</u> of miraculous signs

The devil can perform the miraculous, and as a result, deceive many people. The performance of miracles is no proof that the one doing them is from God. Our Lord Yeshua told us in Matthew 24:24: *"For there shall arise false Christs, and false prophets, and shall shew great signs and wonders; insomuch that, if it were possible, they shall deceive the very elect."* Our Lord's prediction fits perfectly with what the false prophet will do.

Our culture is being prepared for this worldwide deception, and many so-called Christians are involved and do not realize it. We are making claims about miracles today that directly contradict the teaching and warnings of the Bible. We do not deny that God can perform miracles, but the methods and purposes of most miracles being performed in public meetings today simply do not meet Biblical requirements. The deception has already begun!

II Thessalonians 2:9-10 speaks of the ability of the coming political leader to perform the miraculous: *"Even him, whose coming is after the working of Satan with all power and signs and lying wonders, and with all deceivableness of unrighteousness in them that perish; because they received not the love of the truth, that they might be saved."* Satan will counterfeit the true miracles of God and those that were performed by the apostles of our Lord Jesus Christ.

One of the so-called "miracles" which the false prophet will perform is making fire fall from heaven to the earth. Perhaps it is a counterfeit Pentecost or an attempt to duplicate the miracle of Elijah and make people believe that this false prophet is the coming Elijah (who is to come before the return of the Messiah). It may also be an attempt to demonstrate the same kind of power that will accompany the return of the Messiah – II Thessalonians 1:8 says *"in flaming fire."*

2. The <u>PURPOSE</u> of these miraculous sings

The general purpose is to deceive the people of earth; the specific purpose is to encourage those who dwell on the earth to make an image to the beast. It is either a monument to world government or to its leader, the Antichrist. The state now becomes the "god" of the world's populations.

Making the image of the first beast to speak is no longer an impossible task. Computers, as we know, can be programmed to talk. However, this appears to be a convincing miracle causing the people of the world to respond with worship and allegiance.

3. The <u>PERSECUTION</u> that will result

One cannot help but relate the killing of those who refuse to worship the image of the beast to a similar incident in Daniel's prophecy. Nebuchadnezzar made an image of gold and required all the people to worship it or be killed in the fiery furnace. It is the height of depravity to change the glory of the incorruptible God into an image made like corruptible man. This is clearly the message of Romans 1:18-23:

"For the wrath of God is revealed from heaven against all ungodliness and unrighteousness of men, who hold the truth in unrighteousness; Because that which may be known of God is manifest in them; for God hath shewed it to them. For the invisible things of Him from the creation of the world are clearly seen being understood by the things that are made, even His eternal power and Godhead; so that they are without excuse: Because that, when they knew God, they glorified Him not as God, neither were thankful; but became vain in their imaginations, and their foolish heart was darkened. Professing themselves to be wise, they became fools, and changed the glory of the incorruptible God into an image made like to corruptible man, and to birds, and fourfooted beasts, and creeping things."

All who worship such man-made images deserve the judgment of God. Romans 1:32 says: *"Who knowing the judgment of God, that they which commit such things are worthy of death, not only do the same, but have pleasure in them that do them."*

All those who refuse to worship the image of the beast are to be killed. While this is a decree and does not necessarily imply that all were killed, it seems from Revelation 20:4 that this is what will take place. Apart from the 144,000 Jews and the believing Jewish remnant who will be protected by God, it appears that all Gentile believers will be killed because they do not take the mark of the beast or worship its image.

The <u>DEMAND</u> of this religious leader
Revelation 13:16-18

"And he causeth all, both small and great, rich and poor, free and bond, to receive a mark in their right hand, or in their foreheads: And that no man might buy or sell, save he that hath the mark or the name of the beast, or the number of his name. Here is wisdom. Let him that hath understanding count the number of the beast: for it is the number of a man; and his number is six hundred threescore and six (666)."

Many attempts have been made in the past to identify the number 666 with a particular individual. Suggestions have included Roman emperors such as Nero or Caligula, etc. And leaders of the modern history of humanity like Mussolini, Hitler, Lenin, Stalin, etc. Attempts have also been made to identify the Antichrist by assigning numerical equivalents to Hebrew, Greek, or Latin letters – most of these views are totally inadequate.

428

The key phrase seems to be *"for it is the number of a man."*

The entire world is subject to the demand of this religious leader. Every person must receive the mark of the name of the beast. This demand requires complete allegiance to the world government. True believers will refuse the mark and lose their lives.

It will be clear to all what the mark of the beast is and why it must be put on the hand or forehead. Believers will not be caught by surprise; they will have the opportunity and wisdom to refuse such a mark. It appears from Revelation that all believers refuse the mark. Only non-believers take the mark and go along with the demands of world government and its leaders.

We do not have the knowledge of how this all will be achieved; but, one can easily see how simple the process could be with our use of credit cards.

True believers of today will not be here on planet earth to face this deception and demand. They will be *"caught up"* to meet the Lord in the air, and be in heaven during the tribulation on earth! Praise God!

VISIONS OF THE TRIBULATION
Revelation 14:1-20

In this chapter the Apostle John is given a panoramic picture of the tribulation period from the standpoint of the Messiah's victory. We now will view the ultimate triumph of God, the Lamb, and all of His followers, the true believers. It is a preview of coming attractions on the movie screen of human history!

There are at least three major visions of this one chapter:

VISION OF VICTORY
Revelation 14:1-5
VISION OF JUDGMENT
Revelation 14:6-13
VISION OF THE FINAL HARVEST
Revelation 14:14-20

VISION OF VICTORY
Revelation 14:1-5

"And I looked, and, lo, a Lamb stood on the mount Sion, and with Him an hundred forty and four thousand, having His Father's Name written in their foreheads. And I heard a voice from heaven, as the voice of many waters, and as the voice of a great thunder: and I heard the voice of harpists harping with their harps: And they sung as it were a new song before the throne, and before the four beasts, and the elders: and no man could learn that

song but the hundred and forty and four thousand, which were redeemed from the earth. These are they which were not defiled with women; for they are virgins. These are they which follow the Lamb whithersoever He goeth. These were redeemed from among men, being the firstfruits unto God and to the Lamb. And in their mouth was found no guile: for they are without fault before the throne of God.*"*

In chapter 7 we learned that the 144,000 are *"servants of our God"* and represented *"all the tribes of the children of Israel."* We were told that they were *"sealed"* by God *"on their foreheads."* Now we are given additional information about these sealed servants of God.

The words *"and I looked"* appear for the 8th time in the vision of Revelation. They all introduce a key or major vision of the Book. It is critical that we understand God's ultimate triumph over all that is taking place during the tribulation period.

The PROTECTION of God
Revelation 14:1

1. It involves the PRESENCE of the Lamb.

Our Lord Yeshua said in Matthew 28:20: *"and, lo, I am with you always, even unto the end of the world."* Hebrews 13:5 adds: *"for He hath said, I will never leave thee, nor forsake thee."* The Lamb's presence with the 144,000 is indeed reassuring, not only to them, but also to all of us to whom His words of comfort were intended.

2. It involves the <u>PLACE</u> where they are standing.

The Lamb of God is presently in heaven at the right hand of the throne of God where he continues to intercede for us. This picture is not of heaven, though Hebrews 12:22 uses the term *"Mount Zion"* to refer to the heavenly city, the new Jerusalem. This is a picture of the Lamb's ultimate triumph at the end of the tribulation. *"Mount Zion"* is used symbolically of the Messianic age, the Jewish hope of all its history – kingdom promises to the people of Israel with Messiah as its King, reigning in Jerusalem, in fulfillment of God's promise to King David long ago.

3. It involves the <u>PRINT</u> of God's name on their foreheads.

The seal of God upon the foreheads of these Jewish believers is a reminder that they belong to God and to the Lamb. This mark of God's Name is an obvious contrast to the *"mark of the beast."* Is the name of world government on us or are we just "going along" with secular society and its immoral viewpoints? Or, are we claiming the Name that is *"above every name"* and committed to Him and His plans for planet earth? This is a serious battle, a spiritual war for the minds and hearts of the people of this planet.

The **PRAISE** of God
Revelation 14:2-3

"And I heard a voice from heaven, as the voice of many waters, and as the voice of a great thunder: and I heard the voice of harpers harping with their harps: And they sung as it were a new song before the throne, and before the four beasts, and the elders: and no man could learn that song but the hundred and forty and four thousand, which were redeemed from the earth."

It was a *"voice"* that John heard, not *"voices."* This could be referring again to God's voice, for it is like *"many waters"* and *"a great thunder."* Psalm 29:3 says: *"The voice of the LORD is upon the waters: the God of glory thundereth: the LORD is upon many waters."*

The idea of people playing harps in heaven is not foreign to the Bible. Notice the following:

Psalm 144:9 – *"I will sing a new song unto Thee, O God: upon a psaltery and an instrument of ten strings will I sing praises unto Thee."*

Psalm 147:7 – *"Sing unto the LORD with thanksgiving; sing praise upon the harp unto our God."*

Psalm 149:3 – *"Let them praise His Name in the dance: let them sing praises unto Him with the timbrel and harp."*

Psalm 150:3 – *"Praise Him with the sound of the trumpet: praise Him with the psaltery and harp."*

The *"harp"* is a beautiful instrument and a delight to hear when played with skill. Revelation 15:2 mentions those who have been victorious over the beast, his image, and his mark, as *"having the harps of God."* They are singing the song of Moses and the song of the Lamb. Certainly the 144,000 would be included in that "harp orchestra"!

What is the "new song"?

What is the point behind verse 3 that *"no man could learn that song but the 144,000 which were redeemed from the earth"*? In chapter 5 we learned that the 24 elders sing a *"new song"* of praise for their redemption. They represent the church-age believers who are in heaven during the tribulation. They are redeemed by the precious blood of the Lamb of God as well. Perhaps the stanzas of the song are unique as they would express the praise of the 144,000 to God for their redemption, and their unique protection by Almighty God during the days of the tribulation.

The __PURPOSE__ of God
Revelation 14:4-5

"These are they which were not defiled with women; for they are virgins. These are they which follow the Lamb whithersoever He goeth. These were redeemed from among men, being the

firstfruits unto God and to the Lamb. And in their mouth was found no guile: for they are without fault before the throne of God."

1. Their moral <u>PURITY</u>

Many Bible teachers argue that as celibates they would not be encumbered with family responsibilities and so would be uniquely set apart for the preaching of the gospel during this time of trouble and persecution. The Apostle Paul's discussion of the single state in I Corinthians 7: 25-35 is often used to emphasize its importance in such times.

However, If that is the case for the 144,000, would it not also be advisable for the rest of the believers during the tribulation period? In Matthew 25:1-13, our Lord Yeshua spoke of ten virgins, attendants at a wedding. He said that five of them were "wise" and clearly referred to them as believers of the tribulation period. Five were "foolish" and unprepared to meet the Bridegroom when He comes to the earth at the end of the tribulation. Would not the "five wise virgins" represent all tribulation believers and not just the 144,000 Jewish evangelists?

It seems that it would be better to understand the word *"virgins"* in this passage as a reference to moral purity and possibly undefilement from idolatry. They have remained faithful to God.

Paul wrote in II Corinthians 11:2: *"For I am jealous over you with godly jealousy: for I have espoused you to one husband, that I may present you as a chaste virgin to Christ."* Undoubtedly the idea of moral purity is involved in the use of this word *"virgin."*

Since the 144,000 are clearly Jewish believers, there might be a possible connection with the following passages:

Isaiah 37:22 – *"This is the word which the LORD hath spoken concerning him; The VIRGIN, the daughter of Zion, hath despised thee, and laughed thee to scorn; the daughter of Jerusalem hath shaken her head at thee."* (Also found in II Kings 19:21)

Jeremiah 18:13 – *"Therefore thus saith the LORD; Ask ye now among the heathen, who hath heard such things: the VIRGIN of Israel hath done a very horrible thing."*

Jeremiah 31:4 – *"Again I will build thee, and thou shalt be built, O VIRGIN of Israel: thou shalt again be adorned with thy tabrets, and shalt go forth in the dances of them that make merry."*

Jeremiah 31:21 – *"Set thee up waymarks, make thee high heaps: set thine heart toward the highway, even the way which thou wentest: turn again, O VIRGIN of Israel, turn again to these thy cities."*

Lamentations 2:13 – *"What thing shall I take to witness for thee? What things shall I liken to thee, O daughter of Jerusalem? What shall I equal to thee, that I may comfort thee, O VIRGIN daughter of Zion? For thy breach is great like the sea: who can heal thee?*

It is clear that the term *"virgin"* means much more than simply being without a husband and celibate. The use of the term with the Nation of Israel would also lend support to how it is used with the 144,000 Jews in the tribulation.

2. Their faithful <u>PRACTICE</u>

Revelation 14:4 – *"they which follow the Lamb whithersoever He goeth."*

They were willing to go anywhere the Lord wanted them to go and to do whatever He wanted them to do. What marvelous examples they are to all of us who seek to follow our Lord Jesus Christ!

3. Their spiritual <u>POSITION</u>

The 144,000 were *"redeemed from among men, being the firstfruits unto God and to the Lamb."*

The 144,000 are the *"firstfruits"* (meaning that more will follow) of those to be saved during the tribulation. They are possibly the ones referred to in Revelation 11:13 – *"and the remnant were affrighted, and gave glory to the God of heaven."*

Many people have questioned whether or not the 144,000 Jews who are sealed by God could reach all the Gentile nations of the world with the gospel in that short period of time (last half of the tribulation). However, it may be that the miracle of the Day of Pentecost will be repeated and the 144,000 Jewish evangelists will be able to speak in all the languages of the whole world without any previous knowledge of them. The prophecy of Joel 2 which Peter quoted on that day would find its future fulfillment in the tribulation period when the sun is darkened and the moon is turned to blood.

Joel 2:32 says: *"And it shall come to pass, that whosoever shall call on the Name of the LORD shall be delivered: for in mount Zion and in Jerusalem shall be deliverance, as the LORD hath said, and in the remnant whom the LORD shall call."*

These words are planted in our minds when we read Revelation 14:1 – *'And I looked, and, lo, a Lamb stood on the mount Zion, and with Him 144,000, having His Father's Name written in their foreheads."*

The words of Revelation 14:4 says: *"and in their mouth was found no guile"* – there was nothing false in them. The words that follow – *"for they are without fault before the throne of God"* strengthens the view that as *"virgins"* we are talking primarily about moral purity.

VISION OF JUDGMENT
Revelation 14:6-13

The **PROCLAMATION** of the gospel
Revelation 14:6-7

"And I saw another angel fly in the midst of heaven, having the everlasting gospel to preach unto them that dwell on the earth, and to every nation, and kindred, and tongue, and people, saying with a loud voice, Fear God, and give glory to Him; for the hour of His judgment is come: and worship Him that made heaven, and earth, and the sea, and the fountains of waters."

1. The gospel is an **EVERLASTING** gospel!

This is not a different gospel than the one preached in the Bible, the one that grace has brought and centers on the death and resurrection of our Lord Yeshua. There is nothing new here. The gospel is eternal, not localized to certain points of human history.

2. The gospel will reach all **NATIONS**!

Our Lord Yeshua told us in Matthew 24:14: *"And this gospel of the kingdom shall be preached in all the world for a witness unto all nations; and then shall the end come."* The *"end"* is referring to the end of the tribulation.

Some believe that a literal angel will come and proclaim this gospel to the whole world. Angels are used throughout the Book of Revelation to announce God's plans on planet earth. A more likely view is that the angel is proclaiming what is going to happen but that the 144,000 will carry it out.

3. The gospel is the <u>MESSAGE</u> that brings people to God!

Verse 7 says *"Fear God, and give glory to Him; for the hour of His judgment is come: and worship Him that made heaven, and earth, and the sea, and the fountains of waters."*

A gospel that falls short of bringing people to God to give Him glory and worship is insufficient and unable to achieve the purposes of our God!

Interestingly, there are two reasons given for this response to God: One deals with the fact that the hour of His judgment has come! The other reminds us of His creation and His purpose for all things!

The <u>PREDICTION</u> about Babylon
Revelation 14:8

"And there followed another angel, saying, Babylon is fallen, is fallen, that great city, because she made all nations drink of the wine of the wrath of her fornication."

In chapters 17 and 18 we will learn more details about Babylon and its coming fall.

WHAT IS BABYLON?

1. **It refers to the city of Jerusalem!**

Proponents of this view always refer back to Revelation 11:8 – *"the great city, which spiritually is called Sodom and Egypt, where also our Lord was crucified."*

2. **It refers to a rebuilt city of ancient Babylon!**

This has been a very popular view in recent years. The only problem is that the ancient city has not been rebuilt and does not hold the place which Revelation 18 says – affecting all nations of the world.

3. **It refers to the city of Rome!**

This was the view of early church leaders and has been the majority view among premillennialists. The major religious system that seems to include the doctrines and practices of ancient Babylon as well as representing the kind of influence over the nations of the world that Revelation 17 and 18 suggest will be the fact in that day – is the Roman Catholic Church.

Other views speak of major cities of the world that are functioning today. Many hold that it is referring to New York City because of the presence of the United Nations there.

The **REASON** for its fall – *"because she made all nations drink of the wine of her fornication."*

We will speak of more details when we come to Revelation 17 and 18.

The **PUNISHMENT** of those who worship the beast and his image
Revelation 14:9-11

"And the third angel followed them, saying with a loud voice, If any man worship the beast and his image, and receive his mark in his forehead, or in his hand, The same shall drink of the wine of the wrath of God, which is poured out without mixture into the cup of His indignation; and he shall be tormented with fire and brimstone in the presence of the holy angels, and in the presence of the Lamb: And the smoke of their torment ascendeth up forever and ever: and they have no rest day nor night, who worship the beast and his image, and whosoever receiveth the mark of his name."

1. The **EVIDENCE** that such punishment is deserved!

If you worship the beast and his image and/or take the mark of the beast for economic survival, you deserve the punishment of God upon your life.

2. The <u>EXPLANATION</u> of the punishment upon those who worship the beast!

In Revelation 14:8 we read: *"because she made all nations drink of the wine of the wrath of her fornication."* And, verse 10 it adds: *"The same shall drink of the wine of the wrath of God..."*

Psalm 75:7-8 says: *"But God is the Judge: He putteth down one, and setteth up another. For in the hand of the LORD there is a cup, and the wine is red; it is full of mixture; and He poureth out of the same: but the dregs thereof, all the wicked of the earth shall wring them out, and drink them."* The cup out of which they drink is described as the *"indignation"* of God Himself.

3. The <u>EXTENT</u> of this punishment!

No passage is more clear on the eternal punishment of the wicked than this one. Though many attempts have been made to eliminate the concept of eternal retribution, this passage (as well as others) makes it quite clear. All who refuse to put their faith and trust in the Lord and His Messiah will be *"cast into the lake of fire* (Revelation 20:15)." The consequences of the gospel are indeed frightening and awesome! No wonder people laugh at such ideas or try to reinterpret the meaning of these words!

BUT, WILL GOD PUNISH PEOPLE FOREVER?

A very serious question! It appears that His holiness, justice, and righteous character demands it. If there is eternal life for the believer, then simple logic requires that there is eternal punishment for the unbeliever. Matthew 25:46 states clearly: *"And these shall go away into everlasting punishment: but the righteous into life eternal."* To all those who attempt to make a difference between the word *"everlasting"* and the word *"eternal"* – they are exactly the same in the Greek text! Revelation 14:11 says: *"And the smoke of their torment ascendeth up forever and ever."*

The **PATIENCE** of the saints
Revelation 14:12-13

"Here is the patience of the saints: here are they that keep the commandments of God, and the faith of Jesus. And I heard a voice from heaven saying unto me, Write, Blessed are the dead which die in the Lord from henceforth: Yea, saith the Spirit, that they may rest from their labors; and their works do follow them."

    1. The primary **CHARACTERISTIC** of saints.

The phrase that says it all – *"they that keep the commandments of God, and the faith of Jesus."* It refers to our allegiance and loyalty to the teachings of the Bible, and specifically to the doctrine of salvation as found in Jesus Christ. Those believers who have been persecuted and killed for their faith are described in Revelation 6:9 as *"them that were slain for the word of God, and for the testimony which they held."*

2. The future <u>CONDITION</u> of the saints.

This beatitude is one of great comfort and assurance to every believer – *"Blessed are the dead which die in the Lord from henceforth: Yea, saith the Spirit, that they may rest from their labors, and their works do follow them."*

The death of unbelievers is not a blessing, but a tragedy; the judgment of hell will follow. This is also a reminder to all who will suffer martyrdom in the tribulation period that better things will follow after their death. Death is a blessing when we know the Lord personally and have committed our lives to Him, believing that His death for our sins, and His resurrection are solid guarantees and foundations for the future blessings that the Lord has prepared for those who love Him.

Two things describe the future condition of all believers:

    (1)   Eternal <u>REST</u>
    (2)   Eternal <u>REWARD</u>

Nothing we have ever done for the Lord and His people will go unnoticed or unrewarded! Every *"cup of cold water"* given in His Name shall be rewarded – what a blessing awaits us!

VISION OF THE FINAL HARVEST
Revelation 14:14-20

"And I looked, and behold a white cloud, and upon the cloud one sat like unto the Son of man, having on His head a golden crown, and in His hand a sharp sickle. And another angel came out of the temple, crying with a loud voice to Him that sat on the cloud, Thrust in Thy sickle, and reap: for the time is come for Thee to reap; for the harvest of the earth is ripe. And He that sat on the cloud thrust in His sickle on the earth; and the earth was reaped. And another angel came out of the temple which is in heaven, he also having a sharp sickle. And another angel came out from the altar, which had power over fire; and cried with a loud cry to Him that had the sharp sickle, saying, Thrust in thy sharp sickle, and gather the clusters of the vine of the earth; for her grapes are fully ripe. And the angel thrust in his sickle into the earth, and gathered the vine of the earth, and cast it into the great winepress of the wrath of God. And the winepress was trodden without the city, and blood came out of the winepress, even unto the horse bridles, by the space of a thousand and six hundred furlongs (about 200 miles)."

Notice four things about this One Who sat on the cloud:

1. His human **PERSONALITY** – *"one sat like unto the Son of man"*

Jesus Christ is called the *"Son of man"* throughout the gospels. It is a Messianic term referred to in Daniel 7:13-14:

"I saw in the night visions, and, behold, one like the Son of man came with the clouds of heaven, and came to the Ancient of days, and they brought Him near before Him. And there was given Him dominion, and glory, and a kingdom, that all people, nations, and languages, should serve Him: His dominion is an everlasting dominion, which shall not pass away, and His kingdom that which shall not be destroyed."

John 5:26-27 reminds us: *"For as the Father hath life in Himself; so hath He given to the Son to have life in Himself; And hath given Him authority to execute judgment also, because He is the Son of man."*

   2. His moral <u>PURITY</u> – *"and behold a white cloud, and upon the cloud one sat like unto the Son of man"*

The *"clouds of heaven"* are symbols of the Divine and holy presence of God. The word *"white"* emphasizes moral purity and pictures the righteousness of God made possible by the blood of Jesus Christ. Revelation 7:14 says of those who become believers during the tribulation: *"and have washed their robes, and made them white in the blood of the Lamb."*

3. His great <u>POWER</u> – The *"golden crown"* is that which is worn by the King who conquers. Revelation 19:12 says that on His head were *"many crowns* (diadems).*"*

4. His awesome <u>PURPOSE</u> – the *"sharp sickle"* is speaking of the reaping of a harvest, both grain as well as grapes.

The <u>SICKLE</u> of the grain harvest
Revelation 14:15-16

"And another angel came out of the temple, crying with a loud voice to Him that sat on the cloud, Thrust in Thy sickle, and reap: for the time is come for Thee to reap; for the harvest of the earth is ripe. And He that sat on the cloud thrust in His sickle on the earth; and the earth was reaped."

A similar picture is found in the words of our Lord Yeshua in Matthew 13:37-43:

"He that soweth the good seed is the Son of man; The field is the world; the good seed are the children of the kingdom; but the tares are the children of the wicked one; The enemy that sowed them is the devil; the harvest is the end of the world (age); and the reapers are the angels. As therefore the tares are gathered and burned in the fire; so shall it be in the end of this world. The Son of man shall send forth His angels, and they shall gather out of His kingdom all things that offend, and them which do iniquity; And shall cast them into a

furnace of fire: there shall be wailing and gnashing of teeth. Then shall the righteous shine forth as the sun in the kingdom of their Father. Who hath ears to hear, let him hear."

The <u>SICKLE</u> of the grape harvest
Revelation 14:17-20

"And another angel came out from the altar, which had power over fire; and cried with a loud cry to him (the angel that came out of the temple in heaven) *that had the sharp sickle, saying, Thrust in thy sharp sickle, and gather the clusters of the vine of the earth; for her grapes are fully ripe. And the angel thrust in his sickle into the earth, and gathered the vine of the earth, and cast it into the great winepress of the wrath of God. And the winepress was trodden without the city, and blood came out of the winepress, even unto the horse bridles, by the space of a thousand and six hundred furlongs* (about 200 miles)."

In both illustrations the condition of the harvest was considered to be *"ripe"* – ready for the judgment of Almighty God and His Messiah.

Joel 3:12-16 speaks of this powerful illustration:

"Let the heathen be wakened, and come up to the valley of Jehoshaphat: for there will I sit to judge all the heathen round about. Put ye in the sickle, for the harvest is ripe: come, get you down; for the press is full, the vats overflow; for their wickedness

is great. Multitudes, multitudes in the valley of decision: for the day of the LORD is near in the valley of decision. The sun and the moon shall be darkened, and the stars shall withdraw their shining. The LORD also shall roar out of Zion, and utter His voice from Jerusalem; and the heavens and the earth shall shake: but the LORD will be the hope of His people, and the strength of the children of Israel."

The illustrations of the sickle and the harvest of both grain and grapes are picturing the judgment of the Lord that falls on all nations at the end of the tribulation. This judgment occurs in the Valley of Jehoshaphat, which is adjacent to the city of Jerusalem. It is there that all nations will come against Jerusalem.

The picture of the *"winepress"* is vividly presented in Isaiah 63:1-6:

"Who is this that cometh from Edom, with dyed garments from Bozrah? This that is glorious in His apparel, travelling in the greatness of His strength? I that speak in righteousness, mighty to save. Wherefore art Thou red in Thine apparel, and Thy garments like him that treadeth in the winevat? I have trodden the winepress alone; and of the people there was none with Me: for I will tread them in Mine anger, and trample them in My fury; and their blood shall be sprinkled upon My garments, and I will stain all My raiment. For the day of vengeance is in Mine heart, and the year of

My redeemed is come. And I looked, and there was none to help; and I wondered that there was none to uphold: therefore Mine own arm brought salvation unto Me; and My fury, it upheld Me. And I will tread down the people in Mine anger, and make them drunk in My fury, and I will bring down their strength to the earth."

The Messiah will return at the end of the tribulation when all nations have gathered to attack Jerusalem and the Nation of Israel – we call it "The Battle of Armageddon." The entire land of Israel will be the *"winepress"* and the blood of all nations who will attack Israel at that time will flow up to the horse bridles. The Messiah by Himself will conquer all nations and destroy their armies. His garments will be stained by the blood of His enemies. These armies will be assembled on the high plateau of the Nation of Jordan, south of Ammon – at the ancient site and capital named Bozrah. When the battle is over and victory over all nations is won, the Messiah will place His feet on the Mount of Olives and declare victory over the entire world! Praise the Lord!

THE SEVEN LAST PLAGUES
Revelation 15:1-16:21

The scroll with seven seals is now opened. The 7th seal was opened in Revelation 8:1, at which time we were introduced to seven angels with seven trumpets. The seventh trumpet message is the longest and began with the announcement of Revelation 11:15. Within that seventh trumpet message are several signs and visions:

> SIGNS OF THE SEVENTH TRUMPET
> The woman
> The dragon
> The seven last plagues
>
> VISIONS OF THE SEVENTH TRUMPET
> The beast with seven heads
> The beast with two horns
> The 144,000 Jews
> The gospel and judgments
> The final harvest
> The heavenly temple and the seven last
>   Plagues

There are more details in chapters 17-22 and will be discussed later.

The SIGN in heaven
Revelation 15:1-2

"And I saw another sign in heaven, great and marvellous, seven angels having the seven last

plagues; for in them is filled up the wrath of God. And I saw as it were a sea of glass mingled with fire: and them that had gotten the victory over the beast, and over his image, and over his mark, and over the number of his name, stand on the sea of glass, having the harps of God."

The text of Revelation 15:1 says *"I saw another sign in heaven"* – meaning "another of the same kind." The words *"great and marvellous"* connect with verse 3 when we read: *"Great and marvellous are Thy works, Lord God Almighty."*

The words *"sea of glass"* are very different from the *"sea of glass"* that was described in Revelation 4. This one is *"mingled with fire"* and may indicate that those standing on it have gone through the fire of the tribulation period. It is possible that it refers as well to the judgment of God.

The ones standing on this *"sea of glass"* are the martyrs of the tribulation period – the *"great multitude"* of Revelation 7:9-17. The fact that they are *"standing"* implies victory and conquest through their resurrection. What a great encouragement to us all! The Lord has a special ministry for these martyrs of the tribulation period. They will form a marvelous orchestra of harps, a symphony of praise to our God, rejoicing in His ultimate victory over all His enemies and ours.

The <u>SONG</u> of Moses and the Lamb
Revelation 15:3-4

"And they sing the song of Moses the servant of God, and the song of the Lamb, saying, Great and marvellous are Thy works, Lord God Almighty, just and true are Thy ways, Thou King of saints. Who shall not fear Thee, O Lord, and glorify Thy Name? for Thou only art holy: for all nations shall come and worship before Thee; for Thy judgments are made manifest."

What a wonderful song of praise to our God! The music of heaven comes from the hearts who have tasted deeply of the grace of God and His forgiveness and cleansing, but who also know what it means to suffer and to give their lives for the Lord. This is a song of martyrs, and an exhortation to the living about praise and worship.

Exodus 15:1 says that the children of Israel who saw the mighty miracles of God upon the Egyptians *"sang...this song unto the LORD, and spake, saying, I will sing unto the LORD, for He hath triumphed gloriously: the horse and his rider hath He thrown into the sea."*

That song of Moses, recorded in Exodus 15:1-19 is a wonderful song of praise for Who the LORD is, and what He has done!

"The LORD is my strength and song, and He is become my salvation: He is my God, and I will prepare Him an habitation; my father's God, and I will exalt Him. The LORD is a man of war: the

LORD is His Name. Pharaoh's chariots and his host hath He cast into the sea: his chosen captains also are drowned in the Red Sea. The depths have covered them: they sank into the bottom as a stone. Thy right hand, O LORD, is become glorious in power: Thy right hand, O LORD, hath dashed in pieces the enemy. And in the greatness of Thine excellency Thou hast overthrown them that rose up against Thee: Thou sentest forth Thy wrath, which consumed them as stubble. And with the blast of Thy nostrils the waters were gathered together, the floods stood upright as an heap, and the depths were congealed in the heart of the sea. The enemy said, I will pursue, I will overtake, I will divide the spoil; my lust shall be satisfied upon them; I will draw my sword, my hand shall destroy them. Thou didst blow with Thy wind, the sea covered them: they sank as lead in the mighty waters. Who is like unto Thee, O LORD, among the gods? Who is like Thee, glorious in holiness, fearful in praises, doing wonders? Thou stretchedst out Thy right hand, the earth swallowed them. Thou in Thy mercy hast led forth the people which Thou hast redeemed: Thou hast guided them in Thy strength unto Thy holy habitation. The people shall hear, and be afraid: sorrow shall take hold on the inhabitants of Palestina. Then the dukes of Edom shall be amazed; the mighty men of Moab, trembling shall take hold upon them; all the inhabitants of Canaan shall melt away. Fear and dread shall fall upon them; by the greatness of Thine arm they shall be as still as a stone; till Thy people pass over, O LORD, till the people pass over, which Thou hast *purchased. Thou shalt bring them in, and plant them in the mountain of Thine inheritance, in the place, O LORD, which Thou hast made for Thee to dwell in, in the Sanctuary, O Lord, which Thy hands have established. The LORD shall reign forever and ever. For the horse of Pharaoh went in with his chariots and with his horsemen into the sea, and the LORD brought again the waters of the sea upon them; but the children of Israel went on dry land in the midst of the sea."*

(Take a moment and reread this wonderful song of Moses and rejoice in the LORD and His power!)

The <u>SCENE</u> in heaven
Revelation 15:5-8

"And after that I looked, and, behold, the temple of the tabernacle of the testimony in heaven was opened: And the seven angels came out of the temple, having the seven plagues, clothed in pure and white linen, and having their breasts girded with golden girdles. And one of the four beasts gave unto the seven angels seven golden vials (bowls) full of the wrath of God, Who liveth forever and ever. And the temple was filled with smoke from the glory of God, and from His power; and no man was able to enter into the temple, till the seven plagues of the seven angels were fulfilled."

Is there a literal temple in heaven?

Hebrews 8 and 9 seem to argue for the earthly tabernacle and temple being a "copy" of the heavenly one.

Hebrews 8:2 – *"A minister of the sanctuary, and of the true tabernacle, which the Lord pitched, and not man."*

Hebrews 8:5 – *"Who serve unto the example and shadow of heavenly things, as Moses was admonished of God when he was about to make the tabernacle: for, See, saith He, that thou make all things according to the pattern shewed to thee in the mount."*

Hebrews 9:23-24 – *"It was therefore necessary that the patterns of things in the heavens should be purified with these; but the heavenly things themselves with better sacrifices than these. For Christ is not entered into the holy places made with hands, which are the figures of the true; but into heaven itself, now to appear in the presence of God for us."*

Revelation 15:5 – *"And after that I looked, and, behold, the temple of the tabernacle of the testimony in heaven was opened."*

Yes, there is a heavenly temple and the Ark of the Covenant is there! Revelation 15:8 says: *"And the temple was filled with smoke from the glory of God, and His power; and no man was able to enter the temple, till the seven plagues of the seven angels were fulfilled."*

1. The <u>APPEARANCE</u> of the seven angels

Notice that the *"tabernacle of the testimony in heaven was opened."* The *"testimony"* refers to the law, the commandments of God that were placed within the Ark of the Covenant. God's covenant with His people will be kept. He will honor His holy and high standards. His judgment will fall upon those who reject Him and His principles. God will be faithful to what He has said and revealed to His people.

Their clothing (*"clothed in pure and white linen"*) reminds us of the majesty and righteousness of God. They were also *"having their breasts girded with golden girdles"* – a picture of the priests who ministered in the temple, but more likely, a picture of the majesty and greatness of God Himself. Back in Revelation 1:13 we read of our Lord Messiah *"one like unto the Son of man, clothed with a garment down to the foot, and gift about the paps with a golden girdle."* It is the apparel of a sovereign ruler, a picture of majesty.

2. The <u>ASSIGNMENT</u> they were given

One of the four worship leaders of heaven gave the seven angels *"golden vials (bowls) full of the wrath of God, Who liveth forever and ever."*

3. The <u>ATMOSPHERE</u> in the heavenly temple

What an awesome display of God's presence and power! Notice two things in verse 8:

(1)   The <u>INTENSITY</u> of God's power

God's presence was often pictured by a cloud or smoke. Exodus 40:34 says: *"Then a cloud covered the tent of the congregation, and the glory of the LORD filled the tabernacle."* In the wonderful vision of Isaiah 6 we read in verse 4: *"And the posts of the door moved at the voice of Him that cried, and the house was filled with smoke."*

(2)   The <u>IMPORTANCE</u> of God's plan

God's plan includes the coming of God's wrath, and it will be *"fulfilled"* (completed). Until it is finished, no one could enter the temple in heaven, dramatically emphasizing the importance of these seven last plagues in the overall plan of God.

THE SEVEN LAST PLAGUES
Revelation 16:1-21

The <u>COMMAND</u> of a great voice

Revelation 16:1 – *"And I heard a great voice out of the temple saying to the seven angels, Go your ways, and pour out the vials of the wrath of God upon the earth."*

The term *"great voice"* (or *"loud voice"*) is mentioned 20 times in the Book of Revelation, and when used in the singular, it is a reference to the voice of God or one of His mighty angels. God gives this command to the seven angels. He is a God of wrath and power. His holiness and justice require Him to execute judgment upon those who refuse to bow the knee to Him and receive His message of salvation.

FIRST PLAGUE – sores
Revelation 16:2

"And the first went, and poured out his vial upon the earth; and there fell a noisome and grievous sore upon the men which had the mark of the beast, and upon them which worshipped his image."

The target of this first bowl judgment is the people on earth who have received the mark of the beast and worshipped his image. The judgment attacks the health of these earth-dwellers causing tremendous emotional upheaval for a culture obsessed with outward appearance and physical well-being. The affliction is described as a *"noisome and grievous sore."*

SECOND PLAGUE – sea turned to blood
Revelation 16:3

"And the second angel poured out his vial upon the sea; and it became as the blood of a dead man; and every living soul died in the sea."

The second trumpet judgment was similar and was caused by what appears to be a meteor crashing into the sea (probably the Mediterranean Sea). In that judgment, one-third of the creatures died. In this second bowl judgment, the death of every living creature in the sea occurs – one of the major food sources of the world. What an awesome display of the power of God. Imagine the stench alone that will come from these polluted waters. The blood of a dead man is how the judgment is described. It is not merely a different color of the sea that is being pictured; it is the death of millions of sea creatures!

THIRD PLAGUE – fountains of water become blood
Revelation 16:4-7

"And the third angel poured out his vial upon the rivers and fountains of waters; and they became blood. And I heard the angel of the waters say, Thou art righteous, O Lord, which art, and wast, and shalt be, because Thou hast judged thus. For they have shed the blood of saints and prophets, and Thou hast given them blood to drink; for they are worthy. And I heard another out of the altar say, Even so, Lord God Almighty, true and righteous are Thy judgments."

In the third trumpet judgment of chapter 8 one-third of the springs and rivers were affected. In this bowl judgment, all of the world's springs and rivers are affected. The results will be catastrophic! The drinking water of humanity is now completely polluted, causing worldwide panic. The health problems that will accompany such a disaster will only increase the agony of human life. Undoubtedly, people will become aware that the end of the world has come!

The *"angel of the waters"* proclaims the righteousness of God and another angel comes from the heavenly altar and expresses similar praise. While many people often question the ways of the Lord and debate His concern and justice in this world, it is fascinating to see that the angels of God do not!

The angels know that this is a just response to those who have killed the saints and prophets. The world sheds the blood of God's people, and God judges them by turning the water supply of the world into blood. God is answering the prayers of the martyred saints of Revelation 6:9-11 by avenging their blood with this plague!

FOURTH PLAGUE – men scorched with fire
Revelation 16:8-9

"And the fourth angel poured out his vial upon the sun; and power was given unto him to scorch men with fire. And men were scorched with great heat, and blasphemed the Name of God, which hath

462

power over these plagues: and they repented not to give Him glory."

The fourth trumpet judgment also affected the sun, but the two judgments are not the same. The trumpet judgment in chapter 8 strikes the sun, moon, and stars, reducing their light by one-third of their normal output. Here, only the sun is affected, and its impact is not a reduction in light, but an increase in its capacity to bring heat to the earth. What is normally a blessing becomes a curse as men are scorched by the sun's burning rays. It appears that only those non-believers who *"blaspheme the Name of God"* are the ones being affected by this plague. Believers (like Israel in Egypt long ago) will be spared from this global catastrophe – talk about "global warming"! This is no late summer heat wave. The earth will be scorched with *"great heat"* causing severe burning.

One of the purposes of this plague is to demonstrate the power and wrath of Almighty God and to make sure that humanity knows that it is coming from Him!

This plague clearly shows that man's problem is not the environment but the heart controlled by sin and self. Sin blinds us to our real need and refuses to acknowledge what we know to be true.

FIFTH PLAGUE – darkness and pain
Revelation 16:10-11

"And the fifth angel poured out his vial upon the seat of the beast; and his kingdom was full of darkness; and they gnawed their tongues for pain, and blasphemed the God of heaven because of their pains and their sores, and repented not of their deeds."

The darkness strikes the kingdom of the beast, and reminds us of what God did in the plagues of Egypt. This plague is *"full of darkness"* and it causes great pain. In Matthew 25:30 our Lord Yeshua speaks of the eternal consequences of the gospel when He says: *"And cast ye the unprofitable servant into outer darkness; there shall be weeping and gnashing of teeth."* Back in Matthew 8:12 we read: *"But the children of the kingdom shall be cast out into outer darkness: there shall be weeping and gnashing of teeth."* The darkness of this fifth plague is a preview of hell itself.

This fifth plague reminds us of the *"pains and sores"* of unbelievers, and their refusal to repent of their deeds.

SIXTH PLAGUE – Euphrates River dried up
Revelation 16:12-16

"And the sixth angel poured out his vial upon the great river Euphrates, and the water thereof was dried up, that the way of the kings of the east might be prepared. And I saw three unclean spirits like frogs come out of the mouth of the dragon, and out

of the mouth of the beast, and out of the mouth of the false prophet. For they are the spirits of devils, working miracles, which go forth unto the kings of the earth and of the whole world, to gather them to the battle of that great day of God Almighty. Behold, I come as a thief. Blessed is he that watcheth, and keepeth his garments, lest he walk naked, and they see his shame. And He gathered them together into a place called in the Hebrew tongue Armageddon.

1. The **PREPARATION** for battle

One of the great rivers of the world will be dried up! The Euphrates River is the natural boundary that separates the Far East from the Middle East. When it dries up, the kings from the Far East will be able to come and attack Israel. The plural word *"kings"* suggests that there will be several nations involved from the Far East in the Battle of Armageddon.

Is this the same battle as Revelation 9? It does not appear to be so. Revelation 9 is describing a demonic attack that occurs in the tribulation period. This sixth bowl judgment deals with the final battle. Armageddon will bring all nations together against Jerusalem and Israel, the great battle which the Hebrew prophets predicted would take place at the end of the age. It is not the final rebellion, however. That will occur at the end of the 1000 reign of our Lord Jesus Christ, the Messiah of Israel – details found in Revelation 20.

2. The **PRESENCE** of demonic forces

There will be demonic influence in this Battle of Armageddon. We are told that *"three unclean spirits like frogs"* will come out of the mouths of the dragon, beast, and false prophet. The phrase *"like frogs"* implies how they will work on the nations of the world. Verse 14 says *"they are the spirits of devils* (demons), *working miracles."* The whole purpose of these demonic spirits is to *"gather them to the battle of the great day of God Almighty."*

3. The **PROMISE** of the Second Coming

Revelation 16:15 makes it clear when we read: *"Behold, I come as a thief. Blessed is he that watcheth, and keepeth his garments, lest he walk naked, and they see his shame."*

The Second Coming of Jesus Christ to planet earth is NOT the Rapture when believers will meet Him in the air. His coming will be a surprise to the world – *"as a thief."* Our Lord Yeshua told us in Matthew 24:42: *"Watch therefore: for ye know not what hour your Lord doth come."* In Matthew 24:44, it adds: *"Therefore be ye also ready: for in such an hour as ye think not the Son of man cometh."* In Matthew 25:13 we read: *"Watch therefore, for ye know neither the day nor the hour wherein the Son of man cometh."*

Our Lord pronounces a blessing on those who are "watching" and those who "keep their garments" – that is referring to moral purity. We read in I John 3:2-3: *"Beloved, now are we the sons of God, and it doth not yet appear what we shall be: but we know that, when He shall appear, we shall be like Him; for we shall see Him as He is. And every man that hath this hope in him purifieth himself, even as He is pure."*

THREE BEATITUDES SO FAR!

Revelation 1:3 – *"BLESSED is he that readeth, and they that hear the words of this prophecy, and keep those things which are written therein: for the time is at hand."*

Revelation 14:13 – *"BLESSED are the dead which die in the Lord from henceforth: Yea, saith the Spirit, that they may rest from their labors; and their works do follow them."*

Revelation 16:15 – *"BLESSED is he that watcheth, and keepeth his garments, lest he walk naked, and they see his shame."*

WHERE IS ARMAGEDDON?

The term "Armageddon" is found in Revelation 16:12-16 and means "the hill of Megiddo." It was the historic site of many ancient battles. Revelation 14:19-20 describes it as "the great winepress of the wrath of God." In that passage it speaks of the "blood" that comes out of the "winepress" rising to the level of the "horse bridles," and the distance covered as being "a thousand and six hundred furlongs." The Greek word is stadia and a stadion equals 600 ft., making a total of 960,000 ft. - divide by 5280 ft. (1 mile) and you have a distance of 180 miles. There are various viewpoints concerning these facts:

(1) It will be the future radius around Jerusalem
(2) It involves the length of the Jordanian valley
(3) It involves the distance from Megiddo to Bozrah, the capital of ancient Edom (Jordan)
(4) It refers to the entire land of Israel - from north to south

It is a term describing the final battle of all battles – the day when the LORD God brings His vengeance upon a world that has turned its back on Him.

WHAT IS THE LORD DOING AT ARMAGEDDON?

1. It is the day of the Lord's REVENGE!
Isaiah 63:4; Ezekiel 38:19; Nahum 1:2-7

2. It is the day of the Lord's REVELATION of Himself!
Ezekiel 38:23; 39:21-22; Joel 3:16-17

3. It is the day of the Lord's RENNOVATION of the entire planet!

II Peter 3:10-13

WHAT ARE THE MOTIVES BEHIND THIS GREAT BATTLE?

1. The PROBLEM of Jerusalem will be decided!
Zechariah 12:1-3

2. The POWER of God will be displayed!
Isaiah 13:9-13; Ezekiel 38:23

3. The PEOPLE of Israel will be delivered!
Ezekiel 37:25-28; Joel 2:32; Zechariah 12:10; 13:1; Romans 11:25-27

4. The PERSON of the Messiah will be declared! (King of kings and Lord of lords!)
Isaiah 45:22-25; Zechariah 14:9; Revelation 11:15-17; 19:16

5. The PROMISES of God will be done!
Isaiah 46:9-11; 55:10-11; Matthew 24:35

SEVENTH PLAGUE – a great earthquake
Revelation 16:17-21

"And the seventh angel poured out his vial into the air; and there came a great voice out of the temple of heaven, from the throne, saying, It is done! And there were voices, and thunders, and lightnings; and there was a great earthquake, such as was not since men were upon the earth, so mighty an earthquake, and so great. And the great city was

divided into three parts, and the cities of the nations fell: and great Babylon came in remembrance before God, to give unto her the cup of the wine of the fierceness of His wrath. And every island fled away, and the mountains were not found. And there fell upon men a great hail out of heaven, every stone about the weight of a talent: and men blasphemed God because of the plague of the hail; for the plague thereof was exceeding great."

1. The <u>MOTIVE</u> of this great earthquake –
   "a great voice out of the temple of heaven, from the throne, saying, It is done!

This will be the greatest earthquake ever in human history!

2. The <u>MAGNITUDE</u> of this earthquake – *"such as was not since men were upon the earth, so mighty an earthquake, and so great."*

3. The <u>MOVEMENT</u> of this earthquake upon the cities and environment

The *"great city was divided into three parts, and the cities of the nations fell: and great Babylon came in remembrance before God, to give unto her the cup of the wine of the fierceness of His wrath. And every island fled away, and the mountains were not found."*

The *"great city"* is probably referring to the Babylon of the end time – the same verse calls her *"great Babylon."*

4. The <u>MEN</u> of earth respond to this disaster *"men blasphemed God because of the plague of the hail; for the plague thereof was exceeding great"*

Revelation 16:21 says that the hail was *"about the weight of a talent."* Can you imagine such a plague? These hailstones weighed about a hundred pounds each! There has been nothing like this in the history of the world!

It is quite astonishing to read the response of the people of earth to this remarkable disaster. All hope of survival will be gone, and nothing but ruins and evidences of total destruction will be evident. And still, men do not repent, but instead blaspheme God for doing it!

BABYLON THE GREAT
Revelation 17:1-18

"And there came one of the seven angels which had the seven vials, and talked with me, saying unto me, Come hither; I will shew unto thee the judgment of the great whore that sitteth upon many waters."

It is time now to get the details on Babylon the Great. Bible teachers and scholars differ greatly on the identity and influence of this amazing city from the past and its impact upon the present and future of our world.

HISTORY OF BABYLON
Genesis 10:8-10; 11:1-9

"And Cush begat Nimrod: he began to be a mighty one in the earth. He was a mighty hunter before the LORD: wherefore it is said, Even as Nimrod the mighty hunter before the LORD. And the beginning of His kingdom was Babel, and Erech, and Accad, and Calneh, in the land of Shinar."

"And the whole earth was of one language, and of one speech. And it came to pass, as they journeyed from the east, that they found a plain in the land of Shinar; and they dwelt there. And they said one to another, Go to, let us make brick, and burn them throughly. And they had brick for stone, and slime had they for mortar. And they said, Go to, let us

build us a city and a tower, whose top may reach unto heaven; and let us make us a name, lest we be scattered abroad upon the face of the whole earth. And the LORD came down to see the city and the tower, which the children of men builded. And the LORD said, Behold, the people is one, and they have all one language; and this they begin to do: and now nothing will be restrained from them, which they have imagined to do. Go to, let us go down, and there confound their language, that they may not understand one another's speech. So the LORD scattered them abroad from thence upon the face of all the earth: and they left off to build the city. Therefore is the name of it called Babel; because the LORD did there confound the language of all the earth: and from thence did the LORD scatter them abroad upon the face of all the earth."

Babylon is mentioned 286 times in the Bible of which 12 usages are found in the NT, six of those in the book of Revelation. The word "Babel" is used twice – Genesis 10:10 and 11:9. Most of these references are referring to the massive and beautiful city of the Neo-Babylonian period (625-539 BC). With its "Hanging Gardens" and massive walls it has been regarded as one of the "Seven Wonders of the Ancient World." The Greek historian Herodotus (484-425 BC) reported upon visiting the site that its splendor surpassed any city of the known world.

It was also the capital of the 18th century BC King Hammurabi, and was known throughout history as a great center of culture and religion. It was Nebuchadnezzar II (605-562 BC) who brought Babylon to its glory as it was called "The Palace of Heaven and Earth, the Seat of Kingship." In Daniel 4:30 Nebuchadnezzar boasted *"Is not this great Babylon that I have built for the house of the kingdom by the might of my power, and for the honor of my majesty?"*

Ancient Babylon covered an area of 1000 acres making it the largest city of the ancient world, some 15% larger than Nineveh. It had 1179 temples and a population of over 100,000 but could easily have handled over 250,000 people. The famous "Ishtar Gate" was 70 feet high and its arched opening 15 feet wide. Babylon's most significant temple was Esagila ("the temple that raises its head") and was supposedly the home of the god Marduk. According to cuneiform documents the temple was surrounded by an enclosure of about 1410 feet by 720 feet and housed over 50 other temples and shrines. Interesting comment by Jeremiah (50:38*): "it is the land of graven images, and they are mad upon their idols."* Over 6000 figures (idols) were uncovered in the excavations of ancient Babylon and over 10 major altars. There were 180 open-air shrines for Ishtar and 200 identifiable places for other deities.

Adjacent to the temple of Esagila was the tower or ziggurat named Etemenanki called "the foundation house of heaven and earth." It measured about 300 feet square at the base and rose in seven stages to a height of 300 feet. It could very well have been reconstructed and restored from the original "Tower of Babel" mentioned in Genesis 11. The Babylonians believed it was built by the gods.

MYSTERY OF BABYLON THE GREAT
Revelation 17:1-18

THE DETAILS CONCERNING THE WOMAN WHO SITS ON THE BEAST
Revelation 17:1-6

"And there came one of the seven angels which had the seven vials, and talked with me, saying unto me, Come hither; I will shew unto thee the judgment of the great whore that sitteth upon many waters: With whom the kings of the earth have committed fornication, and the inhabitants of the earth have been made drunk with the wine of her fornication. So he carried me away in the spirit into the wilderness; and I saw a woman sit upon a scarlet colored beast, full of names of blasphemy, having seven heads and ten horns. And the woman was arrayed in purple and scarlet color, and decked with gold and precious stones and pearls, having a golden cup in her hand full of abominations and filthiness of her fornication. And upon her forehead was a name written, MYSTERY, BABYLON THE GREAT, THE MOTHER OF HARLOTS AND ABOMINATIONS OF THE EARTH. And I saw the woman drunk with the

blood of the martyrs of Jesus: and when I saw her, I wondered with great admiration."

She has great <u>AUTHORITY</u> that affects all peoples of the earth!

Revelation 17:1 – *"the great whore that sitteth upon many waters."*

Revelation 17:15 – *"The waters which thou sawest, where the whore sitteth, are peoples, and multitudes, and nations, and tongues"*

She has the <u>APPEARANCE</u> of great wealth!

Revelation 17:4a – *"And the woman was arrayed in purple and scarlet color, and decked with gold, and precious stones and pearls…"*

She has many <u>ABOMINATIONS</u> in her history!

Revelation 17:4b – *"having a golden cup in her hand full of abominations and filthiness of her fornication"*

Revelation 18:3 – *"For all nations have drunk of the wine of the wrath of her fornication, and the kings of the earth have committed fornication with her, and the merchants of the earth are waxed rich through the abundance of her delicacies."*

Jeremiah 51:6-8 – *"Flee out of the midst of Babylon, and deliver every man his soul: be not cut off in her iniquity, for this is the time of the LORD's vengeance; He will render unto her a recompence. Babylon hath been a golden cup in the LORD's hand, that made all the earth drunken: the nations have drunken of her wine; therefore the nations are made. Babylon is suddenly fallen and destroyed: howl for her; take balm for her pain, if so be she may be healed."*

    (1) She is called *"the great whore"* – v. 1
          v. 15 – *"where the whore sitteth"*
          v. 16 – *"hate the whore"*

    (2) She is characterized by fornication
          – vv. 2, 4b; 18:3

She has <u>ANTAGONISM</u> toward true believers!

Revelation 18:24 – *"And in her was found the blood of prophets, and of saints, and of all that were slain upon the earth."*

She has an obvious <u>ASSOCIATION</u> with the ancient city of Babylon!

    (1) She is a <u>MYSTERY</u> – word used 22 times
          Revelation 1:20; 10:7; 17:5, 7

    (2) She is a <u>MOTHER</u> – "the mother of
          harlots and abominations of the earth"

THE **DESCRIPTION** OF THE BEAST
UPON WHICH THE WOMAN SITS
Revelation 17:7-15

"And the angel said unto me, Wherefore didst thou marvel? I will tell thee the mystery of the woman, and of the beast that carrieth her, which hath the seven heads and ten horns. The beast that thou sawest was, and is not; and shall ascend out of the bottomless pit, and go into perdition: and they that dwell on the earth shall wonder, whose names were not written in the book of life from the foundation of the world, when they behold the beast that was, and is not, and yet is. And here is the mind which hath wisdom, The seven heads are seven mountains, on which the woman sitteth. And there are seven kings: five are fallen, and one is, and the other is not yet come; and when he cometh, he must continue a short space. And the beast that was, and is not, even he is the eighth, and is of the seven, and goeth into perdition. And the ten horns which thou sawest are ten kings, which have received no kingdom as yet; but receive power as kings one hour with the beast. These have one mind, and shall give their power and strength unto the beast. These shall make war with the Lamb, and the Lamb shall overcome them: for He is LORD of lords, and KING of kings: and they that are with Him are called, and chosen, and faithful. And he saith unto me, The waters which thou sawest, where the whore sitteth, are peoples, and multitudes, and nations, and tongues."

The <u>IDENTITY</u> of the seven heads

(1) Seven heads were on the dragon with seven crowns on the heads!
Revelation 12:3

(2) The beast who arose from the sea had seven heads and ten horns with crowns on the horns!
Revelation 13:1

(3) The beast came out of the bottomless pit and will go into perdition!
Revelation 17:8, 11; 19:20

(4) The beast ceased to exist and then came back to life! *"the beast that was, and is not, and yet is"*

Revelation 13:3 (deadly wound apparently was inflicted on one of its heads – presumably the sixth one)

The seven heads are seven mountains on which the woman sits! The seven heads can be seven kings or seven kingdoms!
Revelation 17:9

NOTE: The first five had already fallen in John's day (Egypt, Assyria, Babylon, Medo-Persia, and Greece). One was existing in John's day – ROME!

The seventh head had not yet come – a future empire with ten divisions – "ten horns" - The seventh head will last only a short time! The eighth will come out of the seven – Revelation 17:11 – cf. Daniel 7:8

The __INVOLVEMENT__ of the ten horns (on the seventh head)!

Revelation 17:12-13 – *"And the ten horns which thou sawest are ten kings, which have received no kingdom as yet; but receive power as kings one hour with the beast. These have one mind, and shall give their power and strength unto the beast."*

Daniel 7:7-8 – *"After this I saw in the night visions, and behold a fourth beast, dreadful and terrible, and strong exceedingly; and it had great iron teeth: it devoured and brake in pieces, and stamped the residue with the feet of it: and it was diverse from all the beasts that were before it; and it had ten horns. I considered the horns, and, behold, there came up among them another little horn, before whom there were three of the first horns plucked up by the roots: and, behold, in this horn were eyes like the eyes of man, and a mouth speaking great things."*

Daniel 7:23-25 – *"Thus he said, The fourth beast shall be the fourth kingdom upon earth, which shall be diverse from all kingdoms, and shall devour the whole earth, and shall tread it down, and break it in pieces. And the ten horns out of this* kingdom are ten kings that shall arise: and another shall rise after them; and he shall be diverse from the first, and he shall subdue three kings. And he shall speak great words against the Most High, and shall wear out the saints of the Most High, and think to change times and laws: and they shall be given into his hand until a time and times and the dividing of time."

The __IMPOSSIBILITY__ which the ten horns will face!

Revelation 17:14 – *"These shall make war with the Lamb, and the Lamb shall overcome them: for He is LORD of lords, and KING of kings: and they that are with Him are called, and chosen, and faithful."*

THE COMING __DESTRUCTION__ OF THIS WOMAN
Revelation 17:16-18

"And the ten horns which thou sawest upon the beast, these shall hate the whore, and shall make her desolate and naked, and shall eat her flesh, and burn her with fire. For God hath put in their hearts to fulfill His will, and to agree, and give their kingdom unto the beast, until the words of God shall be fulfilled. And the woman which thou sawest is that great city, which reigneth over the kings of the earth."

1. The __MEANS__ by which the woman is destroyed!

Revelation 18:8-9 – *"Therefore shall her plagues come in one day, death, and mourning, and famine; and she shall be utterly burned with fire: for strong is the Lord God Who judgeth her. And the kings of the earth, who have committed fornication and lived deliciously with her, shall bewail her, and lament for her, when they shall see the smoke of her burning."*

2. The <u>MOTIVATION</u> behind this destruction of the woman!

Jeremiah 51:6 – *"Flee out of the midst of Babylon, and deliver every man his soul: be not cut off in her iniquity; for this is the time of the LORD's vengeance; He will render unto her a recompence."*

Jeremiah 51:24 – *"And I will render unto Babylon and to all the inhabitants of Chaldea all their evil that they have done in Zion in your sight, saith the LORD."*

Jeremiah 51:29 – *"And the land shall tremble and sorrow: for every purpose of the LORD shall be performed against Babylon, to make the land of Babylon desolation without an inhabitant."*

Jeremiah 51:54-56 – *"A sound of a cry cometh from Babylon, and great destruction from the land of the Chaldeans: Because the LORD hath spoiled Babylon, and destroyed out of her the great voice; when her waves do roar like great waters, a noise of their voice is uttered: Because the spoiler is come upon her, even upon Babylon, and her mighty men are taken, every one of their bows is broken: for the LORD God of recompences shall surely requite.*"

3. The <u>MEANING</u> of the woman!

"that great city" – cf. Revelation 14:8; 16:19; 17:5; 18:2, 10, 19, 21 – seven times the words refer to Babylon. Jerusalem on the earth now is called *"the great city"* in Revelation 11:8 and the heavenly city, the New Jerusalem is called *"that great city"* in Revelation 21:10.

THE FALL OF BABYLON
Revelation 18:1-24

The questions of Bible students throughout history about Babylon have been quite unique and extensive in their applications and understandings. The opening statement of chapter 18, verse 1, says *"after these things."* Does this imply that the fall of Babylon in chapter 18 is different from the destruction of the woman by the ten horns in Revelation 17:16? Is it the religious system that is the meaning of *"Babylon the Great"* in chapter 17 and the political world government that is the judgment of Revelation 18?

Consider the following facts:

1. The usage of the word *"Babylon"* refers to the woman that rides the beast.

2. The context that precedes chapter 17 speaks in Revelation 16:19 of the *"great city"* and *"great Babylon"* that God remembers to judge 'to give <u>HER</u> the cup of the wine of the fierceness of His wrath. The use of the feminine pronoun points to the woman of chapter 17 who sits on the beast with seven heads and ten horns.

3. Revelation 17:1 says that the angel told John *"I will shew unto thee the judgment of the great whore that sitteth upon many waters."* Once again it is the woman's judgment that is being declared. And, Revelation 17:16 speaks of the

destruction of the woman by the ten horns, a political confederacy related to the beast or the Antichrist.

4. Chapter 18 contains many statements about Babylon that are the same in terms of what is said about the harlot woman that rides the beast.

5. Revelation 18:24 says: *"in __HER__ was found the blood of prophets, and of saints, and of all that were slain upon the earth."* Once again we cannot escape the fact that what is being said about Babylon is referring to the woman that rides the beast, NOT the beast itself.

6. Revelation 19:2 has the *"voice of much people in heaven"* rejoicing over the fact that the Lord *"hath judged the great whore, which did corrupt the earth with her fornication..."* If the beast and the political government is the issue of Babylon the Great as well as the woman riding the beast, the illustration becomes quite confusing.

Our conclusion is that the primary usage of the word *"Babylon"* is referring to the religious control over the nations of the world, which would also include the global government of the Antichrist in the end times.

The __PREDICTION__ of the fall of Babylon
Revelation 18:1-3

"And after these things I saw another angel come down from heaven, having great power; and the earth was lightened with his glory. And he cried mightily with a strong voice, saying, Babylon the great is fallen, is fallen, and is become the habitation of devils (demons)*, and the hold of every foul spirit, and a cage of every unclean and hateful bird. For all nations have drunk of the wine of the wrath of her fornication, and the kings of the earth have committed fornication with her, and the merchants of the earth are waxed rich through the abundance of her delicacies."*

The fact that Babylon the Great becomes *"the habitation of demons and evil spirits"* reminds us of the teaching of Isaiah 14 about the real KING of BABYLON!

THE KING OF BABYLON
Isaiah 14:4, 12-27

THE **PERSON** BEHIND THE KING OF BABYLON
Isaiah 14:12-21

1. The REFERENCE to "Lucifer" is a play on Canaanite religion – v. 12a cf. Luke 10:17-20

NOTE: The Hebrew word *helel* means "morning star" – Helel & Ishtar in Canaanite religion attempted a heavenly coup that failed (according to Canaanite mythology).

2. The REALIZATION of how he affected the nations – v. 12b

3. The REASON for his fall – vv. 13-14 (five *"I will"* statements)

> v. 13 – a reminder of the Tower of Babel - Genesis 11:1-9
>
> v. 14 – a reminder of Genesis 3 – *"I will be like the Most High"*

NOTE: The phrase in v. 13 – *"in the sides of the north"* is translated in the Jewish TANAKH – "on the summit of Zaphon" (abode of the gods); NIV: "on the utmost heights of the sacred mountain" – the same thing is found in Psalm 48:2 where the phrase *"sides of the north"* is literally "summit of Zaphon."   The NRSV translates "on the heights of Zaphon."   Mount Zaphon in northern Philistia was considered to be the seat of Canaanite gods.

4. The RESULT cannot be avoided – v. 15 - *"brought down to hell (Sheol) to the sides of the pit"* – the abyss or the bottomless pit – cf. II Peter 2:4; Revelation 9:1-2, 11; 20:1-3

> *"Sheol"* – Hebrew translated into Greek is *"Hades"* and refers both to the *"grave"* and to *"Hell."*

5. The REMEMBRANCE of what he had done would be judged severely by God – vv. 16-21

> (1) His <u>influence</u> over others would be mocked – vv. 16-17
>
> (2) His <u>importance</u> would not be recognized by others – vv. 18-20
>
> (3) His <u>iniquity</u> would bring tragedy and failure to his descendants – v. 21

THE **PURPOSE** OF GOD WILL BE FULFILLED
Isaiah 14:22-27

It is based on the <u>DESTRUCTION</u> of Babylon - vv. 22-23 – *"I will rise up against them, saith the LORD of hosts"*

> *"I will make it..."*
> *"I will sweep it..."*

It is based on the <u>DECISION</u> of the Lord Himself – v. 24 – *"the LORD of hosts hath sworn"*

It is based on the <u>DELIVERANCE</u> God will bring – v. 25

It is based on the <u>DETERMINATION</u> of God in carrying it out – vv. 26-27 – *"For the LORD of hosts hath purposed - who shall disannul it?"*

The **PREDICTION** of the fall of Babylon
Revelation 18:1-3

1. The <u>REAPPEARANCE</u> of another angel – v. 1 (Greek: *allos*) – *"having great power"*

2. The <u>RESULTS</u> of the fall of Babylon – v. 2

Isaiah 13:19-22 – *"And Babylon, the glory of kingdoms, the beauty of the Chaldees' excellency, shall be as when God overthrew Sodom and Gomorrah. It shall never be inhabited, neither shall it be dwelt in from generation to generation: neither shall the Arabian pitch tent there; neither shall the shepherds make their fold there. But wild* beasts of the desert shall be there; and their houses shall be full of doleful creatures; and owls shall dwell there, and satyrs shall dance there. And the wild beasts of the islands shall cry in their desolate houses, and dragons in their pleasant palaces: and her time is near to come, and her days shall not be prolonged."

Jeremiah 51:36-37 – "Therefore thus saith the LORD; Behold, I will plead thy cause, and take vengeance for thee; and I will dry up her sea, and make her springs dry. And Babylon shall become heaps, a dwellingplace for dragons, an astonishment, and an hissing, without an inhabitant."

Jeremiah 51:49 – "As Babylon hath cause the slain of Israel to fall, so at Babylon shall fall the slain of all the earth."

Jeremiah 51:53-56 – "Though Babylon should mount up to heaven, and though she should fortify the height of her strength, yet from Me shall spoilers come unto her, saith the LORD. A sound of a cry cometh from Babylon, and great destruction from the land of the Chaldeans: Because the LORD hath spoiled Babylon, and destroyed out of her the great voice; when her waves do roar like great waters, a noise of their voice is uttered: Because the spoiler is come upon her, even upon Babylon, and her mighty men are taken, every one of their bows is broken: for the LORD God of recompences shall surely requite."

Jeremiah 51:60-64 – *"So Jeremiah wrote in a book all the evil that should come upon Babylon, even all these words that are written against Babylon. And Jeremiah said to Seraiah, When thou comest to Babylon, and shalt see, and shalt read all these words; Then shalt thou say, O LORD, Thou hast spoken against this place, to cut it off, that none shall remain in it, neither man nor beast, but that it shall be desolate forever. And it shall be, when Thou hast made an end of reading this book, that thou shalt bind a stone to it, and cast it into the midst of Euphrates: And thou shalt say, Thus shall Babylon sink, and shall not rise from the evil that I will bring upon her: and they shall be weary. Thus far are the words of Jeremiah."*

3. The <u>REASON</u> for the fall of Babylon – v. 3

    (1) The <u>EXTENT</u> of her influence – *"all nations"* and *"kings of the earth"*

    (2) The <u>EXPLANATION</u> of her seductive ways *"have drunk of the wine of the wrath of her fornication"* and *"have committed fornication with her"*

Revelation 14:8 – *"And there followed another angel, saying, Babylon is fallen, is fallen, that great city, because she made all nations drink of the wine of the wrath of her fornication."*

Revelation 17:6 – *"And I saw the woman drunken with the blood of the saints, and the blood of the* martyrs of Jesus: and when I saw her, I wondered with great admiration."

(3) The <u>EFFECT</u> of her seductive ways – "*the merchants of the earth are waxed rich through the abundance of her delicacies*"

The <u>PLEA</u> to God's people
Revelation 18:4-5

"*And I heard another voice from heaven, saying, Come out of her, My people, that ye be not partakers of her sins, and that ye receive not of her plagues. For her sins have reached unto heaven, and God hath remembered her iniquities.*"

Jeremiah 50:8-10 – "*Remove out of the midst of Babylon, and go forth out of the land of the Chaldeans, and be as the he goats before the flocks. For, lo, I will raise and cause to come up against Babylon an assembly of great nations from the north country: and they shall set themselves in array against her; from thence she shall be taken: their arrows shall be as of a mighty expert man; none shall return in vain. And Chaldea shall be a spoil: all that spoil her shall be satisfied, saith the LORD.*"

Jeremiah 51:45 – "*My people, go ye out of the midst of her, and deliver ye every man his soul from the fierce anger of the LORD.*"

Revelation 18:5 – *"For her sins have reached unto heaven, and God hath remembered her iniquities."*

The word *"reached"* (Greek: *kollao*) is used of putting bricks together with mortar (remember the Tower of Babel!).

The <u>PAYMENT</u> which Babylon will receive
Revelation 18:6-8

"Reward her even as she rewarded you, and double unto her double according to her works: in the cup which she hath filled fill to her double. How much she hath glorified herself, and lived deliciously, so much torment and sorrow give her: for she saith in her heart, I sit as a queen, and am no widow, and shall see no sorrow. Therefore shall her plagues come in one day, death, and mourning, and famine; and she shall be utterly burned with fire: for strong is the Lord God Who judgeth her."

Deuteronomy 32:35 – *"To Me belongeth vengeance, and recompence; their foot shall slide in due time: for the day of their calamity is at hand, and the things that shall come upon them made haste."*

Romans 12:19 – *"Dearly beloved, avenge not yourselves, but rather give place unto wrath: for it is written, Vengeance is Mine; I will repay, saith the Lord."*

1. The <u>EXTENT</u> of that payment – *"Reward her even as she rewarded you"*

2. The **EXPLANATION** of her sins and iniquities
   "How much she hath glorified herself and lived deliciously" and *"she saith in her heart, I sit a queen, and am no widow, and shall see no sorrow"*

3. The **EXPERIENCE** of sorrow – *"so much torment and sorrow give her"*

4. The **EVIDENCE** of her judgment – *"her plagues come in one day, death, and mourning, and famine, and she shall be utterly burned with fire"*

Revelation 17:16 – *"And the ten horns which thou sawest upon the beast, these shall hate the whore, and shall make her desolate and naked, and shall eat her flesh, and burn her with fire."*

5. The **EXECUTION** of this payment – *"for strong is the Lord God Who judgeth her"*

The **PEOPLE** who are affected by the fall of Babylon   Revelation 18:9-19

1. The **SOVEREIGNS** of the earth

Revelation 18:9-10 – *"And the kings of the earth, who have committed fornication and lived deliciously with her, shall bewail her, and lament for her, when they shall see the smoke of her burning, Standing afar off for the fear of her torment, saying, Alas, alas that great city Babylon, that mighty city! For in one hour is thy judgment come."*

Revelation 17:2 – *"the kings of the earth"*
Revelation 17:18 – *"reigneth over the kings of the earth."*
Revelation 18:3 – *"the kings of the earth have committed fornication with her"*
Revelation 18:9 – *"And the kings of the earth, who have committed fornication and lived deliciously with her"*
Revelation 18:23 – *"by thy sorceries were all nations deceived"*

2. The <u>SELLERS</u> of the earth – *"merchants"* –

Revelation 18:11-17 – *"And the merchants of the earth shall weep and mourn over her; for no man buyeth their merchandise any more: The merchandise of gold, and silver, and precious stones, and of pearls, and fine linen, and purple, and silk, and scarlet, and all thyine wood, and all manner vessels of ivory, and all manner vessels of most precious wood, and of brass, and iron, and marble, and cinnamon, and odors, and ointments, and frankincense, and wine, and oil, and fine flour, and wheat, and beasts, and sheep, and horses, and chariots, and slaves, and souls of men. And the fruits that thy soul lusted after are departed from thee, and all things which were dainty and goodly are departed from thee, and thou shalt find them no more at all. The merchants of these things, which were made rich by her, shall stand afar off for the fear of her torment, weeping and wailing. And saying, Alas, also, that great city, that was clothed in fine linen, and purple, and scarlet, and decked with gold, and precious stones, and pearls!*

>   (1) No one buys their merchandise anymore –
>   v. 11 – *"for no man buyeth their merchandise any more"*
>
>   (2) All the things which are dainty and goodly have gone and are found no more v. 14 – *"and thou shalt find them no more at all"*

3. The <u>SAILORS</u> of the earth who trade by sea

Revelation 18:17-19 – *"For in one hour so great riches is come to nought. And every shipmaster, and all the company in ships, and sailors, and as many as trade by sea, stood afar off, and cried when they saw the smoke of her burning, saying, What city is like unto this great city! And they cast dust on their heads, and cried, weeping and wailing, saying, Alas, alas, that great city, wherein were made rich all that had ships in the sea by reason of her costliness! For in one hour is she made desolate."*

The <u>PRAISE</u> of believers
Revelation 18:20

"Rejoice over her, thou heaven, and ye holy apostles and prophets; for God hath avenged you on her."

The __PRONOUNCEMENT__ of Babylon's fall
Revelation 18:21-24

"And a mighty angel took up a stone like a great millstone, and cast it into the sea, saying, Thus with violence shall that great city Babylon be thrown down, and shall be found no more at all. And the voice of harpers, and musicians, and of pipers, and trumpeters, shall be heard no more at all in thee; and no craftsman, of whatsoever craft he be, shall be found any more in thee; and the sound of a millstone shall be heard no more at all in thee; And the light of a candle shall shine no more at all in thee; and the voice of the bridegroom and of the bride shall be heard no more at all in thee: for thy merchants were the great men of the earth; for by thy sorceries were all nations deceived. And in her was found the blood of prophets, and of saints, and of all that were slain upon the earth."

1. A violent __CATASTROPHE__ is stated – *"like a great millstone, and cast into the sea, saying, Thus with violence shall that great city Babylon be thrown down, and shall be found no more"*

2. Severe __CONSEQUENCES__ will hit every activity

(1) No more <u>MUSIC!</u>

(2) No more <u>MANUFACTURING!</u>

(3) No more <u>MARRIAGE!</u>

3. Two basic <u>CAUSES</u> are given

Revelation 18:23b-24 – *"for by thy sorceries were all nations deceived. And in her was found the blood of prophets, and of saints, and of all that were slain upon the earth."*

(1) The <u>SORCERIES</u>
(Greek: *pharmakeia* – drug addictions)

(2) The <u>SLAYINGS</u>
(*"blood of prophets, and of saints, and of all that were slain upon the earth"*)

THE MARRAGE SUPPER AND THE SECOND COMING
Revelation 19:1-21

The <u>PRAISE</u> of God is proclaimed
Revelation 19:1-6

"And after these things I heard a great voice of much people in heaven, saying, Alleluia; Salvation, and glory, and honor, and power, unto the Lord our God: for true and righteous are His judgments: for He hath judged the great whore, which did corrupt the earth with her fornication, and hath avenged the blood of His servants at her hand. And again they said, Alleluia. And her smoke rose up forever and ever. And the four and twenty elders and the four beasts fell down and worshipped God that sat on the throne, saying, Amen; Alleluia. And a voice came out of the throne, saying, Praise our God, all ye His servants, and ye that fear Him, both small and great. And I heard as it were the voice of a great multitude, and as the voice of many waters, and as the voice of mighty thunderings, saying, Alleluia: for the Lord God omnipotent reigneth."

The <u>MULTITUDE</u> who give this praise to God!

This gigantic praise gathering in heaven is composed of several groups who bring continual praise to God. It includes a *"great voice of much people in heaven."* This *"much people"* would include Old Testament believers, and past martyrs, including the prophets of God. This group of heavenly praise would also include church-age believers represented by the 24 elders; they are led in worship by the four living creatures who are cherubim angels. The tribulation martyrs would be there as well, and a summary of it all – *"all ye His servants, and ye that fear Him, both small and great."*

The <u>MOTIVATION</u> for the heavenly multitude praising God!

(1) Because His <u>CHARACTER</u> is revealed in these judgments!

"For true and righteous are His judgments"

(2) Because the <u>CONQUEST</u> of Babylon has been fulfilled!

"for He hath judged the great whore, which did corrupt the earth with her fornication"

(3) Because the <u>COMING</u> of His eternal kingdom has arrived!

"for the Lord God omnipotent reigneth"

The <u>MESSAGE</u> of praise the multitude brings!

The word *"Alleluia"* is the same in all languages of the world, and simply means *"PRAISE THE LORD"* and not a quiet expression of praise but rather the sound of a *"great voice of much people in heaven."*

This outburst of praise sounded like *"many waters"* and the voice of *"mighty thunderings."* Apparently God is going to change the ability of ears to hear that which is loud – because heaven is filled with the word *"loud"*!

This praise involves four major things:

> **SALVATION** – His plan of redemption
> **GLORY** – His preeminence over all
> **HONOR** – His exalted position
> **POWER** – His purposes that will be fulfilled

The **PREPARATION** of the Bride
Revelation 19:7-9

"Let us be glad and rejoice, and give honor to Him: for the marriage of the Lamb is come, and His wife hath made herself ready. And to her was granted that she should be arrayed in fine linen, clean and white: for the fine linen is the righteousness of saints. And He saith unto me, Write, Blessed are they which are called unto the marriage supper of the Lamb. And He saith unto me, These are the true sayings of God."

1. The **INSTRUCTION** to all believers – *"Let us be glad and rejoice, and give honor to Him"*

500

The long-awaited event (the marriage of the Lamb of God) has finally arrived. Will it be in heaven during the tribulation or on earth to begin the Millennial kingdom of our blessed Lord? It would appear from the Biblical record that this great Marriage Supper of the Lamb will be on the earth to begin the kingdom of our Lord. Matthew 8:11 says: *"And I say unto you, That many shall come from the east and west, and shall sit down with Abraham, and Isaac, and Jacob, in the kingdom of heaven."*

But these Old Testament believers are not resurrected until after the tribulation. They are certainly a part of the *"first resurrection"* which refers to believers only. Daniel 12 records the fact of Old Testament believers being resurrected after the tribulation. Daniel 12:12-13 teaches: *"Blessed is he that waiteth, and cometh to the thousand three hundred and five and thirty days. But go thou thy way till the end be: for thou shalt rest, and stand in thy lot at the end of the days."* Apparently there are 75 days after the tribulation is ended. During these days we might see the judgment of all nations for how they have treated God's people Israel during the tribulation – mentioned in Matthew 25. The Nation of Israel will be judged as well.

2. The <u>IMPORTANCE</u> of the bride's apparel

The term *"arrayed in fine linen, clean and white"* clearly refers to the *"righteousness of saints."* Not only does it refers to church-age believers, but to

Israel as well, because both the church and Israel are described as *"the wife of the Lord."*

Matthew 22:1-14 speaks of the *"kingdom of heaven"* as a marriage which a certain king gave for his son. Invitations were sent out, but the people did not respond. Eventually the king sent his servants into the *"highways"* and invited whoever would come. But the people were required to have a wedding garment for the occasion. Here's what Matthew 22:11-14 says:

"And when the king came in to see the guests, he saw there a man which had not on a wedding garment: And he saith unto him, Friend, how camest thou in hither not having a wedding garment? And he was speechless. Then said the king to the servants, Bind him hand and foot, and take him away, and cast him into outer darkness; there shall be weeping and gnashing of teeth. For many are called, but few are chosen."

Without the proper wedding apparel, one cannot attend the wedding supper. The consequences are those used to describe hell itself: *"outer darkness"* and *"weeping and gnashing of teeth."*

3. The <u>INVITATION</u> to the marriage supper

"Blessed are they which are called unto the marriage supper of the Lamb." This is the fourth beatitude in the Book of Revelation.

The church in Laodicea was given an invitation in Revelation 3:20: *"Behold, I stand at the door and knock: if any man hear My voice, and open the door, I will come in to him, and will sup with him, and he with Me."*

The <u>PURPOSE</u> of the believer is revealed
Revelation 19:10

"And I fell at his feet to worship him. And he said to me, See thou do it not: I am thy fellow-servant, and of thy brethren that have the testimony of Jesus: worship God: for the testimony of Jesus is the spirit of prophecy."

Not only is Jesus NOT an angel, but He is the eternal God in human flesh. That is clearly the message of the Apostle John recording in his letters. John is clearly told that angels are not to be worshipped – the only One to worship is our blessed Lord Yeshua! He is the central feature of God prophetic plan, and the Book of Revelation is the one book in the Bible that unveils His Divine character and the glory of Almighty God!

The glorious <u>APPEARING</u> of our blessed Lord Jesus Christ, the Son of God and Savior of the world!

1. The spectacular <u>COMING</u> of our blessed Lord!

"And I saw heaven opened, and behold a white horse; and He that sat upon him was called Faithful and True, and in righteousness He doth judge and make war. His eyes were as a flame of fire, and on His head were many crowns; and He had a Name written, that no man knew, but He Himself. And He was clothed with a vesture dipped in blood: and His Name is called The Word of God."

(1) His <u>NAMES</u> identify Him clearly!

He is called *"Faithful and True"* – but most important of all – His Name is called "THE WORD OF GOD"! This is a favorite word the Apostle John uses to describe the Messiah, our blessed Lord. In John's gospel he said the following in John 1:1-14:

"In the beginning was the Word, and the Word was with God, and the Word was God. The same was in the beginning with God. All things were made by Him; and without Him was not any thing made that was made. In Him was life; and the life was the light of men. And the light shineth in darkness; and the darkness comprehended it not. There was a man sent from God (John the Baptist), whose name was John. The same came for a witness, to bear witness of the Light, that all men through Him might believe. He was not that Light, but was sent to bear witness of that Light. That was the true Light, which lighteth every man that cometh into

the world. He was in the world, and the world was made by Him, and the world knew Him not. He came unto his own, and His own received Him not. But as many as received Him, to them gave He power to become the sons of God, even to them that believe on His Name: Which were born, not of blood, nor of the will of the flesh, nor of the will of man, but of God. And the Word was made flesh, and dwelt among us, (and we beheld His glory, the glory as of the only begotten of the Father,) full of grace and truth."

The **RELIABILITY** of His Name – *"Faithful and True"* – Revelation 1:5 calls Him *"the faithful witness"* and in Revelation 3:14 *"the Faithful and True Witness."*

The **RECOGNITION** of His Name. Isaiah 9:6 says *"and His Name is called Wonderful..."* The Hebrew word means "too difficult to comprehend." There is so much about Him that we simply do not know. But He knows! Revelation 19:12 says: *"and He had a Name written, that no man knew, but He Himself."*

The **REVELATION** of His Name – *"and His Name is called The Word of God."*

The **ROYALTY** of His Name – Revelation 19:16 says: *"and He hath on His vesture and on His thigh written, KING of kings, and LORD of lords."*

(2)   His **NATURE** describes Him powerfully!

His **RIGHTEOUSNESS** – v. 11 – *"and in righteousness He doth judge and make war"*

His **RECOGNITION** of all things – v. 12 – *"His eyes as a flame of fire"*

His **RULE** over all things – v. 12 – *"on His head were many crowns (diadems)"*

His **REVENGE** upon all nations – v. 13 – *"and He was clothed with a vesture dipped in blood"*

This is not referring to the blood He shed on the cross for our sins; this is the blood of His enemies that results from His treading out the winepress of the wrath of God – Revelation 14:20.

Isaiah 63:3-4 – *"I have trodden the winepress alone; and of the people there was none with Me: for I will tread them in Mine anger, and trample them in My fury; and their blood shall be sprinkled upon My garments, and I will stain all My raiment. For the day of vengeance is in Mine heart, and the year of My redeemed is come."*

(3) The **NATIONS** will obey Him completely!

Revelation 19:14-16 – *"And the armies which were in heaven followed Him upon white horses, clothed in fine linen, white and clean. And out of His mouth goeth a sharp sword, that with it He should smite the nations: and He shall rule them with a* rod of iron: and He treadeth the winepress of the fierceness and wrath of Almighty God, and He hath on His vesture and on His thigh a Name written, KING OF KINGS, AND LORD OF LORDS."

THREE THINGS ARE SAID OF HIS POWER AND AUTHORITY OVER ALL NATIONS:

He <u>SMITES</u> them with a sharp sword!

The Word of God is described as a *"sword"* in Hebrew 4:12, although it is referring to the two-edged sword of Roman soldiers. The *"sword"* here in Revelation 19:15 is the long and heavy sword used by the Thracians. The sword is long enough to throw as a spear or javelin.

He <u>SHEPHERDS</u> them with a rod of iron!

Psalm 2:9 – *"Thou shalt break them with a rod of iron; thou shalt dash them in pieces like a potter's vessel."* The shepherd's rod is used for correction.

He <u>STOMPS</u> on them in the winepress!

The *"winepress"* is described as the *"fierceness and wrath of Almighty God."*

(4) The <u>NEWS</u> of His coming will be given to the fowls!

Revelation 19:17-21 – *"And I saw an angel standing in the sun; and he cried with a loud voice, saying to all the fowls that fly in the midst of heaven, Come and gather yourselves together unto the supper of the great God; That ye may eat the flesh of kings, and the flesh of captains, and the flesh of mighty men, and the flesh of horses, and of them that sit on them, and the flesh of all men, both free and bond, both small and great. And I saw the beast, and the kings of the earth, and their armies, gathered together to make war against Him that sat on the horse, and against His army. And the beast was taken, and with him the false prophet that wrought miracles before him, with which he deceived them that had received the mark of the beast, and them that worshipped his image. These both were cast into a lake of fire burning with brimstone. And the remnant were slain with the sword of Him that is upon the horse, which sword proceeded out of His mouth: and all the fowls were filled with their flesh."*

1. The <u>COMING</u> of all birds to the supper of the great God!

Ezekiel 39:17-22 speaks clearly and powerfully of this amazing event known as the "supper of the LORD":

"And, thou son of man, thus saith the Lord GOD; speak unto every feathered fowl, and to every beast of the field, Assemble yourselves on every side to My sacrifice that I do sacrifice for you, even a great sacrifice upon the mountains of Israel, that ye may eat flesh, and drink blood. Ye shall eat the flesh of

the mighty, and drink the blood of the princes of the earth, of rams, of lambs, and of goats, of bullocks, all of them fatlings of Bashan. And ye shall eat fat till ye be full, and drink blood till ye be drunken, of My sacrifice which I have sacrificed for you. Thus ye shall be filled at My table with horses and chariots, with mighty men, and with all men of war, saith the Lord GOD. And I will set My glory among the heathen (nations and/or Gentiles), *and all the heathen shall see My judgment that I have executed, and My hand that I have laid upon them. so the house of Israel shall know that I am the LORD their God from that day and forward."*

2. The final <u>CONFLICT</u> of the tribulation!

Revelation 19:19 – *"And I saw the beast, and the kings of the earth, and their armies, gathered together to make war against Him that sat on the horse, and against His army."*

Whatever their original purpose was, it soon was clear to our Lord's enemies that He is the One that they desire to attack and destroy. The battle quickly becomes "no contest."   II Thessalonians 1:7-10 teaches us:

"And to you who are troubled rest with us, when the Lord Jesus shall be revealed from heaven with His mighty angels, In flaming fire taking vengeance on them that know not God, and that obey not the gospel of our Lord Jesus Christ: Who shall be punished with everlasting destruction

from the presence of the Lord, and from the glory of His power; when He shall come to be glorified in His saints, and to be admired in all them that believe (because our testimony among you was believed) in that day."

3. The **CAPTURE** of the Beast and the False Prophet!

Revelation 19:20 – *"And the beast was taken, and with him the false prophet that wrought miracles before him, with which he deceived them that had received the mark of the beast, and them that worshipped his image. These both were cast alive into a lake of fire burning with brimstone."*

This result of the global leaders of government and religion reminds all of us of what their deception and wickedness will suffer for all eternity. The fact that they are *"cast alive into the lake of fire"* might indicate that their torment and sufferings will be greater than others who will inhabit that awful place of torment.

4. The **CONSEQUENCE** which all nations will face in the future!

Revelation 19:21 – *"And the remnant were slain with the sword of Him that sat upon the horse, which sword proceeded out of His mouth: and all the fowls were filled with their flesh."*

While at times we may have difficulty understanding the meaning and sequence of events mentioned in the Book of Revelation, certain facts are clear:

(1) The <u>PRESENCE</u> of Jesus Christ at His Second Coming to the earth!

(2) The <u>PLAN</u> of God to destroy all nations of the earth!

(3) The eternal <u>PUNISHMENT</u> of the wicked in a place called *"the lake of fire."*

(4) The wonderful <u>PROMISE</u> of resurrection and eternal life for all who believe in the Messiah, our blessed Lord Yeshua!

The MILLENNIUM
Revelation 20:1-15

What is the "MILLENNIUM"?

The word *"Millennium"* is the Latin word for a thousand years. This is the only passage in the Bible the refers to this thousand-year period of time. It occurs six times in this chapter. Some Bible scholars (both past and present) believe that the term is allegorical and is not to be taken literally. We refer to them as "A-Millennialists." They are usually believers in the doctrine that is called "Replacement Theology," the belief that Israel was judged by God through Rome's destruction of the Temple and city of Jerusalem in 70 AD, and the Church replaced the Nation of Israel in God's prophetic program.

THE MILLENNIAL KINGDOM OF THE MESSIAH
Isaiah 9:6-7

Introduction: three viewpoints about the 1000 years (A-Millennial; Post-Millennial; Pre-Millennial)

A-MILLENNIAL – allegorical interpretation – 1000 years is symbolic for the Church ruling and reigning with Christ

POST-MILLENNIAL – Second Coming comes after the 1000 years triumph of the Church ruling and reigning with Christ

PRE-MILLENNIAL – Second Coming of Jesus Christ comes BEFORE the literal, 1000 year reign of the Messiah

There are many viewpoints and Biblical facts that are often ignored in the study of the Millennium. In an effort to inform readers of these wonderful facts, a listing of the major issues of the 1000 year reign of our Lord Yeshua are listed below. May the Lord bless you as you read His Word!

THE COMING OF THE MESSIAH WILL MAKE IT ALL POSSIBLE!

Isaiah 11:1-9 – *"And then shall come forth a rod out of the stem of Jesse, and a Branch shall grow out of his roots: And the Spirit of the LORD shall rest upon Him, the spirit of wisdom and understanding, the spirit of counsel and might, the spirit of knowledge and of the fear of the LORD; And shall make Him of quick understanding in the fear of the LORD; and He shall not judge after the sight of His eyes, neither reprove after the hearing of His ears; But with righteousness shall He judge the poor, and reprove with equity for the meek of the earth: and He shall smite the earth with the rod of His mouth, and with the breath of His lips shall He slay the wicked. And righteousness shall be the girdle of His loins, and faithfulness the girdle of His reins. The wolf also shall dwell with the lamb, and the leopard shall lie down with the kid; and the calf and the young lion and the fatling together; and a little child shall lead them. And the cow and the bear shall feed; their young ones shall lie down together: and the lion shall eat straw like the ox. And the sucking child shall play on the hole of the asp, and the weaned child shall put his hand on the cockatrice's den. They shall not hurt nor destroy in all My holy mountain: for the earth shall be full of the knowledge of the LORD, as the waters cover the sea."*

Zechariah 14:9 – *"And the LORD shall be king over all the earth: in that day shall there be one LORD, and His Name one."*

Revelation 19:11-16 – *"And I saw heaven opened, and behold a white horse; and He that sat upon him was called Faithful and True, and in righteousness He doth judge and make war. His eyes were as a flame of fire, and on His head were many crowns (diadems); and He had a Name written, that no man knew, but He Himself. And He was clothed with a vesture dipped in blood: and His Name is called The Word of God. And the armies which were in heaven followed Him upon white horses, clothed in fine linen, white and clean. And out of His mouth goeth a sharp sword, that with it He should smite the nations: and He shall rule them with a rod of iron: and He treadeth the winepress of the fierceness and wrath of Almighty God. And He hath on His vesture and on His thigh a Name written, KING of kings, and LORD of lords."*

THE CONQUEST OF ALL NATIONS WILL BE ACHIEVED!

Isaiah 59:20-21 – *"And the Redeemer shall come to Zion, and unto them that turn from transgression in Jacob, saith the LORD. As for Me, this is My covenant with them, saith the LORD; My Spirit that is upon Thee, and My words which I have put in Thy mouth, shall not depart out of Thy mouth, nor out of the mouth of Thy seed, nor out of the mouth of Thy seed's seed, saith the LORD, from henceforth and forever."*

Isaiah 60:1-5 – *"Arise, shine; for thy light is come, and the glory of the LORD is risen upon thee. For, behold, the darkness shall cover the earth, and gross darkness the people: but the LORD shall arise upon thee, and His glory shall be see upon thee. And the Gentiles (nations) shall come to thy light, and kings to the brightness of thy rising. Lift up thine eyes round about, and see: all they gather themselves together, they come to thee: thy sons shall come from far, and thy daughters shall be nursed at thy side. Then thou shalt see, and flow together, and thine heart shall fear, and be enlarged; because the abundance of the sea shall be converted unto thee, the forces of the Gentiles shall come unto thee."*

Isaiah 60:18 – *"Violence shall no more be heard in thy land, wasting nor destruction within thy borders; but thou shalt call thy walls Salvation, and thy gates Praise."*

THE CONVERSION OF ISRAEL WILL COME IMMEDIATELY BEFORE IT BEGINS!

Isaiah 62:11-12 – *"Behold, the LORD hath proclaimed unto the end of the world, Say ye to the daughter of Zion, Behold, thy salvation cometh; behold, His reward is with Him, and His work before Him. And they shall call them, The holy people, The redeemed of the LORD: and thou shalt be called, Sought out, A city not forsaken."*

Daniel 12:1-3 – *"And at that time shall Michael stand up, the great prince which standeth for the children of Thy people: and there shall be a time of trouble, such as never was since there was a nation even to that same time: and at that time Thy people shall be delivered, every one that shall be found written in the book. And many of them that sleep in the dust of the earth shall awake, some to everlasting life, and some to shame and everlasting contempt. And they that be wise shall shine as the brightness of the firmament; and they that turn many to righteousness as the stars forever and ever."*

Daniel 12:12-13 – *"Blessed is he that waiteth, and cometh to the thousand three hundred and five and thirty days. But go thou thy way till the end be: for thou shalt rest, and stand in thy lot at the end of the days."*

Micah 7:18-20 – *"Who is a God like unto Thee, that pardoneth iniquity, and passeth by the* transgression of the remnant of His heritage? He retaineth not His anger forever, because He delighteth in mercy. He will turn again, He will have compassion upon us; He will subdue our iniquities; and Thou wilt cast all their sins into the depths of the sea. Thou wilt perform the truth to Jacob, and the mercy to Abraham, which Thou hast sworn unto our fathers from the days of old."

Zechariah 12:10 – "And I will pour upon the house of David, and upon the inhabitants of Jerusalem, the Spirit of grace and of supplications: and they shall look upon Me Whom they have pierced, and they shall mourn for Him, as one mourneth for his only son, and shall be in bitterness for Him, as one that is in bitterness for his firstborn."

THE CONTROL OF SATAN WILL CONTINUE THROUGHOUT THE MILLENNIUM!

Revelation 20:1-3 – "And I saw an angel come down from heaven, having the key of the bottomless pit and a great chain in his hand. And he laid hold on the dragon, that old serpent, which is the Devil, and Satan, and bound him a thousand years, and cast him into the bottomless pit, and shut him up, and set a seal upon him, that he should deceive the nations no more, till the thousand years should be fulfilled: and after that he must be loosed a little season."

THE CROWNING OF ALL BELIEVERS WILL BE EVIDENT!

James 1:12 – *"Blessed is the man that endureth temptation: for when he is tried, he shall receive the crown of life, which the Lord hath promised to them that love Him."*

Revelation 2:10 – *"Fear none of those things which thou shalt suffer: behold, the devil shall cast some of you into prison, that ye may be tried; and ye shall have tribulation ten days; be thou faithful unto death, and I will give thee a crown of life."*

Revelation 20:4-6 – *"And I saw thrones, and they sat upon them, and judgment was given unto them: and I saw the souls of them that were beheaded for the witness of Jesus, and for the word of God, and which had not worshipped the beast, neither his image, neither had received his mark upon their foreheads, or in their hands; and they lived and reigned with Christ a thousand years."*

THE CONSTRUCTION OF THE TEMPLE WILL BE ACCOMPLISHED BY THE MESSIAH!

Isaiah 2:1-5 – *"The word that Isaiah the son of Amoz saw concerning Judah and Jerusalem. And it shall come to pass in the last days, that the mountain of the LORD's house shall be established in the top of the mountains, and shall be exalted above the hills; and all nations shall flow unto it. And many people shall go and say, Come ye, and let us go up to the mountain of the LORD, to the house of the God of Jacob; and He will teach us of His* ways, and we will walk in His paths: for out of Zion shall go forth the law, and the word of the LORD from Jerusalem. And He shall judge among the nations, and shall rebuke many people: and they shall beat their swords into plowshares, and their spears into pruninghooks: nation shall not lift up sword against nation, neither shall thy learn war anymore. O house of Jacob, come ye, and let us walk in the light of the LORD."

Ezekiel 44:4 – "Then brought He me the way of the north gate before the house: and I looked, and, behold, the glory of the LORD filled the house of the LORD: and I fell upon my face."

Amos 9:11 – "In that day will I raise up the tabernacle of David that is fallen, and close up the breaches thereof: and I will raise up his ruins, and I will build it as in the days of old."

Zechariah 6:12-13 – "And speak unto him, saying, Thus speaketh the LORD of hosts, saying, Behold the Man Whose Name is THE BRANCH; and He shall grow up out of His place, and He shall build the temple of the LORD; Even He shall build the temple of the LORD; And He shall bear the glory, and shall sit and rule upon His throne; and He shall be a priest upon His throne: and the counsel of peace shall be between them both."

THE CENTER OF WORLD GOVERNMENT WILL BE IN JERUSALEM!

Psalm 48:1-2 – *"Great is the LORD, and greatly to be praised in the city of our God, in the mountain of His holiness. Beautiful for situation, the joy of the whole earth, is mount Zion, on the sides of the north, the city of the great King."*

Psalm 48:8 – *"As we have heard, so have we seen in the city of the LORD of hosts, in the city of our God: God will establish it forever."*

Isaiah 65:17-25 – *"For, behold, I create new heavens and a new earth: and the former shall not be remembered, nor come into mind. But be ye glad and rejoice forever in that which I create: for, behold, I create Jerusalem a rejoicing, and her people a joy. And I will rejoice in Jerusalem, and joy in My people: and the voice of weeping shall be no more heard in her, nor the voice of crying. There shall be no more thence an infant of days, nor an old man that hath not filled his days: for the child shall die an hundred years old; but the sinner being an hundred years old shall be accursed. And they shall build houses, and inhabit them, and they shall plant vineyards, and eat the fruit of them. They shall not build, and another inhabit; they shall not plant, and another eat: for as the days of a tree are the days of My people, and Mine elect shall long enjoy the work of their hands. They shall not labor in vain, not bring forth for trouble; for they are the seed of the blessed of the LORD, and their offspring with them. And it shall come to pass, that before they call, I will answer; and while they are yet speaking, I will hear. The wolf and the lamb shall feed together, and the lion shall eat straw like the bullock: and dust shall be the serpent's meat. They shall not hurt nor destroy in all My holy mountain, saith the LORD."*

Zephaniah 3:16-17 – *"In that day it shall be said to Jerusalem, Fear thou not: and to Zion, Let not thine hands be slack. The LORD thy God in the midst of thee is mighty; He will save, He will rejoice over thee with joy; He will rest in His love, He will joy over thee with singing."*

THE CELEBRATIONS OF JEWISH WORSHIP WILL BE RESTORED!

Psalm 66:4 – *"All the earth shall worship Thee, and shall sing unto Thee; they shall sing to Thy Name."*

Isaiah 66:20-24 – *"And they shall bring all your brethren for an offering unto the LORD out of all nations upon horses, and in chariots, and in litters, and upon mules, and upon swift beasts, to My holy mountain Jerusalem, saith the LORD, as the children of Israel bring an offering in a clean vessel into the house of the LORD. And I will also take of them for priests and for Levites, saith the LORD. For as the new heavens and the new earth, which I will make, shall remain before Me, saith the LORD, so shall your seed and your name remain. And it shall come to pass, that from one new moon to another, and from one Sabbath to another, shall all flesh come to worship before Me, saith the LORD. And they shall go forth, and look upon the carcases of the men that have transgressed against Me; for their worm shall not die, neither shall their fire be quenched; and they shall be an abhorring unto all flesh."*

Ezekiel 45:18-25 – *"Thus saith the Lord GOD; In the first month, in the first day of the mouth, thou shalt take a young bullock without blemish, and cleanse the sanctuary: And the priest shall take of the blood of the sin offering, and put it upon the posts of the house, and upon the four corners of the settle of the altar, and upon the posts of the gate of the inner court. And so thou shalt do the seventh day of the month for every one that erreth, and for him that is simple: so shall ye reconcile the house. In the first month, in the fourteenth day of the month, ye shall have the Passover, a feast of seven days; unleavened bread shall be eaten. And upon that day shall the prince prepare for himself and for all the people of the land a bullock for a sin offering. And seven days of the feast he shall prepare a burnt offering to the LORD, seven bullocks and seven rams without blemish daily the seven days; and a kid of the goats daily for a sin offering. And he shall prepare a meat offering of an ephah for a bullock, and an ephah for ram, and an hin or oil for an ephah. In the seventh month, in the fifteenth day of the month, shall he do like in the feast of the seven days, according to the sin offering, according to the burnt offering, and according to the meat offering, and according to the oil."*

Ezekiel 46:13-15 – *"Thou shalt daily prepare a burnt offering unto the LORD of a lamb of the first year without blemish: thou shalt prepare it every morning. And thou shalt prepare a meat offering for it every morning, the sixth part of an hin of oil, to temper with the fine flour; a meat offering continually by a perpetual ordinance unto the LORD. Thus shall they prepare the lamb, and the meat offering, and the oil, every morning for a continual burnt offering."*

Ezekiel 48:35 – *"It was round about eighteen thousand measures: and the name of the city from that day shall be, The LORD is there."*

Zechariah 14:16 – *"And it shall come to pass, that every one that is left of all the nations which came against Jerusalem shall even go up from year to year to worship the King, the LORD of hosts, and to keep the feast of tabernacles."*

THE CONFINEMENT OF SATAN TO THE LAKE OF FIRE WILL COME AT THE END OF THE MILLENNIUM!

Revelation 20:7-10 – *"And when the thousand years are expired, Satan shall be loosed out of his prison, and shall go out to deceive the nations which are in the four quarters of the earth, Gog and Magog, to gather them together to battle: the number of whom is as the sand of the sea. And they went up on the breadth of the earth, and compassed the camp of the saints about, and the beloved city: and fire came down from God out of heaven, and devoured them. And the devil that deceived them was cast into the lake of fire and brimstone, where the beast and the false prophet are, and shall be tormented day and night forever and ever."*

THE CONDITION FOR ENTERING THE KINGDOM IS VERY CLEAR!

John 3:3 – *"Jesus answered and said unto him, Verily, verily, I say unto thee, Except a man be born again, he cannot see the kingdom of God."*

John 3:5 – *"Jesus answered, Verily, verily, I say unto thee, Except a man be born of water and of the Spirit, he cannot enter the kingdom of God."*

I Corinthians 6:9-11 – *"Know ye not that the unrighteous shall not inherit the kingdom of God? Be not deceived: neither fornicators, nor idolaters, nor adulterers, nor effeminate, nor abusers of themselves with mankind, nor thieves, nor covetous, nor drunkards, nor revilers, nor extortioners, shall inherit the kingdom of God. And such were some of you, but ye are washed, but ye are sanctified, but ye are justified in the name of the Lord Jesus, and by the Spirit of our God."*

Galatians 5:19-21 – *"Now the works of the flesh are manifest, which are these; Adultery, fornication, uncleanness, lasciviousness, idolatry, witchcraft, hatred, variance, emulations, wrath, strife, seditions, heresies, envyings, murders,* drunkenness, revellings, and such like: of the which I tell you before, as I have also told you in time past, that they which do such things shall not inherit the kingdom of God."

Ephesians 5:5 – "For this ye know, that no whoremonger, nor unclean person, nor covetous man, who is an idolater, hath any inheritance in the kingdom of Christ and of God."

Colossians 1:13-14 – "Who hath delivered us from the power of darkness, and hath translated us into the kingdom of His dear Son: In Whom we have redemption through His blood, even the forgiveness of sins."

II Tim. 4:18 – "And the Lord shall deliver me from every evil work, and will preserve me unto His heavenly kingdom: to Whom be glory forever and ever. Amen."

II Peter 1:10-11 – "Wherefore the rather, brethren, give diligence to make your calling and election sure: for if ye do these things, ye shall never fall: For so an entrance shall be ministered unto you abundantly into the everlasting kingdom of our Lord and Savior Jesus Christ."

Have you made a serious commitment to the Lord Jesus Christ as your Savior – the One Who died and paid for your sins by His blood, and the One Who rose again from the dead the third day to guarantee your own resurrection in the future, and to live forever in Heaven, not Hell?

The <u>BINDING</u> of Satan during the 1000 years   Revelation 20:1-3

"And I saw an angel come down from heaven, having the key of the bottomless pit and a great chain in his hand. And he laid hold on the dragon, that old serpent, which is the Devil and Satan, and bound him a thousand years, and cast him into the bottomless pit, and shut him up, and set a seal upon him, that he should deceive the nations no more, till the thousand years should be fulfilled: and after the he must be loosed a little season."

Satan is alive and well at this time in human history! But, the day is coming when God will bind him and not allow any of his diabolical plans to be fulfilled during the Millennial Kingdom of our Messiah!

   1. The <u>REVELATION</u> of Satan's destiny
       Revelation 20:1 – *"the bottomless pit"*

Who is the angel who has the key to the bottomless pit and a great chain in his hand?

Some argue that this angel is Jesus Christ Himself. The argument is usually found by going back to Revelation 1:18 where we read that our Lord has *"the keys of hell* (Hades) *and death."* However, as we have argued previously, Jesus is not merely an angel even though Old Testament passages call the Messiah *"<u>THE</u> Angel of the LORD."*

Some argue that an angel with this kind of power and authority must be Michael the Archangel. In Revelation 12;7-9 we learned that Michael and his angels fought with the dragon and his evil angels.

Perhaps the safest view is that this angel is simply one of God's unnamed angels who serve Him. The text simply says *"an angel."* The truth is that without giving a name to the angel, it is not possible to be dogmatic.

2. The <u>RECOGNITION</u> of Satan's activity during the tribulation
   Revelation 20:2 – *"that old serpent"*

He continues to deceive all nations, and concentrates his power upon the Beast (Antichrist) and False Prophet.

3. The <u>RESULT</u> that Satan will experience for 1000 years
   Revelation 20:2-3 – *"bound...into the bottomless pit"*

4. The <u>REASON</u> for this binding of Satan
   Revelation 20:3 – *"that he should deceive the nations no more, till the 1000 years should be fulfilled"*

5. The <u>RELEASE</u> of Satan after the 1000 years

Revelation 20:3 – *"and after that he must be loosed a little season."*

The <u>BLESSINGS</u> believers will experience
Revelation 20:4-6

"And I saw thrones, and they sat upon them, and judgment was given unto them: and I saw the souls of them that were beheaded for the witness of Jesus and for the word of God, and which had not worshipped the beast, neither his image, neither had received his mark upon their foreheads, or in their hands; and they lived and reigned with Christ a thousand years. But the rest of the dead lived not again until the thousand years were finished. This is the first resurrection. Blessed and holy is he that hath part in the first resurrection: on such the second death hath no power, but they shall be priests of God and of Christ, and shall reign with Him a thousand years."

1. The <u>RESURRECTION</u> of believers

The *"first resurrection"* consists only of believers. It includes the resurrection of Jesus Christ as the *"firstfruits of them that slept* (I Corinthians 15:23)." It includes church-age believers who are resurrected at the Rapture (I Thessalonians 4:13-18). It will also include all Old Testament believers who will be resurrected at the end of the tribulation period (Daniel 12:12-13); And, it will include all the martyrs of the tribulation period who have come to faith in Jesus Christ as their Lord and Savior. All of these will take part in the *"first resurrection"* for believers only.

2. The <u>RESURRECTION</u> of unbelievers

According to Revelation 20:5: *"But the rest of the dead* (meaning unbelievers) *lived not again until the thousand years were finished."* Revelation 20:13 refers to their resurrection to stand before the Lord and be judged according to their works. If their name is not written in the Lamb's Book of Life, their final destiny is the lake of fire.

3. The <u>REWARD</u> of believers

Revelation 20:6 is the 5th beatitude in the Book of Revelation: *"Blessed and holy is he that hath part in the first resurrection: on such the second death hath no power, but they shall be priests of God and of Christ, and reign with Him a thousand years."* What wonderful things are in store for those who put their faith and trust in the finished work of Jesus Christ our Lord!

The <u>BATTLE</u> at the end of the 1000 years
Revelation 20:7-10

"And when the thousand years are expired, Satan shall be loosed out of his prison. And shall go out to deceive the nations which are in the four quarters of the earth, Gog and Magog, to gather them together to battle: the number of whom is as the sand of the sea. And they went up on the

breadth of the earth, and compassed the camp of the saints about, and the beloved city: and fire came down from God out of heaven, and devoured them. And the devil that deceived them was cast into the lake of fire and brimstone, where the beast and the false prophet are, and shall be tormented day and night forever and ever."

1. The <u>DECEPTION</u> of the nations
    Revelation 20:8 – *"shall go out to deceive the nations"*

The great question is – WHY? The Bible does not tell us all the answers that we would like to have, but there are several possibilities:

> (1) God demonstrates by this one final event that even under the best conditions, mankind's problem is in the heart.

> (2) God demonstrates that Satan's depravity cannot be cured.

> (3) God demonstrates that He is fully justified in exacting eternal punishment.

THE PROBLEM OF "GOD AND MAGOG"

It is not an easy problem to solve. Some believe that this is referring to the same persons and nations of Ezekiel 38-39 – there is no difference.

But, it is possible that the names of these players in the Battle of Armageddon that ends the tribulation are used symbolically to depict the nations Satan has deceived to come and do battle against God and His people. The number of people involved here is *"as the sand of the sea."* Apparently the population of the world has exploded during the thousand years.

2. The <u>DESTRUCTION</u> of the rebellious nations
   Revelation 20:9

God allows these nations to surround the camp of the believers and *"the beloved city"* (Jerusalem), the capital of the kingdom of the Messiah. God's love for Jerusalem is certainly a part of this final act of destroying the nations who rebel against Him. It is the same judgment that God used in destroying Sodom and Gomorrah – *"fire came down from God out of heaven, and devoured them."*

3. The final <u>DESTINY</u> of Satan
   Revelation 20:10

Satan's final destiny is the *"lake of fire"* - the same place where the Beast (Antichrist) and the False Prophet will be. The fact is clear – they will be tormented day and night forever and ever! Yes, Hell is eternal punishment from God!

The <u>BOOKS</u> that will judge the dead
Revelation 20:11-15

There is no more awesome passage in the entire Bible than this one – the GREAT WHITE THRONE judgment of all unbelievers!

1. The <u>DESCRIPTION</u> of the One Who judges
    Revelation 20:11

The Apostle John says: *"I saw a great white throne, and Him that sat on it, from Whose face the earth and the heaven fled away; and there was found no place for them."*

The word *"throne"* appears 45 times in Revelation, but only 16 times in the rest of the New Testament. The One Who sits on the throne in Revelation 4 is God the Father; but the throne is not called *"the great white throne."* In John 5:27 we learn that the Father has given authority to His Son to *"execute judgment also, because He is the Son of man."* The last fact comes from Daniel 7:13-14 and refers to the Messiah of Israel, God's Son and our Savior!

The Bible also speaks of the *"judgment seat of Christ"* where believers will be judged for what they have done in this life. The issue there is not salvation, but rather reward.

If emphasizing a chronological order in the last chapters of Revelation, we might conclude that the renovation of planet earth occurs after the 1000 years rather than at any other time previously. But, it seems more likely that the renovation of the planet spoken of in II Peter 3 happens at the end of the tribulation period. We look for "new heavens" and a "new earth" where we find the righteousness of our Lord controlling the events to come following the tribulation.

> 2. The <u>DEAD</u> who are judged
>   Revelation 20:12-13

"And I saw the dead, small and great, stand before God; and the books were opened: and another book was opened, which is the book of life: and the dead were judged out of those things which were written in the books, according to their works. And the sea gave up the dead which were in it; and death and hell delivered up the dead which were in them: and they were judged every man according to their works."

Some Bible teachers believe that there is only one general judgment of all persons, and one general resurrection. On the basis of Biblical facts, this is impossible. The only judgment that takes place after the 1000 years of the Messianic Kingdom is that of unbelievers.

> (1) Their <u>POSITION</u> in life is not a factor at the Day of Judgment!
> *"the dead, small and great"*

> (2) The <u>PLACE</u> from which they come reveals their identity!

The mention of the *"sea"* shows that the method of burial has nothing to do with God's power to raise them up for this day of judgment. No one will escape! The mention of *"Hades"* confirms that these are the wicked dead. The word *"Hades"* is used 11 times in the New Testament and is to be distinguished from the word *"Gehenna"* which is the final Hell – the lake of fire!

> (3) Their **PRACTICES** in life will be the determining factor of judgment!

Since their final destiny is controlled by the Book of Life, this point of judging them *"according to their works"* is no doubt referring to degrees of their punishment in Hell. The *"books"* were opened, and these *"books"* have recorded the *"works"* of all these unbelievers. Our Lord Yeshua revealed that there were degrees of punishment in Matthew 11:20-24:

"Then began He to upbraid the cities wherein most of His mighty works were done, because they repented not: Woe unto thee, Chorazin! Woe unto thee, Bethsaida! For if the mighty works, which were done in you, had been done in Tyre and Sidon, they would have repented long ago in sackcloth and ashes. But I say unto you, It shall be more tolerable for Tyre and Sidon at the day of judgment, than for you. And thou, Capernaum, which art exalted unto heaven, shalt be brought down to hell: for if the mighty works, which have

been done in thee, had been done in Sodom, it would have remained until this day. But I say unto you, That it shall be more tolerable for the land of Sodom in the day of judgment, than for thee."

3. The final <u>DESTINY</u> of those who are judged at the Great White throne
   Revelation 10:14-15

"And death and hell (Hades) were cast into the lake of fire. This is the second death. And whosoever was not found written in the book of life was cast into the lake of fire."

WHAT DOES THE BIBLE TEACH ABOUT THE REALITY OF HELL?

The Bible uses several words to describe Hell:

1) <u>HADES</u> – used 59 times in the Greek OT and translates the Hebrew word *Sheol* which means "grave," or the "place of the departed."

It is used 11 times in the New Testament and translated with the word "hell." In Greek literature it meant "unseen" and referred to a place of darkness and the abode of departed spirits of unbelievers and demons.

Hades does not refer to a physical grave, but appears to be an intermediate state between physical death and the lake of fire. It is cast into the lake of fire according to Revelation 20:14.

(2) <u>ABYSS</u> – used 8 times, 6 of which are in the Book of Revelation. It refers to an extremely deep place. It is translated by the word "deep" and the words "bottomless pit." In Revelation 9 it appears to be the abode of demonic spirits, and in Revelation 11:7 and 17:8 it is also the place from which the coming world ruler called "the beast" will come. It is also the place where Satan will be bound for 1000 years according to Revelation 20:1, 3.

(3) <u>TARTAROS</u>– only used in II Peter 2:4 as a verb. It refers to the abode of fallen angels or demons. It is mentioned in the apocryphal book of Enoch as the place where fallen angels are confined and are waiting the day of their final judgment.

(4) <u>GEHENNA</u> – used 12 times in the New Testament. It comes from the Hebrew words "Ge-Hinnom" - the valley of Hinnom which was associated with idolatry and human sacrifices to the pagan god Molech and illustrated with fire.

1.   **HELL is the place where all unbelievers will go when they die!**

Luke 16:22 – *"And it came to pass, that the beggar died, and was carried by the angels into Abraham's bosom: the rich man also died, and was buried; and in hell he lift up his eyes, being in torments, and seeth Abraham afar off, and Lazarus in his bosom."*

Revelation 21:8 – *"But the fearful, and unbelieving, and abominable, and murderers, and whore-*

mongers, and sorcerers, and idolaters, and all liars, shall have their part in the lake which burneth with fire and brimstone: which is the second death."

2. HELL is the place where many religious people will go when they die!

Matthew 7:13 – *"Enter ye in at the strait gate: for wide is the gate, and broad is the way, that leadeth to destruction, and many there be which go in thereat."*

Matthew 7:21-23 – *"Not every one that saith unto Me, Lord, Lord, shall enter into the kingdom of heaven; but he that doeth the will of My Father which is in heaven. Many will say to Me in that day, Lord, Lord, have we not prophesied in Thy Name? and in Thy Name have cast out devils? And in Thy Name done many wonderful works? And then will I profess unto them, I never knew you: depart from Me, ye that work iniquity."*

Matthew 8:11-12 – *"And I say unto you, That many shall come from the east and west, and shall sit down with Abraham, and Isaac, and Jacob, in the kingdom of heaven. But the children of the kingdom shall be cast out into outer darkness: there shall be weeping and gnashing of teeth."*

Matthew 23:29-33 – *"Woe unto you, scribes and Pharisees, hypocrites! Because ye build the tombs of the prophets, and garnish the sepulchers of the righteous, and say, If we had been in the days of our fathers, we would not have been partakers with them in the blood of the prophets. Wherefore ye be witnesses unto yourselves, that ye are the children of them which killed the prophets. Fill ye up then the measure of your fathers. Ye serpents, ye generation of vipers, how can ye escape the damnation of hell?"*

3. HELL is the place God has prepared for Satan and demons!

Matthew 25:41 – *"Then shall he say also unto them on the left hand, Depart from Me, ye cursed, into everlasting fire, prepared for the devil and his angels."*

II Peter 2:4 – *"For if God spared not the angels that sinned, but cast them down to hell, and delivered them into chains of darkness, to be reserved unto judgment."*

Jude 6-7 – *"And the angels which kept not their first estate, but left their own habitation, He hath reserved in everlasting chains under darkness unto the judgment of the great day. Even as Sodom and Gomorrah, and the cities about them in like manner, giving themselves over to fornication, and going after strange flesh, are set forth for an example, suffering the vengeance of eternal fire."*

4. HELL is a place of complete darkness!

Matthew 8:12 – *"But the children of the kingdom shall be cast out into outer darkness: there shall be weeping and gnashing of teeth."*

Matthew 22:13 – *"Then said the king to the servants, Bind him hand and foot, and take him away, and cast him into outer darkness; there shall be weeping and gnashing of teeth."*

Matthew 25:30 – *"And cast ye the unprofitable servant into outer darkness: there shall be weeping and gnashing of teeth."*

5.   HELL is a place of torment!

Luke 16:23 – *"And in hell he lift up his eyes, being in torments..."*

Luke 16:24 – *"for I am tormented in this flame"*

Luke 16:25 – *"now he is comforted, and thou art tormented"*

Luke 16:28 – *"lest they also come into this place of torment"*

Matthew 22:13 – *"there shall be weeping and gnashing of teeth"*

Matthew 24:51 – *"And shall cut him asunder, and appoint him his portion with the hypocrites: there shall be weeping and gnashing of teeth"*

Matthew 25:30 – *"And cast ye the unprofitable servant into outer darkness: there shall be weeping and gnashing of teeth."*

Luke 13:27-28 – *"But he shall say, I tell you, I know you not whence ye are; depart from Me, all ye workers of iniquity. There shall be weeping and gnashing of teeth, when ye shall see Abraham, and Isaac, and Jacob, and all the prophets, in the kingdom of God, and you yourselves thrust out."*

6. HELL is a place of unquenchable fire!

Matthew 3:12 – *"but He will burn up the chaff with unquenchable fire"*

Matthew 5:22 – *"shall be in danger of hell fire"*

Matthew 13:42 – *"And shall cast them into a furnace of fire: there shall be wailing and gnashing of teeth."*

Matthew 13:50 – *"And shall cast them into the furnace of fire: there shall be wailing and gnashing of teeth."*

Matthew 18:9 – *"to be cast into hell fire"*

Mark 9:45 – *"to be cast into hell, into the fire that never shall be quenched."*

Mark 9:48 – *"Where their worm dieth not, and the fire is not quenched."*

Revelation 19:20 – *"There both were cast alive into a lake of fire burning with brimstone."*

Revelation 20:10 – *"And the devil that deceived them was cast into the lake of fire and brimstone, where the beast and the false prophet are, and shall be tormented day and night forever and ever."*

Revelation 20:14-15 – *"And death and hell were cast into the lake of fire. This is the second death. And whosoever was not found written in the book of life was cast into the lake of fire."*

Revelation 21:8 – *"shall have their part in the lake which burneth with fire and brimstone: which is the second death."*

7. HELL is a place of everlasting punishment!

Matthew 25:46 – *"And these shall go away into everlasting punishment: but the righteous into life eternal."*

Mark 3:29 – *"But he that shall blaspheme against the Holy Ghost hath never forgiveness, but is in danger of eternal damnation."*

Revelation 14:10-11 – *"The same shall drink of the wine of the wrath of God, which is poured out without mixture into the cup of His indignation; and he shall be tormented with fire and brimstone* in the presence of the holy angels, and in the presence of the Lamb: And the smoke of their torment ascendeth up forever and ever: and they have no rest day nor night, who worship the beast and his image, and whosoever receiveth the mark of his name."

Revelation 20:10 – "And the devil that deceived them was cast into the lake of fire and brimstone, where the beast and the false prophet are, and shall be tormented day and night forever and ever."

Mark 9:48 - "the worm dieth not" - quoted from Isaiah 66:24.

HOW DO WE KNOW THAT WE WILL BE IN HEAVEN AND NOT IN HELL?

(1) REALIZE that you must do more than merely say that you are a believer!

Matthew 5:20 – "For I say unto you, That except your righteousness shall exceed the righteousness of the scribes and Pharisees, ye shall in no case enter into the kingdom of heaven."

Matthew 7:13-14 – "Enter ye in at the strait gate: for wide is the gate, and broad is the way, that leadeth to destruction, and many there be which go in thereat: Because strait is the gate, and narrow is the way, which leadeth unto life, and few there be that find it."

Matthew 7:21-23 – *"Not every one that saith unto Me, Lord, Lord, shall enter into the kingdom of heaven; but he that doeth the will of My Father which is in heaven. Many will say to Me in that day, Lord, Lord, have we not prophesied in Thy Name? and in Thy Name have cast out devils? And in Thy Name done many wonderful works? And then will I profess unto them, I never knew you: depart from Me, ye that work iniquity."*

(2) REPENT of your sin!

Matthew 3:1-2 – *"In those days came John the Baptist, preaching in the wilderness of Judea, and saying, Repent ye: for the kingdom of heaven is at hand."*

(3) RECOGNIZE your need of humility!

Matthew 18:1-4 – *"At the same time came the disciples unto Jesus, saying, Who is the greatest in the kingdom of heaven? And Jesus called a little child unto Him, and set him in the midst of them, and said, Verily I say unto you, Except ye be converted, and become as little children, ye shall not enter into the kingdom of heaven. Whosoever therefore shall humble himself as this little child, the same is greatest in the kingdom of heaven."*

(4) RELY upon the work of the Holy Spirit!

John 3:3-8 – *"Jesus answered and said unto him, Verily, verily, I say unto thee, Except a man be born again, he cannot see the kingdom of God. Nicodemus saith unto Him, How can a man be born when he is old? Can he enter the second time into his mother's womb, and be born? Jesus answered, Verily, verily, I say unto thee, Except a man be born of water and of the Spirit, he cannot enter into the kingdom of God. That which is born of the flesh is flesh; and that which is born of the Spirit is spirit. Marvel not that I said unto thee, Ye must be born again. The wind bloweth where it listeth, and thou hearest the sound thereof, but canst not tell whence it cometh, and whither it goeth: so is every one that is born of the Spirit."*

Titus 3:5 – *"Not by works of righteousness which we have done, but according to His mercy He saved us, by the washing of regeneration, and renewing of the Holy Ghost."*

(5) RECEIVE Jesus Christ as your only Savior from sin, death, and hell!

John 1:12 – *"But as many as received Him, to them gave He power to become the sons of God, even to them that believe on His Name."*

John 3:15-18 – *""That whosoever believeth in Him should not perish, but have eternal life. For God so loved the world that He gave His only begotten Son, that whosoever believeth in Him, should not perish, but have everlasting life. For God sent not His Son into the world to condemn the world; but that the world through Him might be saved. He* that believeth on Him is not condemned: but he that believeth not is condemned already, because he hath not believed in the Name of the only begotten Son of God."

John 3:36 – "He that believeth on the Son hath everlasting life: and he that believeth not the Son shall not see life; but the wrath of God abideth on him."

John 14:6 – "Jesus saith unto him, I am the way, the truth, and the life: no man cometh unto the Father, but by Me."

BOOK OF REVELATION
Understanding the Future

THE LAMB AMONG THE REDEEMED
Part III
Revelation 21-22

THE NEW JERUSALEM
Revelation 21:1-22:5

The Book of Revelation is an unveiling of Jesus Christ in all of His glory! We have given three major facts about Him in the outline of this amazing Book:

LORD OF THE CHURCHES
Revelation 1-3

LION OVER THE NATIONS
Revelation 4-20

LAMB AMONG THE REDEEMED
Revelation 21-22

The word *"lamb"* appears 28 times in this Book. It now takes on special meaning to all who have come to put their trust in Jesus Christ as Lord and Savior. We are introduced to the *"Lamb's wife* (21:10)*"* a spectacular description of the heavenly city, the New Jerusalem, the eternal home for believers.

The word *"heaven"* is used 582 times in the King James Version of the Bible; the plural form *"heavens"* is found another 133 times – a total of 715 times. The Hebrew word *shamayim* is used 458 times; the Greek word *ouranos* in various forms – 288 times – making a total from the original languages of 746 usages.

The phrase *"the kingdom of heaven"* is used 32 times in the NT, all in Matthew; the phrase *"the kingdom of God"* appears 69 times in the NT, 53 of those in the gospels.

II Corinthians 12:2-4 refers to *"one caught up to the third heaven"* in verse 2, and calls it *"paradise"* in verse 4; this leads us to conclude the following:

(1)   The first heaven is the atmosphere around the earth – the *"firmament"* in Genesis 1:8, the place where birds fly – Genesis 1:20

(2)   The second heaven appears to be stellar space where we find the sun, moon, stars, planets, and galaxies – Genesis 1:14-18. In Genesis 15:5 God told Abram to *"look now toward heaven, and tell the stars..."*

Psalm 19:1 – *"the heavens declare the glory of God, and the firmament showeth His handiwork"*

(3) The third heaven which Paul called *"paradise"* in II Corinthians 12:4 appears to be the dwelling place of God.   Psalm 115:3 says *"But our God is in the heavens"* and Psalm 14:2 says *"The Lord looked down from heaven upon the children of men."*

Psalm 103:19: *"The LORD hath prepared His throne in the heavens."* Revelation 4:1-2 says *"a door opened in heaven"* and *"a throne was set in heaven"* – the throne upon which God the Father sits.   Revelation 19:1 says *"a great voice of much people in heaven."*

HEAVEN is the eternal home of true believers!

John 14:1-3 – "Let not your heart be troubled: ye believe in God, believe also in Me. In My Father's house are many mansions; if it were not so, I would have told you. I go to prepare a place for you. And if I go and prepare a place for you, I will come again, and receive you unto Myself; that where I am, there ye may be also."

HEAVEN is a city built by God Himself and the place where God the Father dwells!

Psalm 48:1-2 – *"Great is the LORD, and greatly to be praised in the city of our God, in the mountain of His holiness. Beautiful for situation, the joy of the whole earth, is mount Zion, on the sides of the north, the city of the great King."*

Hebrews 11:16 – *"But now they desire a better country, that is, an heavenly: wherefore God is not ashamed to be called their God: for He hath prepared for them a city."*

Hebrews 12:22-23 – *"But ye are come unto mount Zion, and unto the city of the living God, the heavenly Jerusalem, and to an innumerable company of angels, to the general assembly and church of the firstborn, which are written in heaven, and to God the Judge of all, and to the spirits of just men made perfect."*

Revelation 21:1-2 – *"And I saw a new heaven and a new earth: for the first heaven and the first earth were passed away; and there was no more sea. And I John saw the holy city, new Jerusalem, coming down from God out of heaven, prepared as a bride adorned for her husband."*

Revelation 21:10 – *"And he carried me away in the spirit to a great and high mountain, and shewed me that great city, the holy Jerusalem, descending out of heaven from God."*

HEAVEN is a city of enormous size and beauty!

(1)   The <u>DIMENSIONS</u> will handle all believers!

Revelation 21:16-17 – *"And the city lieth foursquare, and the length is as large as the breadth: and he measured the city with the reed, twelve thousand furlongs.   The length and the breadth of it are equal.   And he measured the wall thereof, an hundred and forty and four cubits, according to the measure of a man, that is, of the angel."*

(2)   The <u>DESCRIPTION</u> of its beauty is dazzling beyond our ability to imagine it!

Rev. 21:18 – the wall which is 218 feet thick is made of "jasper" (probably a "diamond").   It is a city made of "pure gold, like unto clear glass." It has 12 gates – 12 gigantic pearls! It has 12 foundations, made of 12 different precious stones!

Revelation 22:5 – no night, no need of sun, moon, and stars – Rev. 21:23; 22:5.

HEAVEN is the place where believers go when they die!

II Corinthians 5:8 says: *"absent from the body, and...present with the Lord"*

Hebrews 12:22-23 teaches: *"But ye are come unto mount Zion, and unto the city of the living God, the heavenly Jerusalem, and to an innumerable company of angels, to the general assembly and church of the firstborn, which are written in heaven, and to God the Judge of all, and to the spirits of just men made perfect, and to Jesus the Mediator of the new covenant..."*

HEAVEN is a place of reward for believers!

Matthew 5:12 says: *"Rejoice and be exceeding glad; for great is your reward in heaven."*

HEAVEN is a place that is far better!

Philippians 1:23 – *"to be with Christ; which is far better"*

Revelation 14:13 – *"Blessed are they who die in the Lord for they shall rest from their labors"*

HEAVEN is a city for believers only!

Revelation 21:24 – *"And the nations of them which are saved shall walk in the light of it: and the kings of the earth do bring their glory and honor into it."*

Revelation 21:27b – *"but they which are written in the Lamb's book of life."*

The details that describe the NEW JERUSALEM are indeed spectacular and amazing!

The INTRODUCTION to the New Jerusalem
Revelation 21:1-8

"And I saw a new heaven and a new earth: for the first heaven and the first earth were passed away; and there was no more sea. And I John saw the holy city, NEW JERUSALEM, coming down from God out of heaven, prepared as a bride adorned for her husband. And I heard a great voice out of heaven saying, Behold, the tabernacle of God is with men, and He will dwell with them, and they shall be His people, and God Himself shall be with them, and be their God. And God shall wipe away all tears from their eyes; and there shall be no more death, neither sorrow, nor crying, neither shall there be any more pain: for the former things are passed away. And he that sat upon the throne said, Behold, I make all things new. And He said

unto me, Write: for these words are true and faithful. And He said unto me, It is done. I am Alpha and Omega, the beginning and the end. I will give unto him that is athirst of the fountain of the water of life freely. He that overcometh shall inherit all things; and I will be his God, and he shall be My son. But the fearful, and unbelieving, and the abominable, and murderers, and whoremongers, and sorcerers, and idolaters, and all liars, shall have their part in the lake which burneth with fire and brimstone: which is the second death."

1. The <u>PATTERN</u> of things in the universe will be changed!

    (1)   Our physical <u>ENVIRONMENT</u> will be brand new!
    "a new heaven and a new earth"

    (2)   Our present <u>EVENTS</u> will pass away!
    "for the first heaven and the first earth were passed away; and there was no more sea"

<u>NOTE:</u> The phrase *"no more sea"* tells us how the environment will change. Does this mean the removal of water from the planet? No – there will be a river in the heavenly city. All the passages that deal with water and the sea are referring to the Millennial Kingdom of the Messiah, not the eternal state of the believers.

      (3)   Our future <u>EXPERIENCE</u> will be totally different!
"And God shall wipe away all tears from their eyes...the former things are passed away"

2. The <u>PRESENCE</u> of a new city will be the main attraction in eternity!
"prepared as a bride adorned for her husband"

      (1)   The <u>CHARACTER</u> of the city
"holy" – no more sin!

      (2)   The <u>CONTRAST</u> of the city
"new" – unlike the old city!

      (3)   The <u>COMING</u> of the city
"coming down from God out of heaven"

      (4)   The <u>COMPARISON</u> of the city
"as a bride"

3. The <u>PURPOSE</u> of God will be fulfilled!
"Behold, the tabernacle of God is with men, and He will dwell with them"

4. The <u>PAST</u> will be removed – v. 4
"for the former things are passed away"

5. The <u>PROMISES</u> of God will be realized!

(1)　Based on His **ABILITY** to do it!
(2)　Based on the **ACCURACY** of His Word!
(3)　Based on His **AUTHORITY** to do it!
(4)　Based on the **ASSURANCE** He gives!

The **INVITATION** to the New Jerusalem
Revelation 21:9-10

"And there came unto me one of the seven angels which had the seven vials full of the seven last plagues, and talked with me, saying, Come hither, I will shew thee the bride, the Lamb's wife. And he carried me away in the spirit to a great and high mountain, and shewed me that great city, the holy Jerusalem, descending out of heaven from God."

1.　The **ANNOUNCEMENT** of the angel

This angel is one of the seven who had the seven last plagues – how interesting; The blending of God's wrath and judgment with God's promise of eternal blessing is a reminder of God's character; He manifests both attributes throughout all His dealings with humanity.

2.　The **ABILITY** of John to see it

In chapter 17 John was carried away in the spirit to the wilderness; but, here he is taken to *"a great and high mountain."* The holy city is far more wonderful than the sight of the harlot on the beast with seven heads and ten horns. John is once again transferred or transported into the future in the realm of the spirit (in contrast with the flesh). He is an eyewitness of those events and tries to describe them in the language of his day. What an incredible experience this first-century apostle must have had!

3. The **APPEARANCE** of the city
   v. 11a – *"having the glory of God"*

The New Jerusalem reflects all that God is and does. The city is a wonderful manifestation of the glory and character of Almighty God.

The **IMPACT** of this city upon John
Revelation 21:11b-21

1. The **SHINING** of its light.

Revelation 21:11b – *"and her light was like unto a stone most precious, even like a jasper stone, clear as crystal."*

Many scholars believe that the *"jasper stone"* is the same as a "diamond." Of course when light is focused on a diamond, the array of beautiful colors that is manifested is indeed incredible!

2. The **STRUCTURE** of this city.

Revelation 21:12-14 – *"And had a wall great and high, and had twelve gates, and at the gates twelve angels, and names written thereon, which are the names of the twelve tribes of the children of Israel:*

On the east three gates; on the north three gates; on the south three gates; and on the west three gates. And the wall of the city had twelve foundations, and in them the names of the twelve apostles of the Lamb.

3. The <u>SIZE</u> of this city.

Revelation 21:15-17 – *"And he that talked with me had a golden reed to measure the city, and the gates thereof, and wall thereof. And the city lieth foursquare, and the length is as large as the breadth: and he measured the city with the reed, twelve thousand furlongs. The length and the breadth and the height of it are equal. And he measured the wall thereof, an hundred and forty and four cubits. According to the measure of man, that is, of the angel.*

The wall measures 216 feet – is this the height of it or the width of it? By the way it is expressed it would usually be referring to its width – that would be one tremendous size, regardless of which direction was being measured.

A *"furlong"* is approximately 600 feet, which means that each side would be about 1400 miles – which makes this city considerably larger than the city Ezekiel spoke about during the time of the Millennial Kingdom of the Messiah (last nine chapters of Ezekiel). It is possible that the height of the city might make it a cube or a pyramid – we simply do not know. But the measurements for our human comprehension are beyond the average person's ability to fathom.

4. The <u>STONES</u> of this city.
   Revelation 21:18-21

Years ago a gemologist in Southern California was asked to analyze this city and the gems associated with it. His reply was that the sight of this city would be beyond our human eyes to capture. It was awesome in every respect and would be stunningly beautiful beyond words!

"And the building of the wall of it was of jasper (probably a diamond); and the city was pure gold, like unto clear glass. And the foundations of the wall of the city were garnished with all manner of precious stones.

> *First foundation* = JASPER
> *Second foundation* = SAPPHIRE
> *Third foundation* = CHALCEDONY
> *Fourth foundation* = EMERALD
> *Fifth foundation* = SARDONYX
> *Sixth foundation* = SARDIUS
> *Seventh foundation* = CHRYSOLYTE
> *Eighth foundation* = BERYL
> *Ninth foundation* = TOPAZ
> *Tenth foundation* = CHRYSOPRASUS
> *Eleventh foundation* = JACINTH
> *Twelfth foundation* = AMETHYST

And the twelve gates were twelve pearls: every several gate was of one pearl: and the street of the city was pure gold, as it were transparent glass."

It seems like only one English word fits this scene – WOW!

The <u>IMPORTANCE</u> of the LORD's presence and the Lamb of God Himself!
Revelation 21:22-27

"And I saw no temple there: for the Lord God Almighty and the Lamb are the temple of it. And the city had no need of the sun, neither of the moon, to shine in it: for the glory of God did lighten it, and the Lamb is the light thereof. And the nations of them which are saved shall walk in the light of it: and the kings of the earth do bring their glory and honor into it. And the gates of it shall not be shut at all by day: for there shall be no night there. And they shall bring the glory and honor of the nations into it. And there shall in no wise enter it any thing that defileth, neither whatsoever worketh abomination, or maketh a lie: but they which are written in the Lamb's book of life."

1. The <u>PLACE</u> of worship will be the Lord Himself!

There is no temple in the eternal state. There is no building or structure in the heavenly city to which we must come for worship. The Millennial Kingdom of our Messiah will have a temple, but not the heavenly city, the New Jerusalem. The Lord God Almighty and the Lamb are the only temple we will need. They are the fulfillment of all we have symbolized by our worship: they are the objects of our praise.

All symbols that help us focus on the Lord will be rendered useless by the glory of God's presence, a reminder to us not to place too much importance on present symbolism. What makes the New Jerusalem so special is that we will finally be *"with the Lord"* forever and ever. He is the only temple we will need in the eternal state.

2. The <u>PRESENCE</u> of the Lord will eliminate the need for the sun and the moon!

The New Jerusalem seems to be unique in what is missing: no more death, sorrow, crying, or pain, and no temple, and no need of the sun or moon or lamp; no more curse – what a wonderful place it will be with all of these things gone forever!

Verse 23 tells us: *"And the city had no need of the sun, neither of the moon, to shine in it: for the glory of God did lighten it, and the Lamb is the light thereof."*

Isaiah 60:1-3 – *"Arise, shine; for thy light is come, and the glory of the LORD is risen upon thee. For, behold, the darkness shall cover the earth, and gross darkness the people: but the LORD shall arise upon thee, and His glory shall be seen upon thee.*

And the Gentiles shall come to Thy light, and kings to the brightness of Thy rising."

Isaiah 60:19 – *"The sun shall be no more thy light by day; neither for brightness shall the moon give light unto thee: but the LORD shall be unto thee an everlasting light, and thy God thy glory."*

    3. The <u>PURPOSE</u> of God for all nations will be fulfilled!

God's original purpose is that all the nations will worship Him. His plan during this present age is to bring people to Himself out of every nation, tribe, tongue, and people.

Psalm 66:4 – *"All the earth shall worship Thee, and shall sing unto Thee; they shall sing to Thy Name."*

Isaiah 66:23 – *"And it shall come to pass, that from one new moon to another, and from one sabbath to another, shall all flesh come to worship before Me, saith the LORD."*

I Peter 2:9 – *"But ye are a chosen generation, a royal priesthood, an holy nation, a peculiar people; that ye should shew forth the praises of Him Who hath called you out of darkness into His marvellous light."*

    4. The <u>PURITY</u> of the heavenly city

Revelation 21:24-27 – *"And the nations of them which are saved shall walk in the light of it: and the kings of the earth do bring their glory and honor into it. And the gates of it shall not be shut at all by day: for there shall be no night there. And they shall bring the glory and honor of the nations into it. And there shall in no wise enter into it any thing that defileth, neither whatsoever worketh abomination, or maketh a lie: but they which are written in the Lamb's book of life."*

(1)   The <u>SALVATION</u> of the nations

What a wonderful day it will be when all nations that are saved will *"walk in the light of it."* The *"kings of the earth"* will *"bring their glory and honor into it."* Praise the Lord!

(2)   The <u>SACRIFICES</u> of worship that will be brought to this city

Verse 26 says: *"And they shall bring the glory and honor of the nations into it."* The whole population of the New Jerusalem will be focused on the worship of Almighty God – what a day that will be!

(3)   The <u>SINFULNESS</u> of the nations will be no more!

Yes, nothing will be in the New Jerusalem that defiles or works abominations (immorality and idolatry) or operates by lying to others – that will be no more – praise the Lord! The only people that will occupy the heavenly city are those who are written in the Lamb's book of life!

The INSIGHTS about the river, the tree of life, the throne of God, and the light
Revelation 22:1-5

"And he shewed me a pure river of water of life, clear as crystal, proceeding out of the throne of God and of the Lamb. In the midst of the street of it, and on either side of the river, was there the tree of life, which bare twelve manner of fruits, and yielded her fruit every month: and the leaves of the tree were for the healing of the nations. And there shall be no more curse: but the throne of God and of the Lamb shall be in it; and His servants shall serve Him: And they shall see His face; and His Name shall be in their foreheads. And there shall be no night there; and they need no candle, neither light of the sun; for the Lord God giveth them light: and they shall reign forever and ever."

1. The **PICTURE** of eternal life will be portrayed by a river and a tree!

The river is *"a pure river of water of life,"* and the *"tree of life"* and its *"leaves"* are for the *"healing of the nations."* The *"tree of life"* was originally in the Garden of Eden and symbolizes eternal life for all who believe.

2. The **PLACE** from where the river comes!
   "proceeding out of the throne of God and of the Lamb"

The source of eternal life is the LORD Himself! When we are *"born again by the Holy Spirit"* we are *"born of God."* In John 7:37-39 our Lord Yeshua spoke of *"rivers of living water"* which the Holy Spirit would produce in the heart of all believers.

"In the last day, that great day of the feast, Jesus stood and cried, saying, If any man thirst, let him come unto Me, and drink. He that believeth on Me, as the scripture hath said, out of his belly shall flow rivers of living water. (But this spake He of the Spirit, which they that believe on Him should receive: for the Holy Ghost was not yet given; because that Jesus was not yet glorified.)

3. The <u>POSITION</u> of the river and the tree!

The street of the city is *"pure gold, like transparent glass* (Revelation 21:21)" and seems to be dividing down the middle by the river. The *"tree of life"* is located on both sides of the river, perhaps a continuous hedge-like appearance on either side of the river, possibly implying a row of trees rather than a single tree.

It is difficult to ascertain the meaning of the river and the tree. Is this a literal tree with fruit on it from which we may freely eat, or is this to be taken symbolically? The questions are easier than the answers. Eating and drinking are common symbols portraying faith in and communion with the Lord. It is possible that such actions will continue forever as a constant reminder of the ground upon which we will enjoy the blessings of eternity. We are saved by faith alone in the Person and work of the Messiah, our blessed Lord Yeshua!

4. The <u>PURPOSE</u> of the leaves of the tree!

We are told in Revelation 22:2 that *"the leaves of the tree were for the healing of the nations."* The *"tree of life"* is the key to the perpetual health of all peoples who find themselves in the eternal state. It is hard to conceive of the need for healing in the eternal state when all pain, sickness, and death has been removed forever! It is probably a reason for regarding the *"tree of life"* as a symbol of eternal life, bringing health and eternal life to all who have believed in the Lord.

5. The <u>PRACTICES</u> of believers in the eternal state!

The following teaches what we will be doing forever:
What we <u>SERVE</u> – *"and His servants shall serve Him"*
What we will <u>SEE</u> – *"they shall see His face"*

There is a wonderful old song, whose words and music were done by a famous country singer – Stuart Hamblen. The title is "UNTIL THEN."

> My heart can sing when I pause to remember
> A heartache here, is but a stepping stone;
> Along a trail that's winding always upward;
> This troubled world is not my final home!

CHORUS:
But until then my heart will go on singing;
Until then with joy I'll carry on;
Until the day my eyes behold the city;
Until the day God calls me home!

The things of earth will dim and lose their value;
If we recall, they're borrowed for awhile;
And things of earth that cause the heart to tremble;
Remembered there, will only bring a smile!

This weary world with all its toil and struggle;
May take its toll of misery and strife;
The soul of man is like a waiting falcon;
When it's released, it's destined for the skies!

MESSIAH IS COMING SOON!
Revelation 22:6-21

Three times in these sixteen verses we read the words of our Lord Jesus Christ that capture His final message to our hearts:

"I AM COMING QUICKLY!"

The words *"I come quickly"* are found in Revelation 2:5, 16; 3:11; 22:7, 12, 20. We also have the words *"I will come on thee as a thief"* in Revelation 3:3 and *"Behold, I come as a thief"* in Revelation 16:16. II Peter 3:10 also says: *"But the day of the Lord will come as a thief in the night."* The Apostle Paul added in I Thessalonians 5:2: *"the day of the Lord so cometh as a thief in the night."* The idea of coming *"quickly"* is that which is sudden, soon, and surprising! No time for additional preparation!

There are eight grammatical forms of the word translated *"quickly."* The Greek noun *tachos* refers to speed or quickness and is only used with the preposition *en* – and speaks of that which is of short duration, or soon, or suddenly – used in Revelation 1:1 and 22:6 – translated often in the King James Bible with the word *"shortly."* This noun form is found 7 times in the New Testament.

Two forms of the word are used as adjectives: the word *tachos* found once in James 1:19 – *"let every man be swift to hear"* and the word *tachinos* which is used twice in II Peter 1:14 and 2:1.

568

Five forms of the word are used as adverbs. The word *tachu* used 11 times and in Revelation 2:5, 16; 3:11; 11:14; 22:7, 12, 20. The word *tacha* is found twice in Romans 5:7 and Philemon 1:15.

The word *tacheos* is found 10 times in the NT; the word *tachion* is used 5 times and is a comparative form of the words meaning *"more quickly"* as in Hebrews 13:19, 23. The final form of the word is *tachista* and is a superlative of the other words meaning the *"quickest"* or the *"soonest possible"* and is found once in Acts 17:15 and translated in English as *"with all speed."*

These eight forms of a Greek word are used 39 times in the New Testament and refer to speed, suddenness, and surprise.

THE IMPACT OF THE BOOK
Revelation 22:6-9

"And he said unto me, these sayings are faithful and true: and the Lord God of the holy prophets sent His angel to shew unto His servants the things which must shortly be done. Behold, I come quickly: blessed is he that keepeth the sayings of the prophecy of this book. And I John saw these things and heard them. And when I had heard and seen, I fell down to worship before the feet of the angel that shewed me these things. Then saith he unto me, See thou do it not: for I am thy fellow-servant, and of thy brethren the prophets, and of them which keep the sayings of this book: Worship God."

1. The **RELIABILITY** of its message – *"These sayings are faithful and true"* – cf. 21:6

2. The **RESPONSE** we should give to its message – *"keepeth the sayings of the prophecy of this book"*

3. The **REACTION** of John – *"I fell down to worship before the feet of the angel which shewed me these things"*

4. The **REBUKE** of the angel – *"See thou do it not; for I am thy fellow-servant, and of thy brethren the prophets, and of them which keep the sayings of this book: WORSHIP GOD!"*

THE IMPORTANCE OF THE BOOK
Revelation 22:10-15

"And he saith unto me, Seal not the sayings of the prophecy of this book: for the time is at hand. He that is unjust still: and he which is filthy, let him be filthy still: and he that is righteous, let him be righteous still: and he that is holy, let him be holy still. And, behold, I come quickly; and My reward is with Me, to give every man according as his work shall be. I am Alpha and Omega, the beginning and the end, the first and the last. Blessed are they that do His commandments, that they may have right to the tree of life, and may enter in through the gates into the city. For without are dogs, and sorcerers,

and whoremongers, and murderers, and idolaters, and whosoever loveth and maketh a lie."

1. It reveals the <u>CLIMAX</u> of God's plan of the ages!
      Revelation 22:10-11

<u>NOTE</u>: The words *"seal not"* remind us of Daniel 8:26; 12:4, 8-10.

Daniel 8:26 – *"And the vision of the evening and the morning which was told is true: wherefore shut thou up the vision; for it shall be for many days."*

Daniel 12:4 – *"But thou, O Daniel, shut up the words, and seal the book, even to the time of the end: many shall run to and fro, and knowledge shall be increased."*

Daniel 12:8-10 – *"And I heard, but I understood not: then said I, O my Lord, when shall be the end of these things? And He said, Go thy way, Daniel: for the words are closed up and sealed till the time of the end. Many shall be purified, and made white, and tried; but the wicked shall do wickedly; and none of the wicked shall understand; but the wise shall understand."*

      (1) Notice that any desired <u>CHANGES</u> in the eternal state of believers and non-believers is impossible! (marked by the simple word *"still"*)

      (2) Notice the enormous <u>CONTRAST</u> in

the destiny of believers and non-believers – *"filthy"* vs. *"righteous"* and *"holy."*

2. It reveals the <u>COMING</u> of Yeshua HaMashiach *"Behold, I come quickly; and My reward is with Me"*

3. It reveals the Divine <u>CHARACTER</u> of our Lord Yeshua – *"I am Alpha and Omega, the beginning and the end, the first and the last"*

4. It reveals the <u>CONSEQUENCES</u> of the gospel – vv. 14-15

THE FINAL INVITATION OF THE BOOK
Revelation 22:16-21

"I Jesus have sent Mine angel to testify unto you these things in the churches. I am the root and the offspring of David, and the bright and morning star. And the Spirit and the bride say, Come. And let him that heareth say, Come. And let him that is athirst come. And whosoever will, let him take the water of life freely. For I testify unto every man that heareth the words of the prophecy of this book, If any man shall add unto these things, God shall add unto him the plagues that are written in this book: And if any man shall take away from the words of the book of this prophecy, God shall take away his part out of the book of life, and out of the holy city, and from the things which are written in this book. He which testifieth these things saith, Surely I come quickly. Amen. Even so, come, Lord

Jesus. The grace of our Lord Jesus Christ be with you all. Amen.

1. The <u>PERSON</u> from Whom the invitation comes
      v. 16 – "I Yeshua (Jesus)..."

    (1)   He is the <u>ROOT</u> of David!

Psalm 132;11-12 – *"The LORD hath sworn in truth unto David; He will not turn from it; Of the fruit of thy body will I set upon thy throne. If thy children will keep My covenant and My testimony that I shall teach them, their children shall also sit upon thy throne forevermore."*

Isaiah 11:1 – *"And there shall come forth a rod out of the stem of Jesse, and a Branch shall grow out of his roots."*

Isaiah 53:2 – *"For He shall grow up before Him as a tender plant, and as a root out of a dry ground: He hath no form nor comeliness; and when we shall see Him, there is no beauty that we should desire Him."*

    (2)   He is the <u>STAR</u> of Bible prophecy –

Numbers 24:17-19 – *"I shall see Him, but not now: I shall behold Him, but not nigh: there shall come a Star out of Jacob, and a Sceptre shall rise out of Israel, and shall smite the corners of Moab, and destroy all the children of Sheth. And Edom shall be a possession, Seir also shall be a possession for his enemies; and Israel shall do valiantly. Out of Jacob shall come He that shall have dominion, and shall destroy him that remaineth of the city."*

Revelation 2:28 – *"And I will give him the morning star"* (message to the overcomers in the church of Thyatira).

2. The <u>PEOPLE</u> who give the invitation –
   v. 17a – "the Spirit and the bride"

3. The <u>PREREQUISITE</u> in this invitation –
   v. 17b – *"him that is athirst"* and *"whosoever will"*

4. The <u>PROMISE</u> of this invitation – v. 17c
   "the water of life"

5. The <u>PRICE</u> of this invitation – v. 17d –
   "freely"

<u>NOTE:</u> The word *"freely"* is a translation of the Greek word *dorean*. Its usage in John 15:25 translates as *"without a cause."* It makes an interesting point in connection with our justification as in Romans 3:24.

6. The <u>PUNISHMENT</u> for rejecting the invitation
   vv. 18-19

The Bible is *"inspired of God"* and that does not refer to the writers, but to what was written. The

Holy Spirit controlled the writers so that what was written was exactly what God wanted.

When we speak of the revelation of God, we are dealing with the issue of authority. The Bible is the Word of God; we don't make it the Word of God by how we interpret it or apply it. God is finished giving us His Divine revelation in written form. There will be no further communication from God regarding what is soon to take place. All that God wanted to say, He has already said. No more is to be given. Anyone who claims to receive direct communication from God today is deceiving himself and disobeying the clear teaching of the Bible.

7. The <u>PROPHECY</u> that makes this invitation so important – v. 20

(1) It is an <u>EVENT</u> that will happen quickly!

(2) It is the <u>EXPECTATION</u> of every believer!

And, we all say with the Apostle John – *"Even so, come, Lord Jesus."*